TREACHEROUS ALLIANCE

TREACHEROUS ALLIANCE

the secret dealings of israel, iran, and the united states

trita parsi

yale university press / new haven and london

A Caravan book. For more information, visit www.caravanbooks.org.

Set in Minion and Franklin Gothic types by The Composing Room of Michigan, Inc. Printed in the United States of America.

Library of Congress Cataloging-in-Publication Data
Parsi, Trita.
Treacherous alliance : the secret dealings of Israel, Iran, and the United States / Trita Parsi.
p. cm.
Includes bibliographical references and index.
ISBN 978-0-300-12057-8 (hardcover: alk. paper)
1. Iran—Foreign relations—Israel.   2. Israel—Foreign relations—Iran.
3. United States—Foreign relations—Middle East.   4. Middle East—Foreign relations—United States.   I. Title.
DS274.2.I75P37 2007
327.5694055—dc22

2007018945

A catalogue record for this book is available from the British Library.

10   9   8   7   6   5   4   3   2   1

To Amina
For your love, for your laughter
and for standing firm when weaker hearts succumb

And to Darius, my eternal love
I hope to be as good of a parent to you as my parents were to me

CONTENTS

part three. looking ahead

PREFACE

Israeli-Iranian relations remain a mystery to most analysts in spite of the profound impact that these countries' tensions have had on the Middle East and on U.S. national security. The political sensitivity of the issue has prompted most U.S. experts to refrain from studying the subject in detail. Instead, the poor state of relations between these two former allies has been treated either as an inexplicable phenomenon or as purely the result of deep-seated ideological antagonism. All the while, its impact on U.S. foreign policy has been conveniently ignored at a great cost to U.S. national interests. While it is widely believed that the key to peace in the Middle East is the resolution of the Israeli-Palestinian conflict, little attention has been given to the key geopolitical rivalry between Israel and Iran, which has had a decisive influence on this and other regional conflicts.

In examining the ups and downs in Israeli-Iranian relations and the triangular relationship between the United States, Israel, and Iran, I have focused on geopolitical forces and developments rather than on ideology, fleeting political justifications, or simplistic Manichean perspectives. I argue that the major transformations of Israeli-Iranian relations are results of geopolitical—rather than ideological—shifts and that a negotiated resolution of their strategic rivalry will significantly facilitate the resolution of other regional problems rather than the other way around.

The current enmity between the two states has more to do with the shift in the balance of power in the Middle East after the end of the Cold War and the defeat of Iraq in the first Persian Gulf War than it does with the Islamic Revolution in 1979. Though the Iranian revolution was a major setback for Israel, it didn't stop the Jewish State from supporting Iran and seeking to improve its relations with the Khomeini government as a counter to Israel's Arab enemies. Ironically, when Iranian leaders called for Israel's destruction in the 1980s, Israel and the pro-Israel lobby in Washington lobbied the United States *not* to pay attention to Iranian rhetoric. Today, even though Iran's revolutionary Islamist zeal is far from what it was in the 1980s, things have changed quite a bit. The Iranian government, in turn, has pursued a double policy throughout this period: In the 1980s, Iran made itself the most vocal regional supporter of the Palestinian cause. Yet its rhetoric was seldom followed up with action, since Tehran's strategic interest—reducing tensions with Israel and using the Jewish State to reestablish relations with the United States—contradicted Iran's ideological imperatives. After 1991 and the efforts by the United States and Israel to create a new Middle East order based on the Israeli-Palestinian peace process and on Iran's prolonged isolation, however, Iran's ideological and strategic interests overlapped, and Tehran decided for the first time to become a front-line opponent of the Jewish State. At this stage, both Israel and Iran used their influence to undermine U.S. foreign policy initiatives that they deemed beneficial to the other. Iran worked against the peace process, fearing that it would be left isolated in the region, and Israel sought to prevent a U.S.-Iran dialogue because it feared that Washington would betray Israeli security interests if Iran and the United States were to communicate directly. To this day, that logic prevails in both capitals, and it is fueling the tensions in the region.

This is a book about foreign policy. My focus is on the relations between these states and not on internal developments that—while important—have little or no impact on their respective foreign policies. Nor do I seek to provide a deeper explanation of the ideologies espoused by the leaders of these states. Instead, these ideas and worldviews are considered relevant only to the extent that they influence Iran's and Israel's foreign policy. This approach does not mean, though, that these ideologies are wholly irrelevant or that the belief in them is put under question. On the contrary, both Israeli and Iranian leaders have strongly held ideologies and worldviews, which they take most seriously. Whether these ideologies are the chief determining factor in Israeli-Iranian relations, however, is a different question altogether.

Precisely because of the sensitivity of this issue, very little has been written about Israeli-Iranian relations or their impact on U.S. foreign policy. It has been almost two decades since a book on Israeli-Iranian relations was published in English, and many of the analyses about Iran produced in the United States in this period have suffered from Western analysts' lack of access to Iran and Iranian officials. This has particularly affected the study of convoluted issues such as the relations between the United States, Iran, and Israel. To avoid these pitfalls, the bulk of this book is based on 130 in-depth interviews I've conducted with Iranian, Israeli, and American officials and analysts.

Through these face-to-face interviews with the decision-makers themselves, I have been able to map out firsthand accounts of events and the thinking that underlie strategic decisions, while at the same time going beyond the talking points and public justifications Iran and Israel have developed to conceal the true nature of their tensions. Many of these accounts and rationales have never been made available to the public before. The interviews with Iranian officials in particular have been very revealing and have penetrated areas that thus far have rarely—if ever—been discussed openly in Iran, mindful of the censorship that print media there face regarding sensitive issues such as Israel. The same is true to a certain extent in Israel, where the problem may not have been government censorship, but rather that reporting has focused almost exclusively on the perceived military threat from Iran and has neglected the underlying strategic calculations of Israeli and Iranian decision-makers.

To ensure the reliability of the interviewees and their accounts, an extraordinarily large number of people have been interviewed, and their accounts have been cross-checked. No argument in the book is dependent on one or two quotes alone. The cross-referencing and the large pool of interviewees have also ensured that the accounts presented in the book reflect the essence of the exchanges, even though exact recollections are difficult to reproduce after twenty years.

The interviewees have been selected based on their direct involvement in the formulation of Iranian, Israeli, or American foreign policy, or on their knowledge of that process. Quotes have been attributed to these officials or analysts in all but a few cases. Though they are too numerous to name them all here, a few are worth mentioning because of their access to highly valuable and previously undisclosed inside information.

In regards to Iran's policy on Israel under the Shah, Iran's UN Ambassador in the late 1970s, Fereydoun Hoveyda; and Iran's Minister of Economics, Alinaghi Alikhani (a close associate of the Shah's Court Marshall, Assadollah Alam); have all provided invaluable insights into the Shah's strategic thinking. For the postrevolutionary era, Iran's UN Ambassador and Deputy Foreign Minister Dr. Javad Zarif, former Deputy Foreign Ministers Dr. Abbas Maleki, Dr. Mahmoud Vaezi, and Dr. Hadi Nejad-Hosseinian, as well as former Chairman of the Foreign Relations Committee in the Iranian Parliament Mohsen Mirdamadi; former advisor to President Mohammad Khatami, Mohammad Reza Tajik; the political editor of *Resalat*, a conservative daily newspaper in Iran, Amir Mohebian; and Ali Reza Alavi Tabar, editor of several reformist newspapers; have all provided priceless insights into the Islamic Republic's calculations.

In Israel, invaluable information has been offered by former head of the Mossad Efraim Halevi; former Foreign Minister Dr. Shlomo Ben-Ami; former Defense Minister Moshe Arens; Deputy Defense Minister Dr. Efraim Sneh; Director of Military Intelligence Maj. Amos Gilad; former UN Ambassador Dr. Dore Gold; former Head of the Foreign Ministry David Kimche; former representative to Iran Uri Lubrani; former Defense Attaché to Iran Yitzhak Segev; former head of the Israeli Committee on Iran David Ivry; former Advisor to Prime Minister Yitzhak Rabin Yossi Alpher; former UN Ambassador Itamar Rabinovich, and financier of the Iran-Contra dealings, Yaacov Nimrodi. Also, as the American Israel Public Affairs Committee's point person on Iran, Keith Weissman has shared his insight into the strategizing of the pro-Israel lobby. (My interview and discussions with Keith took place before he was charged with espionage and left the organization.)

Finally, inside accounts of Washington's calculations have been provided by National Security Advisors Dr. Zbigniew Brzezinski, Lt. Col. Robert McFarlane, Gen. Brent Scowcroft, and Dr. Anthony Lake, as well as Assistant Secretaries of State Robert Pelletreau and Martin Indyk; Secretary of State Colin Powell's Chief of Staff Larry Wilkerson; the current Bush administration's first Special Envoy for Afghanistan, Ambassador James Dobbins; Ambassador Dennis Ross; and Dr. Gary Sick, who served as principal White House aide for Persian Gulf affairs from 1976 to 1981.

These interviewees have been intricately involved in Iran's, Israel's, and the United States' foreign policy decision-making and as a result present a unique and largely unknown picture of the three countries' approach to each other. The Iranian perspective, in particular, has largely been unknown to Western audiences, which as a result has significantly impaired the analysis of Iran in the West. A key reason why the analysis of this book differs greatly from the conventional wisdom regarding the U.S.-Israel-Iran triangle is because it is based on the perspectives and accounts of high-level decision-makers from *all three countries*. In addition, for the latter chapters of the book, I myself, in my capacity as an advisor to a U.S. Congressman, have had access to some of the hidden dealings between the three countries. This position has provided me with a firsthand account of some of the developments spelled out in this book, which I have sought to recount as accurately as possible.

The book addresses the state of Israeli-Iranian relations from the creation of the Jewish State in 1948 to the present. This is done in three separate parts. First, I address the historic context of the U.S.-Israel-Iran triangle during the Cold War. Both the Israeli-Iranian entente under the Shah, as well as their secret ties under the Islamic Republic, are discussed in this section. I examine the formation of the Israeli-Iranian entente and the Shah's betrayal of Israel through the 1975 Algiers Accord, as well as Israel's extensive efforts to patch up U.S.-Iran relations in the 1980s and Iran's double policy versus Israel—denying its right to exist on the one hand while accepting its support and paying lip service to the Palestinian cause on the other. The second part of the book shows how the geopolitical earthquake following the collapse of the Soviet Union and the defeat of Iraq in the 1991 Gulf War dramatically altered the way Iran, Israel, and the United States related to one another. In the new Middle East emerging after this geopolitical rupture, Israel and Iran viewed each other no longer as potential security partners, but as rivals for defining the balance of the Middle East. Here I discuss Iran's transition to being an active opponent of Israel and Tel Aviv's 180-degree shift toward opposing rather than supporting a U.S.-Iran rapprochement, as well as both Iran and Israel's efforts to undermine U.S. policies in the region that they deemed beneficial to the other. In the final section of the book I discuss the options Washington currently is considering, as well as the one policy the Bush administration seems loath to pursue but that has the highest chance of taming the Israeli-Iranian rivalry and reducing the risk for a disastrous war that can engulf the Middle East—and America—for decades to come.

ACKNOWLEDGMENTS

There is not enough room here to thank everyone who deserves credit for this book, and I cannot thank enough the ones I do mention. First and foremost, I am forever indebted to Francis Fukuyama, my advisor at Johns Hopkins University School of Advanced International Studies (SAIS), where I wrote the PhD dissertation on which this book is based. His guidance, criticism, and assistance have been crucial, and they go beyond the particular advice he's given regarding my dissertation and this book. He is one of our era's most prominent political thinkers, and I have been fortunate enough to have had the opportunity to be influenced by his wisdom. Likewise, neither this book nor the analysis behind it would have been possible absent the help I received from Charles Doran at SAIS. Doran's power cycle theory constitutes the book's analytical bedrock. Through this theory, the interplay between the cyclical nature of states' power and role ambitions is taken into account. In the case of Israeli-Iranian relations, Iranian role ambitions are pivotal to understanding Iran's behavior toward Israel—both before and after the revolution. Furthermore, the advice and thoughtful criticism of Zbigniew Brzezinski and Jakub Grygiel have been immensely helpful. And of course, I am forever indebted to Ruhi Ramazani, the dean of Iranian foreign policy studies. I have been extremely fortunate and honored in receiving his advice and assistance, and I hope to be able to continue my study of international relations and Iranian foreign policy in his tradition and to uphold the standard he has set.

Roane Carey provided endless insights and suggestions for the book, for which I am immensely thankful. My agent, Deborah Grosvenor, helped clean up my book proposal and made it sellable. And thanks to Clayton Swisher for his support and for helping me make the connections. I am also indebted to Professor David Menashri, Col. Shmuel Limone of the Israeli Ministry of Defense, and Professor Elliot Cohen for their help in setting up interviews in Israel. This book is built on the groundbreaking work Professor Menashri has done on Israeli-Iranian relations in the past few decades. I am equally grateful to Ambassador Javad Zarif, Dr. Mustafa Zahrani, and Afshin Molavi for their help in arranging interviews in Iran. Also, I owe much gratitude to Johns Hopkins SAIS for giving me the opportunity to investigate in-depth this important issue, and to George Perkovich at the Carnegie Endowment for International Peace for providing me with an office to write this book over the summer of 2006. Chris Rogers at Yale University Press and Professor Nikki Keddie provided invaluable help in transforming my original writings into an acceptable manuscript.

Above all, I must thank my family: my wife, Amina, without whose love, friendship, and endless patience I couldn't do without; my son Darius, the pride of my life; my brother Rouzbeh, whose dispassionate search for truth has inspired me; and, last but not least, my parents, without whom nothing would have been possible. I am to them eternally grateful.

TREACHEROUS ALLIANCE

1

introduction:
an eight-hundred-pound gorilla

The Iranian president is a Persian version of Hitler.

—Israel Deputy Prime Minister Shimon Peres,
referring to Iran President Mahmoud Ahmadinejad

[Israel and the U.S. need to establish] a broader strategic
relationship with Iran.

—Prime Minister Shimon Peres to President
Ronald Reagan, September 1986

"This regime that is occupying Qods [Jerusalem] must be eliminated from the pages of history."[1] With these words, spoken at an obscure conference in the Iranian capital of Tehran in October 2005, Mahmoud Ahmadinejad, the hard-line Iranian president, brought to the boiling point a rivalry between Iran and Israel that has been simmering for more than fifteen years. Always treated as a peripheral conflict, Israeli-Iranian tensions were often avoided by decision-makers in Washington, who focused on the Israeli-Palestinian dispute or on Iraq President Saddam Hussein's impulse for conquest. In doing so they failed to recognize that the geopolitical rivalry between Israel and Iran has—since the end of the Cold War—been the underlying conflict that defined the context of almost all other matters in the region. Sooner or later, even the most nearsighted politicians would see this eight-hundred-pound gorilla in the room. By pulling Ayatollah Ruhollah Khomeini's poisonous anti-Israel rhetoric from the dustbin of history, Ahmadinejad made sure it was sooner rather than later.

Still, even though the world has turned its attention to the Israeli-Iranian standoff, the nature of the conflict remains largely misunderstood. Ahmadinejad's questioning of the Holocaust, and Israel's demonization of Iran as a modern-day Nazi Germany, reflect a fundamental clash of ideologies, most Americans believe. On one side there's Israel, portrayed by its defenders as a democracy in a region beset by authoritarianism and an eastern outpost of Enlightenment rationalism. On the other side there's the Islamic Republic of Iran, depicted by its enemies as a hidebound clerical regime whose rejection of the West and whose aspiration to speak for all Muslims everywhere are symbolized by its refusal to grant Israel a right to exist. These ideologues have rejoined a battle in which there can be no parley or negotiated truce—only the victory of one vision and one value system over the other. Or so it would seem. Blinded by the condemnatory rhetoric, most observers have failed to notice a critical common interest shared by these two non-Arab powerhouses in the Middle East: the need to portray their fundamentally strategic conflict as an ideological clash.

After the end of the Cold War and the defeat of Iraq in the 1991 Persian Gulf War, the strategic considerations that had put Iran and Israel on the same geopolitical side in the latter part of the twentieth century evaporated. Soon enough, absent any common foes, Israel and Iran found themselves in a rivalry to redefine the regional order after the decimation of Iraq's military. Fearing that Israel's strategic weight would suffer if Iran emerged as the undisputed power in the Middle East, Israeli politicians began painting the regime in Tehran as fanatical and irrational. Clearly, they maintained, finding an accommodation with such "mad mullahs" was a nonstarter. Instead, they called on the United States to classify Iran, along with Saddam Hussein's Iraq, as a rogue state that needed to be "contained." Israel's change of heart on Iran was initially met with skepticism in Washington, though the Israelis advanced the same argument they do today, namely that Iran's nuclear program would soon afford the black-turbaned clerics access to the bomb. "Why the Israelis waited until fairly recently to sound a strong alarm about Iran is a perplexity," Clyde Haberman of the *New York Times* wrote in November 1992. Haberman went on to note: "For years, Israel remained willing to do business with Iran, even though the mullahs in Teheran were screaming for an end to the 'Zionist entity.'"[2]

But for Israel, rallying Western states to its side was best achieved by bringing attention to the alleged suicidal tendencies of the clergy and to Iran's apparent infatuation with the idea of destroying Israel. If the Iranian leadership was viewed as irrational, conventional tactics such as deterrence would be impossible, leaving the international community with no option but to have zero tolerance for Iranian military capabilities. How could a country like Iran be trusted with missile technology, the argument went, if its leadership was immune to dissuasion by the larger and more numerous missiles of the West? The Israeli strategy was to convince the world—particularly Washington—that the Israeli-Iranian conflict wasn't one between two rivals for military preeminence in a fundamentally disordered region that lacked a clear pecking order. Rather, Israel framed the clash as one between the sole democracy in the Middle East and a totalitarian theocracy that hated everything the West stood for. In casting the situation in those terms, Israel argued that the allegiance of Western states to Israel was no longer a matter of choice or mere political interest, but rather of survival, or at the very least of a struggle of good against evil.

Eventually the "mad mullah" argument stuck. After all, the Iranians themselves were the greatest help in selling that argument to Washington, because they too preferred an ideological framing of the conflict. When revolution swept Iran in 1979, the new Islamic leadership forsook the Persian nationalist identity of the regime of the overthrown Shah of Iran, Mohammad Reza Pahlavi, but not its yen for Iranian great-power status. Whereas the Shah sought suzerainty in the Persian Gulf and parts of the Indian Ocean regions, while hoping to make Iran the Japan of western Asia, the Khomeini government sought leadership in the entire Islamic world. The Shah's means for achieving his goal were a strong army and strategic ties to the United States. The Ayatollah, on the other hand, relied on his brand of political Islam and ideological zeal to overcome the Arab-Persian divide and to undermine the Arab governments that opposed Iran's ambitions. But whenever Iran's ideological and strategic goals were at odds, Tehran's strategic imperatives prevailed. So in the 1980s, when Iran was involved in a bloody war with Saddam Hussein's Iraq, the Iranians were careful not to follow up its diatribes against Israel with any concrete actions. Though ideology played a critical role in the revolution's early years, Iran's policy on Israel was to bark a lot, but never bite. The revolutionary regime's ideology and lurid rhetoric successfully veiled a fairly consistent pursuit of realpolitik.

After the Cold War, this double policy became all the more important because Israel was transformed from a partner that Iran needed to keep at arm's length to an aggressive competitor that had penetrated Iran's growing sphere of influence. But it was not possible to rally the Arab Muslim masses to Iran's side for the sake of Iran's power ambitions. So Iran turned to ideology once more to conceal its true motives, while utilizing the plight of the Palestinian people to undermine the Arab governments that supported the

Oslo process of the 1990s. Iranian speechwriters took the lead in inveighing against Israel's "never-ending appetite for Arab lands," its oppression of the Palestinians, its disregard for UN Security Council resolutions, and the "insult to Islam" embodied in its continued occupation of Jerusalem, site of the Haram al-Sharif, or dome of the rock, the third-holiest site in Islam. To this day, the rhetoric of Tehran preaches that its struggle against Israel is not about geopolitical gains or even about Iran itself, but rather about justice for the Palestinians and honor for Islam. With the Israeli-Palestinian conflict cast in these terms, and fearing a backlash from their own populations, pro-Western Arab rulers have to tread carefully not to belittle the announced goals of Tehran. In the eyes of many Arab states, the power of Iran's rhetoric has made public opposition to Iran equivalent to acquiescence in or even approval of the Israeli and U.S. stance on the Palestinian issue. Indeed, anti-Iranian statements such as Jordanian King Abdallah's warning in late 2004 of a "Shiite crescent" stretching from Iran through post-Saddam Iraq into Lebanon, and Egyptian President Hosni Mubarak's denunciation in early 2006 of Iraqi Shias as Iranian loyalists, have been poorly received by the Arab public. Tehran's pro-Palestinian reputation is one reason why.

The ideological pronouncements emanating from Ahmadinejad and other Iranian figures are an effect, rather than a cause, of Iran's strategic orientation. Likewise, Israeli Prime Minister Ehud Olmert's description of Iran as a "dark and gathering storm casting its shadow over the world" in his May 24, 2006, speech to Congress shouldn't be taken at face value. For now, both Iran and Israel seem to calculate—or miscalculate—that portraying their struggle in ideological and apocalyptic terms will provide each with a critical edge against the other in their efforts to define the order of the Middle East to their own benefit. But the dangers of this risky game are reaching intolerable levels and are dragging other actors into it. Israel has threatened to bomb Iran. The Bush administration has made similar threats, insisting that its own military option in relation to Iran remains on the table. Washington has even considered using nuclear weapons against Iran, according to press reports.[3] And Tehran continues to call Israel a fabricated entity with no legitimacy and no future in the Middle East. Forgotten behind the threats, the slogans, and the sound bites are not only a political and strategic reality but also a human reality and millennia of Iranian-Jewish friendship.

There are few Western cities where Persian pop music blasts at full volume in shopping malls. Yet this is a daily, natural occurrence at Jerusalem's high-security downtown bus terminal. Here, in the equivalent of New York's Penn Station, eighteen-year-old Israeli soldiers wait for their rides home, assault rifles slung over their shoulders, Persian pop legends Moin and Ebi pounding in their ears. Most of the CD stores here are owned by Iranian Jews, and over the past twenty years they have created a market for Persian pop in the very heart of the Jewish State. When one scratches the surface of the ferocious Israeli-Iranian enmity, an affinity between the two cultures emerges. In many ways they are more alike than different. Both tend to view themselves as somewhat superior to their Arab neighbors. Many Iranians think of the Arabs to their west and south as culturally inferior; as brutes who had the good fortune to have Persians as neighbors who could civilize and refine them. Similarly, having defeated the Arabs in numerous wars, most Israelis have little respect for their capabilities. "We know what the Arabs can do, and it isn't much," an Israeli analyst told me arrogantly, months before the war with Hezbollah in 2006 might have sobered him a bit. Incapable of suppressing their sense of superiority or of convincing the Arabs to let go of their own stereotypes of Persians and Jews, Israelis feel they are left with no option but to view true peace as unattainable. Some Israelis have all but given up the dream of living at peace with their neighbors, whether through true friendship or minimal but mutual recognition and acceptance, and have settled for a vision of "no war, no peace" built on a bedrock of Israeli military preponderance. The Iranians drew a similar conclusion centuries ago. "The Arabs are out to get us," Israelis and Iranians often think as they go about their daily lives.

Perhaps most importantly, both view themselves as culturally and politically disconnected from the region where they are forced to face their regional foes through the lens of a Manichean mindset. Ethnically, the Jews of Israel are surrounded by a sea of Arabs who may not always have been at war with Israel, but who have never been at peace with Israel. Culturally, Ashkenazi Jews from Eastern Europe dominate Israeli society, even though the profile of Mizrahi, or Oriental, Jews has risen in recent years. And religiously, of course, Israel is unique regionally and globally as the only state based on the Jewish faith. In perhaps a natural response to the long Jewish history of persecution, Israel has a penchant for mistrusting the outside world. According to this mindset, international institutions and global alliances can never substitute for Israel's own ability to protect itself. At the end of the day, a UN Security Council resolution can never protect Israel as well as two hundred nuclear warheads, Israelis believe. "These are weapons of peace," an Israeli general told me proudly, failing to see the contradiction in terms.

The Iranians aren't terribly different. Proud heirs to a civilization that precedes Islam by at least two millennia, they are the first to point out to Westerners that they are not Arabs. Iran, or the Land of the Aryans, as it is believed to mean, is largely populated by peoples speaking Indo-European tongues. Persian (or Farsi) is linguistically closer to French and Swedish than it is to Arabic, although it includes many Arabic words and is written in the Arabic script. And though Iran was Islamized in the seventh century B.C., the Persians kept their language, cultural traditions, and the special quality that to this day connects them to their Zoroastrian past. The Iranian New Year, Nowruz (New Day), has been celebrated in Iran for more than three thousand years and remains the largest Iranian holiday today, far out-shining any Islamic festival. When Ashura, the Shia Muslim day of mourn-ing commemorating the martyrdom of Hussain ibn Ali, the grandson of Prophet Muhammad, at the Battle of Karbala in the year A.D. 680, coincides with Nowruz, a day of rejoicing, the Zoroastrian soul of Iran wins in spite of the wishes of Iran's clerical rulers.

Even as Muslims, the Iranians distinguish themselves from their sur-roundings by following the Shia line of Islam rather than the much larger and dominating Sunni camp. And like Israelis, Iranians are deeply suspicious of the outside world. While Jews have been persecuted and have survived a Holocaust, Iranians have fought colonization, annexation, decades of for-eign intervention, and, last but not least, an eight-year war with Saddam Hussein's Iraq, in which virtually the entire world—including the United States—sided with Iraq. When Saddam invaded Iran in 1980, the UN didn't consider it a threat to international peace and security; it took the Security Council more than two years to call for withdrawal of the invading forces. (Compare that to Saddam's 1990 assault on Kuwait, when a Security Council Resolution [UNSR 660] passed within twelve hours of the invasion, de-manding an immediate and unconditional withdrawal of Iraqi forces.) An-other five years passed, mainly because of American procrastination, before the UN addressed Saddam's use of chemical weapons against Iranian sol-diers and civilians. (The United States and Western European countries ei-ther directly sold components for chemical weapons to Saddam or knew and quietly approved of such sales.) Even then, Washington ensured that the UN resolutions would be watered down to protect Saddam. The United States later cited these same crimes to justify its invasion of Iraq in 2003. For the Iranians, the lesson was clear: When in danger, Iran can rely on neither the Geneva Conventions nor the UN Charter for protection. Just like Israel, Iran has concluded that it can rely only on itself.

Jews and Iranians are no strangers to each other. Their cultures, religions, and histories are intimately intertwined and date back to biblical times. The origins of their relations can be traced to the eighth century B.C., when the Assyrian king Tiglath-pileser III forcibly resettled thousands of Jews in Media (northwestern Iran). Another group of Jews was resettled in Ecbatana (Hamadan) and Susa in 721 B.C. by his successor, Sargon II. To this day, Hamadan constitutes a major center for Iranian Jews. Hamadan is also reputed to be the burial site of Queen Esther, King Xerxes' wife, who saved the Jewish people from persecution in the fifth century B.C. This occasion is still celebrated by Jews in the Purim festival (Esther 3:1–9:32). Furthermore, the grave of the Old Testament prophet Daniel lies outside modern day Susa, in southwestern Iran.[4] The most significant wave of Jewish settlers arrived after the Persian king Cyrus the Great sacked Babylon in 539 B.C. and liberated the Jews from Babylonian captivity. The Jews appreciated the Persian king so much that they elevated him to the status of a God-sent savior, the only non-Jew to achieve that standing in the Bible (Ezra 1:1–7). Even though the Persians allowed the Jews to return to Israel and paid for the reconstruction of the temple in Jerusalem, many chose to immigrate to Persia. The twenty-five thousand Jews of modern-day Iran are direct descendents of those who chose to settle in what was then the world's sole superpower.

What is perhaps more important, and arguably explains why Persian Jews have been such an integral part of Iran throughout history, is that, unlike other Diasporas, Iranian Jews didn't flee to Iran. They moved there voluntarily, and, ever since, through good times and bad, Iran has been their home. Even today, under the Islamic Republic, Iran hosts the largest Jewish community in the Middle East outside of Israel, even though tens of thousands have left for Israel or the United States.[5] The books of Esther, Ezra, Nehemiah, and Daniel give favorable descriptions of the relationship of the Jews to the court of the Persians. Like other subjects in the Persian Empire, the Jews enjoyed religious freedom and followed their own legal code in personal matters such as marriage and family law. This mild treatment made the Jews less resistant to Persian influences on the Jewish faith. The Persian Zoroastrians shaped many of the key tenets of modern Judaism. From the Persians the Jews obtained the concepts of linear time, eschatology, angelology, and demonology, as well as concepts such as heaven and hell, which later influenced Christianity and Islam.[6] Most importantly, however, it was under Persian influence that Judaism became a monotheistic religion. The Zoroastrians were the first to believe in one universal god, Ahura Mazda, and contact with the Persians helped the Jews transcend their own tribal, henotheistic conception of god (the idea that each people have their own singular god). This is vividly seen in the literary works dating from the time of the Achaemenian empire, when the Jews began to describe a single god as opposed to pronouncing their god as the greatest among many other gods—which was the conception embraced by earlier Jewish prophets and figures.[7]

Some two hundred thousand Iranian Jews and their descendants live in Israel. Some of them belong to the highest levels of the Israeli political elite. In the Islamic Republic, these individuals would never have been able to excel in their careers. Long before reaching prominence, they would have been stopped by the glass ceiling that separates religious minorities, seculars, and disbelievers from those considered to be capable of being loyal to the Islamic Republic. Current Israeli President Moshe Katsav and Deputy Prime Minister (and former Chief of Staff of the Israel Defense Forces [IDF] and Defense Minister) Shaul Mofaz were both born in Iran. The recently resigned IDF chief of staff, Dan Halutz, was born to Persian immigrants.

When Katsav worked at the UN, a favorite pastime of his was to embarrass Iranian diplomats at various events by seeking to converse with them in Persian. Forbidden to talk to Israeli officials (at least in public), the Iranian diplomats could rid themselves of the unrelenting Katsav only by leaving the events. Katsav found that profoundly amusing. Mofaz and Halutz approach Iran with a bit less humor; they are some of the most hawkish Israeli leaders regarding Iran. When asked in a press conference in January 2005 how far Israel would go to stop Iran's nuclear program, Halutz, a former pilot, gave a chilling response: "Two thousand kilometers." That's the distance between Israel and Iran. For other Iranian Jews—both in Israel and in Iran—the tensions between the two countries have caused major pain and anxiety. Since the Iranian revolution there has been an unwritten understanding between Iran's Jewish minority and the Iranian authorities. As long as the Jews of Iran oppose Zionism and the Israeli state, they would be protected in Iran and given a great deal of religious freedom. "This arrangement, which makes a clear separation between being a Jew and being a Zionist, was the community's idea; they brought it to the Khomeini regime after the revolution," noted David Menashri, Israel's most prominent expert on Iran, himself an Iranian-born Jew.[8] Khomeini issued a "fatwa," a religious decree, declaring that Jews were to be protected.[9]

Few Iranian Jews take Ahmadinejad's anti-Israel rhetoric seriously, and they point to the fact that little has changed for Iranian Jews under him. "Anti-Semitism is not an eastern phenomenon, it's not an Islamic or Iranian phenomenon—anti-Semitism is a European phenomenon," Ciamak Mor-sathegh, head of the Jewish hospital in Tehran, explained.[10] Iran's forty synagogues, many of them with Hebrew schools, haven't been touched. Neither has the Jewish library, which boasts twenty thousand titles, or Jewish hospitals and cemeteries. Still, Iran's Jews have not sat idly by. The Jewish member of the Iranian Majlis, or parliament (most religious minorities are guaranteed a seat in the parliament), Maurice Mohtamed, has been outspoken in his condemnation of Ahmadinejad's comments. "When our president spoke about the Holocaust, I considered it my duty as a Jew to speak about this issue," Mohtamed told the *Guardian*. "The biggest disaster in human history is based on tens of thousands of films and documents. I said these remarks are a big insult to the whole Jewish society in Iran and the whole world."[11] Haroun Yashayaei, the chairman of Iran's Jewish Council, quickly followed suit, sending Ahmadinejad a strongly worded letter protesting his remarks.[12] The Jewish community won support from Mohammad Khatami, Ahmadinejad's more moderate predecessor. "We should speak out if even a single Jew is killed," the reformist president said in widely published remarks in early 2006. "Don't forget that one of the crimes of Hitler, Nazism and German National Socialism was the massacre of innocent people, among them many Jews."[13]

Iranian Jews in Israel have faced similar dilemmas. Quite understandably, Ahmadinejad's questioning of the Holocaust and his call for Israel to be moved to Europe have sparked fears of a revival of fascism among Ashkenazi Jews. But Iranian Jews in Israel have been less alarmed, though equally angered. "European Jews do not know Ahmadinejad as well as Iranian Jews, so his pronouncements about the Holocaust are more effective with them," explained Soli Shavar, a Persian Jew who teaches at Haifa University. "[The Iranian Jews] know [where] the jargon and rhetoric of the radical element comes from."[14] After all, many Iranian Jews in Israel see Iran up close—a perspective that other Israelis never experience. During Khatami's presidency, travel between the two countries via Turkey was made easier, and the direct telephone lines—which have never been cut—are used more frequently as prices plummet. Persian Jews travel from Israel to Turkey, where they mail back their Israeli passports and take out their Iranian passports as they hop on the next flight to Tehran. Some Jews who have lost their Iranian passports even go to the Iranian consulate in Istanbul and request new ones, fully disclosing their new Israeli nationality. Surprisingly, the Iranian authorities don't seem to mind.

With all their cultural similarities, there is also much that separates the two. The differences between Iranians and Israelis are something the Persian Jews deal with daily. Culturally and economically, some Iranian Jews prefer their Persian birthplace to their Jewish homeland. Many of the recent Iranian immigrants to Israel came for economic and not political reasons. Thinking that Israel was an economic paradise, they left their lives in Iran to make better ones in Israel. But to many, Israel has not lived up to their expectations, and now they dream of returning to Iran. Some have acted on those dreams. According to Orly Halpern of the *Jerusalem Post,* Jerusalem's Jaffa Road and Rehov Ben-Yehuda are lined with Iranian shopkeepers who say they are desperate to go back—some to visit, some to live. "In Iran, everyone says that in the land of Israel, it's great. They give you a house, they give you money. Life is easy," an Iranian Jewish immigrant told Halpern. "We came here and we were in shock. There it's difficult, but not as difficult as here," she said, adding that her "heart aches for Iran."[15] Other Iranian immigrants clearly prefer Israel, and some tensions exist between recent and more established immigrants from Iran. Older immigrants tend to be somewhat suspicious of the more recent arrivals, at times accusing them of favoring the Iranian government.

As similar as Israelis and Iranians are, recent Iranian immigrants to Israel experience difficulty in overcoming the cultural shock. The contrast between the traditional values of Iranian society and the liberal currents of Israeli society—defined by the norms and culture of its European immigrants rather than by its Middle Eastern geography—could not be greater. I once had a conversation with an elderly Iranian Jew whom I sat next to during the bus ride from Jerusalem to Tel Aviv. Ehsaq (Isaac), as he was called, spared no love for the clerics in Tehran, but he liked to reminisce about the country in which he had spent most of his life. After all, Israel was only the most recent chapter in his long life, and he had never really managed to make the Jewish State his home. He didn't quite fit in. In typical Iranian fashion, Ehsaq felt compelled to share the bread he had brought with him for the hour-long bus ride with his fellow Ashkenazi passengers, scaring the daylights out of the more reserved European Jews, who could not quite determine if Ehsaq's dark features made him an Oriental Jew (Mizrahi) or a local Arab. Embarrassed, Ehsaq returned to his seat. After a moment of silence, he burst out in Persian with a thick Isfahani accent, "Farhang nadaran" (They're uncultured). This criticism against Israel is commonly heard among Iranian Jews.

Like most Russian Jews who immigrated to Israel after the fall of the Berlin Wall, the Iranian Jews still prefer their own language over Hebrew

and cling to their Iranian culture with great devotion. They celebrate the
Nowruz with such fanfare that festivities in Los Angeles or Tehran would
pale in comparison. "I am proud to be Jewish, I am proud to be an Israeli,
but I have nothing in common with these people," Ehsaq complained to me.
"I don't want my children to live like they do," he said dismissively of the liberal ways of the European Jews. Misunderstandings between the two groups
are not uncommon. Iranians tend to speak circumspectly, avoiding spelling
out their intentions or objectives at all cost. With great finesse and redundant politeness, they deliver their message behind layers and layers of nuance and deliberately misleading compliments. Israelis are the opposite. It's
the clash between *taarof* and *chutzpah.*

Taarof is an Iranian social principle, a concept of insincere politeness.
For instance, Iranians invite each other to dinner not necessarily because
they mean it, but to show politeness. The expectation is that the invited
party will respond with equal politeness—by turning the invitation down.
The impolite thing to do would be to accept the invitation on its first offering. An invitation should be considered sincere only if it has been offered
roughly three times, after which, of course, it would be immensely rude to
decline it. Vagueness, symbolism, and endless nuance are inherent in the
Iranian culture and language. "*Taarof* is a sign of respect, even if we don't
mean it," Nasser Hadian of Tehran University explained, in a statement
Americans and Israelis would find blatantly contradictory.[16] For Iranians,
however, there is no contradiction. They understand *taarof* and why insincere politeness is still a sign of utter respect.

The Israelis have a different cultural trait, *chutzpah,* meaning "audac-
ity" or "gall." They tell a joke to explain the concept. A spoiled twelve-year-
old boy argues with his parents, and in a moment of rage he kills them both.
He is immediately caught and taken to jail to await trial. As he is brought
into the courtroom he throws himself at the feet of the judge and cries out:
"Have mercy with me! After all, I am just a poor orphan!" Unlike many Iranians, Israelis don't tend to hide what they mean to say. They can't help
themselves but to be absolutely direct without a single redundant word or
any effort to reflect the nuances that inevitably characterize all social situa-
tions—a trait that Iranians and Iranian Jews simply find crude and offensive. While an Iranian would go to great lengths to avoid using the word
"no," many Israelis thrive on categorical imperatives. Getting a nuanced answer from an Israeli can be as tricky as getting a straight answer from an
Iranian. In the clash between *taarof* and *chutzpah,* no one wins. Only confusion reigns.

As much as they can find each other rude and impolite, or insincere and disingenuous, Israelis and Iranians also hold an exaggerated and almost mythical view of each other. The respect and awe the two rivals have for each other cannot be mistaken. "Iranians are perceived as masters of deception, and I think their mythical stature arises not solely because Israelis know Iranians and appreciate their abilities, but because they are so unlike Arabs," an Israeli expert on Iran told me. "When we classify our enemies, Arabs are the hard heads who would operate along exactly the same guidelines forever and ever, because they're Arabs. They are narrow-minded. Unsophisticated. Iranians are something that is much harder to characterize for Israelis because they are so much like us."

Some Israelis point to the biblical story of Queen Esther as an indication of Iranian mastery of the art of manipulation. According to the legend, Esther was the daughter of a Jewish merchant living in the city of Susa during the reign of Xerxes (486–465 B.C.). Her beauty caught the eye of the Persian king, who made her his queen, unaware of her Jewish heritage. Once on the throne, Esther learned of a conspiracy in the kingdom to kill all the Jews, orchestrated not by the Persians but by another minority group, the Amalekites. Esther approached the king and invited him and the key conspirator, Haman, to attend a banquet she had prepared, at which she would reveal to the Persian emperor a petition. At the banquet, Xerxes curiously asked Esther about the request. "Now what is your petition? It will be given you," he said, according to the Bible. But rather than making her wish known, Esther promised to reveal it if the king and Haman would join her for dinner the following day as well. There again, the king asked about her request. Esther had waited patiently for the right moment and it had now arrived. "If it pleases your majesty, grant me my life—this is my petition," she said. "For I and my people have been sold for destruction and slaughter and annihilation." Bewildered, the king demanded to know who had requested the death of his queen. "Haman," Esther replied confidently, knowing that her plan and patience had paid off. Haman was hanged, and the Jews of Persia were saved.

"In the Bible, Esther acts completely Persian," explained Shmuel Bar of the Interdisciplinary Center in Herzliya and a veteran of the Israeli intelligence community. "She deceives, conceals her intentions, manipulates and convinces stronger parties to fight her battles."[17] According to the Shalem Center in Jerusalem, Israelis today should learn from Esther's manipulative "Iranian" instincts and employ it in their diplomacy. But the infatuation with Esther may reveal more about the Israelis themselves than about the

Iranians. "We like to think of ourselves as master tricksters," an Israeli expert on Iran commented. "Consider this: When you define someone as your worst enemy, you say a lot about yourself." Ironically, in Europe, where the currents of anti-Semitism have been strong historically, the title "masters of deception" was given to the Jewish people—and not to the Iranians. Many Israelis are wary of the stereotypes they have of the Iranians, arguing they are exaggerated at best and misleading at worst. "These myths are created by the old Iran hands; let's call them the 'Lubranis' [a reference to Uri Lubrani, the Israeli envoy to Iran in the 1970s who remains active on Iran affairs at the Ministry of Defense]," explained Ehud Yaari, a veteran Israeli television journalist. "I don't buy the myth that the Iranians have seven thousand years of diplomacy under the turban of Rafsanjani." But even Yaari could not deny the esteem Israelis have for the Iranian nation. "I miss Iran. A lot," he told me while reminiscing about the "good old days" before the revolution, when intelligence cooperation between the two countries was extensive and Israeli tourists flocked to visit Iran—the only Middle Eastern country where Israelis were welcome at the time.[18]

Iranians, on the other hand, refuse to express open admiration for the abilities of the Israelis and try to hide their concerns and fears behind inflammable rhetoric and ideological façades. Iranians angrily dismiss any suggestion that Israel is a rival with Iran for a leadership position in the region. How can that be, they ask with unmasked irritation? With all the problems Iran has with the Arabs, Israel's problems are far worse, they insist. At least Iran has Islam in common with the Arabs, and Iran is a "real country"—not an artificial state built on occupied Arab land, as they usually argue. "Nobody will accept Israeli hegemony, even if there is a two-state solution," Mustafa Zahrani, head of the Iranian Foreign Ministry's think tank IPIS, told me in his office in northern Tehran in August 2004. "Israeli actions are illegitimate, and their population is very small. They cannot be the dominating power. Just accepting them to continue to exist is too much, let alone being the hegemon," he said.[19] But behind Zahrani's harsh words lies the Iranian fear of facing a rival in the region that may be small, that may be culturally foreign to the region, but that holds an ace up its sleeve that Iran covets—the support of the United States of America.

On July 12, 2006, war broke out between Israel and Hezbollah, a Lebanese guerrilla and political group supported by Iran. On that day, a Hezbollah unit crossed the Israeli-Lebanese border and kidnapped two Israeli soldiers and killed another three. Israel immediately launched a rescue mission that not only failed, but also led to the death of five more Israeli soldiers. To Hezbollah, this was a medium-size border clash; the purpose of the raid was to acquire Israeli prisoners, which Hezbollah could use to win the release of Lebanese and Palestinian fighters held by the Israelis. To Israel, and to its neoconservative supporters in the Bush administration, this was an act of war—not only by Hezbollah, but by Iran as well.

Within hours, Israel handed Hezbollah a response it hadn't expected; massive air strikes against Hezbollah strongholds and missile launchpads, as well as against Lebanon's civilian infrastructure. It was shock and awe, Israeli style. The Israelis even bombed Lebanese oil storage tanks and tarmacs at Beirut's airport, making it impossible for airplanes to take off or land. That move stranded up to twenty-five thousand Lebanese-Americans in the midst of the fighting, but the Bush administration didn't seem to mind. On the contrary, prominent neoconservatives, who for years had urged the Bush administration to take on Iran, were ecstatic. William Kristol of the *Weekly Standard* urged the Pentagon to counter "this act of Iranian aggression with a military strike against Iranian nuclear facilities. Why wait?" Describing the fighting in ideological terms—"an Islamist-Israeli war"— Kristol warned against appearing weak and concluded, "This is our war, too."[20] Never mind that Hezbollah, though a close ally of Iran and of Syria as well, has repeatedly demonstrated that it can come to important political and military decisions on its own, without Iranian approval or tutelage. To the neoconservatives and Israel's supporters on the right in America, the war in Lebanon represented a crucial step in their plan to turn Iran into the next Iraq.[21] Only a day after the war began, one of Washington's most aggressive Iran hawks, Michael Ledeen of the American Enterprise Institute, called for the United States to expand the fighting into a regional war: "The only way we are going to win this war is to bring down those regimes in Tehran and Damascus, and they are not going to fall as a result of fighting between their terrorist proxies in Gaza and Lebanon on the one hand, and Israel on the other. Only the United States can accomplish it."[22]

That same day, another supporter of the Bush administration's Middle East policy, John Gibson, wrote an editorial for the Fox News Channel in which he argued that Iran (that is, Hezbollah) hadn't attacked Israel. It had actually attacked the United States. "It's really a war by Iran on us."[23] Though President Bush didn't follow the advice of his neoconservative brethren, Washington did everything it could to prolong the war and thus give Israel time to destroy as much of Hezbollah as possible. "A cessation of violence is crucial, but if that cessation of violence is hostage to Hezbollah's next decision to launch missiles into Israel or Hamas's next decision to abduct an Israeli citizen, then we will have gotten nowhere," Secretary of State Condoleezza Rice told Fox News. President Bush himself responded to calls for an immediate cease-fire from the international community by urging them not to neglect the strategic opportunity the war provided. "What we're saying is, let's not lose sight of the broader context," Bush said on CNN.[24] Clearly, Bush's hope was that Israel's anticipated decapitation of Hezbollah would weaken Iran's spreading influence in the region and put an end to its challenge to America and Israel's regional dominance. Neutralizing Hezbollah would also deprive Iran of its deterrence and retaliatory capabilities, paving the way for a war with Tehran in which it wouldn't be able to strike back at the Jewish State. "War with Iran is inevitable," Ephraim Sneh, Israel's deputy defense minister, told me at a conference in southern Europe on July 28, 2006, halfway through the war. "Lebanon is just a prelude to the greater war with Iran," he said with frightening certainty.

After a war that left more than fifteen hundred people dead, mostly Lebanese civilians, displacing nine hundred thousand Lebanese and three hundred thousand Israelis, severely damaging Lebanon's infrastructure, and disrupting normal life across all of Lebanon and northern Israel, Sneh's prediction stands as an ominous warning. But if it comes to pass, the conflict won't be limited to Israel and Iran. It will be a regional war, pulling in other countries and nonstate actors alike. And it will be America's war, too, just as the neoconservatives have so desperately wished. (Unlike Iraq, Iran can inflict devastating harm on the United States due to its asymmetric military capabilities spread throughout the region.)

Today America stands at a dangerous crossroads, with the Iraq occupation rapidly collapsing in civil war and chaos, even as the U.S. military has been stretched to its limit. There is a great deal of confusion as to how America got mixed up in an Israeli-Iranian rivalry that is about neither ideology nor religion. Before it can find a path toward a peaceful future, Washington must first relearn the past and deal directly with the eight-hundred-pound gorilla.

part one

the cold war era

2

an alliance of necessity:
the secret friendship of the shah

The Arabs could tolerate the substance of close Iran-Israel relations
as long as this was not apparent from surface indications.

—De-classified Memorandum of Conversation, U.S. embassy
in Tehran, Iran, October 14, 1972

After the First World War, the British controlled Palestine in quasi-colonial
fashion, in a mandate sanctioned by the League of Nations. The Zionist
movement, which had begun at the end of the previous century and encouraged Jewish immigration to Palestine with the eventual goal of creating
a Jewish State, flourished under the mandate. The growing Jewish population clashed repeatedly with the Arab majority, which was unalterably opposed to a Jewish State and which itself wanted independence from Britain.
At various periods during the mandate, the British suppressed both Arab
and Jewish guerrilla rebellions. Exhausted after the Second World War, fi-
nancially broke, and torn between bitterly opposing demands from the
Arab and Jewish populations, the British finally threw in the towel and
asked the UN to settle the problem. On May 15, 1947, the United Nations
created a Special Committee on Palestine, UNSCOP, to recommend a resolution. Iran was selected to be part of the eleven-state committee.

After several months of laborious hearings a plan was presented with the
support of only eight of the committee's eleven members. The majority favored a partition of Palestine and the creation of independent Arab and
Jewish States, with Jerusalem to be placed under international administration. Iran, together with India and Yugoslavia, opposed this idea and pre-

dicted that partition would lead to more rather than less violence.[1] At the time, Iran was ruled by Shah Mohammad Reza Pahlavi, the second emperor in the Pahlavi dynasty. His father, Reza Shah, had staged a coup d'état in February 1921 and ousted the ruling Qajar dynasty. Twenty years later, Reza Shah was deposed by the British and the Russians, who put his young son, Mohammad Reza, on the throne. Even before the creation of the Jewish State, Mohammad Reza Shah had predicted that partition of Palestine would lead to decades, if not centuries, of violence. Only through the creation of a single federal state containing both Jewish and Arab constituent states could peace be established, the Pahlavi regime maintained. Against Tehran's quiet objections, the partition plan was adopted by the General Assembly as Resolution 181 on November 29, 1947. Fighting immediately broke out between Jews and Palestinians, and less than six months later David Ben-Gurion declared the independence of the State of Israel. Iran, which together with twelve other nations voted against partition, chose not to formally recognize the new nation, a decision the Shah stuck to throughout his thirty-seven-year reign.[2]

At Israel's inception, Iran faced a dilemma that has characterized its dealings with the Jewish State ever since. The Shah knew that the creation of a non-Arab, pro-Western state in the Middle East could improve Iran's security by absorbing the attention and resources of the Arab states, which were Iran's traditional rivals in the region. But if the Shah were to officially recognize Israel or publicly support its creation, part of that Arab wrath would fall on Iran. Thus it behooved Iran to tread a path between overt hostility and overt alliance. For the next three decades, the Shah handled this balancing act with great astuteness.

CAUGHT IN THE SUPERPOWER GAME

The two clear winners of the Second World War were the United States and the Soviet Union. But their defeat of the Axis powers entangled them in a global rivalry, and soon after the war they began carving up the world into their respective spheres of influence. The Middle East was no exception; its abundance of oil made it a particularly valuable piece in the geopolitical chess game played by Washington and Moscow, which drew regional states into their respective camps. In return for their cooperation, those states were offered friendship and protection. For Iran, the choice was clear. Centuries of war between Iran and Russia had bred in the Shah a natural suspicion of Soviet intentions. The Communist ideology was a real threat to the Shah's rule in Iran, where the uneven distribution of wealth created fertile ground for pro-Soviet groups such as the Iranian Tudeh ("People's") Party. The Shah hoped that joining the Western camp would entitle Iran to economic and military assistance from the United States in order to prevent Soviet adventurism in the Middle East and the Persian Gulf.

Israel's strategic options were more complex. The newly created Jewish State depended on the West for capital investment, but it was also in dire need of immigration from the Jewish communities in both the East and West to grow and survive. With the demographic balance tilted strongly against it—by 1948 there were approximately 1.35 million Arabs and 650,000 Jews in historic Palestine—Israel could not prosper without more Jewish immigrants. While Ben-Gurion always favored the United States as a primary patron, in the country's early days many Israelis felt an emotional and ideological affinity for the Soviet Union, because not only did strong socialist sentiment exist in Israel, but many Israelis identified the Soviet Union as the country primarily responsible for defeating Nazism. For the Shah, who saw the world primarily through the prism of the Cold War, Israel's ambiguous relations with the Soviet Union and its efforts to cultivate ties with both superpowers made it suspect. The Shah adopted a policy of "calculated ambivalence," maintaining a healthy distance from the Jewish State while waiting for it to clarify its allegiances. For the first two years of Israel's existence, Iran recognized it neither de facto nor de jure. But as Tel Aviv distanced itself from the Soviet camp, and as its pro-Western orientation solidified, Iranian suspicions were dispelled.[3] In 1951, the Mossadeq government in Iran recognized Israel as a fact in the region but still refused de jure recognition, meaning that it did not officially establish relations with the Jewish State.[4] Still, the de facto recognition had significant political implications—it essentially meant that Iran recognized the creation of the state of Israel and would not seek or support its undoing.

But choosing the Western camp did not resolve Israel's security dilemma. Israel was a lone state for Jews in a sea of hostile Arab states, some of which were developing closer ties to the Soviet Union. Since breaking the circle of Arab enmity appeared impossible, Israel put its faith in reaching out to the non-Arab states of the region, including Iran. This outlook gave birth to Ben-Gurion's doctrine of the periphery, a foreign policy concept that came to dominate Israeli strategic thinking till the end of the Cold War. The doctrine held that the improbability of achieving peace with the surrounding Arab states forced Israel to build alliances with the non-Arab states of the periphery—primarily Iran, Turkey, and Ethiopia—as well as with non-Arab minorities such as the Kurds and the Lebanese Christians.

This network of alliances would drive a wedge between Israel's enemies, weaken the Arab bloc, and halt the spread of pan-Arabism in the region, the reasoning went.[5]

Meanwhile, Iran's relationship with the Arab states was swiftly deteriorating.[6] Though Iran sympathized with Arab nationalism and its quest for Arab independence from the European colonial powers (Iran was, after all, still emerging from its own painful history of British and Russian interference), the Shah felt increasingly uncomfortable with its pro-Soviet expressions.[7] In Egypt, for example, the free officers' coup of 1952 ousted King Farouk and achieved final independence from Britain, slowly drifting into the Soviet orbit as a result. By no choice of their own, Iran and Israel soon found themselves facing a common security dilemma. Both feared Soviet designs on the region and the threat of radical pro-Soviet Arab states, and both saw the pan-Arab, anti-Western regime in Cairo, led by Gamal Abdel Nasser, as the main villain of the Middle East.[8] Next to Israel, Iran's pro-Western emperor was one of Egypt's prime targets.[9] Iran was particularly concerned about the territorial expansionism of pan-Arabism and Arab claims over Iran's southern oil-rich province of Khuzestan because this pushed Arab nations to ally against Iran even though their respective national interests may have dictated a different course.[10] "The Iranians felt like [they were] surrounded by the Arabs. And the Arabs always adopted policies that were anti-Iranian," said Fereydoun Hoveyda, who served as Iran's ambassador to the UN during the 1970s while his brother, Amir Abbas Hoveyda, served as the Shah's prime minister.[11]

By the late 1950s, an Israeli-Iranian entente had taken shape, fueled by the solidification of Egyptian-Soviet relations and the emergence of Nasser as the leader of the Arab masses after the 1956 Suez war. The collusion of Israel, Britain, and France in the attack on Egypt in 1956 cemented Nasser's and the wider Arab world's suspicion and hostility toward both their former colonial masters and Israel. But Ben-Gurion, ever so cautious and suspicious of the outside world's attitudes toward the Jewish State, feared that Iran and the periphery states wouldn't enter into full strategic relations with Israel unless pressured by the United States. On July 24, 1958, he sent a personal letter to U.S. President Dwight Eisenhower in which he warned about the spread of pan-Arabism and Communism in the Middle East, and requested U.S. support for Israel as a means of defending Western interests. He wrote that "with the purpose of erecting a high dam against the Nasserist-Soviet tidal wave, we have begun tightening our links with several states on the outside of the perimeter of the Middle East—Iran, Turkey and

Ethiopia. . . . Our goal is to organize a group of countries, not necessarily an official alliance, that will be able to stand strong against Soviet expansion by proxy through [Egyptian President] Nasser, and which might save Lebanon's freedom and, maybe in time, Syria's."[12] Eisenhower heeded Israel's call and offered America's backing to the periphery alliance.

Compatibility between Iran and Israel went beyond their two common threats. Israel's impressive economic growth and the Arabs' refusal to sell oil to Israel made Tel Aviv desperate for a commodity that Iran possessed in abundance.[13] After the 1956 Suez crisis, Iran helped finance the construction of an eight-inch oil pipeline from Eilat in southern Israel through Beersheba to Israel's Mediterranean coastline. This pipeline, called the Eilat-Ashkelon pipeline, connected the gulf of Aqaba and the Mediterranean and enabled Iranian oil exports to bypass the strategically vulnerable Suez Canal. Lessening the dependence on the Egyptian-controlled Suez was of utmost importance to the Shah because 73 percent of Iran's imports and 76 percent of its oil exports passed through the canal. The deal, which took several days to conclude, was brokered in the suburbs of Tel Aviv in the summer of 1957 during a secret visit by a representative of the National Iranian Oil Company. The pipeline was laid in a record-breaking one hundred days and came into operation in late 1957, transporting Iranian oil to Israel at the price of $1.30 per barrel. The pipeline was later upgraded to a sixteen-inch pipe after direct negotiations between Israeli Prime Minister Levi Eshkol and the Shah in 1958. This was the first direct meeting between an Israeli cabinet minister and the Shah.[14] Though neither Iran nor Israel acknowledged the oil trade or the pipeline cooperation, their relationship was an open secret and the subject of intense Arab criticism. Fearing that the Shah might abandon the project because of his Arab sensitivities, Washington granted the pipeline project its strong support only after receiving reassurances that Iran's financial interest in seeing to the completion of the pipelines outweighed Tehran's interest in appeasing Arab sentiments. Washington clearly sensed that the Shah wanted to keep Israel at a healthy distance and wanted assurances that pressure from the Arab states wouldn't prompt the Shah to renege on his commitments to the pipeline.[15]

And there were other reasons for the cultivation of stronger Israel-Iran relations: Iran had a sizable Jewish community, which Israel was eager to bring to the Jewish State, and Tehran was willing to provide Iraqi Jews with a safe passage to Israel as well. Iran, in turn, coveted Israel's influence in Washington and was in dire need of advanced Israeli technology for its own economic growth. Israel's expertise in irrigation was highly valued by the technology-starved Iranians. The arid and uninviting climate and terrain of Iran and Israel opened up opportunities for extensive cooperation in the field of agriculture, even though political factors motivated this coopera- tion more than Iran's agricultural needs. The Shah often ordered his min- istries to hire Israeli consultants as a means of cementing the relationship— even though their expertise wasn't always needed and their skill sets often were irrelevant to their assigned projects. "We had Israelis who weren't even agriculturalists who didn't collect salary, yet they were still involved in the projects," Iran's former deputy minister of agriculture explained.[16] But hir- ing redundant Israeli consultants was a politically safe way for the Shah to balance his public distance from the Jewish State.[17] Nonetheless, while there was a political aspect to the technological exchange, the Israelis did provide Iran with badly needed know-how and expertise. According to Arieh Eliav, former Israeli labor minister, Israel trained some ten thousand Iranian agricultural experts.[18] Last but not least, Israel and Iran's common non-Arab makeup provided the two with an emotional dimension to their growing cooperation.[19]

AN UNBALANCED PARTNERSHIP

Clearly, as the most powerful country on Israel's periphery, Iran was a criti- cal factor in Tel Aviv's political grand strategy. But Israel wasn't equally im- portant to Iran despite Iran's need for Israeli technology. Throughout the 1950s, Iran viewed Israel primarily as a vehicle to prevent Soviet—and not Arab—advances in the region.[20] The Soviet Union constituted Iran's pri- mary threat because it was eyeing the oil reserves of the region and using Nasser's Egypt as its surrogate to penetrate the Persian Gulf.[21] "The Shah saw these Soviet twin pincers coming down through Afghanistan and Iraq," explained Charles Naas, who served as an American diplomat in Iran at the time.[22] Clearly, Iranian fears of the Soviet Union benefited the United States because it made Iran all the more eager for the Western superpower's pro- tection. Soviet support for the pan-Arab states, in turn, caused the Arab danger to Iran to be seen in Tehran as a mere extension of the Soviet threat, while the pan-Arab ideology was perceived more as a facilitator than as the root of this threat.

The Shah strongly believed that in the face of Soviet subversion or even a direct assault, no one could guarantee Iran's security but Iran itself.[23] This conviction was partly born out of a conversation between the Shah and an American ambassador in the late 1940s. At the time, the Shah was young, inexperienced, and impressionable. He had seen how Iran's weakness had enabled the great powers to control the destiny of his country. This was an affront he was determined to change. "America would never go to war with the Soviets on account of Iran, to save Iran," the ambassador told the Iranian monarch matter-of-factly. The Shah never forgot that conversation.[24]

The Soviets, on the other hand, did little to alleviate the Shah's fears. Moscow supported leftist Iranian opposition groups such as the Mujahedin-e Khalq, the Tudeh Party, and the Fedayeen-e Khalq in the hope that a Communist revolution would make Iran a Soviet satellite.[25] In a December 1974 interview with Beirut's *al-Hawadis* newspaper, the Shah emphasized that Iranian nervousness about pan-Arabism was rooted in Moscow's influence over the Arab governments that championed that ideology. With the Arabs, the Shah pointed out, Iran did not seek any enmity, even though the Palestinians supported Iranian opposition groups. What the Shah sought to avoid was a situation in which the activities of Palestinian and Arab nationalists would enable the Soviets to up the ante on Iran. "We have stood and we will stand at the side of the Palestinians, despite the fact that some of the groups of the resistance trained Iranian saboteurs to infiltrate our territory, kill our people, and blow up various installations," he said. "We know how to discriminate between the justness of the Palestinian question and the wrongdoing directed against us by some Palestinians. What I fear is that the Palestinians may allow international circumstances to make their cause a tool of Soviet or some other international strategy. Egypt, Saudi Arabia, Syria, and the other Arab states would do well to help the Palestinians avoid such pitfalls."[26] With time, however, the Arab threat came to play a greater role in Iranian strategic thinking. As the Arab threat to Iran increased, so did Iran's military need for Israel and—paradoxically— its need to keep Israeli dealings secret.

A NOT-SO-SECRET MARRIAGE OF CONVENIENCE

Iran preferred to keep most of its collaboration with Israel out of the public eye. On the one hand, the Shah believed that overt relations with Israel would harm Iran's standing with the Arab nations and fuel Arab opposition to Iranian policies in the Persian Gulf. On the other hand, he needed Israel in order to balance the threat from the Soviets and pro-Soviet Arab states. To minimize the visibility of his Israeli dealings, the Shah decided to have interactions with Israel handled by Iran's dreaded secret police—Sazeman-e Ettela'at va Amniyat-e Keshvar (Organization of Information and State Security, or Savak).[27] In 1957, the Shah ordered the Iranian intelligence service to establish relations with the Israeli intelligence agency, the

Mossad, and manage Iran's sensitive dealings with the Jewish State, which often kept the Iranian Foreign Ministry in the dark. Iranian military and secret police operatives were secretly trained by Israeli intelligence officers in both Iran and Israel. Israel also trained four hundred Iranian pilots, paratroopers, and artillery men and sold Iran high-tech military equipment.[28] According to one former Iranian ambassador, the Mossad also trained the Savak in torture and investigative techniques as well.[29]

Still, Tehran kept secret the visits of its officials to Israel. The Iranians traveled to Israel via Turkey and never had their passports stamped upon arrival in the Jewish State. This procedure ensured that the travel logs listed only a visit to Turkey and no trace of the Israel leg of the trip.[30] (To this day, Iranian Jews traveling to Israel follow the same route with the tacit approval of the Iranian government.) Even the deployment of Iranian diplomats in Israel was kept secret. During the 1970s, six Iranian diplomats manned the Iranian secret mission in Israel, but their records indicated that they were serving in Bern, Switzerland. The Iranian embassy in Israel was referred to as "Bern 2" in Iranian Foreign Ministry documents.[31] The Iranians even tried to withhold the true location of their posting from American diplomats, despite the United States's awareness of both the existence and the activities of the Iranian diplomats in Israel.[32] Although Israel had grown accustomed to Iran's secretive approach, and though Israel was well aware of the Shah's precarious balancing act between living up to Iran's obligations as a Muslim nation and neutralizing the tide of Arab radicalism, Iran's contradictory policy and stance on Israel was never fully accepted in Tel Aviv. If Iran, a predominantly Muslim nation, were to openly recognize Israel, it would help advance Israel's quest to convince the Arabs that the Jewish State was a permanent feature of the Middle East. After all, Israel had proven its utility to the Shah and to Iran's national interest, yet the Iranian emperor refused to grant Israel full recognition.

Ben-Gurion's first visit to Iran in 1961 set the precedent on the secretive protocol.[33] The groundbreaking visit was kept secret, and successive trips of Israeli prime ministers to Iran simply followed the same protocol. A few years later, Israeli diplomats in Tehran urged Prime Minister Golda Meir to take a more aggressive line with the Shah on this matter and change the protocol. By bringing its relations with Iran into the open, Iran would have no choice but to recognize Israel de jure, decision-makers in Tel Aviv figured. The Israelis jumped on every opportunity to make their dealings with Iran public.[34] Meir's advisers proposed putting a sign on the building of the Israeli mission in Tehran to clearly identify it as such. She dismissed this proposal but accepted the recommendation of the head of the Israeli mission, Meir Ezri, to convince Western powers such as the United States and the United Kingdom to pressure the Shah into publicly recognizing Israel. But the Shah wouldn't budge, and he further rebuked the Israelis by refusing for more than three years to meet with Israel's representative to Iran.[35]

Throughout the 1970s, Iran succeeded with its diplomatic acrobatics of maintaining a geostrategic alliance with a state it did not officially recognize, and of permitting a large Israeli presence in Tehran without officially recognizing its mission as the embassy of the Jewish State. The Israeli flag wasn't flown at the mission and Israeli diplomats did not participate in ceremonies that protocol required other diplomats to attend. But in all matters except ceremony, the Israeli mission functioned like any other embassy. Despite the unofficial nature of the relationship, the head of the Israeli mission was commonly referred to as the Israeli ambassador to Iran, and by the 1970s he enjoyed ready access to the Shah. Israeli officials visited Iran frequently and met with the Shah one-on-one, often without the knowledge of the Iranian Foreign Ministry.[36] Although the symbolic value of winning the recognition of a major Muslim state in the Middle East was significant, Israel was careful not to push this issue too hard because it could negatively affect the substance of its relations with Tehran.[37] At the end of the day, it was an arrangement that, while not optimal, still worked to Israel's benefit. According to Amnon Ben Yohanan, a high-ranking Israeli diplomat serving in Tehran in the 1970s, the Israelis "were willing to forgo the ceremonial trappings of diplomacy as long as the real substance was present, while the Arabs could tolerate the substance of close Iran-Israel relations as long as this was not apparent from surface indications."[38] Iran, in turn, needed Israel militarily but had to keep its dealings with the Jewish State out of the public's eye to avoid attracting the attention of the pan-Arab governments.

THE GROWING IRANIAN-EGYPTIAN ENMITY

The Shah learned the hard way how public knowledge of his Israeli dealings undercut Iran's strategic interest. In July 1960, a foreign journalist asked whether Iran had decided to recognize Israel. Without further reflection, the Shah pointed to Iran's de facto recognition of Israel in 1951 by the Mossadeq government and said that "Iran has recognized Israel long ago."[39] The Shah's comments provoked a fiery response from Egypt's Nasser, who hastily cut diplomatic relations and embarked on a venomous propaganda campaign against Iran.[40] But Nasser wasn't concerned primarily about Iran's relationship with Israel. Rather, the Shah's unguarded statement provided the Egyptian leader with an opportunity to expand Egypt's influence in the Persian Gulf and to counter Iran's expanding relations with the Persian Gulf Arabs. Increasingly, the center of anti-Iranian Arab propaganda shifted from Baghdad—Iran's traditional Arab rival in the region—to Cairo.[41] Egypt's aggressive posture and willingness to collaborate with Moscow were not taken lightly in Tehran. The Shah viewed the risk of a military engagement with Egypt, either directly or through Iraq, as substantial. "Iran was under direct threat of the military activities of the Egyptians in the Persian Gulf area," a former Iranian intelligence officer involved in the Iranian-Israeli collaboration explained. "[The Egyptians] were trying to build up naval forces that could be sent to the Persian Gulf in support of Iraq in direct military confrontation with Iran."[42]

If Iran was weakened by Egypt and Iraq, the Arab side would be bolstered and the Iraqi army would be freed up to participate in a potential Arab attack on Israel. But as long as Iran balanced Iraq and diverted the Iraqi armed forces eastward and away from the Jewish State, Israel was provided with a small but important window of safety. So Israeli intelligence provided Iran—whose military was constantly preparing for potential Iraqi or Egyptian attacks—with extensive intelligence on Egyptian military movements and planning. Together with Turkey, the Iranian and Israeli intelligence services constantly monitored Soviet-Egyptian-Iraqi military cooperation. The three non-Arab countries observed Soviet military shipments destined for Egypt and Iraq as they made their way from the Black Sea to the Persian Gulf through the Suez Canal. But as the 1960s came to a close, the strategic context that had inspired the Israeli-Iranian entente in the early 1950s was slowly withering away.[43]

3

rise of israel, rise of iran

Protect me!

—President Richard Nixon to the Shah,
selling the Twin Pillar policy, May 1972

The essence of the Iranian-Israeli entente of the 1950s and 1960s wasn't the inevitability of a non-Arab alliance against the Arab masses, but a congruence of interests formed by Iran's and Israel's common vulnerabilities. They shared interests because they shared common threats. The balance of power and not the non-Arab makeup of the two countries—paved the way for the Iranian-Israeli entente. But the logic of the balance meant that the very basis of the alliance was threatened if either country overcame its differences with its neighbors or if one gained enough power to deal with the threats on its own. Because Arab-Israeli hostilities ran deeper than Arab-Persian grievances, Tel Aviv needed Tehran more than Tehran needed Tel Aviv. Iran was thus more likely to betray Israel than the other way around.

The late 1960s and early 1970s saw significant changes to the geopolitical map of the Middle East: Israel won a stunning victory against the Arabs in the 1967 war; the threat to Iran and Israel from Iraq increased; the superpowers' strategic relationship shifted from containment to détente; Egypt abandoned its alliance with the Soviet Union and shifted toward the Western camp after the 1973 Yom Kippur war; Iran experienced a rapid and unprecedented economic growth and hence regional influence; and the British decided to withdraw its fleet from the Persian Gulf, which enabled the Shah to play a dominant role in the affairs of the region and beyond. All of these factors challenged the equilibrium on which the Israeli-Iranian entente was founded.

THE 1967 WAR

The 1967 war marked a major change in the Shah's perception of Israel. The Jewish State's crushing defeat of its Arab neighbors and its seizure of Egyptian, Jordanian, and Syrian territories compelled Iran to reevaluate its regional relationships. The Shah's reluctance to see the balance between Israel and the Arabs shift too much in favor of Tel Aviv wasn't motivated by a fear of Israel turning into a threat to Iran.[1] After all, Iran was at the time a nation of forty-one million and was many hundreds of miles away from Israel, a nation of only four million. Geopolitical realities, at least at the time, prevented Israel from becoming a threat to Iran.[2] If Israel ever were to turn on Iran, Tehran could always modify its position in the region and move closer to the moderate Arab bloc. "We weren't feeling insecure because of Israeli strength in the region," explained Mehdi Ehsassi, Iran's deputy UN ambassador during the 1970s. "[There] is a geopolitical element in which Iranians will feel better if the Israelis are not weak."[3]

In its balancing game, Iran did not want Israel to be weak, but neither did it want Israel to be too strong. A weakened Israel would bolster the Arabs and the Soviets and prompt them to turn their focus toward Iran. If Israel became too strong, on the other hand, it would bring both benefits and disadvantages. Certainly, Iran benefited from the weakening of the Arab states, but with Israel's rise in power came also a growing Iranian suspicion of Israeli expansionism. The 1967 war had transformed Israel from an embattled state into an aggressive state, the Shah believed. This created several problems for Iran. Ever wary of the power and position of his neighbors, the Shah did not want Israel to become a dominant state in the region that could challenge Iran's quest for preeminence or its strategic significance in Washington. More importantly, a more aggressive and dominant Israel would complicate the Shah's balancing act of maintaining strong relations with Israel without angering Iran's Arab neighbors.[4] Israel's refusal to return Arab territories taken in the Six-Day War did just that. Contrary to Tel Aviv's expectations, the crushing of Nasser's army did not prompt the Shah to move closer to Israel and recognize the Jewish State de jure. Instead, despite warm congratulatory notes sent to Israeli officials by Iranian generals, the Shah froze all joint Iranian-Israeli projects and adopted a tougher public line against Tel Aviv.[5] In an interview with a Yugoslavian newspaper in late 1967, the Shah stated that "any occupation of territory by force of arms shall not be recognized. A permanent solution for the existing differences between Arab states and Israel must be found within the framework of the UN charter."[6]

Washington likewise perceived Iran's attitude shift and sought clarifications on the matter.[7] As it turned out, the shift wasn't cosmetic, it was substantive. On November 22, 1967, the UN Security Council adopted Resolution 242, calling for the "withdrawal of Israeli armed forces from territories occupied in the recent conflict" and emphasizing "the inadmissibility of the acquisition of territory by war." Together with the United States and the United Kingdom, Iran supported the resolution and privately pressured Israel to let go of the occupied territories.

The Iranians also turned to the Americans to pressure Israel to adopt a more flexible position in its dealings with the Arabs. Tehran's belief was that Israel's insistence on retaining occupied Arab territories would only prolong and aggravate the conflict.[8] But the Shah was also thinking of Iran's own interest and the long-term strategic consequences of Israel's actions. Just as Egypt had earlier taken advantage of Iran's political proximity to Israel to advance its interest in the region at the expense of Iran, Iranian criticism of Israel's expansionist policies gave way to a warming in Iranian-Arab relations.[9] In addition, upholding the key principle of Resolution 242— that acquisition of territory by war was inadmissible—was important to protect Iranian territories from possible Arab or Soviet expansionism. It was "very important to stress the principle that you cannot get territory through war," explained Ambassador Fereydoun Hoveyda, former head of the Permanent Mission of Iran to the UN. "So when Israel said that the West Bank was part of Eretz Israel [Greater Israel]," he continued, "it was important that this was pointed out as not acceptable—not to please the Arabs, but because we had problems with Baluchistan and Azerbaijan. [Resolution] 242 was important to us."[10] These areas of Iran have historically been home to small yet potentially problematic ethnic separatists, and Iran wanted to establish firm principles that could prevent them from seceding or falling into the hands of Iran's neighbors. As Tel Aviv realized Iran's lack of appreciation for Israel's rise in power, a new suspicion of the Shah's intentions emerged in Tel Aviv.[11] Israeli fears proved justified as changes in Egypt drew Iran even closer to the Arabs.

THE END OF THE NASSER ERA AND EGYPT'S DEFECTION

The Arabs' devastating defeat under Nasser's leadership in the 1967 war forced Cairo to review its strategy of advancing its leadership in the Arab world by siding with Moscow and challenging the United States and Iran. Nasser's dreams of reinvigorating Egypt's past glory came crashing down on him, and he was forced to reduce his regional ambitions. As Egypt explored a reorientation away from the Soviet Union under Nasser's successor, Anwar Sadat, an opening emerged between Iran and Egypt that had a profound effect on Iran's relations with Israel: Egypt moderated its foreign policy and recognized Iran's public support for the Arab position on Resolution 242. This represented an important step toward defusing Arab-Iranian tensions.[12]

Through Kuwaiti mediation, Iranian–Egyptian back-channel discussions began in 1969. Iran had two conditions for resumption of ties with Egypt: first, Tehran insisted that Cairo issue an apology to Iran for its previous provocations toward Iran. Second, the first step toward normalization had to be taken by Egypt. Recognizing his weakness, Nasser acquiesced and accepted the harsh terms laid forth by the Shah. He grudgingly agreed to a joint communiqué announcing the resumption of full diplomatic relations in August 1970. A month later he died and was succeeded by Anwar Sadat, whose eventual pro-American orientation intensified the Iranian-Egyptian rapprochement.[13] In July 1972, the new Egyptian president made a significant shift toward the Western camp by expelling more than ten thousand Russian military advisers. Before making this radical shift in allegiance Sadat consulted with the Shah, who was delighted by Sadat's pro-Western inclinations and offered economic incentives for Egypt's reorientation.[14]

But even before the expulsion, despite the fact that the Shah sought to retain strong security ties to Israel, he began taking increasingly visible steps toward the Arabs.[15] For instance, the Shah forbade Iranian officials from attending the twenty-second anniversary of the inception of the Jewish State at the Israeli mission in Tehran.[16] The Shah also incensed his Israeli allies by refusing to invite the Israeli head of state to the celebrations marking 2,500 years of the Persian Empire in October 1971; the presence of Israel's president would have caused an Arab boycott of the festivities.[17] The lavish celebrations received negative press in the United States, which the Shah interpreted as Israeli retaliation for the noninvitation. The Iranian monarch was prone to conspiracy theories and believed that the U.S. media was controlled by Jewish interests. He attributed any criticism of Iran in the American media as an Israeli effort to undermine him. The Israelis may have been irritated by the Shah's media prejudice, but they also took advantage of it. In his discussions with the Shah, Shimon Peres, who was Israel's defense minister at the time, often threw in promises of providing favorable press for

Iran in the United States in order to win Iranian concessions on other matters. "Even though we couldn't deliver on those promises, it didn't hurt us
that the Shah *believed* that we did have those powers," explained a former Israeli diplomat to Iran.[18]

Privately, the Shah was even harsher in his disapproval of Israeli policies. In a secret meeting between the Shah and Israeli Foreign Minister Abba
Eban in Tehran on December 14, 1970, the Iranian monarch repeatedly impressed upon Eban that a peaceful solution had to be reached and that Arab
territories had to be returned.[19] This was anathema to the legendary Eban.
The thaw between Iran and Egypt revealed the inherent weakness in the Israeli-Iranian entente. As Iran's wealth and power increased, primarily the
result of increased oil revenues, Tehran was less willing to automatically side
with Israel once it realized that its prospects of resolving its disputes with
the Arabs had become more favorable. At the same time, Iran's rise and its
improved relations with the Arabs increased Israel's fears that it was becoming less useful to Tehran.[20] The asymmetry in relations was evidenced
by the eagerness of Israeli officials for political cooperation between the
two countries, an enthusiasm that their Iranian counterparts could not
muster.[21]

From Iran's perspective, Egypt's shift toward the West was a significant
strategic victory. The defeat of Nasser's pan-Arab ideology and the break in
Egyptian-Soviet relations rid the Arab bloc of the country that could present the most potent challenge to Iran or that could best champion anti-
Persian propaganda.[22] The emergence of a moderate, pro-Western Arab
power significantly altered Iran's strategic calculations. For instance, under
Sadat's leadership, Egypt effectively ceased to be viewed as a threat by
Tehran. "The biggest advantage [Iran] got from Nasser to Sadat," a former
deputy commander in chief of the Iranian navy recalled, "was the fact that
the agitation against Iran in neighboring Arab countries was reduced.
There was no one there to agitate them against Iran."[23] For Israel, however,
Egypt's shift to the West left its strategic environment more complex and its
alliances less clear-cut. Israel did not have any clear reasons to view the ascendancy of Sadat as positively as did Iran. Israel's conflict with Egypt ran
deeper and was less dependent on superpower politics in comparison with
Iran's beef with the Arabs. In general, the threat of pan-Arabism was a more
imminent threat to Israel than it was to Iran. Decision-makers in Tel Aviv
perceived it as an existential threat, a force uniting and mobilizing Arab resources aimed at the destruction of the Jewish State, while Iran viewed it as
a function of Soviet designs and to a certain extent a threat to Iran's regional

leadership aspirations. Israel's concern was well founded. Israel had a territorial dispute with Egypt, and while Egypt's Western orientation put a stop to its pan-Arab tirades against Iran, it did little to temper Cairo's enmity toward Tel Aviv. For Israel, Egypt under Sadat remained a threat, as the Yom Kippur war later demonstrated.

Consequently, the shift in Iranian thinking became all the more problematic for Israel. A few months before Sadat expelled the Soviet advisers, Golda Meir paid her first visit to Tehran in her capacity as prime minister of Israel. According to routine practice, Meir's plane landed at night on an out-of-the-way runway at Mehrabad airport. Again, the Shah urged Israel to take a more moderate stance with Egypt. Soviet inroads with Iraq's new Baathist regime necessitated the detachment of Egypt from the Soviet bloc, the Iranian monarch argued. From the Shah's point of view, Israel did not understand the changes taking place in the Middle East and did not pay enough attention to the needs and interests of its allies. Meir left Tehran distraught. She later complained to her aides that "after renewing relations with Egypt, the Shah is no longer what he was."[24]

THE GROWING IRAQI THREAT AND DÉTENTE

After Sadat broke with the Soviet Union, Moscow turned its focus to Iraq. Quickly, Iraq started to replace Egypt as Iran's main Arab foe, though Iraq's emerging strongman, Saddam Hussein, wasn't—at least not yet—as potent as Nasser had been. Sadat's rejection of Nasser's militant pan-Arabism permitted Iran to end all its military planning targeting Egypt, particularly plans to deny any possible infiltration or insurgency activity by Egypt through Iraq.[25] Planning against Iraq continued and intensified, however.[26] Baghdad's hosting of Iranian opposition elements and its Treaty of Friendship with the Soviet Union, which involved a fifteen-year Soviet military and economic commitment to Iraq, fueled Iranian suspicions regarding the Baathist regime's hostile intentions. The treaty was signed on April 9, 1972, at the height of the Egyptian-Iranian rapprochement.[27] Though the Shah claimed to have little regard for Iraq, referring to it as "a miserable little dwarf," U.S. hesitation over selling arms to Iran could make his country vulnerable to Iraq's growing armies. Throughout the early 1970s, Iran's military spending was driven primarily by the perceived threat from Iraq.[28]

Israel faced the same threat and viewed the growing power of Iraq with great anxiety. Iraq had never been a full participant in the Arab wars against Israel, but strategists in Israel feared that if Iraq emerged as a contender for the leadership of the Arab world and was willing to take on Israel in a future

Israeli-Arab war, the balance might tip in favor of the Arabs. An Arab alliance with Iraq's full participation could overrun Jordan and quickly place the Iraqi army on Israel's eastern front. "There was a big Israeli fear that Iraqi divisions would descend on Israel together with other Arab armies," Shmuel Bar of the Israeli think tank Interdisciplinary Center in Herzliya explained.[29] The view of Iraq as the wild card in Israeli threat assessments was widespread in the 1970s, despite the demonstrated power of the Egyptian and Syrian armies in the 1973 war. "Iraq was the *real* enemy of Israel," recalled Lt. Gen. Yitzhak Segev, Israel's military attaché to Iran.[30]

At a time when the Arab-Iranian rapprochement was causing friction between Tehran and Tel Aviv, the emerging Iraqi threat helped provide a solid geopolitical basis for the continuation of the clandestine Israeli-Iranian entente. In spite of Tehran's flirtation with Egypt, Iran's vulnerability toward the Soviet Union and Iraq continued to plague the Shah. In reality, the Soviet threat to Iran was growing, not because of direct Soviet advances against Iran but because of America's weakening determination to protect Iran. As the U.S.-Soviet strategic relationship shifted from containment to détente, creating a competitive yet peaceful coexistence between the United States and the Soviet Union, Israel and Iran's differing attitudes vis-à-vis superpower politics became a lesser factor in their bilateral relations. Clearly, Israel wasn't as consumed by the Cold War as Iran was. In Israel's view, a pro-Western Arab government wasn't necessarily a lesser threat to Israel's security, and neither would a pro-Soviet state automatically become an enemy of the Jewish State.[31]

But with détente, the dynamics changed. It put the final nail in the coffin of the regional military arrangement of CENTO (the Central Treaty Organization between Iran, Pakistan, Turkey, and the United States), which enabled the CENTO states to adopt more independent foreign policies and to reduce tensions with the Soviet Union without risking friction with the United States.[32] But détente also decreased the superpowers' willingness to take risks and left their allies in regions such as the Middle East less confident about the superpowers' inclination to guarantee their security. Along with the rise of the Iraqi threat to Israel and Iran, this new uncertainty of American reliability in countering Soviet (and Arab) influence in the region made Israeli-Iranian cooperation all the more important.[33]

THE BRITISH WITHDRAWAL

Détente and American overextension because of the war in Vietnam also brought with them unprecedented opportunities for Iran. The Shah had long dreamt of resurrecting Iran's past glory and clearing it from its super-power dependence. Most importantly, he wanted Iranian preeminence in the Persian Gulf—these waters were Iran's backyard and critical to the country's security. They should be guarded by Iran and not by foreign pow-ers, the Shah reasoned. So when the British announced, in 1969, that they would withdraw all of their troops east of the Suez Canal and end their mil-itary control of the Persian Gulf, the Shah saw an opportunity to increase Iran's profile decisively and expand its role in regional decision-making. With the Vietnam War still raging, the United States was in no position to seize strategic control of the Persian Gulf. So the regional states had to fend for security on their own. The vacuum left by the United Kingdom simply begged Iran to step in. The Shah lobbied hard for Iran to be granted the role of policeman of the Persian Gulf, which eventually led to U.S. President Richard Nixon's Twin Pillar policy. This important regional development deepened American reliance on Tehran—rather than the other way around—and increased Iranian influence in Washington.[34]

Under the Twin Pillar policy, the United States left the security of the Persian Gulf to the region's two most powerful states, Iran and Saudi Ara-bia. But because Iran was the most populous nation and the strongest mili-tary power in the area, and because it was the main country straddling the strategic Strait of Hormuz, most of the security burden fell on it, much to the Shah's satisfaction.[35] Gholam-Reza Afkhami, an adviser to the Shah, be-lieves that the seeds of the policy may have been laid in 1966 during a visit by Nixon to Iran. Nixon, who at the time held no public office, spent several hours with the Shah in a private audience. During the talks, the Shah argued that the United States was becoming overextended and that its heavy mili-tary presence throughout the world would soon create ill feelings toward Washington. Instead, the Shah suggested, the United States should encour-age regional powers that had the ability to uphold stability to take on a greater role in security matters. This approach would leave the regional powers more content with U.S. global leadership while creating a more sus-tainable foundation for regional security.[36] Whether the Shah's advice to Nixon was a determining factor in the decisions he later made as president is debatable. The idea of "regional influentials" was well established in Washington foreign policy circles at the time and emerged independently of the Shah's wishes. Nevertheless, it was an argument that the Shah repeated to American officials as often as possible.[37]

By the end of the 1960s, the Shah, who had pursued a policy of increased independence from the United States, needed Washington less than America needed Iran. This was partly because of Iran's increased oil revenues, and partly a result of the United States's overextension in Southeast Asia. Ally or not, the Shah did not hesitate to take advantage of his growing leverage.[38] Nixon and National Security Advisor Henry Kissinger made a brief stop in Tehran in May 1972 on the way back from their historic first visit to the Soviet Union, setting in motion the policy of détente. During several hours of discussions with the Shah, Nixon spelled out the concept of the Twin Pillar policy and the role he envisioned for Iran in Persian Gulf security matters. To make the policy more appealing, Nixon offered the Shah carte blanche on the purchase of almost all non-nuclear U.S. arms. As the meeting reached its conclusion, Nixon looked the Shah in the eye and exclaimed, "Protect me!"[39] Despite strong protests from the U.S. military, Nixon adopted the unprecedented policy of granting one of its allies in the Middle East unlimited access to almost all U.S.-produced non-nuclear weapons. Although Kissinger later denied that such carte blanche was ever granted to Iran, a secret memorandum dated July 25, 1972, found in the U.S. embassy in Tehran in 1979 during the hostage crisis, refutes his claim. In that memo to Secretary of Defense Melvin Laird and Secretary of State William Rogers, Kissinger wrote that the president has reiterated that "in general, decisions on the acquisition of military equipment should be left primarily to the government of Iran. If the Government of Iran has decided to buy certain equipment, the purchase of U.S. equipment should be encouraged tactfully where appropriate, and technical advice on the capabilities of the equipment in question should be provided."[40]

At the height of America's vulnerability, the Shah astutely advanced Iran's interests and role, winning concessions from Washington that other U.S. allies dared not dream of. Since the 1960s Iran had experienced an unprecedented growth in its military and economic powers. In the 1968–1973 period, Iran's gross national product (GNP) grew in real terms at an average annual rate of 12 percent, and gross domestic investment averaged an annual increase of more than 15 percent. In 1973 and 1974, its GNP grew at even higher rates, by 34 percent and 42 percent respectively, arising from the Organization of Petroleum Exporting Countries (OPEC) oil embargo. Iran's oil revenues jumped from $5.4 billion in 1973 to $19.4 billion in 1974.[41]

But with greater power came greater responsibilities and greater vulnerabilities. The Shah understood this and sought to increase his role in the region by filling the vacuum left by Britain's departure, increasing American dependence on Iran, and—perhaps most importantly—winning Arab acceptance of Iran's growing importance. However, just when geopolitical forces—above all, the rise of the Iraqi threat—seemed to call for closer cooperation between Iran and Israel, the Shah's ambitions to become the preeminent power in the region put a shadow over Israeli-Iranian relations.

4

iran's quest for supremacy

> We could benefit from the friendship [of Israel],
> but they weren't our real friends.
>
> —Former Iranian diplomat stationed in Israel

Regional primacy has been the norm rather than the exception for Iran throughout its three-thousand-year history. Between 550 B.C. and A.D. 630, Persia was one of the world's leading powers, defeating the armies of Babylon, Assyria, Egypt, Athens, and Rome. The Persians established the world's first empire, stretching from Libya in the west to Ethiopia in the south, Bulgaria in the north, and India in the east. In the empires of the Parthian and Sassanian dynasties, mighty Rome found its match. Iran has vast natural resources, a unique geostrategic position, a vibrant culture, and a population that dwarfs those of most of its neighbors. Well aware of these advantages, the Iranians have consistently aspired to the role of primus inter pares in regional politics.[1] These realities did not escape the Shah, who dreamt of resurrecting Iran's past glory and turning it into the mighty power it had once been. Only under Iranian supremacy, the Shah believed, could the region flourish and find an escape from war and bloodshed. Iran was the "only nation capable of maintaining peace and stability in the Mideast," he wrote on his deathbed in *Answer to History.*[2] In the minds of the Iranians, their country was the natural hegemon in the Persian Gulf; the weakness of Iran's neighbors disqualified them from legitimately aspiring to that position.[3] "No one could match Iran's power, Iran's culture, or Iran's history," explained Gholam-Reza Afkhami, former adviser to the Shah. "It's important to realize this in order to understand why [the Shah] did what he did. And also why everyone else in the world said that he was arrogant."[4]

Washington was well aware of the Shah's aspiration for imperial grandeur and found Iran's motivation legitimate even though its ambitions often clashed with those of Washington.[5] The Shah's ambitious economic reforms, as well as his lavish military spending, were all aimed at actualizing Iran's potential as the region's most powerful nation. By the early 1970s, there were clear indications that Iran had reached this position. During the late 1960s and 1970s, Iran quickly outgrew its neighbors in terms of economic and military strength, making it the "obvious major power in the region."[6] On February 12, 1971, the Shah's minister of court wrote in his diary that Iran was "rapidly assuming leadership not only over the Persian Gulf, but over the Middle East and the entire oil-producing world."[7] Iran's oil revenues jumped from the millions into the billions. Much of this oil revenue was used to modernize and expand Iran's military, as well as to grant loans to Iran's Arab neighbors. The Shah went on an arms shopping spree, increasing Iran's military expenditures from $6.10 billion in 1973 to $12.14 billion in 1974. By 1976, Iran's military expenditures had tripled, reaching an astounding $18.07 billion.[8] Meanwhile, Israel's military spending remained more or less constant through the 1970s, while that of the Arab nations surged, mainly because of the rising price of oil. The logic of balance of power dictated that the rise of these Arab powers should cause Iran to solidify its ties to Israel, decision-makers in Tel Aviv reasoned. But as they did many times before, the Israelis miscalculated the intentions of the Shah and the grander game he was preparing for Iran.[9]

BEYOND MILITARY SUPREMACY

Every blessing has a downside. For Iran, its rise in power necessitated changes in its foreign policy to win recognition from states with which Iran traditionally had less than favorable relations. Without this recognition, Iran wouldn't be able to enjoy the fruits of its new position. The Shah knew very well that as a state gains power, its sphere of influence grows. To sustain its newly won position of power, it becomes sensitive to developments on the outskirts of that sphere—and, to maintain a certain level of control over such developments, the state needs a political role equivalent to its new economic and military capabilities. That role, however, cannot simply be seized—it must be granted to the state by its neighbors. If these neighbors find the policies of the rising state problematic and illegitimate, they may opt to band together to oppose the rising power rather than accommodate its new geopolitical weight.[10] By gaining recognition from its neighbors, Iran would gain a voice in regional decision-making by taking on a leadership position in bodies such as OPEC and in regional security arrangements. With this voice, Iran could ensure that its neighbors would take its interest and wishes into consideration and forestall developments that could challenge Iran's position of power. The Shah believed "that the only way this could happen would be for Iran to have some [political] control over the way oil moved, in the same way the Americans did."[11] The Shah knew that Iran now needed a political role commensurate with its growing economic power. With this role, he sensed Iran would have an opportunity to change the terms of regional statecraft in its favor by shelving the costly and destabilizing doctrine of balance of power. Simply put, Iran felt that it was becoming strong enough to end the balancing game and befriend its Arab foes from a position of strength. After all, if Iran didn't jump at this opportunity, it could later be forced to adjust relations from a position of weakness.

"If Iran becomes strong enough to be able to deal with the situation [in the region] all by itself, and its relationship with the United States becomes so solidified so that you won't need [Israel], then strategically the direction was to gravitate to the Arabs," explained Afkhami.[12] In the mid-1970s, Iran was extremely self-confident, perhaps even overconfident. With everything going its way, the Shah didn't feel that caution was warranted. "Iran felt at that time that it was in a position to change the political structure of the region and to assume a pivotal status," said Davoud Hermidas-Bavand, a former Iranian diplomat who, unlike many of his colleagues, chose to stay in Iran after the revolution.[13] The Iranian game, commented a senior Israeli official stationed in Iran in the 1970s, "was to be a player. Iran wanted to be important to all parties, be part of the game."[14] The Shah despised it when his neighbors made decisions without consulting him first. By having a say in every regional decision—just as a global power requires a voice in every global decision—the Shah could ensure that the materialization of his long-sought dream of making Iran the region's preeminent power could be sustained. "For the Shah, projection of power was to have a role in which he would be considered and consulted for all decisions," a former Iranian diplomat explained.[15] But what the Shah considered leadership aroused fear among its neighbors. While the U.S. government understood and was somewhat sympathetic toward Iran's aspirations ("The Iranian voice and position had to be taken very seriously. . . . In the very difficult and nasty world that we all live in, that's not unreasonable," said Charles Naas, who

served as an American diplomat in Iran at the time), others ultimately concluded that what originated as a defensive strategy for sustaining Iran's
power soon turned into a hegemonic policy.[16] Bridging the Arab-Persian
divide while keeping Israel on its side became increasingly difficult for the
Shah. With Iran's power rising, the balance between strategic ties with Israel
and recognition by the Arabs began to tilt in favor of Iran's historic enemies.

THE EMERGENCE OF IRAN'S ARAB OPTION

Tensions between Arabs and Persians have deep historic roots. The scars of
the Arab invasion in the seventh century and the Islamization of Iran are
still vivid; Iranians continue to pride themselves on successfully resisting
the Arabization of their country. While Iran largely accepted Islam, much of
Iran's ethnic and cultural identity remained unchanged, unlike that of other
nations in the Middle East. Iran became an Islamic state, but not an *Arab*
state. As much as this gratifies Iranians, it causes resentment among Iran's
Arab neighbors. Three hundred years after the Arab invasion of Iran, cultural antagonism between the Arab and Iranian peoples blossomed into a
war of words, dubbed the *Shu'ubiya*. This war, which featured an exchange
of colorful insults, served to reinforce the Persian identity of the Iranian nation and the idea that becoming a Muslim need not be tantamount to becoming an Arab. This millennium-old dispute, deeply rooted in the minds
of both Arabs and Persians, has created a unique type of bigotry that has
adversely affected relations between the two peoples. Whereas the Arabs believe themselves to be ethnically superior to the Iranians, Persian antagonism is more rooted in a sense of cultural supremacy.[17] This mindset continued into the twentieth century and still exerts a powerful hold. In fact,
many argue that Arab-Persian animosity has grown stronger in recent
decades.[18] With the rise of Iranian and Arab nationalism in the nineteenth
and twentieth centuries, these tensions reached new levels. In Iran, Reza
Shah (father of Mohammad Reza Pahlavi), inspired by the purist doctrines
of President Kemal Atatürk of Turkey, attempted to re-create the Persian
Empire and reduce the influence of Arab culture, language, and religion in
Iranian society. On the other hand, Arab-Iranian animosity was exploited
and exaggerated by pan-Arabists as a means to unite the Arab masses.

Bridging the Persian-Arab divide was one of two factors complicating
Iran's quest in the 1970s to reach a position of preeminence. On the one
hand, Shah Mohammad Reza Pahlavi needed to keep a measure of stability
in the region in order to deprive the United States and the Soviet Union of a
pretext to meddle in Iran's sphere of influence. The Shah had managed to

win suzerainty over the Persian Gulf through the exit of the British; he wasn't about to lose it to Washington or Moscow.[19] On the other hand, absent Arab-Persian reconciliation, the Arabs would be loath to recognize Iran's rising power and its claim for a larger political role in the region. The Arabs viewed Iran's rise and the Shah's Persian nationalism with great suspicion and were reluctant to grant Iran their political blessings. Even the smallest Arab sheikdom could potentially undermine Iran's quest to obtain Arab legitimacy and assume the role of regional leader.[20] Simply put, to be recognized and accepted as the regional leader, "Iran had to cater to the wishes of the Arabs."[21]

Time and again the Shah failed to overcome Arab suspicion and resistance. In 1972 he tried to create a multilateral organ for Persian Gulf security in order to formalize and create regional legitimacy for Nixon's Twin Pillar policy. The Iranian campaign failed because of Arab refusal to participate, rooted in Arab qualms about the Shah's perceived hegemonic aspirations.[22] An Iranian leadership role in the oil cartel OPEC, another body that was critical to Iran's internal and external development, also necessitated improved Iranian-Arab relations. Here, too, the Shah failed.[23] As its economic situation improved because of skyrocketing oil revenues, Iran started to utilize this power for political objectives.[24] The Shah attempted to improve relations with the Arabs by providing them with generous financial aid.[25] In 1974 alone, the Shah granted $850 million in loans to Egypt, $7.4 million to Jordan, $30 million to Morocco, and $150 million to the pro-Soviet government in Syria.[26] "The Syrians needed [our oil] badly. We were actually buying their friendship with these kinds of bribes," recalled Mehdi Ehsassi, former Iranian deputy UN ambassador. "The Shah knew very well that we [were] not going to be good friends, but [this] could help."[27]

But Iranian financial aid could go only so far, particularly because the pan-Arab governments could turn to the oil-rich Arab sheikdoms of the Persian Gulf for financial support. Increasingly, the Shah realized that Iran's ties with Israel were preventing a genuine warming in Arab-Iranian relations. Arab criticism of his ties with Israel could no longer be dismissed. In a letter to the Shah, the distinguished Arab oil expert Sheikh Tariki spelled out Arab frustrations with Iran: "You are aware of what Israel is doing to your Muslim brothers, you know how it is desecrating the al-Aqsa mosque and its soldiers setting foot in the mosque and minaret. Yet you insist on forging close relations with it, and supplying it with crude oil which plays a basic role in propelling its armed forces against your Muslim brothers. After all this, do you imagine it is possible to have neighborly relations with the Arabs?"[28]

The stronger Iran grew, and the more the Shah needed Arab acceptance of Iran's political aspirations, the more sensitive he became regarding Arab criticism. Out of this political context emerged a new orientation for Tehran—Iran's Arab option; that is, the gravitation toward the Arab position in its conflict with Israel. This meant that Israeli objections became increasingly irrelevant to Iran. The Shah "did not have to play to [the Israeli] tune. . . . The Shah was very, very much worried about an Arab leader criticizing him, but he wouldn't worry if [Israel Prime Minister Menachem] Begin criticized him," a former deputy commander in chief of the Iranian navy commented. For instance, Iran displayed increased sensitivity toward Arab feelings on Israeli-Iranian military cooperation. Military ties with Israel were confined to the army and air force because those armed forces "were inside Iran and weren't seen from the outside. . . . We couldn't have our ships running around the Persian Gulf with Israeli [Gabriel] missiles on board," the navy commander explained.[29] Well aware that his strong ties to Israel prevented Iran from fulfilling its role as a regional leader, the Shah sought opportunities to show that Iran's disapproval of Israeli policies went beyond a reluctance to grant full diplomatic recognition to Israel. In practice, too, Iran was prepared to show its independence to the Arabs. The first test of Iran's new considerations came with the Arabs' show of strength in the Yom Kippur war.

ISRAEL "CAUGHT WITH ITS PANTS DOWN"

Israel's apprehensions about Sadat's intentions were confirmed with the Yom Kippur war. On October 6, 1973, the armies of Egypt and Syria caught Israel by surprise and dispelled the Israel Defense Forces' image of invincibility, gained only six years earlier during the 1967 war.[30] Israel had overestimated its deterrence and underestimated the capabilities of the Arab armies. "Mighty Israel was caught with its pants down in 1973," was how one Israeli scholar put it.[31] Though Israel eventually beat back the attacking Arabs, its near defeat prompted Middle Eastern nations to reassess their perceptions of the balance of power. The war damaged the perception of Israel's strength, which had significant impact on the political map of the region.

The Yom Kippur war presented both challenges and opportunities for Iran. On the one hand, Iran did not want to see an Arab victory that would allow those nations to discount Israel entirely and focus fully on Iran.[32] Israel was acutely aware of this inherent weakness in its relations with Iran, as well as with the periphery doctrine as a whole. Just as Israel tried to undermine improvements in Arab-Iranian relations, Tel Aviv recognized that Iran had an interest in sustaining a certain level of enmity between Israel and its Arab neighbors. "The Shah was very clever," Yitzhak Segev, Israel's former military attaché to Iran, explained to me at his house outside Tel Aviv. Browsing through an album with pictures of his former Iranian colleagues—mostly generals under the Shah—Segev admitted the limits of the Israeli-Iranian entente. "The moment that he found out that all Arab countries are hostile against Israel, it was very good for him to continue to push all Arabs to be against Israel. . . . Israel would be the subject that would take all the Arab anger [away from Iran]," Segev acknowledged.[33] On the other hand, an Israeli victory could have rendered Iran's efforts to moderate the Arab bloc more difficult. The emergence of a pro-Western Egypt was a godsend for the Shah, as it significantly reduced the Arab threat against Iran. A decisive Israeli victory could lead to the fall of the Sadat regime and Egypt's return to the radical pro-Soviet Arab camp, Tehran reasoned.[34]

A swift victory for *either* side would have been negative for Iran, since it would boost the prestige and standing of the victorious power. Iran's position was best maintained by ensuring that neither side came out of the conflict with an unqualified victory, since that could challenge Iran's steady path toward regional primacy.[35] Extended warfare, however, brought with it another danger: the great powers would be given a pretext to reenter the Persian Gulf. Such a scenario was viewed with utmost concern in Tehran.[36] Consequently, Iran was careful "not to put any gas in the fire [of the war]."[37] Tehran was primarily concerned that the Soviet Union would take advantage of U.S. overextension because of war in Vietnam and challenge Iran's primacy in the Persian Gulf, which in turn would jeopardize Iran's control over the flow of oil and, as a result, its ability to set the pace for internal and external growth.[38]

Instability or prolonged warfare could provide the Soviet Union with such an excuse, which fueled the Shah's worries about Israel's increasingly aggressive foreign policy. As a result, though Iran wanted the Arabs and the Israelis to be wary of each other, it did not want them to engage in warfare that could have the unintended consequences of bringing the major powers back into the area. A secret U.S. State Department document, dated April 1974, spelled out the Shah's worries in detail:

> The Shah takes a close interest in our détente with the USSR and the possibility that it might free Soviet resources for the Middle East. The

Shah believes Soviet activity in the Middle East indicates a continuing use of proxies such as Iraq and South Yemen to accomplish Soviet foreign policy goals. The Shah remains concerned by the potential for instability—and Soviet Exploitation of it—in neighboring countries. He is concerned about radical movements in the Persian Gulf; Iraqi hostility towards Iran. . . . He recognizes the need for, and has been seeking, improved relations and cooperation with the more moderate Arab governments. . . . Establishing this cooperation is not easy because of longstanding Arab wariness toward Iran.[39]

But the Soviet Union wasn't the only potential contender for leadership in the Persian Gulf. Iran's ally and supporter, the United States, was also viewed as a rival by the Shah, albeit a nonhostile one.[40] The Shah publicly opposed the American military presence in the region, because he "wanted no restraints on his ambition to dominate the [Persian] Gulf, and he saw the U.S. Navy base in Bahrain as a rival to his own suzerainty."[41] According to Afkhami, "If the Americans were in the region, then Iran could not possibly have the role that it wanted."[42] Though Iran sought to strengthen U.S. willingness to protect it from Soviet or Arab aggression, it still did not want a U.S. military presence in what it considered to be its domain. By establishing a stable regional framework under its leadership, Iran could prevent both Washington and Moscow from penetrating the Shah's Persian waters.[43]

With these goals in mind, the Shah trod carefully during the Yom Kippur war to prevent either side from winning and to avoid instability and prolonged warfare, all the while distancing Iran from Israel to demonstrate to the Arabs the benefits Iranian leadership would have for the Arab states. So, much to Israel's disappointment, Iran officially maintained a position of neutrality throughout the war, in spite of the Arab states' rising power. Unlike the situation with the 1967 war, Tehran now viewed the Arabs' war aspirations as legitimate.

Tehran directly aided the warring Arab states, a clear contradiction of its entente with Israel. Sadat personally called the Shah in the first days of the war to request crude oil supplies. The Shah agreed, and within twenty-four hours a large shipment was delivered to Cairo. The Shah's generosity and act of friendship made a lasting impression on Sadat.[44] Iran extended medical aid to the Arabs and provided Saudi Arabia with Iranian pilots and airplanes to help resolve logistical problems. Iranian planes brought a Saudi battalion to the Syrian side of the Golan Heights. There, it picked up wounded Syrian soldiers and brought them to Tehran for treatment.[45] "It's the very least I could do, given that the Saudis are our fellow Muslims, and I've long been keen to cement our friendship," the Shah told Court Marshall Asadollah Alam.[46] These measures immediately paid dividends for Iran, as both Iraq and Sudan agreed to normalize relations with Tehran. To add insult to injury, the Shah prevented Jewish Australian volunteers for the Israeli army from reaching Israel via Tehran.[47]

The Iranian monarch even helped the Soviets aid the Arab side. In early October 1973, the Soviets requested Iranian permission to send military equipment to Baghdad (to be used in the war with Israel) through Iranian airspace. The Shah rejected the Soviet request but allowed four civilian Soviet airplanes to fly spare parts to the Arabs. The Shah did not consult the United States and did not inform Washington about his decision until ten days after the request had been made. Iran's deputy foreign minister, Ahmad Mirfendereski, later gave permission for five additional Soviet overflights. This unauthorized decision cost Mirfendereski his job, though it remains unclear whether his decision contradicted the Shah's strategic wishes or whether he was fired for making the decision without proper authorization. According to a former Iranian navy commander, the problem wasn't one of substance but of procedure. "The problem was that *he* [Mirfendereski] made the decision. Had he asked for the Shah's advice, he would probably have OK'd [the overflights] as well."[48]

Yet, at the same time, Iran refused to join the Arab oil embargo against Israel and continued to supply Israel with oil throughout the conflict. Iran had an official policy of disallowing the use of oil as a political weapon. "We never accepted oil embargoes against any country," explained a former Iranian ambassador. "We didn't believe in using that weapon."[49] This policy enabled Tehran always to be in a position to sell oil to all parties of a conflict.[50] In addition, Iran also supplied the Israel Defense Forces with arms, including badly needed heavy mortars.[51]

Rather than pursuing a policy of balance of power, in which the rise in Arab power would have necessitated stronger Iranian support for Israel, the Shah opted to balance both Arabs and Israelis by helping *both* sides. "We didn't have Israel as a friend to have the Arabs as enemies," a former Iranian Ambassador explained.[52] Iran wasn't tied to either side of the conflict, he argued, and could not automatically side with Israel, even though the two countries agreed on many things. "Politics is politics," commented Ambassador Fereydoun Hoveyda, former head of the Permanent Mission of Iran to the UN, coldly. "At the end of the day, Iran follows its own national interest."[53]

Politics or not, the Jewish State felt betrayed by the Shah. Israeli leaders believed that their initial setbacks in the war made the Shah reconsider his strategy of allying with Israel. The Israelis "were very anxious and very apprehensive about the shift in the Shah's attitude towards them and the Arab world after the Yom Kippur war," explained Professor Soli Shavar of Haifa University.[54] Israeli officials routinely tried to convince Iran to reverse its policy, arguing that Iran did not know who its real friends were.[55] Though Iran and Israel were not tied by any formal alliance, Israel expected Iran to behave as an Israeli ally in practice, mindful of their common geostrategic objectives and their intelligence cooperation. But while Israel pursued a policy of balancing the Arabs through its relations with Iran, which it viewed as a natural ally and friend—Tehran's perspective was more complex. Tehran kept its foreign policy dispassionate and pragmatic, with little room for concepts such as friendship. Iran never defined itself as being on Israel's side, and it distinguished between "friends" and "friendship." "We could benefit from the friendship [of Israel], but they weren't our real friends," an Iranian diplomat stationed in Israel told me matter-of-factly.[56] Shortly after the war, Egypt and Iran jointly introduced a UN resolution calling for the establishment of a nuclear-weapons-free zone in the Middle East. Mindful of Israel's nuclear monopoly in the region, the target of the resolution was all too obvious.[57]

5

sealing demise in the moment of triumph

We lost all confidence in him. He was crazy. He was an idiot.

—Yaacov Nimrodi, Israel's military attaché to Iran,
on the Shah and his decision to sign the Algiers Accord

I was cursing Iran all the way to Tehran.

—Eliezer Tsafrir, head of the Mossad's operations
in northern Iraq, on his reaction to the Algiers Accord

The Yom Kippur war forced Israel to reexamine the nature of its relations with Iran. In a time of war, when Israel faced an existential threat, the Shah did not come to Israel's aid to balance the Arabs. Instead the Shah, aiming to solidify Iran's own position in the region, balanced Iran's relations between the two sides.

The war had shown that Egypt's turn to the West did not necessarily translate into avoidance of war with Israel. With or without Nasser, Egypt remained a formidable foe and a serious threat. At the same time that Israel was confident about the longevity of Iraqi-Iranian tensions, it was also insecure regarding Iranian-Egyptian relations—and the effects of those relations on Israel's ties to Iran. The Shah never shared with the Israelis his plans of action vis-à-vis Egypt, whereas such information sharing was common in regards to Iraq.[1] This made Egypt all the more problematic for Israel. Soviet support for the Arabs during the war also showed that the Communist empire's intentions, power, and offensive capabilities could be a dangerous threat. At the same time, the powers on Israel's eastern front were gaining strength. Israel had faced the combined armies of its Arab neighbors thrice in twenty-five years. None of those wars saw the Iraqi army's full participation, however. And because Iraq had both the aspiration and the potential to become the most powerful Arab country, much sleep was lost in Israel over Baghdad's continued hostile intentions. Iraq had improved its offensive capabilities through the acquisition of Scud missiles and had developed the ability to overrun Jordan and place itself on Israel's eastern front within forty-eight hours. All in all, in spite of Iran's cooling attitude toward Israel, the Jewish State was in greater need of Iran after the war than before it. Israel simply had no choice but to reinvest in its relations with Tehran, since it lacked maneuverability to pursue other policies or alliances.

To reinvigorate its ties to Iran, in 1973 Israel appointed Uri Lubrani as the new head of its mission in Tehran. Born in Germany in 1926, Lubrani joined the Haganah (the Defense), a Jewish paramilitary organization and forerunner of the Israeli Defense Forces, in what was then the British Mandate of Palestine, at an early age. After the Israeli state was created, he joined the Foreign Ministry and was appointed to several high-level posts, including adviser to Prime Minister David Ben-Gurion on Arab affairs. Lubrani's closeness to Ben-Gurion may account for the eagerness with which Lubrani developed Israel's relations with periphery states, as Ben-Gurion had always been a strong advocate of the periphery strategy. From 1965 to 1968, Lubrani served as ambassador to Uganda, Rwanda, and Burundi, where his industrious intelligence efforts soon made him one of the best-informed men in those countries—a man that the U.S. State Department often turned to for intelligence. He later went on to serve as Israel's ambassador to another critical periphery state, Ethiopia.[2]

Lubrani quickly acquired a deep respect for Iran's cultural and national cohesiveness. "During my first visit to Iran, I visited a small village," Lubrani recalled over tea at his house in Tel Aviv. "It was a poor village; they didn't have running water and other basic facilities. But in the evening, the villagers gathered to hear one of their elders recite the *Shahname*."[3] The *Book of Kings*, or the *Shahname*, was written in the tenth century. It is an astounding literary work, telling the story of the Iranian nation from mythological times to the era of the Persian Empires. According to many scholars, the *Shahname*, and the cultural and political unity that it both reflected and provided, helped ensure Iran's successful resistance to Arabization, thus allowing it to remain a Persian-speaking nation. "The scene of these poor villagers listening to this man reciting the *Shahname* by heart had a lasting impact on me. Iran wasn't rich, it wasn't developed, but it was a civilization,"

Lubrani continued. Over the years, Lubrani went on to become one of the Jewish State's foremost experts on Iran. His understanding of and admiration for Iranian culture deeply affected Israel's view of Iran as a friend— and as a foe.

Tel Aviv tried to use Lubrani's appointment as an opportunity to raise Israel's diplomatic profile in Iran. Lubrani attempted to offer his credentials to the Shah—a procedure reserved for incoming ambassadors only—to force de jure recognition of Israel on the Shah. Israel's expectations proved unrealistic, though, as no Iranian official came to greet Lubrani at Mehrabad airport. To make matters worse, Lubrani's request to meet with the Shah was left unanswered for more than three and a half years.[4]

Israel had good reason to worry about its ties to Iran. After the war, Iran started exploring opportunities to reduce its dependence on Israeli pipelines for exporting oil to Europe. The Eilat-Ashkelon pipeline had somewhat outlived its strategic usefulness because it was originally built for Iran to circumvent territory controlled by Nasser's anti-Iranian government. Israeli fears that Iran would discontinue its use led to diplomatic efforts to dissuade the Shah from any such actions. "The Israelis were very afraid. The visits of Israeli leaders, Yigal Allon, Rabin, Peres . . . were to get further assurances from the Shah that he would continue the flow of oil. This was the main issue between Israel and Iran after the Yom Kippur war," Israeli professor Soli Shavar explained.[5]

Not long after the cease-fire in 1973, Washington initiated disengagement talks between Egypt and Israel. Iran played an active role in the negotiations, though the Israelis were frustrated with the Shah's position. Throughout the negotiations Iran expressed support for the Egyptian position—the return of all occupied territory in exchange for peace, which the Shah argued was based on logic and justice—while criticizing the "rigid and unwise" Israeli position of seeking recognition from the Arab states first. Tehran pressured Tel Aviv by freezing all military cooperation and ending the purchase of Israeli arms. Iranian officials indicated to Lubrani that Iranian-Israeli relations would remain frozen as long as negotiations between Egypt and Israel were deadlocked. In addition, the Shah urged U.S. President Gerald Ford to increase American pressure on Israel. The Shah's impatience with Israel prompted officials in Tel Aviv to worry that Iran could go so far as to sever all ties.[6] In an interview with an American journalist working for the Beirut daily *al-Hawadis,* the Shah openly rejected the Israeli strategy of seeking security through the conquest of territory:

Israel is making a big mistake in relying on the occupied Arab territories for its security. . . . In these days of long-range planes flying at 80,000 feet, and ground-to-ground missiles which go over any obstacle, there is no such thing as secure borders for Israel. . . . The only security for Israel is an international guarantee of its former borders. . . . Has Israel enough men to occupy the entire Arab world? Can she go to Algeria? Can she fight Saudi Arabia? Furthermore, can Israel sustain such military expenditures for the next ten years? Who has to pay for it? You Americans, for what? For supporting a very immoral question—the occupation by force of the land of some country by another country?[7]

As discouraging as these signals were to Israel, the Shah's greatest act of treachery toward the Jewish State—from Israel's perspective—was yet to come. Israel believed that the Shah would continue to "openly criticize Israel in order to sweeten the Arabs" while keeping private all substantive disagreements with Israel.[8] Little did Tel Aviv expect that on the severest disagreement between Israel and Iran—the sudden end to Iran's support for Israeli aid to the Iraqi Kurdish rebellion through the signing of the 1975 Algiers Accord—the Shah wouldn't consult with Israel at all.

ISRAEL, IRAN, AND THE KURDS OF IRAQ

Descendents of the ancient Medes, as the legend goes, the Kurds have been living in the mountains of Iraq, Turkey, and Iran for millennia. Because they are of Iranian stock, their ethnic, cultural, and linguistic ties to Iran are strong. Yet many Kurds have sought independence—or at least autonomy—from the governments of Iraq, Turkey, and Iran, arguing that they deserve their own country since they cannot express their cultural identity freely in countries dominated by non-Kurds.[9] The Kurdish question has been a problem for these governments, but it has also provided them with an opportunity to weaken each other. Historically, Kurdish discontent has been far greater in Turkey and Iraq—where even the existence of Kurds was denied for decades—than in Iran. Because of this, Iran has been better able to use the Kurdish issue to undermine its neighbors.

In the early 1960s, Mullah Mustapha Barzani, a prominent Kurdish guerrilla leader in Iraq, sought military support from the Israelis in order to fight the Iraqi army. Israel clearly shared an interest in weakening Baghdad, particularly by allying with a non-Arab people. But the Mossad (Israeli intelligence agency) quickly concluded that no meaningful support to the Iraqi Kurds could be extended without the cooperation of Iran. While

Tehran also benefited from the Iraqi government's preoccupation with its rebellious Kurds, the Shah was deeply mistrustful of Barzani, whom he suspected was a Communist. According to the head of the Mossad's operations in Iraqi Kurdistan, Eliezer Tsafrir, the Iranians "didn't like Mullah Mustapha Barzani because they thought he was a 'Red Mullah' . . . because he spent twelve years in Russia as a political refugee."[10]

The Shah initially rejected the suggestion, citing Barzani's presumed ties to the Soviet Union and the potential repercussions that Kurdish victories in Iraq could have on Iran's own Kurdish minority. The Shah was also hesitant about Israel's intentions, knowing full well that Israel supported Kurdish sovereignty—which went well beyond the idea of weakening Baghdad.[11] As the Shah had suspected, Israel had told Barzani that he could count on unconditional support from the Jewish State. After all, the creation of a non-Arab state in the middle of the Arab heartland wasn't a scenario Israel felt it had to fear. "We told the Kurds . . . [that] whatever they do, we are supporting them—in war and in peace," explained Tsafrir, who was in charge of the Mossad's training of the Kurdish fighters. "In a way, our common interest with the Kurds was more complete than the Iranian interest with the Kurds."[12] In spite of the Shah's hesitations, Israel managed to bring both the Iranians and Barzani—who had his own apprehensions about the Shah's motivations—on board after several months of lobbying. The United States was informed about the cooperative efforts and agreed to lend limited clandestine support. Iran, too, wanted its role in the collaboration to be inconspicuous.

The first agreement was sealed in May 1965, in Mustapha Barzani's own headquarters in Iraqi Kurdistan.[13] Dressed in traditional Kurdish costumes, Savak, the Shah's secret service, and Mossad officials crossed the Iraqi border by foot to reach the headquarters of the Kurdish guerrillas. Israel offered to train, fund, and arm Barzani's forces in order to stage a large-scale offensive against the Iraqi army.[14] The funding and the arms shipments were to be channeled through Savak, which also provided the Israelis with a land corridor into Iraqi Kurdistan. Iranian cooperation enabled a steady flow of Israeli arms, doctors, medical supplies, and instructors to make their way to Iraqi Kurdistan from Israel via Iran.[15]

During President Richard Nixon and National Security Advisor Henry Kissinger's visit to Tehran in May 1972, the Shah convinced the United States to take on a much larger role in what up to then had been a largely Israeli-Iranian operation. The CIA and the State Department advised against U.S. participation on the basis that the Kurds would inevitably be betrayed by Tehran, but Kissinger decided otherwise and argued that this was a concrete way for the United States to demonstrate its support for Iran.[16] Though the operation was very successful insofar as it disabled Baghdad from challenging the Shah's primacy in the Persian Gulf and distracted the Iraqi army from the Palestinian cause, Iraq's power was still rising, and Washington, Tehran, and Tel Aviv all viewed Baghdad's pro-Soviet tilt, anti-Iranian orientation, and pan-Arab tendencies with great concern.[17] From Israel's perspective, the operation also gave Tel Aviv access to Iraq's large Jewish population and enabled Israel to repatriate Iraqi Jews. The demographic component of Israel's foreign policy was of pivotal importance to the Jewish State, whose small population in relation to its Arab neighbors made it particularly eager to encourage Jewish immigration to Israel from the Diaspora. Savak helped smuggle Iraqi Jews through Iraqi Kurdistan to the northern Iranian city of Rezaieh, where they were turned over to Jewish organizations that resettled them in Israel.[18]

Soon after Nixon and Kissinger's Tehran visit, covert American financial aid started to flow to the Kurdish guerrillas, or *peshmerga* (those who face death), as they call themselves.[19] According to Yaacov Nimrodi, an Iraqi Jew who served as the Israeli army's first military attaché in Tehran, Israel had a few platoons deployed in Iraqi Kurdistan. They trained the Iraqi peshmerga and commanded them in battle but rarely involved themselves in the actual fighting.[20] The Iranian military presence was greater, with one anti-aircraft battalion, one artillery battalion, and a few Savak operatives. The Iranians, too, avoided fighting on the front lines against the Iraqi army.[21]

In March 1975, however, the Kurdish operation came to a sudden end as Iran pulled the rug from under Israel and its primary lever against Iraq. Algeria's president, Houari Boumédienne, had informed the Shah that Iraq's de facto ruler, Saddam Hussein, planned to attend the OPEC summit in Algiers in order to negotiate an end to Iraqi-Iranian hostilities, including their border dispute over the Shatt al-Arab/Arvand Rud waterway. On March 3, 1975, the Shah left for Algeria, and, three days later, Boumédienne announced that the conflict between Iran and Iraq was over.[22] The two countries reached a border agreement that called for each side to refrain from interference in the other's internal affairs and that established a division of control over the Shatt al-Arab/Arvand Rud waterway, a long-standing territorial objective of Iran.[23] Through this Algiers Accord, the waterway dispute was clearly resolved in Iran's favor and was initially hailed by many as one of the Shah's foremost triumphs, as it boosted Iran's status as the paramount power in the Persian Gulf. "Now at long last I've been able to tear up the Shatt al-Arab treaty," the Shah triumphantly told Asadollah Alam, his Court Marshall, when he returned to Tehran.[24]

The agreement took Israel and the United States by complete surprise. The Shah neither consulted nor informed his Israeli and American allies about the negotiations with the Iraqis, nor did he indicate that the collaboration with the Kurds was in jeopardy.[25] According to Gary Sick, who served as an Iran expert on the National Security Council during the Carter and Reagan administrations, "[The deal] was done before anyone was notified, that was the key thing. [The Shah] got an offer, he grabbed it, completed it, came back, gave the orders and let the United States and Israel know that the game was over."[26] Charles Naas, the Iran desk officer at the State Department, found out about the agreement through the press. "Bang, there it was. One morning I went in, and there was the agreement," he recalled.[27]

According to Iranian officials, however, the failure to consult wasn't surprising. "Dictators are autocrats. . . . The Shah considered himself an equal to the United States; he didn't feel that he needed to consult the Americans."[28] Much indicates that the Shah's decision to sign the Algiers Accord was made on the spot. Even senior Savak officials were taken by surprise, and a passage in the diary of Assadollah Alam supports this theory. The Shah returned to Tehran early in the morning of March 7, 1975, and called Gen. Nematollah Nassiri, head of Savak, and ordered him to immediately end the operations in Iraqi Kurdistan and to offer the Kurdish guerrillas refuge in Iran.[29] In the Shah's characteristically autocratic style, the accord was never given to the Iranian Parliament for ratification, leaving little room for a critical assessment of some of its provisions, including a little-known transfer of oil-rich Iranian territory to the Iraqi state.[30]

The Israelis and the Kurds were stunned to see their Iranian allies just pack up and leave. While Tel Aviv had no illusions that Iran sooner or later would put an end to the Kurdish operations, they never expected it to end in such a "dramatic and sad way," as Eliezer Tsafrir put it.[31] The Savak was at first too embarrassed to inform the Israeli Mossad operatives in Iraq that their collaboration would end. Instead, they explained that there was to be a routine replacement of troops. A day later, on March 9, Uri Lubrani was summoned by a senior Iranian official and told of the details of the agreement.[32] By this time, Washington had already been aware of Iran's intentions for a few days without sharing the information with the Jewish State, adding insult to injury for Tel Aviv.[33]

For Israel, this wasn't just another one of the Shah's symbolic moves in favor of the Arabs—this was a matter of life and death. The Shah's swift pullout put Israeli soldiers in harm's way. Tsafrir had only two hours to flee Barzani's Iraqi Kurdistan headquarters to Iran (where his family was stationed) in the face of the Iraqi army advance. "I was cursing Iran all the way to Tehran. I was terribly disappointed," Tsafrir told me.[34]

Tehran showed little understanding for the Israeli protests. The Shah viewed the operation primarily as Iranian, and as a result the agreement or viewpoint of Israel wasn't of much importance. "I would put myself in the place of the Shah," a former member of the Shah's cabinet told me. "Here I am, not a small country, thirty-five million people, I have oil behind me, I have so many educated people. Why the hell would I care about a bunch of goddamn Jews?"[35] To the Iranians, this was the rule rather than the exception—the Shah was simply never in the habit of consulting the Israelis on issues that he considered to be in Iran's national interest.[36] In the view of a former Iranian ambassador to South Africa, "Our priority was Shatt al-Arab . . . and that we improved relations with Iraq. . . . Our national interest was first."[37] The Iranian position was that time for consultations with Washington and Tel Aviv did not exist. The negotiations took no longer than a few hours over the span of two days, March 5–6, 1975, and were very intense.[38] The Shah managed to sleep only two hours a night while in Algiers—he also had to negotiate OPEC matters—and was exhausted upon his return.[39]

Iranian officials maintained that the United States and Israel were well aware that Iran and Iraq were negotiating their waterway dispute since early 1974 in Istanbul. Those talks were led by Ambassador Abdul Rahman Sadrieh, one of the Iranian Foreign Ministry's most prominent diplomats, and his Iraqi counterpart, Ambassador Talib Shabib. The talks were not kept secret, and both Washington and Tel Aviv followed their progress. Sooner or later, an agreement would have been reached, the Iranians argued, and it was simply naïve of Washington and Tel Aviv to believe that a resolution to the waterway dispute would not encompass an end to Iranian interference in northern Iraq.[40] Tehran reacted negatively to the international uproar against its treatment of the Kurds, pointing to Saddam Hussein's own admission during the Algiers talks that the Kurds would have been eliminated by the Iraqi army long ago had it not been for Tehran's intervention. "They've [the Kurds] suffered defeat after defeat," the Shah complained to Alam. "Without our support they wouldn't last ten days against the Iraqis." Still, the Shah agreed only reluctantly to meet with Barzani on March 11 in

Tehran, because he, according to Alam, was "embarrassed to meet the man face to face."[41]

Whether time for consultations existed or not, decision-makers in both Tel Aviv and Washington were infuriated by the Shah's decision. Kissinger, who had been the key advocate for U.S. involvement in the Kurdish operations, sent an emissary to Switzerland, where the Shah was vacationing shortly after the Algiers summit, to better understand the Shah's motivations. The emissary brought with him a strongly worded letter in which Kissinger reiterated the U.S. position that the Kurdish operation should continue. Uncharacteristically, Kissinger did not offer the Shah any congratulatory notes for his diplomatic victory.[42] For Washington, the Algiers Accord was a wake-up call, because it realized that Iran's interests had started to deviate from those of its own. "This was the first major divergence [of interest]. We were taken aback by this," Naas said.[43] Despite this insight, the United States refrained from reacting too harshly to the Shah's policy reversal, partly because of Iranian exceptionalism in U.S. foreign policy. Washington had for some time turned a blind eye to the Shah's maverick tendencies. "We didn't view Iran, at least not at the embassy, as a compliant state," recalled Henry Precht, the Iran desk officer at the U.S. State Department in the late 1990s.[44]

The Israelis, however, did not mince words in criticizing the Shah. Overnight, a major component of Israel's strategic policy had been cancelled by Iran. Lubrani objected strongly to Tehran's decision but was rebuffed by a senior Iranian official, who explained that Israel's weakness "was that she allowed sentiment to interfere with politics."[45] Israeli decision-makers felt that they had been personally betrayed by the Iranian monarch. "[The Shah] did what [British Prime Minister Neville] Chamberlain did with Hitler in abandoning Czechoslovakia," Tsafrir bitterly commented.[46] The Kurdish saga made Israel painfully aware of its vulnerable position vis-à-vis Iran, and Tel Aviv's confidence and trust in the Shah was shaken. "That was [the Shah's] big mistake. We lost all confidence in him. He was crazy. He was an idiot," Nimrodi commented resentfully.[47]

Though Israel could tolerate the Shah's political games and his flirting with the Arab bloc, Tel Aviv viewed any hints of a change in the Shah's strategic outlook most seriously. By not informing Israel of his decision to end the Kurdish operations, Tel Aviv was left with the impression that Iran's "links with the Jewish State had become more expedient than imperative." Yitzhak Rabin, who was then Israel's prime minister, flew to Tehran to seek an explanation from the Shah. Well aware of Israel's hope that Iran and Israel would see eye to eye on potential regional threats, the Shah said that he believed war with Iraq was inevitable and that the treaty would buy Iran time.[48] "The Algiers Accord is not worth the paper it is written on," the Shah told Lubrani in order to reassure Tel Aviv that the basis for their alliance—the common threat picture—remained solid.[49] But in reality, Iran and Israel's threat perceptions had started to diverge.

UNCHAINING IRAQ

Iran took full advantage of Nixon's carte blanche on purchases of almost all non-nuclear American weaponry. As Iran's arms purchases ballooned, it increased the size of its army from 225,000 in 1972 to 385,000 in 1975.[50] The Shah's intemperate arms spending helped save the American economy from the oil crisis of the early 1970s, since much of the money the United States spent on Middle East oil was channeled right back to Washington through the Shah's military shopping. From 1972 to 1977, Iran accounted for one-third of all American arms sales.[51] Still, Iran's growth enabled the Shah to adopt increasingly independent—and at times unilateral—policies, which fueled Washington and Tel Aviv's suspicions of the Shah's dangerous ambitions.[52]

By pulling the rug from under Israel in Iraq, the Shah helped make the eastern front even more threatening to Israel. The Arab states' antagonistic intentions toward Israel hadn't been tempered by the Shah's rise in power and his improved relations with Iran's Arab neighbors. The uneven growth between Iran and Israel paved the way for differing Iranian and Israeli assessments of the Arab threat. According to former Iranian Finance Minister Alinaghi Alikhani, "The common threat picture [between Iran and Israel] was diverging," even though they still shared many common enemies.[53]

But as happened many times before, Iranian actions that increased Israel's vulnerability to the Arabs also increased Israel's need for security cooperation with Iran. Though Tehran's actions were detrimental to Israeli interests, Tel Aviv nonetheless could not afford to retaliate. Rather, Israel was made even more dependent on Iran, because losing Tehran when Egypt was moving closer to Washington and Iraq was becoming more powerful would have been disastrous for the Jewish State.

Meanwhile, Iran's growing wealth and power did little to alleviate the Arab threat; Arab suspicion and mistrust of Iran remained intact. As the Shah himself pointed out, Iraq in particular remained a threat through its rearmament, its championing of the Arab cause, and its support for Iranian opposition elements, including Ayatollah Khomeini, who was then living in exile in Iraq, and whose popularity and influence among opposition elements in Iran were growing. By signing the Algiers Accord, Iran nullified its key lever against Baghdad (that is, support for the Kurdish insurgency) and undermined the security of Israel.

The Shah was well aware that it was Iran's support for the Kurdish insurgency that had prevented Iraq from taking military action against Iran, so ending the support for the Kurds made little sense if the Shah was thinking solely in terms of regional balance. Deserting Israel and the Kurdish rebels was a clear indication that the Shah was abandoning the logic of balance of power. The Shah stated as much in an interview with Arab journalist Muhammad Hassanein Haykal in April 1975, only one month after the signing of the Algiers Accord: "We followed the principle 'my enemy's enemy is my friend,' and our relations with Israel began to develop. But now the situation has changed. . . . I think occasionally of a new equilibrium in the region. . . . Perhaps [it] can be integrated into an Islamic framework."[54]

As in many of his previous strategic decisions, the Shah was motivated by the goal of winning Arab recognition for Iran's regional leadership. Since Iran's success in receiving Arab support for Iranian dominion over the Persian Gulf had been limited at best, the elimination of the Iraqi threat—the sole remaining country in the region that could and actually did aspire to challenge Iran's bid for regional leadership—became all the more important. The Shah hoped that Baghdad's implicit acceptance of Iranian dominion through the Algiers Accord could lead the way for other Arab countries to follow suit, since the terms of the agreement were perceived by regional states as being clearly in Iran's favor. As the Shah had expected, in the Arab view the accord sanctioned Iran's number-one position in the Persian Gulf and established Iran's primacy in regional affairs.[55] Furthermore, Iran's swift and unilateral decision to sign the accord—without consulting the United States—further emphasized Tehran's independence and leadership. Essentially, the Shah refrained from conferring with Washington and Tel Aviv because he "thought that the time had come for him to take certain measures without necessarily [consulting] everybody else; because it was a statement about where Iran had arrived," according to one of his advisers.[56]

Initially, the Shah's diplomatic coup seemed successful. It temporarily calmed the Iraqi-Iranian rivalry. For instance, at the Persian Gulf security conference in Muscat, Oman, in 1978, there was neither an Iranian-Iraqi nor an Arab-Persian clash. Rather, the conference failed because of a confrontation between Iraq and Saudi Arabia essentially over the number-two position in regional matters. Iraq believed that the Arab states should have minority status vis-à-vis Iran within the common security arrangement, and that Iraq should be the dominant voice within that minority. The conference failed to advance regional security because Saudi Arabia refused to accept this position.[57]

But it soon became clear that the Algiers Accord was a major strategic misstep by the Shah—just as Israel had argued at the time. Rather than winning time for Iran, it won time for Saddam Hussein. Though the Shah gained symbolic recognition by his main rival of being the dominant power in the region, the quelling of the Kurdish uprising freed Baghdad from its Kurdish chains. Iraq's resources were now free to focus on armament and ascendancy. It enabled Iraq to consolidate its power and significantly increase the size of its army and its military spending on Soviet arms—Iraq's military spending more than doubled between 1975 and 1980—while Iran entered a period of steady relative decline. The shifting of the balance in Baghdad's favor fed the Iraqi perception that the terms of the Algiers Accord were unjust, fueling Saddam's appetite for revenge.[58]

By 1978, Savak officials started to quietly admit to Israeli officials that the Algiers Accord had lifted a heavy burden from Iraq, enabling Baghdad to strengthen its offensive capabilities. "Saddam Hussein only waited for an opportunity to invade Iran," argued Tsafrir. Saddam's opportunity came just five years after the Accord was signed, shortly after the fall of the Shah.[59] In addition, the Shah's unilateralism had undermined Iran's credibility as an ally in Washington and Tel Aviv, and among the Kurds. In retrospect, the Shah's signing of the Algiers Accord exchanged Iran's real but unrecognized supremacy for a short-lived but acknowledged preeminence. In his moment of triumph, the Shah sealed his own demise. "The agreement was a disaster," a former Iranian navy admiral admitted to me.[60]

6

megalomania

> I say quite openly that I wish Iran to play a role in the Indian
> Ocean. I have no objection to America being present;
> indeed I shall actively defend your interests.
>
> —Shah Mohammad Reza Pahlavi to U.S. Vice President
> Nelson Rockefeller, March 24, 1976

Within the context of the pragmatic entente between Iran and Israel,
Tehran's conduct on the Kurdish question marked the continued weakening—but not breakdown—of the alliance. Despite the Algiers Accord,
Iraqi-Iranian relations remained tense until the end of the Shah's reign, and
Tehran and Tel Aviv continued to share many geostrategic interests even
though one crucial element of cooperation had been eliminated. Thinking
beyond threats, the Shah made it his primary goal in the region to solidify
Iran's position by securing Arab support for Iran's aspiration to be primus
inter pares.

Though Israel wasn't a contender for regional leadership, Tehran's ties
to the Jewish State hindered Iran's efforts to achieve that position.[1] Increasingly, Israeli-Iranian relations were shifting from an alliance between two
embattled states to interactions between a would-be hegemon and a state
that was more a burden than an asset in the former's quest for primacy. Israel was also an encumbrance for the Shah for domestic political reasons
even though he paid little attention to Iranian public opinion on foreign
policy matters. While the Israeli public supported Tel Aviv's relations with
Tehran—one of the few regional states with whom Israel could boast joint

intelligence operations—the opposite was true in Iran. Even though the Iranians were apprehensive and suspicious of their Arab neighbors, those sentiments did not translate into a favorable view of Israel.[2] The Jewish State was commonly seen as an aggressive, imperialist power. The most serious public outburst of anti-Israeli feelings took place in 1967 during a soccer match in Tehran between the national teams of Iran and Israel. The event quickly turned into an anti-Israeli demonstration in which balloons with swastikas were distributed and an effigy of Moshe Dayan was hoisted and spat on.[3]

The Iranian public's views on Israel were rooted primarily in the influence of Iran's religious circles and the general anti-imperialist sentiments of ordinary Iranians. Also, at a time when voicing open criticism of the Shah could land one in jail, directing anger toward Israel was a safe way for ordinary Iranians to express discontent with the Shah's rule.[4] These public outbursts may have led outside observers to think that anti-Israel sentiment in Iran was deeper than it actually was, yet Israeli officials stationed in Iran did not escape these negative attitudes. In one of many incidents, the car of Yitzhak Segev, Yaacov Nimrodi's successor as Israel's military attaché to Iran, was spray-painted with Nazi and anti-Israeli slogans—"Heil Hitler" and "Israel out." "In the Bazaar, when I mentioned that I am Israeli, [they] would not take money from my hand," Segev explained to me. "The basics of anti-Judaism based on Shi'ism were clear to us."[5]

Anti-Israeli sentiments were not limited to the public; such attitudes existed within the government as well. The sentiments of government officials, however, were rooted more in political than in religious attitudes. According to a former Iranian official, "Even those technocrats that were helping Israel, in their hearts they were really unhappy that Israel was doing these things to the Palestinians."[6] Within the government, the Foreign Ministry was known to be particularly critical of Iran's relations with Israel, whereas the army and the Savak favored stronger ties.[7] The Foreign Ministry argued that the Arab bloc was growing in importance, since all the nonaligned countries were siding with the Arabs against Israel. But the ministry was fighting an uphill battle to influence Iran's Israel policy, since the Shah and the Savak systematically left it in the dark on these matters. Often, a former Iranian diplomat explained, "we didn't even know what was going on."[8] The distrust between the military and the Foreign Ministry was exemplified by an incident in which Gen. Hassan Toufanian, the Shah's trusted general in charge of army procurement, discovered that Israel's military attaché to Iran, Yaacov Nimrodi, had forged a dead Iranian air force general's letterhead and signature to sell Second World War weaponry to an African state through the Swiss government. Toufanian notified the head of the Israeli mission, Meir Ezri, and the two agreed that Nimrodi should be asked to leave Iran but that the matter should be kept secret in order to preclude the Foreign Ministry from blowing "the incident out of proportion in view of their pro-Arab tendencies."[9]

The Shah himself was known for his suspicions of—and at times contempt for—Israel and world Jewry.[10] The Iranian monarch had an exaggerated belief in Jewish influence in Washington, believing that American Jewry controlled the U.S. media, among other things.[11] His overblown estimation of the Jewish lobby's influence caused many headaches for Israel, but it also provided Israel with a degree of deterrence. "The Shah believed— quite erroneously—that every op-ed in the New York Times was the work of Israel—so he didn't want to antagonize Israel," commented a senior Israeli official stationed in Iran.[12] As the image in America of the Shah's rule deteriorated in the 1970s and was increasingly characterized by human rights abuses and lack of democracy, the Iranian emperor's need of the Jewish lobby's good offices grew. This enabled Israel to offer Iran the support of the Jewish lobby in return for Iranian concessions. But according to Ambassador Hoveyda, former head of the Permanent Mission of Iran to the UN, Shimon Peres gave the Shah only empty promises. Offering the support of the Jewish lobby "was a cheap trick on the part of Shimon Peres. It didn't cost him anything. He would [offer help], but he would do nothing."[13]

Yet for most Iranians, anti-Israel sentiments did not reflect a deeper anti-Semitism. Regardless of the discrimination various minorities experienced under Islamic Iran, the Jewish community in Iran thrived in both culture and trade—thanks greatly to the policies of the Pahlavi dynasty. By the early twentieth century, the community numbered in the tens of thousands, and they played an increasingly important political role. Jewish Iranians participated heavily in the Constitutional Revolution of 1906, and they put their weight behind the constitutionalists to form a National Consultative Majlis (parliament) instead of an Islamic Majlis, as demanded by the religious hierarchy. Reza Shah, the founder of the short-lived Pahlavi dynasty, put an end to the segregation of religious minorities and fully integrated them into the larger Iranian society. He also permitted the Jewish Agency to open an office in Tehran to help Jews emigrate, despite opposition from religious circles in Iran.[14] Reza Shah's policies deeply affected the reaction of Iranian Jews to the creation of Israel. While the founding of the Jewish State prompted a mass exodus of Sephardic Jews to Israel from Arab countries, Iranian Jews did not follow suit. By March 1951, only eight thousand of Iran's one-hundred-thousand-strong Jewish community had made Israel their new home.[15] And according to a study at Tehran University from 1974, most of those Iranian Jews who did emigrate opposed the notion that anti-Semitism existed in Iran; they made Israel their new home overwhelmingly for economic and not ideological reasons.[16]

THE ZIONISM-EQUALS-RACISM RESOLUTION

In November 1975, only months after the signing of the Algiers Accord, the Arab states at the United Nations brought to a vote a resolution equating Zionism—the founding ideology of the Jewish State—with racism based on the argument that Zionism justified racial discrimination. UN General Assembly Resolution 3379 determined "that Zionism is a form of racism and racial discrimination" and called for an end to all forms of racial discrimination, including Zionism. The resolution was passed on November 10, 1975, with seventy-two voting for it and thirty-five against, with thirty-two states abstaining. Much to Israel's disappointment, Iran cast its vote in favor of the resolution. The ambivalent feelings of Iranian Foreign Ministry bureaucrats about Israel turned out to be a critical factor influencing Iran's vote.

The Arab UN bloc put the Iranian delegation under intense pressure to support the resolution, arguing that a Muslim nation like Iran could not remain silent about Israel's treatment of the Palestinians. A passionate debate emerged between Tehran and its New York delegation. Tehran's initial position was to abstain, but the Iranian UN delegation, particularly its lower-ranking diplomats, convinced Tehran to reverse its position by stressing the political benefits of a favorable vote. These Iranian career diplomats tended to agree with the claims of the resolution and were concerned about the wider implications of Iran's ties to Israel.[17] Pleasing the United States and Israel while frustrating the developing countries in the region with which Iran sought improved relations had an increasingly high political cost for Iran. "We didn't want to give the image that we were blindly following the U.S. and Israel," explained Ambassador Mehdi Ehsassi, who served as a member of the Iranian UN delegation at the time.[18] From Iran's perspective, voting in favor of Resolution 3379 was compatible with Tehran's policy of voting with the Non-Aligned Movement and showing increased consideration for Arab sensitivities.[19] Tehran was eventually convinced by the argument that a vote in favor would be "part of Iran's policy of moving closer to the Arabs in order to achieve its independence and leadership role."[20]

Hoveyda, who cast Iran's vote, explained that Iran's leadership aspirations played a critical role in the debate between Tehran and its UN Mission. "[Because of the Shah's] policy of hegemony in the Persian Gulf, he couldn't evade this vote," Hoveyda said. Iran's policy of leadership prevented it from abstaining.[21]

After the fact, though, the Shah had yet another change of heart. The Iranian monarch, who micromanaged the affairs of the state and who involved himself in both big and small decisions, contacted the Iranian UN mission on November 11 with new instructions. Fearing that a vote in favor of the Non-Aligned Movement and the Arab bloc but against the United States would create problems for Iran, the Shah ordered the Iranian UN delegation to oppose the resolution, only to be informed that the vote had taken place the night before and that, per his earlier instructions, the Iranian vote had been cast in its favor.[22] The Israelis did not fail to express their anger at Iran's public insult to the creed of the Jewish State. At the bimonthly luncheon between the deputy heads of the Israeli and Iranian UN mission in New York, the Israeli deputy ambassador made sure that his Iranian colleague understood the full extent of Israel's dissatisfaction. In Tehran, the head of the Israeli mission brought up the issue directly with the Shah, but the Iranian monarch refused to discuss the resolution, dismissing it as irrelevant.[23] The Shah's arrogance was reflective of his new self-image as a geopolitical mastermind who in less than three decades had transformed Iran from a backward developing state into a modern industrial and regional power. Success did little to temper the Shah's aspirations.

THE CAESAR IN THE SHAH

The Shah believed that power made states more responsible. He himself, however, was an exception to that rule. As his power rose, so did his appetite for more power. But perhaps more importantly, as Iran's power suddenly began to decline as a result of the rise of Iraq (which had just been freed from the Kurdish insurgency by the Algiers Accord), the Shah's reaction was to rid himself of all possible constraints.[24] Ironically, the Shah viewed the accords as not only a huge victory but a testament to his wise policies. Having reached his objectives in the Persian Gulf, the Shah upped the ante and started to eye the Indian Ocean states and beyond, effectively overextending Iran through his unlimited aspirations. At a meeting with U.S. Vice President Nelson Rockefeller on March 24, 1976, the Shah spelled out his vision and ambitions: "My policy is honest and straightforward and I have no hidden agenda. I say quite openly that I wish Iran to play a role in the Indian

Ocean. I have no objection to America being present; indeed I shall actively defend your interests."[25] The Shah first extended Iran's navy to the twentieth parallel, and then moved even farther south to the tenth parallel. Iran's navy started to patrol the coast of East Africa, demonstrating its potency.[26] In light of these developments the Shah felt that Iran could not remain indifferent to the political situation in Somalia, so he commanded his army to intervene in the East African state. "It was the outcome of the megalomaniac perception of the Shah, of himself and the status of Iran," noted former Iranian diplomat Davoud Hermidas-Bavand.[27]

Washington viewed these developments with caution, worrying about where the Shah's ambitions could take him.[28] "[The Shah] wasn't trying to just be the hegemon of the region; he wanted to become a power on the world stage," said Henry Precht, former Iran desk officer at the U.S. Department of State.[29] Israeli officials had also recognized Iran's overextension and what they described as the "Shah's megalomania," as well as the dangers it posed to Iran and to Israeli-Iranian relations.[30] In the view of Iraq specialist Andrew Parasiliti, the Shah's increasingly ambitious policy after 1975 was an attempt to maintain Tehran's position at a time when it was losing ground to Baghdad because of Iraq's growing massive armament under Saddam Hussein.

Though many of the Shah's advisers were aware of the dangers of his polices, few were in a position to express their views to the Iranian autocrat. "Why should we be the dominant power in the Indian Ocean? It was ridiculous," lamented Alinaghi Alikhani, a former minister in the Shah's cabinet. "Our people were poor. . . . Even our army wasn't that good, since all the spare parts were made in the U.S.—we were completely dependent."[31] To make matters worse, the Shah's already autocratic style of governing was reaching absurd levels. A declassified State Department paper prepared before the Shah's visit to the United States on August 22, 1967, said that the "Shah rules as well as he reigns. He makes all the important and many unimportant decisions for the government of Iran."[32] By the mid-1970s, the Shah's propensity to micromanage the affairs of the state had become chronic. "All of a sudden he thought that he was more intelligent than everybody else," explained Hoveyda.[33] The Shah stopped consulting his advisers and insisted on making all the analyses and decisions himself. Competition between different parts of the government in providing the Shah with data—particularly between the Savak and the Foreign Ministry—intensified. Eventually information was provided to the Shah raw—without any analysis or processing, leaving him to do both the analysis and decision-making. "There wasn't a single cable from the mission which wouldn't go to the Majesty himself. . . . [He] had to know everything about the foreign relations. . . . He would say yes or no, and he was the only one that could decide."[34]

On no issue was this more flagrant than on Iran's relations with Israel. Minister of Court Assadollah Alam repeatedly declined invitations from high-level Israeli officials because such meetings "would not go down well with His Imperial Majesty who likes to keep certain things exclusive to himself."[35] The Shah increasingly became a one-man government. Cabinet meetings turned into farces; neither national security, oil policies, army spending, nor the Shah's nuclear program were ever addressed at the cabinet level.[36] The same was true for Israeli-Iranian relations. "I attended cabinet meetings for about six years. At no time did we have a strategic discussion on Israel," a former cabinet minister explained to me.[37] Much like his approach toward the Arab states, the Shah tried to keep the nature of his ties with Israel out of the sight of his own people and even his own government. In the end, his distrustful and secretive habits contributed to his own downfall. As instability spread in Iran, the Shah's tendency to punish advisers who merely reported on negative developments grew stronger, leaving few who dared to tell him anything at all. By the time reality hit him, it was too late.

7

the rise of begin and the israeli right

A country like yours, with F-14s, with so many F-4s, with the
problems surrounding you, [must have] a good missile force.

—Israeli Defense Minister Ezer Weizman to Iran's
Gen. Hassan Toufanian, July 1978

June 21, 1977, marked the victory of the right in Israel. After several decades of Labor Party domination of the Israeli political scene, the Likud Party, under the leadership of Menachem Begin, finally took over the Israeli Knesset and the executive branch. As it turned out, Israel's step to the right became a source of friction between Tel Aviv and Tehran.[1] Born in Poland in 1913, Begin was a student and later rival of Ze'ev Jabotinsky, the founder of Revisionist Zionism and the intellectual father of the Israeli right. After moving to Palestine after the outbreak of the Second World War, Begin played a key role in the rise of the Israeli right and led the Irgun Zvai Leumi (National Military Organization), a militant Jewish organization responsible for numerous bombings in the British Mandate of Palestine in the 1940s. The British government offered a reward of £10,000 for information leading to his arrest, but he repeatedly evaded capture. Begin later cofounded the Herut Party and radicalized Jabotinsky's teachings into neo-Revisionism.[2] Unlike Jabotinsky, Begin and his cohorts, many of them Holocaust survivors, did not share the belief that the world would understand and support the implementation of the Zionist dream, though they shared Jabotinsky's fundamental belief that an inevitable blood feud existed between Arabs and Jews.[3] Moreover, Herut, like its Revisionist predecessor, had an ideological attachment to "Eretz Israel" (Greater Israel), which it defined as not only all of British Mandate Palestine, but also territory east of the Jordan River, in what would later become the country of Jordan.

In the mid-1970s, Herut formed a coalition with other like-minded parties called the Likud. The coalition moved to center stage the ideological component of the debate regarding the borders of the Jewish State. According to Shlomo Avineri, former director general of the Israeli Foreign Ministry, Begin's ideological attachment to the West Bank (which he insisted on calling Judea and Samaria) went beyond Israel's legitimate security concerns. Begin belonged to the "territorial" school, which argued that Israel should hold on to as much of what they considered historic Israel as possible, since the more territory Israel held, the more "Jewish" the state would become. By increasing one's territorial claims, one becomes a stronger Zionist, whereas any compromise on the territories of historic Israel is tantamount to a compromise in one's faith in Zionism, followers of this school believe.[4] While the Likud was closer to this line of thinking, the Labor Party was associated with the "sociological school," which argued that the internal structure of Israeli society took precedence over the extent of its territory. A territorially larger Israel would encompass more Palestinians and would as a result be *less* Jewish. Given the higher birthrates of the Palestinian population, the Jews would eventually become a minority in their own country if the West Bank and Gaza were annexed by Israel. Accordingly, the sociological school viewed territorial aggrandizement as a recipe for catastrophe.[5] The "territorialists" recognized the dangers of the demographic problem but believed that it was outweighed by the imperative of maintaining control of Eretz Israel.

Capitalizing on the general dissatisfaction with the Labor Party following the Yom Kippur war, Begin ran on a territorialist platform and made the right-wing ideology of Jabotinsky the dominating thought in Israel.[6] He was the first Israeli prime minister to refer to the West Bank as Judea and Samaria and consider them integral parts of the Land of Israel. Immediately after being elected, he visited the Israeli settlement of Elon Moreh in occupied Palestine and declared it to be part of "liberated Israel." In October 1979, the Israeli Supreme Court ruled that the Elon Moreh settlement was illegal and had to be evacuated.[7] Despite the Supreme Court ruling, Begin's minister of agriculture, Ariel Sharon, announced plans to settle over one million Jews in the West Bank in the coming twenty years, in stark defiance of UN Security Council Resolution 242. With Begin came also a new Israeli security doctrine. Begin was determined to establish Israeli hegemony in the region, "a new balance of power in which Israel would be completely dominant," according to Ilan Peleg. Begin had been openly critical of what he described as Israel's posture of deterrence during his years in opposition. He adopted an offensive posture, "characterized by grandiose expansionist goals," in order to grant Israel strategic superiority. The idea of Israel as a regional military superpower gained support among the Israeli public during Begin's tenure.[8]

In addition, as a result of the Holocaust generation's radicalization of Jabotinsky's teachings, an ideological dimension was added to Israel's doctrine of the periphery. Israel was no longer seeking alliances with the non-Arab states of the region just to weaken the Arab states in Israel's vicinity and convince them of the benefits of peace with the Jewish State, but, rather, alliances with the non-Arab states were now seen as necessary because of the perceived *impossibility* of reaching peace with the Arabs. Non-Arab Iran fitted in perfectly well with the Likudnik Israeli worldview, particularly because of Iran's own ancient civilization—which many Israelis viewed as superior to that of the Arabs—and ancient practice of diplomacy. While Israeli officials tended to view themselves as culturally superior to their Arab neighbors, they viewed Iran as an equal. There was an Israeli idea that they "could deal with the Iranians because they're Iranians."[9] For Iran, Likud's aggressive foreign policy made Begin's victory the Shah's second foreign electoral setback in less than eight months, as Democratic U.S. presidential candidate Jimmy Carter defeated Gerald Ford in November 1976. Since the early years of the Kennedy administration, the Shah had developed a very tense relationship with the Democratic Party. He detested Kennedy's focus on human rights and feared that Carter—who argued for the promotion of human rights and the reduction of U.S. arms sales in general—would have "Kennedy type pretensions."[10] From the Shah's vantage point, a Democrat in the White House made the United States a less reliable ally against Communism. In Israel, however, the Shah preferred the Labor government, which was in power while he had been developing Israeli-Iranian relations over the previous two decades, and whose leadership had good working relations with both the Shah and his advisers.[11] "We could get along with the Labor Party easier because you could talk to them more forcefully and they would listen," commented an Iranian official serving the Pahlavi regime.[12]

Begin's aggressive approach was bad news for Iran. Since the 1967 war, Iran had viewed Israel as an increasingly belligerent state. Iranian diplomats often expressed Tehran's disapproval of Israel's military doctrine, arguing that Israel could not achieve peace and acceptance in the region by "living by the barrel of a gun."[13] The Shah lent support to the Arab position when he rejected Israel's claim to the West Bank by arguing that "the era for the occupation and usurpation of the lands by force was long past."[14] According to a secret U.S. State Department brief, the Shah had urged the United States back in the early 1970s to pressure Israel to make peace: "The Shah feels the U.S. should make every effort to bring about an early resolution to the Arab-Israeli situation. He is on record as opposing the Judaization of Jerusalem and supporting Israeli withdrawal from all occupied Arab territories and restoring the legitimate rights of the Palestinians."[15]

In an interview with *U.S. News & World Report* in 1976, the Shah called for Israel to implement UN Resolutions 242 and 338 and recognize a Palestinian state as a reality: "I have always expressed the opinion that resolutions 242 and 338 must be implemented. We can't just accept fait accompli—the acquisition of land by force—because if you accept it one place, why should you oppose of someplace else [sic]? . . . The PLO should be at Geneva in some form, because you cannot ignore the existence of so many Palestinians. We have got to accept this. Just as we accept the existence of Israel, we have to accept the existence of the Palestinians, too. It is a reality."[16]

In early 1977, a few months prior to Begin's election, Iranian Prime Minister Amir Abbas Hoveyda toured the Middle East and issued several joint communiqués with his Arab counterparts. In Rabat, Iran, and Morocco he "stressed that the Middle East crisis can be solved only on the basis of the withdrawal of Israel from all Arab land it has occupied and the restoration of the Palestinian people's inalienable right to national existence."[17] A month later, a joint statement issued with Egypt in Tehran "condemned Israel for its policy and practices in the occupied territories designed to change the demographic composition and geographical character of those territories." Such a policy, the two countries held, was a serious threat to peace in the Middle East.[18] In May, a similar statement was issued with the Kuwaiti government.[19] From Iran's perspective, criticizing the Israeli position was simply the politically correct thing to do at the time, and, mindful of Israel's vulnerable position vis-à-vis Iran, the criticism did not carry much political cost.[20] Israel's shift to the right, and Begin's—from the perspective of the Shah—stubborn policies posed severe challenges to Iran's strategy and objectives, which were hampered by Iran's relative decline. The Shah saw Begin as a hard-liner whose inflexible policies would undermine Sadat's will for peace, and he threatened to curtail Iranian-Israeli military cooperation unless Begin adopted a more flexible position. He instructed Gen. Hassan Toufanian, who ran Iran's military procurement programs, to "go slow" with the secret Iranian-Israeli military projects.[21] Tehran also feared that Israel's expansionist policies in the West Bank would fuel instability and provide the Soviet Union with an opportunity to strengthen its presence in the Middle East. "If the Arabs were not accommodated in some way, then the chances of the Soviets to return and penetrate [the region] would increase, because [the Arabs] had nowhere else to go," an adviser to the Shah commented. In addition, the Shah was building the legitimacy of his leadership by promoting peace between the Israelis and the Arabs.[22] The Shah's long-standing decision not to recognize Israel de jure was partly rooted in a fear that such a move would disable future Iranian mediation between Israel and the Arabs.[23]

But Begin's hard-line policies rendered the Shah's role as a peacemaker more difficult, which in turn reflected badly on Iran's performance as a regional leader in the eyes of the Arabs.[24] Further warfare would bring unpredictable consequences that could tilt the balance in the region against Iran while drawing more attention to Iran's unpopular ties to Israel. Begin was well aware of the Shah's sensitivities, and soon after his election victory he sent Foreign Minister Moshe Dayan to Tehran to reassure the Shah that Israel would pursue peace. Dayan's message was repeated to Toufanian during their meeting in Tel Aviv on July 18, 1977. The secret minutes of the meeting reveal that Dayan reassured Toufanian that Israel wanted peace "without any preconditions and without any buts and ifs." Furthermore, Dayan explained that "all points are open to negotiations, and that Israel is prepared to sit down with her Arab neighbors without any preconditions," but that Israel would "not negotiate with the PLO and would not agree to a PLO state being established." Toufanian responded that the Shah also advocated a peaceful settlement with the Arabs and that once "His Imperial Majesty will be assured that this is the policy pursued by the present Israel Government, . . . cooperation between the two countries would be further developed and deepened."[25] Toufanian's conditional approval reflected Iran's doubts regarding Begin's sincerity.

On November 9, 1977, Sadat made a courageous attempt to break the Arab-Israeli deadlock by offering to address the Israeli Knesset.[26] The Shah strongly supported Sadat's gambit in the hope that it would compel Israel to adopt a more flexible position.[27] "Sadat has less of a complex about peace than anyone else, including the Israelis," he told *Newsweek* magazine. "I wish Israel had fewer complexes."[28] The unexpected Egyptian offer put much pressure on Israel, which correctly suspected that Sadat's peace offer would strengthen Iran's "Arab option"—gravitating toward the Arab position in its conflict with Israel. Immediately after Sadat's address, Begin dispatched Dayan to Tehran with the official purpose of giving the Iranian monarch a firsthand account of the Egyptian president's talks. The Shah took the opportunity to yet again warn Israel not to take Soviet intentions lightly. The Shah argued that the Soviet Union was arming Iraq and Syria to sabotage any efforts toward peace. "Israel would do well to take into account that these countries, at the initiative and backing of Soviet Russia, would again make war on Israel."[29] But Dayan's initial demands revealed that Israel's primary objective with the visit was to temper Iran's Arab option. Dayan requested that the Shah officially announce his arrival in Tehran, contrary to the practices of Iran and Israel's clandestine relations. Dayan also proposed that their diplomatic missions be raised to the status of official embassies—that is, Iranian de jure recognition of Israel. Recognizing Israel's attempt to negate his ability to exercise the Arab option, the Shah rejected Dayan's proposals, citing the influence of Iran's Islamic leaders on Iranian public opinion. Even before Dayan's trip, Tel Aviv had tried to use the Sadat visit to further publicize Israeli-Iranian relations, much to Iran's annoyance. The Israeli Foreign Ministry extended an invitation to the head of the Iranian mission to Israel to be the first official to greet Sadat upon his arrival at Ben-Gurion Airport. Mindful of the media attention the visit would attract, Iran could ill-afford the sight of one of its officials greeting the Egyptian president in Israel. The head of the Iranian mission politely declined the offer.[30]

Sadat's unprecedented trip to Israel raised hopes for the peace process, but it quickly bogged down again during follow-up talks in Ismailia, Egypt, in December. In a strong show of support for Sadat's position, the Shah visited Egypt on January 9, 1978, and told reporters that "I think Egypt is doing precisely what we believe is right." The Shah shifted blame to Israel by declaring that the ball was in Israel's court.[31] A month later, the Shah further pressured Israel publicly by decrying the Israeli attitude as "incomprehensible, uncompromising and stubborn."[32] The Shah's harsh remarks came only days before Begin's visit to Tehran. Though the Shah was tough on the Israeli prime minister, impressing on Begin that Israel must appreciate Sadat's vulnerable position in the Arab world because of his unilateral decision to visit Jerusalem, the Iranian monarch also indicated that Iran did not intend to side completely with the Arabs. The Shah did not consider taking "positions antagonistic against Israel in defense of the Arabs," according to Gholam-Reza Afkhami, an adviser to the Shah.[33] The reason for this stance was because, as Iran's power was declining and Iraq's was rising,

Tehran's security need for Israel was on the rise once more, much to Tel Aviv's delight.

PROJECT FLOWER

Only two years after the signing of the Algiers Accord, Iran began to realize that the agreement hadn't hampered Iraq's rise as a threat. Furthermore, Iran's sense of security was undermined by President Carter, who pursued a softer approach toward the Soviets. The Shah was highly critical of U.S. conduct in the Cold War and argued that Washington had increasingly become an unreliable ally. He feared that with the United States incapable of standing firm against Communism, the Soviets would find opportunities to make advances in the Middle East. In late 1977, the Shah told an Israeli official who inquired about Iran's unprecedented arms spending that he was convinced that war with the pro-Soviet Arab bloc was coming. The Iranian monarch believed that Iraq—instigated by the Soviet Union and with the full support of regional Arab states—would attack Iran in spite of the Algiers Accord. To make matters worse, the Iranians feared that the United States would treat the war as a local conflict and refrain from taking sides, leaving Iran to fend for itself, even though Iraq would fight with full Soviet backing.[34] Soviet sales of Scud missiles to Iraq, which significantly increased Iraq's offensive capabilities, did not improve matters.[35] In the November 1977 *Newsweek* interview the Shah spelled out Iran's dilemma:

> Q: You are still frequently accused of having "la folie des grandeurs" in your arms purchases. . . . Are you trying to achieve a sort of self-sufficiency because of what you perceive to be U.S. unreliability?
>
> Shah: It's not only U.S. unreliability as we witnessed in Vietnam, Cambodia, Laos and during the India-Pakistan wars. It's also U.N. impotency. We have settled our differences with Iraq, but their military buildup continues. And I wonder how many of your editorial writers and congressmen realize that Iraq has more planes, tanks, and guns than we do—[even] ground-to-ground SCUD missiles. Nor are we just in another state. Look at our borders. What would happen if what remains of Pakistan were to disintegrate? If we don't assume [our own] security in the region, who will do it?[36]

The Shah felt that Iran needed deterrent capabilities against the Iraqi Scuds and turned to the United States to purchase Pershing missiles. But the

Carter administration denied Iran's request, citing the missiles' potential to carry nuclear warheads.[37] Frustrated, Tehran was left with no choice but to turn to Israel—as so often happened when Washington refused to share advanced technologies with Iran. The Jewish State was willing to offer "technology that the West wouldn't give to [Iran]."[38] The Iraqi acquisition of Scud ballistic missiles prompted the initiation of one of the most secretive and controversial collaborations between Iran and Israel—Project Flower. The Shah instructed Gen. Toufanian to turn to the Israelis for missile technology. The Israeli response went beyond just a sale of American missiles. Tel Aviv proposed a collaboration that would use Iranian funds and Israeli know-how to develop a missile with a range of two hundred miles. Israel contended that Tehran needed indigenously produced ballistic missiles in its arsenal, and the Shah was all ears. "You must have ground-to-ground missiles," Israeli Defense Minister Ezer Weizman told Toufanian. "A country like yours, with F-14s, with so many F-4s, with the problems surrounding you, [must have] a good missile force."[39] The initial discussions had already begun under the Rabin government. The Shah and then–Defense Minister Shimon Peres signed an agreement in April 1977 in Tehran, together with five other oil-for-arms contracts totaling $1 billion.[40] The objective was to extend the range of an existing Israeli missile and replace American-supplied parts so that Israel could legally export it without Washington's approval. The Israeli missile included American-made inertial navigation equipment and a guidance system that Tel Aviv was forbidden to make available to other countries.

Begin's election victory led the Shah to put Project Flower on hold, but the decision was reversed in 1978 after Iran received reassurances from Weizman that Israel was serious about peace with the Arabs. Iran made a down payment of $280 million in oil from Kharg Island in the Persian Gulf, and Israel began the construction of a missile assembly facility near Sirjan, in south-central Iran, and a missile test range near Rafsanjan, from where the missile could be fired two hundred miles north into the desert, and south into the Gulf of Oman.[41] Toufanian watched the missile being test-fired during a visit to Israel. "It was beautiful, beautiful, a fully developed missile," Toufanian recalled in an interview with the *New York Times*.[42] The project provided the Iranians with indigenous missile technology that could protect Iran from both Saddam Hussein and Moscow and lessen its dependence on foreign military supplies.[43] "The important thing is really our neighbor Russia," Toufanian told Weizman. "Their aim has never changed. This is to come to all these waters. We are obliged to develop some type of deterrence force."[44] For the Israelis, the projects reinvigorated the alliance with Tehran at a time when it was under increased pressure from the Arabs and from the Shah's leadership aspirations, while offering Israel a guaranteed oil supply as well as financing for advanced military research. Though Israel was uncomfortable with its dependence on Iranian oil—the U.S. State Department estimated that three quarters of Israel's oil imports originated from Iran in 1970—and though Tel Aviv made efforts to seek new suppliers and stockpile oil in storage facilities in the Negev Desert, the oil purchases also enabled Israel to create a market for Israeli goods and technology in Iran.[45] This would show the Arab states— Israel hoped—that cooperation with and acceptance of Israel would carry great benefits.

A critical aspect of Project Flower was that the missiles could be fitted with nuclear warheads, although this possibility wasn't pursued at the time. The matter was never discussed openly, but the Iranians interpreted Israeli signals as indications that this possibility could be explored down the road. "When you read these pages," Toufanian explained, referring to secret Israeli documents describing Toufanian and Weizman's discussions, "there is no doubt about it." Though Iran wasn't pursuing nuclear weapons at the time, that "did not mean we would not be interested in another decade," the Shah's trusted general recalled. At a later stage, the Israelis and Iranians discussed possibilities to enhance the missiles so that they could be launched from submarines. What was most astonishing about the project was that both countries went to great lengths to keep the Americans in the dark. Washington was well aware that Tel Aviv and Tehran held many secret meetings, but neither the full extent of them nor their substance was clear to the Americans. "Israel built a lot of things for the Iranians that we did not know about," former Assistant Secretary of State for Near Eastern Affairs Harold Saunders said. "But it surprises me that the Israelis would have brought the Iranians into the development of a missile that may have been part of their nuclear program." Gary Sick, who served on the National Security Council, was equally stunned. He said he was "surprised to learn that two countries closely allied with the United States were conducting joint military operations without talking to us about them."[46]

The 1979 revolution put an end to Iran's involvement in Project Flower. Later, in the 1990s, Iran's Islamic leadership contacted Toufanian in Washington, D.C., and tried to convince him to share the details of the project, as well as help Iran regain the money it had transferred to Israel in 1978. Toufanian refused to cooperate.[47] The military cooperation between Israel and

Iran was a testament to the rigidity of Iran and Israel's common threat assessments. While the geostrategic environment of Iran and Israel was shifting, the foundation of their entente—the twin perils of Soviet advancement and Arab power—showed remarkable endurance, notwithstanding the Shah's quest for regional preeminence. For Iran, the Israeli-Iranian connection was a deterrent against the Arab regimes, because Israel could use an Arab attack on Iran to strike Iraq's western flank.[48] Although the peace talks with Egypt alleviated some Israeli concerns regarding Cairo's intentions, Tel Aviv continued to sense a threat from its eastern neighbor. Weizman emphasized Israeli worries about the combined armies of Egypt, Syria, and Iraq in his discussions with Toufanian: "The last thing we want and the last thing we need is war. You must remember that Egypt, Jordan, Syria, are all around us, they now possess over 5,000 tanks and over 1,300 fighting airplanes. Iraq can move in forty-eight hours with quite a force. . . . I don't want to go into strategy but you only have to look at the map and see what happens to a small country like ours if we go all the way back to the old borders without real security."[49]

Sensing Iran's wariness of Iraqi rearmament, the Mossad readdressed the issue of aiding the Iraqi Kurds with Savak. Iran's recognition that the termination of the collaboration with the Kurds had permitted Iraq's rise in power gave Israel hope that Tehran might consider reopening the Kurdish corridor. Tehran considered the proposal but never offered a definite reply, according to the Israelis. A senior Iranian government official, however, maintains that secret Savak documents show that cooperation between Israel, Iran, and the Barzani Kurds recommenced in 1978, although on a much smaller scale. Only four Savak agents were involved in and aware of the operations.[50]

Nevertheless, Iran's relative decline, the Carter administration's softer approach toward the Soviet Union, and Iraq's rising power all served to push Iran back toward Israel. Though Israel did not take any specific actions to intensify the common Iranian and Israeli threat perception, save occasional efforts to undermine Iranian-Arab relations, just as the Shah benefited from continued Israeli-Arab tensions, the Jewish State profited from the Shah's continued and increased sense of threat from Baghdad and Moscow. From Israel's perspective, particularly the neo-Revisionists in the Likud, Iran continued to be the cornerstone of its peripheral doctrine. To Israel, the logic of the Israeli-Iranian alliance was enduring—if not permanent. According to Eliezer Tsafrir, head of the Mossad in Iran and Iraq in the 1960s and 1970s,

Whatever the name of Iran—Pars, Elam, Media—and whatever the name of Iraq—Babylon, Assyria, Akkad, Sumer—there was always a rivalry and sometimes war [between the two]. . . . The Iranians know this—and this is why I am optimistic about Iranian-Israeli relations in the future. "Koroush-e Kabir" [Cyrus the Great] knew that there is a common interest between the two sides of the Middle East—Iran and Israel. That is why Koroush let Ezra and Nehemja come back and rebuild the temple. It was obviously an interest of his in order to dominate Babylon [Iraq]. Iran is Moslem but not Arab, and [to keep this balance] Iran needs another [non-Arab] people [who share that] common interest.[51]

Amid the Shah's efforts to regain the initiative in the tilting balance in the region, internal upheaval in Iran forced the Iranian monarch to divert attention to his domestic vulnerabilities. Unrest was growing; indeed, seven months after Begin's visit to Iran, the Israeli prime minister tried to convince Carter and Sadat at the Camp David talks that the Shah was finished.[52]

8

enter the sign of god

Allahu Akbar, Khomeini Rahbar.
(God is Great, Khomeini is our leader.)

—Military Attaché Yitzhak Segev and Mossad Chief
Eliezer Tsafrir, cheering Khomeini's return to Iran, in
Shahyad Square/Meidan-e Azadi, February 11, 1979

On February 11, 1979, the Persian dynasty was replaced with an Islamic one. The revolution was a momentous event not only for Iran—it also sent shockwaves throughout the entire Islamic world. Through a popular revolution a pro-American dictatorship in the oil-rich Middle East had been replaced with the modern world's first theocratic regime. The Middle East would never be the same again. The Shah's swift downfall took the West by surprise, though signs of growing discontent in Iran were hardly hidden. The Israelis were equally dismayed but did not experience the same surprise. Built on the back of the vibrant Jewish Iranian community, Israel's informal intelligence network in Iran was far superior to that of the United States.[1] Iranian officials had indirectly revealed the vulnerability of the Shah by turning to their Israeli counterparts for support and advice. More often than not, the Savak turned to the Mossad for assistance in interrogating the growing number of opposition activists.[2]

At times, the behavior of the Iranian officials was comical. For instance, in 1978 the chief of the Iranian air force, Gen. Amir Hossein Rabii, urged Israel's military attaché, Yitzhak Segev, to ask Israeli Foreign Minister Moshe Dayan to "tell the Shah what is the reality in Iran. . . . The Shah is sitting on a very high chair. Everyone just say yes, yes, yes. You can't criticize, you can't tell him all these things." The Israeli military attaché obliged and brought Dayan to Iran. Dayan quickly concluded that the Shah had become incapable of making decisions. And without the Shah making decisions, the Iranian government was effectively paralyzed. Segev argued that a military coup was the only way to save the Pahlavi regime. But the Iranian generals were too afraid of challenging the Shah's authority or of even explaining to him the full extent of the instability. Simply organizing a meeting between the generals without the Iranian emperor's permission was tantamount to a coup d'état in the paranoid mind of the Shah. The generals managed to gather courage to take action only after the Shah fled the country on January 16, 1979, but by then the Carter administration had signaled that it wanted to see democratic reforms in Iran. Washington's decision destroyed the last glimpse of hope among the generals, and many of them saw no other solution than to flee the country.[3]

As the Shah fled, he handed power over to Shahpour Bakhtiar, a prominent opponent of the Shah's rule who was not trusted by the Iranian monarch, the Islamists, or the leftists. The Mossad offered its support to Bakhtiar, who hinted that it would be helpful if Israel did "something to quiet Khomeini," the hard-line Iranian ayatollah who spearheaded the opposition to the Shah from his base outside of Paris. Bakhtiar offered to have the Shah make the request directly to Tel Aviv, but Israel rejected Bakhtiar's demand, reminding the new Iranian premier that Israel wasn't the "police of the world."[4] (A decade later the roles were reversed. According to press reports, Iranian agents entered Bakhtiar's home in Paris—where he had taken refuge—and brutally murdered him.) By the time Bakhtiar had been given the premiership, Israel's El Al flights were the only connection between Iran and the outside world; all other airlines had cancelled their flights to Iran because of the instability and violence. Dayan wanted to keep the Israeli personnel in Iran as long as possible, hoping that their presence would compel the revolutionary government to maintain Iran's ties to Israel.[5] However, to appease public opinion and the religious opposition, one of Bakhtiar's first orders of business was to break off ties with the apartheid regime in South Africa and end oil exports to Israel.[6] Israeli gestures to Bakhtiar proved useless, as his reign was short-lived. On February 1, Ayatollah Khomeini returned to Iran after fifteen years in exile and was cheered there by millions. He immediately declared war on the Bakhtiar government. Ten days later, Bakhtiar resigned.[7]

Upon his arrival, the ayatollah—literally "Sign of God"—was flown to

Shahyad Square in southwestern Tehran (renamed Meidan-e Azadi, Freedom Square, after the revolution), where millions of his supporters had gathered to greet him. There, next to the religious revolutionaries, stood Israel's military attaché—Yitzhak Segev—and the head of the Israeli Mossad in Iran—Eliezer Tsafrir—observing the proceedings while trying to fit in. A mullah—an Islamic cleric—passed by the two Israelis and asked them in Persian why they weren't carrying pictures of the angry-looking Ayatollah. They apologized—in perfect Persian—and were handed two large pictures of the "Father of the revolution." They then joined the crowd in chanting "Allahu Akbar, Khomeini Rahbar" (God is Great, Khomeini is our leader). As Khomeini's helicopter approached, Segev detected a familiar figure sitting next to the ayatollah. "Inside the helicopter was [Gen.] Rabii," the Shah's right-hand man who only months earlier had conspired to kill Khomeini.[8] A few weeks later, Rabii was executed by the revolutionaries. Those were dangerous days to be an Israeli in Tehran. The Jewish State began to evacuate most of its citizens, but a few dozen were deliberately kept in Tehran per the instructions of Dayan. On February 10, a day before Bakhtiar's resignation, the final El Al flight arrived in Tehran to evacuate the last Israelis. But an early curfew forced the flight to take off hastily, without its human cargo, and many Israelis were stuck at the airport till the next morning. The following day, a mob attacked the Israeli mission. Segev called Gen. Toufanian in desperation and requested Iranian military intervention. But Segev's request was denied. "I'm sorry, General," Toufanian replied, "but I am unable to assist you."[9] As the mob broke through the gates, Segev and three other employees fled through a side exit. The mission was plundered and set on fire.

Having lost the Israeli mission, the Mossad set up safe houses in Tehran to protect the few remaining Israelis. By now a new government had been installed by Khomeini. The Mossad had made contact with elements of the opposition before the Shah's fall, and they had little hope of establishing friendly relations with the revolutionary government.[10] Nevertheless, a final effort was made to clarify whether they could stay or whether they had to leave, knowing very well that it would be much harder to send Israeli officials back to Iran than to try to keep them there and present the new government in Tehran with a fait accompli. Tsafrir, who headed the Mossad's evacuation efforts, contacted Khomeini's deputy prime minister, Amir Abbas Entezam, and asked for permission to stay. Entezam, after consulting Prime Minister Mehdi Bazargan and an aide to Foreign Minister Karim Sanjabi, answered in the negative and instead urged the Israelis to leave. A few days later, on February 18, Bazargan severed all relations with Israel, including oil sales and air links. With that, an era of Israeli-Iranian relations came to an abrupt and unforeseen end.[11]

THE PALESTINIAN QUESTION ACCORDING TO THE REVOLUTIONARIES

The new regime defined itself in counter-Pahlavi terms: everything with the Pahlavi dynasty was simply wrong, including its ties to Israel. Though discontent with the Shah's clandestine relations with Tel Aviv wasn't a driving force of the revolution, anti-Israeli sentiments were espoused by all the major revolutionary factions. The Left opposed Israel because Tel Aviv was close to the United States. They saw the Jewish State as an outpost of American imperialism in the Middle East and likened Israel's treatment of the Palestinians to the apartheid regime's treatment of Blacks in South Africa.[12] The religious forces, on the other hand, viewed Israel as an illegitimate state and a usurper of Muslim land.[13] The religious revolutionaries maintained that Israel was "by its very nature against Islam and the Qur'an," and that it was the religious duty of every Muslim to confront it.[14] The creation of the Jewish State was nothing less than an affront to Islam, and the Islamic world's troubles were rooted in secularism and divergence from the real Islam. Since the revolution had created the only real Islamic state, Iran had a duty to struggle for Islam and Islamic justice everywhere, the fundamentalists believed.[15] This line of thinking was in many ways new to Iran's clerical circles. While many among the clerics supported the Palestinian cause from an anti-imperialistic perspective, it was Ayatollah Khomeini who gave the conflict a religious dimension.[16]

Imam Seyyed Ruhollah Khomeini Al-Mosawi was born into a religious family with an established clerical heritage in the city of Khomein in central Iran on May 17, 1900. He entered into religious studies at an early age and was accepted into the seminary in Arak and Qom, renowned for its scholastic brilliance under the leadership of Ayatollah Sheikh Abdol-Karim Haeri-Yazdi. In 1963, Khomeini publicly denounced the Shah's government and was imprisoned for eight months, after which he was exiled, first to Turkey and then later to Iraq, where he continued his anti-Shah sermons. In 1978, Saddam Hussein had had enough of the fiery ayatollah and expelled him, evidently in part because of Iranian pressure.[17] Khomeini then lived in France until his triumphant return to Iran in 1979. By the time he set foot in France, Khomeini had become one of the most influential opponents of the Pahlavi dynasty. Unlike other Iranian critics of Israel, Khomeini did not concern himself much with the plight of the Palestinian people. Rather, he

couched his criticism of the Jewish State in religious language and positioned Israel as an enemy of Islam.[18] Israel was a "cancer" that would destroy Islam and Muslims if not removed from the region; it was a state that
did not want the Qur'an to exist.[19] Khomeini's neglect of the Palestinian
dimension of the Palestinian-Israeli conflict fitted well with his worldview. He elevated the interest of the Muslim community *(umma)* and deni-
grated the very idea of secular national interests and nationalism *(melli-
garai)*, and argued that the international system was the "creature of a
weak human mind," which must be replaced with a divine Islamic world
order. "Islam is not peculiar to a country, to several countries, a group,
or even the Muslims. Islam has come for humanity. . . . Islam wishes to
bring all of humanity under the umbrella of its justice," he wrote in the
late 1970s.[20]

This worldview added an ideological dimension to Iran's foreign policy,
which was further fueled by the religious bloc's failure to view Iran as a state.
Rather, the clerics initially defined their allies and enemies based on their
respective perspectives on Islam.[21] In addition, Iran's revolutionaries entered the political scene with much disdain for the United States, the result
of Washington's support for the Shah. Often, no distinction was made between Washington and Tel Aviv; while the United States was the "Great Satan," Israel was "Little America." Consequently, opposition to Israel became
a defining characteristic of Islamic Iran, in which the Jewish State and Zionism were seen as enemies of Islam and ideological threats to Iran's Islamic
identity.[22]

AN UNINVITED GUEST

The Palestinians had a long history of active support for the Iranian op-
position to the Pahlavi regime. Many of the Iranian revolutionaries had
trained in PLO camps, and the Palestinians expected the revolution to bring
about a major change in Iran's outlook on the Palestinian-Israeli conflict.
Without prior notice to the revolutionary government, PLO leader Yasser
Arafat traveled to Iran on February 18, 1979, together with fifty-eight other
PLO officials.[23] Though the revolutionaries were caught off guard, several
Iranian officials greeted Arafat at the airport and provided the Palestinians
with high-end accommodations at the former Government Club on Fe-
reshteh Street in northern Tehran.[24] At an official ceremony that same
week, attended by both Prime Minister Bazargan and Foreign Minister Sanjabi, the compounds of the Israeli mission to Iran were handed over to the
PLO, and the name of the street on which it was located was renamed Pales-

tine Street. Furthermore, Arafat traveled throughout Iran and set up PLO offices in various Iranian cities, including the southwestern city of Ahvaz in the province of Khuzestan, which has a sizable Arabic-speaking population.[25]

Several members of Arafat's entourage ultimately stayed for more than a year, manning the PLO offices in Iran. During his trip Arafat also met with Ayatollah Taleqani, his longtime Iranian supporter, whose involvement in the Palestinian issue preceded that of Khomeini.[26] But immediately after Arafat's arrival in Tehran, tensions between the PLO and the revolutionaries began to surface. On the first day of his visit, Arafat had a two-hour meeting with Khomeini. Much to Arafat's surprise, Khomeini was quite critical of the PLO and lectured the Palestinian leader on the necessity of getting to the Islamic roots of the Palestinian issue and away from Arafat's leftist and nationalistic tendencies. "They just didn't hit it off well," according to an Iranian analyst.[27] Ibrahim Yazdi, Iran's foreign minister in the first revolutionary government, informed the U.S. embassy staff that Khomeini had appealed to the PLO to adopt an Islamic orientation and replicate the methodology of Iran's nonviolent revolution. The Iranians argued that an Islamic orientation would increase the prospects of a Palestinian victory and would prevent Marxists and radical elements among the Palestinians from taking over.[28] In reality, however, the Iranians needed to redefine the Palestinian issue in order for Iran to be able to play a leadership role in it. If it was defined as an Arab cause, then Iran could have no major role. The two revolutionaries did not meet again.

In their own minds, the Iranian revolutionaries had created an image of the Palestinians and their struggle that simply did not correspond to reality. "None of [the Palestinians] were religious. Most of them drank alcohol, and they wanted to watch films," an Iranian official who hosted the Palestinians complained. The ideological differences between the Iranian revolutionaries and the PLO representatives put a dark cloud over their relations, and the gap between them steadily grew. "Were these really the Palestinians? The Palestinians whose level we had a desire to reach?" the Iranians asked themselves.[29] The Palestinians, in turn, had already begun to understand after Arafat's meeting with Khomeini that Islamic Iran would lend the Palestinians only verbal and rhetorical support. The significant Palestinian investments in the Iranian opposition to the Shah would simply not yield a high return.[30] For instance, in spite of his anti-Israeli rhetoric, Khomeini decided against a request to send Iranian F-14s to aid the Syrian air force against Israel in the ongoing fighting in Lebanon, indicating yet again that Iran did not intend to take an active role on the Arab side against Israel beyond its verbal condemnations of the Jewish State.[31] Though Arafat had the support of Ayatollah Taleqani, the ailing ayatollah was becoming increasingly marginalized in Iranian politics, and opponents of the PLO were gaining ground. Some revolutionaries, such as the U.S.-educated Mostafa Chamran, Iran's minister of defense, supported the Shi'a Amal movement in Lebanon, which was at odds with the PLO. Others, like the commander of the Iranian Revolutionary Guards Corps, had close ties to Arafat's rival, George Habash of the Popular Front for the Liberation of Palestine (PFLP).[32]

Iranian-PLO ties further suffered as Iran's relations with its Arab neighbors deteriorated. Just as Khomeini lectured Arafat on the evils of secularism, he accused other Arab states of having deserted Islam. Soon enough, tensions emerged between Tehran and the Gulf Cooperation Council (GCC) states. The Khomeini government began to publicly accuse the PLO and PFLP of fueling tensions between Arabs and Persians in Ahvaz, and several prominent clerics questioned, from a security perspective, the sensibility of having a PLO office in Ahvaz, mindful of its large Arabic-speaking population.[33] Only months after the Ahvaz offices had been set up, they were shut down and the PLO embassy in Tehran was put under close scrutiny. In order to balance this act against the Palestinians and appeal to the broader Arab and Muslim masses, Khomeini turned to his rhetorical resources to cover up Iran's real policies. The Ayatollah declared August 17 as Quds (Jerusalem) Day and urged Muslims worldwide to demonstrate on that day in support of the Palestinians.[34] In reality, however, the celebrations of Quds Day demonstrated only Iran's unwillingness to deliver concrete support to the Palestinians.

Khomeini's tense relations with the PLO did not remain a secret for long. A confidential memo sent to Washington from the U.S. embassy in Tehran in September 1979 stated that "Iran enthusiastically and unreservedly supports the Palestinian cause," but that "relatively little is said about the PLO itself," and that the Iranians will not permit any PLO interference in domestic Iranian affairs, particularly in Khuzestan.[35] But just like Israel, the PLO knew that Iran was too important to give up on. Until the outbreak of the Iraq-Iran war, the PLO continued to invest in various Iranian factions in order to outmaneuver Khomeini and his lukewarm attitude toward active, nonrhetorical Iranian engagement in the Palestinian cause.[36]

As Arafat strengthened his ties with the Mujahedin, his relations with Khomeini further deteriorated, and by November 1980 the Iranian-Palestinian honeymoon was over, as Khomeini refused to recognize a Palestinian mediation effort to win the release of American diplomats taken hostage by Iranian students at the Iranian embassy.[37]

9

ideological shifts, geopolitical continuities

> Imagine if you could topple Saddam and establish an Islamic Republic over there. . . . [T]hat would change the balance of everything, you could dominate the region, you could dominate the entire Middle East.
>
> —An Iranian political strategist on Iran's ambitions at the outset of the revolution

By the time of the 1979 revolution, Iran's power in the region was declining in comparison with its neighbors—particularly Iraq. Already by 1978, Iran's position as the region's undisputed power rested on shaky ground. The chaos that swept the country with the revolution served only to make matters worse. Iran's military spending fell from $16.6 billion in 1978 to $7.7 billion in 1979, and scores of Iranian officers either fled the country or were killed by the revolutionaries, thereby dissipating much of the country's military know-how. Between 1979 and 1980, Iran's armed forces lost more than one hundred thousand men; at the same time, Iraq's army swelled and outnumbered the Iranian army for the first time. By 1980, Iraq outspent Iran on its military for the first time as well.

Paradoxically, Iran's declining power only increased the ambitions of the revolutionaries. Though U.S. policy-makers predicted that Ayatollah Khomeini would pursue an extremely nationalist foreign policy, they also believed that he would reject the Shah's political aspirations.[1] But Iran's Islamic ideology, though resentful of the international order and the idea of nation-states, was no less ambitious than the realpolitik outlook of the Shah with the notion of Iranian regional leadership at its center. While the Shah sought approval of and legitimacy for his bid for leadership through finan-

cial aid to and military protection of the surrounding Arab states, the revolutionaries sought the same through political Islam. But while the Shah believed that his aspirations could be achieved within the framework of the
existing order, the revolutionaries felt they needed to redefine the framework of state-to-state interaction and its founding principles in order to reverse Iran's decline and restore its bid for leadership.

Though the methods and justifications of the Pahlavi and Khomeini regimes differed considerably, their strategic goals were remarkably similar—
regional leadership and primacy. The one big difference, however, was that
the revolutionaries topped the Shah's megalomania: beyond merely seeking the role of first among equals in the Indian Ocean and western Asia region, the Khomeini government sought to lead the entire Islamic world.
Both the Shah (after 1976) and the revolutionaries desired a political role
that outstripped Iran's resources.[2]

The revolutionaries believed that for Iran's leadership to be viable, the
entire order of the region needed to be changed. Just as the Iranian masses
had dethroned the U.S.-backed Shah and established an Islamic government, the revolutionaries argued, so the Arab masses should dethrone their
U.S.-backed sheikhs and establish governments based on Islamic principles. The Shah's quest to win legitimacy for Iranian regional leadership—
based on American backing, strong ties and military aid to the region's
moderate Arab governments, and financial aid to Arab states such as Syria,
combined with public distancing from Israel—ultimately failed to persuade the Arabs to grant Iran the role to which it aspired. Historic Arab-
Persian suspicions, as well as resentment of the Shah's entente with Israel,
would deny Iran that role. But by exporting the revolution and spreading
the ideology of political Islam, Iran hoped to bridge the Persian-Arab divide
and establish a regional values system that would include Iran in a leadership role. An Iranian politician belonging to the reformist camp explained
Iran's thinking as follows: "Imagine if you could topple Saddam and establish an Islamic Republic over there. . . . That [regional domination] was the
whole idea. You have an Islamic Republic in Iraq, an Islamic Republic in
Iran. These are the two most powerful states in the region. And that would
change the balance of everything, you could dominate the region, you could
dominate the entire Middle East."[3]

Unlike the strategy of the Shah, who based Iran's position in the region
on an alliance with Washington, the new regime neither had that option nor
believed in the usefulness of such a strategy. Instead, the new leadership favored an approach based on Iran's integration and reconciliation with its

immediate neighbors rather than on cooperation with remoter states. "Iran is situated in a region where it is considered a minority, where the population in the region is not necessarily close to Iran," explained Iran's ambassador to the UN, Javad Zarif. "But at the same time, that is the immediate neighborhood of Iran, and Iran needs to somehow find an appropriate relationship with its immediate neighborhood, which would reduce the anxieties that exist in Iran due to the fact of being surrounded by predominantly Sunni surroundings and then quite a bit of Arab surroundings."[4]

Iran's long-term security and its bid for leadership was best achieved by befriending Iran's Arab neighbors rather than by balancing them through Iranian military preponderance and alliances with extraregional states, the revolutionaries argued. The importance of bridging the Arab-Persian divide through political Islam was visible from the outset of the revolution. Khomeini's clash with Arafat was over the Palestinian leader's pan-Arab nationalist struggle against Israel at the expense of an Islamic-inspired resistance. Khomeini's criticism of Arafat reflected Iran's need to establish a values system through which its leadership aspirations could be realized. This line of thought wasn't necessarily new to Iranian foreign policy. The Shah had reached the same conclusion in 1975 when he signed the Algiers Accord, and he even toyed with the idea of relying on Islam to win the Arabs' trust. Yet, as much as he recognized Iran's dilemma in being a Persian state in a sea of Arabs, he never resorted to the excesses of the revolutionaries.

A GREAT LOSS FOR AMERICA, A DEVASTATING BLOW TO ISRAEL

The Iranian revolution tilted the balance in the Middle East by drawing Iran away from the Western camp. For America, it was a disaster. In the midst of the Cold War, Washington had lost a critical ally tasked with maintaining stability in the ever so vital Persian Gulf region and with keeping the Soviets out. Though Khomeini was contemptuous of the atheists in the Kremlin and rejected a tilt toward the Soviet Union—his slogan read "Neither West nor East"—Washington still feared that Iran would fall into the hands of the Red Empire. But at the outset, all options remained open for Khomeini and Carter. Although the Ayatollah's rhetoric was defiant and scornful of the United States, he initially did not intend to sever ties with Washington. As long as the United States respected Iran's independence, a new relationship could emerge, he reasoned.

Declassified CIA documents show that Washington was well aware that Khomeini recognized areas of common interest between the two countries and that he favored the continuation of oil sales to the United States.[5] Washington too was eager to ensure that the revolution wouldn't lead to a complete break with Iran, because that surely would benefit Moscow. But the radical cleric found himself out-radicalized when a handful of Iranian leftist students stormed the U.S. embassy on November 4, 1979, and took all diplomats and employees hostage. Khomeini first refrained from endorsing the hostage-taking but was soon convinced by left-leaning elements among his supporters to back the students and their demand for the United States to hand over the Shah.[6] (The cancer-stricken Iranian "King of Kings" had been fleeing from state to state, in the hope that President Carter would eventually grant him refuge in the United States.)

What began as an amateurish plan to take a few American diplomats hostage for a few days soon turned into an unprecedented international ordeal. Humiliated, Carter severed all diplomatic ties with Tehran, and America never looked at Iran with the same eyes again. Conversely, the Iranians began to view Washington as a threat—not necessarily a direct military threat but a long-term political threat stemming from America's refusal to accept Iran's revolution and thus Washington's determination to jump on every opportunity to reverse it.[7] To this day Iran is wrestling with the disastrous consequences it brought on itself as a result of the hostage-taking.

The ramifications of the Cold War were less of a factor for Israel's strategic calculations than were its immediate security concerns and the threats it faced from the Arab states—whose pro- or anti-U.S. tilt was of secondary importance to the Jewish State. Rather, Israel was guided by the periphery doctrine even though Tel Aviv had succeeded in breaking the circle of Arab enmity surrounding it through the peace treaty with Egypt—the most powerful and populous Arab state.[8] Within that strategic framework, Iran's location at the perimeter of the Arab world, its economic and military ties to Israel, its oil, and its traditional enmity with Iraq and the Soviet Union made it next to irreplaceable.[9] After twenty-five years of Israeli political investments in Iran, the ties to Tehran had become a crucial element of Israel's regional strategy.

Unquestionably, losing Iran would have been a great strategic setback for the Jewish State. That prospect made it all the more important for Israel to seek to maintain its ties even under the new regime. Israel had suffered the loss of a peripheral ally only a few years earlier through the collapse of Haile Selassie's government in Ethiopia in 1974. But Israel successfully rebuilt its alliance with that country's new Communist rulers. Iran was far more valuable to Israel than Ethiopia, so it was clearly worth fighting for.[10]

"We had very deep relations with Iran, cutting deep into the fabric of the two peoples," explained David Kimche, who headed the Israeli Foreign Ministry at the time. "It was difficult for people to accept the fact that all of this intimacy was thrown out of the window. So there were a lot of attempts during the first year after the revolution to see if we could revive the relations with [Iran]."[11] Israel was also concerned about the faith of Iran's one-hundred-thousand-strong Jewish community. The dilemma was that an aggressive policy vis-à-vis Tehran could put the Iranian Jews in danger, while a softer approach would likely not be able to remove the dangers facing them. Israel simply did not have many cards to play.[12]

Though the Israeli intelligence service knew that the revolution would likely mean the end of Iran's official relations with Israel, the Jewish State was torn between those who wanted to mount a counterstrike to save the Pahlavi regime and those who believed that the new regime would soon collapse and be replaced by a leadership that would adapt to Iran's geopolitical realities and recognize its need for Israel.[13] The former group was dominated by Israelis who had had extensive contacts with the Pahlavi regime. They felt strongly that the revolution was a temporary phenomenon. Soon enough, the "real" Iran would reemerge.

Ariel Sharon, an ambitious Israeli military commander and politician who later became Israel's prime minister, belonged to the first camp. During a cabinet meeting at the height of the revolution, he proposed that Israeli paratroopers be dispatched to Tehran to save the Shah.[14] The proposal was voted down. Whatever the differences between these two camps, however, the periphery doctrine dominated the thinking of both. "These people continued to see Iran from the prism of the periphery doctrine, and believed that Iran was a natural ally of Israel," commented Yossi Alpher, a former Mossad official.[15] According to Alpher, the logic of the periphery doctrine was so "thoroughly ingrained" in the Israeli mindset that it had become "instinctive." For the Israelis not to view Iran as a natural ally was simply hard to fathom.[16]

With the rise of neo-Revisionist Zionism, the periphery doctrine was also given an ideological dimension. David Ben-Gurion originally devised the strategy for the purpose of weakening the Arab states while demonstrating to them the benefits of concluding peace with Israel by showcasing Israel's contributions to the economic and technological development of the peripheral states. The Arab states would soon realize that they too could benefit from these advancements if they made peace with Israel, he argued.

So peace with the Arabs and Israel's acceptance in the region wasn't only a possibility, in the view of the father of the periphery doctrine it was its goal.

The neo-Revisionists, however, were not as optimistic. Prime Minister Begin believed that the Arabs understood only the language of force, leaving Israel with no choice but to seek military preponderance. According to this view, because Israel would never be accepted in the Middle East peace wasn't achievable through negotiation and compromise but could be won only through the complete military defeat of Israel's neighbors.[17] Yitzhak Shamir, Begin's successor as Likud Party leader, shared this view and strongly believed that a real peace with the Arabs was unachievable.[18] To the neo-Revisionists, the periphery doctrine not only made strategic sense; it also was compatible with their worldview. So even when the strategic logic of the periphery doctrine was weakened—through the cold peace with Egypt and through Iran's new anti-Israeli ideology—its ideological dimension kept the doctrine alive.

Israel failed to question the wisdom of the doctrine even when Iran began developing ties to radical Shias in Lebanon by the mid-1980s. Paradoxically, the loss and weakness of Iran intensified the threat Israel sensed from Iraq, which in turn increased Tel Aviv's need for relations with Tehran. Though Israel had concluded a peace with Egypt, its relations with the Arab world and the Soviet bloc remained hostile. So while its southern front, that is, the Egyptian front, had been pacified, its eastern front remained all the more vulnerable as a result of the rise in Iraqi power and the loss of Iran as a counterweight to Iraq. From Tel Aviv's perspective, Iraq was the single greatest regional threat to Israel's security, while Iran—in spite of its ideology, its harsh rhetoric, and its vocal support of the Palestinian issue—was seen as a nonthreat. For all practical purposes, to Israel, Iran continued to be a partner in balancing the Iraqi threat.[19]

GEOPOLITICAL REALITIES VS. IDEOLOGICAL FANTASIES

Indeed, much to the chagrin of the revolutionaries, the geopolitical realities of the region remained surprisingly unchanged—in spite of the reinvention of Iran's identity from a Persian monarchy under Pahlavi to an Islamic Republic under Khomeini. Israel and Iran continued to share fundamental common threats. Consequently, Iran's geopolitical realities remained largely immune to the worldviews and ideologies espoused by Tehran's new leadership—Iran was still surrounded by hostile Arab states to the south and west and an aggressive Russian superpower to the north.[20]

At first, because of Iran's wish to redesign the entire Middle East order,

it rejected alliances with Arab states that shared Tehran's geopolitical dilemmas but whose ideologies clashed with Iran's. For instance, Egypt lost its
leadership role in the Arab world and was shunned by the Arab states after
signing the Camp David Accord with Israel. Sadat tried to break out of his
country's isolation by reaching out to Iran immediately after the death of
the Shah. But Khomeini took the opportunity to win legitimacy in the Arab
world by rejecting Sadat's offer and by accusing Cairo of betraying the
Palestinians.

By May 1980, Iran had severed all relations with Egypt.[21] But as the
Khomeini government was soon to find out, Iran's Arab neighbors were not
receptive to Iran's brand of political Islam. Islamic unity, and an Islamic order, hardly suited the existing Arab regimes, and even those that did support
an Islamic order, like Saudi Arabia, were hostile to Iran's Shia brand of Islam. (Tensions between the Shia and Sunni branches of Islam date back
centuries.) Iran's challenge to the existing political systems among the Arab
states was particularly troubling for the Arab kingdoms with strong ties to
Washington, whose form of Islam was branded "American Islam" by Khomeini. Revolutionary Iran was also feared by the rulers of states with major
Shia populations such as Iraq, Bahrain, and Saudi Arabia, whose oil-rich
Eastern Province is heavily Shia. While the Arabs had been wary of the
Shah's ambitions, they were terrified of Khomeini's political designs and
Iran's attempts to export the revolution.[22] The tables had been turned—the
pan-Arab threat to Iran had been replaced with an Islamic—and a specifi-
cally Shia Islamic—threat to the Arabs.[23]

Nor did the revolution change Iran's fear of the Soviet Union. In December 1979 Russian troops invaded Afghanistan, putting Iran's armed
forces on high alert. Tehran feared that Moscow would take advantage of
the political disorder in Iran in order to achieve its long-term goal of reaching the warm waters of the Persian Gulf. The Soviet empire continued to
pose three specific challenges to Tehran, despite the revolution. At the ideological level, the Shah had opposed Communism as a result of his adherence
to Western capitalist values, while the followers of Khomeini viewed Moscow's atheism as a threat to Islam. Strategically, the Kremlin's political designs for the region remained the same. The revolutionary regime's foreign
policy elite, headed by President Abolhassan Bani-Sadr and Foreign Minister Sadegh Ghotbzadeh, were deeply suspicious of Moscow and worried
that the Soviets would take advantage of the collapse of Iran's armed forces
and launch an attack.[24] Politically, both the Shah and Khomeini faced a
leftist opposition supported—directly or indirectly—by Moscow. The key

difference for the new leadership was that Iran could no longer rely on Washington's support to counter the Soviet challenge, rendering Iran all the more vulnerable to Soviet designs.

Tehran's regional ambitions, its aim to spread political Islam, and its tensions with Washington quickly translated into an Iranian-Israeli enmity, as Israeli intelligence had suspected long before the revolution took place. Iran's ideological opposition to the Jewish State was unmistakable, and its suspicious outlook caused it to see an Israeli hand behind many of the challenges it faced. For instance, the Khomeini regime believed that Israel aided the Kurdish rebellion in northwestern Iran that began only months after the revolution.[25] "[W]e looked at Israel from the perspective that it was a supporter and agent of the U.S. in the region," explained Mahmoud Vaezi, a former deputy foreign minister of the Islamic Republic.[26] Yet geopolitical factors pushed the two countries toward each other, in spite of Iran's ideological opposition to and suspicion of Israel. Feelers were sent from both capitals, though Tel Aviv was clearly the most eager to revive its old cooperation with Tehran.

Only months after the revolution, in spite of the break in relations, Tel Aviv offered to send back a number of American-built Iranian tanks that the Shah had shipped to Israel to be refurbished. Iran accepted the offer.[27] Israel constantly sought ways to woo the Khomeini government but found Tehran rather ambivalent about the usefulness of the Jewish State. On the one hand, the two countries did share common interests resulting from the threats they faced in the region. On the other hand, any open dealings with Israel would discredit Khomeini's purist stance on the Palestinian issue and his argument that the Islamic world must turn to Iran's leadership to win its freedom and independence. The balancing act between these two objectives meant that Iran would turn to Israel only as an absolute last resort. As long as Iran enjoyed other alternatives, the revolutionaries believed, shunning the Jewish State should be the natural policy of the Islamic Republic, much to Israel's frustration. But the leverage Israel could not create against Iran by itself was provided by the militant students who seized hostages at the U.S. embassy. The hostage-taking of American diplomats was followed by a limited international embargo, the freezing of Iranian assets abroad, and an end to U.S. sales of arms and spare parts to Iran. As Iran's standing in the world plummeted, and as American pressure increased Iran's international isolation, Israel found the leverage over Tehran it needed to cultivate ties with Iran's angry ayatollahs.[28]

AN ETHIOPIA REDUX IN THE MAKING?

In early 1980, only months after the eruption of the hostage crisis, Ahmed Kashani, the youngest son of Grand Ayatollah Abol Qassem Kashani, who had played a key role in the nationalization of the Iranian oil industry in 1951, visited Israel—most likely the first Iranian to do so after the revolution—to discuss arms sales and military cooperation against Iraq's nuclear program at Osirak. Though he presented himself as a "concerned private citizen," his trip resulted in Begin's approval of the shipment of tires for Phantom fighter planes as well as weapons for the Iranian army. Begin's decision completely contradicted U.S. interest and Washington's explicit policy of isolating Iran to secure the release of the American hostages. Carter was infuriated by Begin's insensitivity toward the trauma America was undergoing. After a harsh exchange between the two tough-minded leaders, Carter reprimanded Israel by putting on hold future sales of spare parts to the Jewish State.[29]

But Begin's defiance paid off. Ayatollah Khomeini reciprocated the Israeli move by permitting large numbers of Iranian Jews to leave Iran. Thousands crossed the border to Pakistan by bus, where they were flown to Austria and allowed to immigrate to the United States or Israel.[30] According to Mohammad Reza Aminzadeh, an Iranian officer who defected in 1985, the deal was negotiated by a certain Colonel Uri of the Israeli army, who visited Iran in early 1980.[31] Iran's willingness to deal with Israel revealed how Tehran's predicaments were limiting its ability to pursue its ideological goals. Already at this early stage, the revolutionaries showed their inclination to comfortably put ideology aside to advance their own security and interests. At one point, Khomeini was informed by one of his associates that a large shipment of arms that Iran was considering bidding on originated in Israel. The associate sought the Ayatollah's approval to go ahead with the purchase. Khomeini asked whether it was necessary to discuss and inquire about the source of the weaponry when making the purchase, to which the associate replied no. "Then," Khomeini calmly concluded, "we don't care."[32]

Increasingly it was becoming clear that Iran's rhetoric against Israel did not match its actual policy. At the same time that Iran was secretly dealing with the government of Israel, it was openly condemning the Jewish State and questioning its right to exist. For instance, on August 14, 1980, the Iranian Foreign Ministry called for an end to oil sales to countries that supported Israel. After much fanfare, the threat was never acted upon.[33] "The ideological opposition to Israel," explained a Tehran-based expert on Iranian foreign policy, "played a role for this regime *before* the revolution."[34] Once in power, the revolutionaries acted according to different principles. A key pillar of the revolutionary government's foreign policy was "rhetorical opposition to Israel but practical collaboration . . . with the Jewish State."[35]

Clearly this wasn't an ideal arrangement for Israel, but the logic of the periphery doctrine compelled Israel to continue to woo the Iranians. Sadat's rising popularity in the United States and Begin's own frosty relations with Carter complicated Israel's strategic options. If the U.S.-Arab rapprochement post–Camp David solidified even further, then Israel's need for a regional counterbalance to the Arabs—Iran—would increase accordingly. The doors to win Iran back needed to be kept open. "From the Israeli perspective, this was a long-term and strategic plan; it was the peripheral policy," commented Gary Sick, who served in the U.S. National Security Council at the time. "They were trying to do an Ethiopia with Iran."[36] But on September 22, 1980, the Shah's prediction that Iraqi dictator Saddam Hussein would attack Iran when given the opportunity was fulfilled—only five years after the signing of the Algiers Accord. Rather than Israel finding itself more dependent on Iran, it was Tehran that suddenly found itself in desperate need of Israel's access to American arms.

10

saddam attacks!

Three Whom God Should Not Have Created: Persians, Jews and Flies

—Title of book by Khairallah Tulfah, Saddam Hussein's maternal uncle

Rather than winning Arab friends, the Khomeini government's policies won it only enemies. Iran's efforts to challenge the regional status quo turned it into a pariah state, shunned by most and feared by all.[1] Iran's claims to leadership of the world's oppressed Muslims put it at odds with Iraq—which sought to uphold the pan-Arab flag after Egypt's fall from grace with the signing of the Camp David Accord with Israel—and Saudi Arabia, which, as the birthplace of Islam and custodian of Islam's holiest sites, viewed itself as the undisputed caretaker of and ultimate authority on the Islamic faith.[2]

The ayatollah had few options for breaking out of the circle of isolation imposed on Iran by the United States, the Arab bloc, and the Soviet Union. Iran lacked diplomatic sophistication, regional friends, and the oil revenues of the Shah (because of a sharp decline in Iranian oil production as a result of the chaos of the revolution) to buy off enemies. Iran's weakness was a blessing for its many enemies, however. Saddam, who was eagerly awaiting an opportunity to resurrect the ancient glories of Iraq, realized that several circumstances were in his favor. He knew that other Arab nations, mindful of the threat they felt from Iran, would likely support Iraq (in fact, Saddam would coordinate his attack on Iran with Saudi Arabia and Kuwait). And the vacuum created by Egypt's eviction from the Arab League (after Sadat broke with Arab ranks and signed the Camp David Accord with Israel) begged for a new leader to fill the void left by Sadat.[3] In addition, Iran's army seemed to be in tatters and its defenses around the disputed Shatt al-Arab/ Arvand Rud waterway minimal. Iran was a tempting target. Saddam calculated that he could take control over not only the waterway but also the oil-rich Khuzistan province of southwestern Iran. A successful invasion of Iran would make Iraq the dominant power in the Persian Gulf region and strengthen its lucrative oil trade. Iraq was at the time also improving its relations with the United States, and it is widely believed that Washington saw many benefits from an Iraqi attack on Iran.

Having broken diplomatic relations with Iran in June 1980, Iraq declared the Shatt al-Arab part of its territory on September 17, effectively voiding the Algiers Accord. Saddam launched a full-scale invasion of Iran on September 22, claiming as a pretext an alleged Iranian assassination attempt on Iraq's foreign minister, Tariq Aziz. The Iranian defense was at first disorganized, and Iraq advanced easily toward Ahvaz, the capital of Khuzistan. Without American spare parts, much of Iran's air force was paralyzed, giving the Iraqis air superiority and greater offensive capabilities. But as its penetration into Iran continued, Iraq encountered unexpected resistance. Rather than turning against the clerical regime, Iranians rallied around their leadership with ferocious zeal. Within two months, an estimated one hundred thousand Iranian volunteers reached the war front. The Iraqis soon found that the Iranian military was still a formidable foe, in spite of the chaos and difficulties it faced. By 1982 Iran recovered the areas previously lost to Saddam's army and took the war into Iraqi territory. What Saddam thought would be a swift and elegant victory turned out to be an eight-year war of attrition that cost roughly one million lives.

The war reinforced Soviet and Arab hostility toward Iran, which in turn strengthened Israel and Iran's shared threat perception. In spite of the thaw in Iraqi-American relations, Moscow feared that an Iranian victory would create an imbalance in the region, so it extended support to Iraq. Moscow's arming of Iraq aggravated the Khomeini regime—which referred to the Soviet Union as the "other Great Satan"—and by 1983 Iran had expelled several Soviet diplomats and executed numerous members of Iran's Communist Party, allegedly for spying for Moscow.[4] And as Saddam had calculated, the Persian Gulf sheikhdoms generously funded the Iraqi war machine. In return, the Iraqi dictator closely coordinated his war decisions with the leaders of Saudi Arabia, Kuwait, and Jordan.[5]

Between September 1980 and spring 1982, Saudi Arabia—which was particularly fearful of an Iranian victory and the boost that it would give to

Iran's ideological zeal—provided Iraq with $1 billion per month. Thanks to the bankrolling of the Gulf Arabs, Iraq spent several billion dollars more on arms during this period than did both Iran and Israel. Within the region, Iraq's military expenditure was second only to that of Saudi Arabia throughout the 1980s, and the size of its military increased tenfold in less than a decade, reaching 1,000,000 by 1988 and 1,400,000 by 1990. Baghdad's offensive capabilities grew accordingly and included stockpiles of chemical weapons, the components of which were provided by Western powers. By the latter years of the war, Iraq demonstrated the reach of its offensive weaponry by striking the Iranian capital—three hundred miles from the Iraqi defense lines—with ballistic missiles. With such weaponry, Iraq had suddenly also put Israel within its reach.[6]

The war also placed further strain on Iran's ties with the PLO, which supported Saddam, leaving Iran with little credibility in its quest for Muslim leadership against Israel.[7] The united Arab front against Iran was unmistakable once Saudi Arabia, Bahrain, Kuwait, Qatar, United Arab Emirates, and Oman formed the Gulf Cooperation Council in 1981, a security body essentially aimed at balancing Iran.[8] "On the one hand, we did not recognize Israel, and on the other hand, we were at war with a secular Islamic state," commented Amir Mohebian, the political editor of *Resalat*, a conservative daily newspaper in Iran. "We felt that the world was against us."[9]

Reality had caught up with the ideologues in Tehran. By invading Iran, Saddam Hussein had actualized the Arab threat against Iran and intensified the geostrategic forces that had created the Israeli-Iranian axis decades earlier. Ideological zeal could carry Iran only so far, and the revolutionary leaders debated intensively within their closed circles whether such a thing as a "national interest" existed or whether ideology alone should guide state action. As the hardships of the war increased, the debates increasingly tilted in favor of the pragmatists.[10] Though this trend had begun only months after the victory of the revolution, Saddam's assault and Iran's isolation intensified the shift in Iranian foreign policy—in its conduct though not in its rhetoric—away from ideology and toward practicality and expediency.[11] After all, Iran couldn't take on the invading Iraqi army without expanding its channels to Israel and Washington in order to purchase arms and spare parts for its U.S.-built weaponry.[12]

As the concept of national interest started to dominate, many began to argue that channels to the United States needed to be opened, even if Israeli intermediaries were to be used.[13] All contacts with the Israelis had to be discreet, however, because open channels would discredit Iran's ideological credentials. But rather than reverting to the early foreign policy patterns of the Shah, with his alliance with Israel and the West, the revolutionaries reached a different conclusion, one that was closer to the Shah's thinking after the signing of the Algiers Accord. Saddam's invasion—far from convincing Iran to give up on the idea of befriending its Arab and Sunni neighbors and throw in its lot with Israel—paradoxically intensified the Khomeini government's belief that finding an accommodation with the Arabs was critical for Iran's standing and long-term security.

Out of Iran's strategic dilemma, with ideological and strategic forces pulling its foreign policy in different directions, emerged a multilayered strategy that continues to bewilder political analysts and foreign leaders alike. Instead of opting to balance the Arabs by aligning with Israel, or to seek accommodation with the Arabs by taking the lead against Israel, Tehran chose to do both by differentiating between its operational policy and its rhetoric. On the one hand, Iran collaborated secretly with Israel on security matters, and, on the other, it took its rhetorical excesses against Israel to even higher levels to cover up its Israeli dealings.[14] This policy, which may well have emerged as a compromise between factions of varying degrees of ideological zeal within the government, aimed to make Iran's ideological and strategic interests reinforce each other. Those goals included long-term security as a non-Arab state in the Middle East, a position of primacy within the region in spite of the Arab-Persian and Sunni-Shia divide, and, finally, ideological purity to protect the identity of the revolution and use Iran's Islamic ideology as a vehicle to facilitate the achievement of the previous two goals.

At the ideological level, the interests of the Islamic world needed to be taken into account; that is, independence from the great powers, the plight of the Palestinian people, and access to and control of the holy sites in Jerusalem. And though the revolutionaries "did not see a [military] threat coming from Israel, at least not in the short term," the Jewish State was considered an ideological threat to political Islam.[15] These moral duties, as Iran's former Deputy Foreign Minister Mahmoud Vaezi described them, overshadowed Iran's strategic interest at times, particularly during the early years of the revolution.[16]

Iran's strategic imperatives, on the other hand, reinforced its ideological opposition to Israel in the view of the revolutionaries. To manage its relations with the surrounding Muslim states, "Iran required, from a strategic point of view, to take a very harsh position against Israel in order to—if not remove—at least alleviate some of the animosity that was inherent in the approach of its neighbors [against Iran]," explained Iran's Ambassador to the UN Javad Zarif. "This is from a strategic point of view in addition to the ideological aspects of Iranian support for the Palestinians."[17] The revolutionaries vehemently rejected the idea of relying on remoter states such as Israel or the United States to balance the Arabs precisely because Iran would never be able to become a regional leader if it was dependent on others for its security. When "Iran was being attacked with chemical weapons, all of the [treaties with Iran] that people had signed turned out to be meaningless," explained Gary Sick, who served on the National Security Council during the Carter and Reagan administrations. "[The Iranians] concluded that they couldn't rely on anybody outside themselves."[18]

The key function of Iran's anti-Israel stance was to alleviate Arab threats to Iran or at least make it more costly for Arab governments to support Iraq. "We believed that our opposition against Israel would help convince the Islamic and Arab world that Iraq's attack on Iran was wrong," *Resalat* political editor Mohebian admitted.[19] At a strategy meeting, Iranian Foreign Minister Ali Akbar Velayati, who often played a balancing role in the internal debates between the more ideological factions in the government and the proponents of a "national interest" approach, lent his support to the ideologues. "Ideology is one of the few levers Iran has left," he argued. It was a source of influence that Iran couldn't afford to discard.[20] Just as the Shah had done, the revolutionaries utilized the unpopularity of the Jewish State among the Arab populace to advance Iran's status in the Muslim world and reduce the threats it faced from the Arabs. Unlike the Shah, however, the revolutionaries couldn't pursue overt relations with Israel because of Iran's renewed regional focus—open relations with Israel would undermine the goal of reaching a rapprochement with Iran's Arab neighbors.

But political Islam and opposition to Israel served other strategic purposes as well. Having failed to export its revolution and topple the surrounding Arab regimes, Iran sought to exploit and widen the gap between the Arab populations—"the Arab street"—and their unpopular and corrupt governments by appealing to the Arabs' religious pride and their frustration with the Arab governments' impotence vis-à-vis Israel and the superpowers.

Iran made numerous attempts to expel Israel from the United Nations, sponsored a children's drawing and writing contest on the theme "Israel Must Be Erased from the Earth" in various Islamic countries, and pledged to send Iraqi prisoners of war to fight Israel in Lebanon.[21] It even proposed the creation of an Islamic army to oust Israel from occupied Arab territories.

"Iran has declared that it wants to actively participate in the task of liberating Palestine," Velayati told reporters. The more anti-Israel Iran appeared, the more sympathy it would win among the Arab populations and the more difficult it would be for the Arab governments to challenge and oppose Iran, the revolutionaries reasoned. But the strategy backfired. It further isolated Iran and increased the Arab governments' fear of Iranian ambitions. "Our appeal wasn't the governments of the Islamic world, but their peoples, the street," Mohebian explained. "But that scared the Arab governments even more and they increased their support to Saddam."[22]

But Iran's venomous rhetoric against Israel was just that—words. In a victory of realism over ideology, Tehran was careful not to translate this rhetoric into concrete actions, because Iran could ill afford a confrontation with the Jewish State in the midst of its war with Iraq. "Iranian decision-makers were very clever to not substitute or replace Israel as a direct threat to Iran," former Deputy Foreign Minister Abbas Maleki explained to me. "Because at that time, Iraq was the threat."[23]

In a three-hour conversation with his close associates during the early days of the war, Ayatollah Khomeini spelled out the Islamic Republic's approach to the Palestinian conflict. According to the Father of the Iranian revolution, and the person embodying its ideology, the Israeli-Palestinian conflict was primarily a *Palestinian* issue. At the second level, it should involve the Arab states neighboring Israel, and only at the third level should it involve Iran and other Islamic states. As a result, Iran should never be more involved in the conflict than the Palestinians themselves and their Arab neighbors, and Iran should not be a frontline state against Israel. Direct confrontation with the Jewish State should be left to the Palestinians themselves and their immediate Arab neighbors. "We never wanted to get directly involved in the fights against Israel," explained Ali Reza Alavi Tabar, who belongs to the reformist faction of the Iranian government.[24] Khomeini also told his associates that in the event of an agreement between the Palestinians and the Israelis, Iran should lend its support to the agreement by standing behind the Palestinians.[25]

During the early years of the Iraq-Iran war, Khomeini was given ample opportunity to demonstrate Iran's differentiation between rhetoric and operational policy. On June 6, 1982, when Israel invaded Lebanon, several leaders of Lebanon's Shia community, including the head of what later became the Lebanese Hezbollah, were in Tehran for a conference. News of the attack came when the conference was in session, and the Shia leaders immediately turned to Iran for help. Khomeini agreed and sent a high-level delegation, including the Iranian defense minister and some elite troops, to Syria to look into Iran's potential role. On June 11, the Iranians arrived in Syria, but they soon concluded what Khomeini had suspected all along— that the Lebanon war was a diversion to take Iran's focus away from Iraq. Saddam had on the eve of the Lebanon war offered peace with Iran and called on Tehran to join Baghdad in fighting Israel. Khomeini had refused. Now, despite the lobbying efforts of Iran's ambassador to Syria, Ali Akbar Mohtashamipour, and the head of the Iranian Revolutionary Guards Corps, Mohsen Rafiqdoost, to dispatch ten thousand Iranian soldiers to southern Lebanon to open a two-front war, Khomeini quickly changed his orders and commanded the Iranians to return to the war front with Iraq, declaring that the road to Qods (Jerusalem) went through Karbala, Iraq.[26]

This wasn't an isolated incident. In 1986, fighting broke out between Hezbollah and the pro-Syrian SSNP (Syrian Social Nationalist Party) as a result of Syria's efforts to bring Hezbollah under its control. This put Iran's ally in Lebanon at odds with Iran's ally against Iraq. Tehran chose the latter.[27] Khomeini's decision reaffirmed Iran's ideological goals while ensuring that those goals wouldn't necessarily be actively pursued. The "liberation" of Jerusalem would remain a rhetorical vehicle to win legitimacy in the Arab world, but not an ideal to be pursued for its own purpose with concrete actions, in order not to jeopardize Iran's short-term security needs. "It reaffirmed that our policy towards the region had a soft-power and hard-power side. We always declare our views and our beliefs. But that does not mean that we need to operationalize these views into actual policy," argued former Deputy Foreign Minister Vaezi.[28] By avoiding direct entanglement in the Palestinian issue, Iran could attend to its more immediate needs. "It was a deep strategic decision," insisted former Deputy Foreign Minister Abbas Maleki. "If Ayatollah Khomeini at that time did not oppose this move, Iran would not have been able to fight Saddam."[29] This potentially explosive policy of vehemently opposing Israel—on which Iran was desperately dependent for arms supplies—without translating that rhetoric into practical efforts can be understood only in light of the centrality of Iran's ambition to lead the Islamic world.

Perhaps more importantly, Iran's support for Hezbollah was motivated more by its efforts to spread its brand of political Islam to take on a leadership position in the Islamic world than by its opposition to Israel. "If we concentrate on the point that Lebanon is considered the heart of the Arab countries in the Middle East, a platform from which different ideas have been directed to the rest of the Arab world," Iran's ambassador to Lebanon explained, "we can conclude that the existence of an Islamic movement in that country will result in Islamic movements throughout the Arab world."[30]

Saddam's invasion of Iran made the divergence of U.S. and Israeli interests in regards to Iran unmistakable. Unlike its Washington ally, Israel regarded the war with great concern. Iran appeared weak, and an Iraqi victory would leave Israel in a far more vulnerable position.[31] Baghdad would become the undisputed hegemon over the Persian Gulf, with the world's third-largest oil reserves and an army more than four times the size of Israel's. It would make the threat of the "eastern front" worse than ever before. Although Iraq was flirting with the United States, and some in the Reagan administration—like Donald Rumsfeld, President Reagan's special envoy to Iraq—were flirting back and toying with the idea of making Saddam their new ally in the Persian Gulf, an Iraqi-Western rapprochement would have little bearing on Baghdad's hostility toward Israel.[32] An Iranian victory, as unlikely as it appeared at the outbreak of the war, did not particularly worry Israel. Because Iran was a thousand miles away, its ability to participate in a war against Israel was minimal, even if it had come out of the war victorious.[33] "Throughout the 1980s, no one in Israel said anything about an Iranian threat—the word wasn't even uttered," said Professor David Menashri of Tel Aviv University, Israel's foremost expert on Iran.[34]

At the height of Iran's ideological zeal, Israel's fear of an Iraqi victory, its dismissal of the dangers of Iran's political ideology, and its efforts to win Iran back and revive the periphery doctrine all paved the way for Israel's policy of arming Iran and seeking to defuse tensions between Washington and Tehran.[35] Even though the Arab core and the non-Arab periphery in many ways had exchanged roles by the late 1970s through the stabilization and moderation of the Sunni heartland and the radicalization of the Shia, Persian periphery, the Israeli leadership either failed to recognize this or chose to focus on the capabilities of these different elements, rather than on their ideology, rhetoric, or intentions. The war vindicated Israel's reliance on the periphery doctrine, many Israelis believed. A majority of senior Israeli officials, including Yitzhak Rabin, continued to believe that Iran was a "natural ally" of Israel.[36] Stopping Saddam was paramount, and if "that meant going along with the request for arms by the Iranians, and that could prevent an Iraqi victory, so be it," asserted David Kimche, former head of the Israeli Foreign Ministry.[37] But there was more. Inducing Washington to reach out to Iran had the benefit of not only stopping Iraq and reviving the periphery doctrine; it would also distance the United States from the Arabs and ultimately "establish Israel as the only real strategic partner of the United States in the region."[38]

So three days after Iraqi troops entered Iranian territory, Israeli Foreign Minister Moshe Dayan interrupted a private visit to Vienna to hold a press conference to urge the United States—in the middle of the hostage crisis—to forget the past and help Iran keep up its defenses.[39] Two days later, Israeli Deputy Defense Minister Mordechai Zippori told the Israeli daily *Maariv* that Israel would provide military aid to Iran if it changed its hostile approach to the Jewish State: "Israel has the possibility to extend significant aid to Iran and enable it, from the logistical point of view, to continue its war with Iraq. Of course this cannot take place as long as there is no serious change in the extremist Iranian regime."[40]

Israel moved swiftly on several fronts. In Zurich, Iranian and Israeli officials reportedly met to conclude an arms deal. Israeli Col. Ben-Youssef and his Iranian counterpart, Col. Zarabi, the director of Iran's military-industrial complex, discussed numerous proposals, including an agreement that would allow Israeli technicians to train the Iranian army in retooling and refitting Iran's American-made weapons for Israeli-made parts.[41] In Washington, Israel's ambassador to the United States, Ephraim Evron, lobbied Secretary of State Edmund Muskie to soften the Carter administration's stance on arms sales to Tehran while relaying Tel Aviv's concerns about the implications of an Iraqi victory. Against Washington's wishes, Begin went back on his word to Carter and resumed the sale of arms and spare parts to Iran. During Carter's last meeting with Begin, on November 13, 1980, Begin reiterated Israel's interest in resurrecting relations with Iran. He explained Tehran's request for support and Tel Aviv's inclination to oblige. Carter flat out rejected the idea and reminded Begin that sales to Iran would violate the U.S. embargo. Though Begin promised to comply, he wasn't seriously deterred. As soon as Reagan was sworn into office in January 1981, the clandestine Israeli arms sales resumed.[42] The Reagan administration, for its part, kept the embargo in place but turned a blind eye to the Israeli arms sales. Secretary of State Alexander Haig, known for his sympathies with Israel, gave Kimche an informal green light to go ahead with the sales in early 1981.[43]

Later, in September 1981, Sharon met again with Haig, Secretary of Defense Caspar Weinberger, and CIA Director William Casey and brought up the need to support Iran. In his autobiography, Sharon wrote that he told the Americans that Khomeini's extremist ideology "did not negate the importance of Iran as a key country in the region" and that it was to the West's long-term benefit to keep low-key contacts with Khomeini's government, particularly the military circles in Tehran. Rather than emphasizing Israel's need for Iran to balance Iraq, Sharon warned the Americans of the dangers of the Soviet Union using the war to enter Iran and take control over its energy resources. A treaty from 1921 between Iran and Russia allowed Moscow to intervene against the troops of any power using Iran as a base of operations against Russia.[44] This could happen, Sharon warned the Americans, if Iraq continued its war against the Iranians.[45] All in all, according to Ahmad Haidari, an Iranian arms dealer working for the Khomeini regime, roughly 80 percent of the weaponry bought by Tehran immediately after the onset of the war originated in Israel.[46]

As the war progressed without the fall of the revolutionary government, Israeli thinking increasingly shifted from counting on the Khomeini government's collapse to seeking the strengthening of moderate elements within it.[47] Though the Israelis began to realize that the Khomeini regime wasn't going to collapse any time soon, they still viewed its Islamic nature and extremist views as a historical parenthesis. The real, geostrategically oriented Iran that would resume the Shah's strategic cooperation with Israel would soon reemerge. This made it all the more important for Israel to support Iran in the war, because an Iranian defeat not only would strengthen the Arab front against Israel, it would also reduce the chances of reviving Israel's alliance with Iran, because the next regime would be weak and dependent on Iraq. Strengthening moderates within the Iranian regime could facilitate the process of reestablishing Israel's ties to Iran, and the one element in Iran that could change the situation for the better comprised professional officers in the Iranian army. "There was a feeling that if we in Israel could somehow maintain relations with the army, this could bring about an improvement of relations between Iran and Israel," Kimche explained.[48]

But Israel wasn't united in its enthusiasm for supporting Iran in the war. A small minority camp continued to advocate active Israeli involvement in dethroning Khomeini. Uri Lubrani, Israel's representative to Iran in the 1970s, argued on *BBC Panorama* on February 8, 1982, that Israel could stage a military coup against Khomeini, but that Washington was slow in giving its blessing to the plan. Sharon flirted with helping Reza Pahlavi, the son of the late Shah.[49] Others argued that the peace with Egypt had made the entire periphery doctrine obsolete, because it proved that peace with the Arabs was possible. The idea that Iran and Iraq were unable to threaten Israel while they were still at war with each other was "a shortsighted approach because it didn't recognize that the longer this went on, the more heavily armed they could become and the more extreme either side could become," argued Yossi (Joseph) Alpher, a former Mossad official and senior adviser to former Israeli Prime Minister Ehud Barak.[50]

Shortsighted or not, Israel wasn't giving up on the idea of rebuilding its relations with Tehran. It may have been Israel's extensive contacts in the Iranian army that paved the way for Israel's most decisive intervention during the war. On June 7, 1981, eight Israeli F-16s and six F-15s left the Etzion air base in what was known as Operation Opera. The target of their mission was the Iraqi research plutonium reactor at Osirak, which was suspected of developing material for weapons of mass destruction. The strike force quickly destroyed the reactor site, setting back Iraq's nuclear weapons program several years. All the jets returned safely to Israel by dusk in what was deemed an impeccable operation. According to London's *Sunday Telegraph*, Israel was aided by Iranian photographs and maps of the nuclear installations.[51] The Osirak attack was discussed by a senior Israeli official and representative of the Khomeini regime in France only one month earlier, according to Ari Ben-Menashe, who was intimately involved in Israeli-Iranian contacts in the early 1980s. At the meeting, the Iranians explained details of their unsuccessful attack on the site on September 30, 1980, and agreed to permit Israeli planes to land at an Iranian airfield in Tabriz in event of an emergency.[52] Whether Iran played a role in the Osirak bombing or not, Iraq used the Israeli attack in its propaganda to undermine Iran's efforts to win legitimacy for its leadership role in the Islamic world. Iran, the Iraqis said, was fighting Israel's war.

A month later, on July 18, an Argentine cargo plane carrying Israeli arms destined for Iran crashed near the Soviet-Turkish border, creating an international furor. Both Iran and Israel denied the affair, but Israeli support for Iran was becoming an increasingly open secret.[53] While this gave a further boost to Saddam Hussein's propaganda efforts against Iran, the PLO protested what it viewed as Iran's double standard in its policy toward the Palestinians.[54] But the arms sales continued unabated. All in all, Iran purchased over $500 million worth of arms from Israel in the 1980–1983 period, according to the Jaffee Institute for Strategic Studies at Tel Aviv University. Most of it was paid for through deliverance of Iranian oil to Israel. The CIA tracked approximately $300 million of those sales, and many intelligence officers were surprised by the Reagan administration's unwillingness to stop the Israeli-Iranian transactions.[55]

In May 1982, Israeli Defense Minister Ariel Sharon told NBC that Tel

Aviv had supplied Iran with arms and ammunition because it viewed Iraq as "being dangerous to the peace process in the Middle East."[56] Sharon added that Israel provided the arms to Iran because it felt it was important to "leave a small window open" to the possibility of good relations with Iran in the future.[57] While Iran sought to keep its trade with Israel as secret as possible, Israel reaped some benefit by publicizing it, particularly since the Reagan administration had decided to turn a blind eye to Israel's dealings with Iran. The more publicity Israeli-Iranian cooperation received, the more isolated Iran became from the Arab world, and this in turn increased Iran's dependence on Israel. "Any relations with Israel or any perception of relations with Israel would seriously jeopardize [Iran's] most important strategic foreign policy goal, and that was rapprochement with the countries of the region," Ambassador Zarif explained. Even in the more revolutionary times, the goal of capturing the hearts and minds of the peoples in the Islamic world was a paramount objective.[58] Tehran considered public disclosures of its dealings with Israel as attempts by either the United States, Israel, or Iraq to defame Iran and to undermine its foreign policy.[59]

Khomeini reacted angrily to these revelations. In a speech on August 24, 1981, he vehemently denied the allegations and argued that Iran's enemies were trying to undermine the revolution by spreading false rumors of Israeli-Iranian cooperation.

> They are accusing us of importing arms from Israel. This is being said against a country which rose to oppose this condemned Zionist clan from the very beginning. . . . For over twenty years, in speeches and statements, we have spoken of Israel and its oppression, whereas a great many Islamic countries did not even take a step along this road in opposing Israel. This man Saddam who resorted to play-acting and, as reported, forced Israel to bomb his [nuclear] centre in order to save himself from the disgrace he himself created by attacking Islamic Iran—his aim in doing this was to camouflage this crime and give the impression that Israel opposes Saddam, that it opposes the Iraqi Ba'thist government. This would then give him a pretext, that Israel opposes Saddam, that it has ties with us. That is childish nonsense. They are trying to make other Islamic countries believe that we are supporting Israel. But, ever since we began this affair, this movement, one of our most important issues was that Israel should be eliminated.[60]

Israel, for its part, was dealing with its own ideological disconnections. Undoubtedly, its dealings with Iran went beyond the short-term calculations of balancing the Iraqi threat. Though Tehran accepted Israel's military aid, Iran's unwillingness to acknowledge Israel's utility or to extend the cooperation to other areas left Israel without durable strategic ties with the key non-Arab peripheral state. Israel mistook pragmatism in Iranian business dealings with nuances in Iranian views regarding Israel. "In the Iranian worldview," commented Shmuel Bar of the Institute of Policy and Strategy in Herzliya, Israel, "you can do business with Satan himself, but Satan always remains Satan."[61] But for Israel, faced with no decent options, instinct prevailed. And out of Israel's desperate wish to revive the periphery doctrine and rebuild the U.S.-Israeli-Iranian axis came the scandal of the decade, the Iran-Contra operation.

scandal

> Israel and Iran need each other. It has always been
> this way and will always remain the same.
>
> —Israeli analyst, 1986

The world was a different place in 1983 than it is today. As a special envoy of President Ronald Reagan, Donald Rumsfeld was courting Saddam Hussein in Baghdad; Israel was lobbying Washington not to pay attention to Tehran's calls for the destruction of the Jewish State; neoconservatives were masterminding a rapprochement with Khomeini's government; and Iran—not the United States—was considered out of touch with reality for fantasizing about a rising Shia crescent.

Rather than countering Iran's influence in the region and warning the West of Iranian hegemony, Israel, by invading Lebanon, inadvertently handed Iran its only success in exporting its revolution to the Arab world. The June 6, 1982, invasion was ostensibly in response to an attempt by Palestinian militants to assassinate Shlomo Argov, Israel's ambassador to the United Kingdom. But Ariel Sharon, then Israel's defense minister, had been planning a Lebanon invasion to wipe out the PLO presence there for many months—at least as early as late 1981. Although the PLO had been observing a cease-fire with Israel since the summer of 1981, Sharon and Prime Minister Menachem Begin calculated that if they could destroy the PLO presence in Lebanon, they would both derail the PLO's growing diplomatic strength and quell nationalist Palestinian ferment in the occupied territories.

Southern Lebanon had traditionally been the home of Lebanon's disenfranchised Shia Muslim community. The Shias initially welcomed the Israelis because of their own competition with Palestinian refugees for local resources and their resentment of the PLO's often heavy-handed rule of the south. But the Shias were dismayed when the Israelis overstayed their welcome by creating a "security zone" in the south. They soon turned against Israel as it blocked the Shias' access to northern markets and began dumping Israeli goods into their local economy, causing indigenous economic interests to suffer.[1] In addition, Israel's invasion had been immensely destructive and only added to the misery of Lebanese who had already been suffering from seven years of civil war. Close to 20,000 Lebanese were killed in the invasion, and another 450,000 were displaced. In September 1982, under Sharon's direction, a Lebanese Christian militia unit entered the Palestinian refugee camps of Sabra and Shatila in Beirut. With tacit Israeli approval, the militia raped, killed, and maimed as many as several thousand civilian refugees. Approximately one quarter of those refugees were Shias who had fled the violence in the south.[2]

The plight of the Shias under Israeli occupation made them receptive to Tehran's message. Faced with a mighty Israeli opponent, the Shias desperately needed an external ally, and Tehran was more than willing to play the part—not so much to act out its anti-Israeli sentiments but rather to find a stronghold in an Arab country. Tehran badly needed progress in exporting its revolution. It had failed in Iraq and Bahrain, in spite of the majority Shia populations of those countries. Now, thanks to the Israeli invasion of Lebanon, Iran was given the opportunity to plant the seeds of an Islamic revolution in the Levant. Out of the Israeli invasion emerged a new and invigorated Shia movement, inspired by Iran's revolution. Initially just a small number of armed groups of young men organized under the banner of Islam and dedicated to fighting the Israeli occupation, over time they banded together—through Iranian help and assistance—into what has proved to be one of Israel's most formidable foes—the Lebanese Hezbollah.[3]

Not only did Hezbollah provide Iran with a foothold in the Levant, it also presented Iran with an even more valuable card: an abundance of potential American hostages. Reagan had sent 1,800 marines to Lebanon in August 1982 to broker a peace and to forestall a wider regional conflict. The marines formed a multinational force along with French and Italian troops. But as the multinational force was increasingly perceived to be taking sides in the war rather than serving as a peace force, Hezbollah began targeting them. The attacks culminated in the suicide truck-bombing of the marine barracks in Beirut on October 23, 1983, in which 241 servicemen were killed. Twenty seconds after this attack, another bomb killed fifty-eight French paratroopers in a building housing the multinational force four miles away. In succeeding years, Hezbollah kidnapped several U.S. citizens and other Westerners. The hostages provided Iran with a valuable negotiating card with the United States, and Israel with a compelling opening to push the United States to strike a deal with Iran.

ISRAEL'S STRATEGIC BREATHER

By 1983, the mood in the Reagan administration had shifted. Iranian forces had expelled the Iraqis from Iranian soil, and Saddam Hussein had made a peace offer, including the payment of war damages to Iran. But Ayatollah Khomeini opted to continue the war into Iraqi territory, insisting on the slogan "War, war till victory." In spite of Iran's disorganized and chaotic defense, Tehran had put up a good fight against the invading Iraqis, and Israel's fears of a swift Iraqi victory had been allayed. Now that the war had bogged down both Iraq and Iran, it provided Israel with a "strategic breather" while strengthening Israel's regional position.[4]

Ironically, through the war Iran fulfilled Israel's goals for it as a periphery state by tying down Iraq and neutralizing Israel's eastern front.[5] And by providing military assistance to Iran, Israel contributed to its own security by further splitting the Arabs. "Our big hope was that the two sides would weaken each other to such an extent that neither of them would be a threat to us," explained David Kimche, the head of the Israeli Foreign Ministry.[6] The logic was simple: as long as Iraq and Iran fought each other, neither one could fight Israel.[7] At a roundtable discussion at Tel Aviv University in January 1988, Defense Minister Yitzhak Rabin spelled out Israel's strategic reasoning: "What is good for Israel is a no win situation in the Iraq-Iran war. This is in Israel's strategic interest and the political mileage that Israel has gotten out of it has been invaluable. The peripheral pact [with Iran under the Shah] only neutralized the Arab inner circle, but did not strategically diminish the threat. Whereas with the Iraq-Iran war, a balance of threat has been created for Israel."[8]

But maintaining Israel's strategic breather was an imprecise science. The war could quickly turn in Iraq's favor and present Israel with a nightmare. Iran's impressive defensive capabilities reinforced Israel's support for the periphery doctrine. The Israelis thought that the cultivation of moderates within the Iranian government could help soften the official Islamist ideology and steer Iran's policy closer to Israel's. It was thought that these

moderates could assume power once the ailing Khomeini died.[9] The ayatollah wasn't getting any younger, and the succession struggle could bring
about a unique opportunity for Israel to influence Iran with the aim of
restoring the periphery alliance.[10] Pursuing this option became all the more
important as Washington showed increasing signs of tilting toward Iraq in
the war.

OPERATION STAUNCH

Khomeini's decision to continue the war into Iraqi territory strengthened
the hands of those in the Reagan administration who advocated shutting
down Iran's access to arms. These officials were particularly disturbed by Israel's assistance to the ayatollah. Already in March 1982, the United States
had begun to provide Saddam Hussein with intelligence and military support, contrary to Washington's official position of neutrality on the war.[11]
The U.S. tilt toward Iraq made Washington all the more reluctant to condemn Iraq's use of chemical weapons, even though U.S. intelligence confirmed Iranian accusations of "almost daily" Iraqi chemical attacks against
Iranian soldiers and Kurdish insurgents.[12]

In late 1983, Reagan sent Rumsfeld as a special envoy to Baghdad to
meet with Saddam Hussein and pave the way for improved U.S.-Iraqi relations by increasing America's support for Iraq in the war. During this visit,
Rumsfeld also conveyed to Iraqi Foreign Minister Tariq Aziz a secret Israeli
offer to assist Iraq. Aziz, however, refused the offer and even declined to accept the Israeli letter to the Iraqi dictator.[13] The Israeli feeler was intended
to see whether improved U.S.-Iraqi relations also could lead to better relations between Israel and Iraq. Aziz's refusal even to accept the letter ensured
that there would be no doubt in Tel Aviv about Baghdad's intentions. Washington's gravitation toward the Jewish State's most formidable Arab foe at a
time when Iraq refused to improve its relations with Israel was most alarm-
ing to the Israelis. The rapprochement could significantly shift the balance
in the region if it led to American acceptance of an Iraqi military victory, Israel feared.

Aziz's rather undiplomatic gesture toward Israel did little to quell
Washington's enthusiasm, much to Israel's dismay. State Department officials capitalized on the warming U.S.-Iraqi ties and presented a plan named
Operation Staunch, aimed at preventing U.S. allies from reselling American
military equipment to Iran. The plan was adopted in 1984, and Iranian
arms sources quickly dried up.[14] Tel Aviv grudgingly complied with the new
American directive, though it never fully cut off its Iranian channels.

Operation Staunch, America's failure in Lebanon, Hezbollah's hostage-taking, Israel's failure to woo Iraq, and the persistent doctrine of the periphery paved the way for what was to become the scandal of the decade—the Iran-Contra affair. No longer was the aim to win Khomeini's Iran back to the West, but rather to strengthen moderates within Iran who could turn Tehran toward the West once Khomeini had left Iran's political scene. "It is important that the West have a foothold in Iran after it turns around," argued Yitzhak Shamir, who briefly succeeded Begin as Israeli prime minister in 1983–1984.[15] To his left, David Kimche of the Labor Party concurred: "There were the ultraextremists and there were, let's say, the moderate extremists. . . . They were all extremists, they were all fanatics, but there were the ones who were absolutely dangerous, and there was another group . . . who would be willing to come to terms with the West. . . . They were still against Israel, but they were much less extremist than that first group. [W]e felt that if that first group were to inherit Khomeini's place, that would be a direct threat to us . . . whereas if the second group were to inherit Khomeini's place, there would still be hope. . . . [W]e certainly had nothing to lose."[16] The strength of the periphery thinking among Israeli leaders at the time cannot be underestimated. Israeli analysts still believed that the Khomeini regime was—unlike the laws of geopolitics—just a temporary phenomenon. "These laws have proven themselves to be true from the days of Cyrus to the present time. . . . Israel and Iran need each other. It has always been this way and will always remain the same."[17] An unnamed Israeli official told the *Manchester Guardian Weekly* in 1986 that "the basic geo-political interests which originally dictated an Israeli-Iranian link were far from being a mere whim of the Shah's. . . . These common interests will remain valid when the present religious fervor on which the Khomeini regime is based has run its course and began [sic] to wane."[18]

ISRAEL'S PLOT

The idea to go around Operation Staunch to bring Iran—with or without Khomeini—back to the West was first plotted at a meeting in Hamburg in late 1984 between Kimche; Al Schwimmer, an Israeli arms dealer who served as a close adviser to Israeli Prime Minister Shimon Peres; Yaacov Nimrodi, who had served as Israeli military attaché to Iran in the 1960s and '70s; and Iranian arms dealer Manuchehr Ghorbanifar, who was close to the faction of Hashemi Rafsanjani, the powerful head of the Iranian parliament.[19] Kimche had, a few months earlier, entered into a dialogue with elements of the Iranian regime who sought to shift Iran's foreign policy toward a more pro-Western stance.[20] Although the Iranians had forced the Iraqis out of Iran, the war continued to grind on, and Iran was in desperate need of arms. Through Ghorbanifar, the Iranians had approached both the Saudi and the Egyptian governments but were denied assistance.

The Iranians even tried to reach out directly to the United States. On June 14, 1985, TWA Flight 847 en route from Athens to Rome was hijacked by Hezbollah. The hijackers demanded the release of Shia prisoners held in Kuwait, Israel, and Spain in return for the hostages, among them several Americans. Hoping to win goodwill with Washington, Tehran intervened to put an end to the hostage taking. Iran sent a message to the U.S. National Security Council declaring that it "wanted to do as much as it could to end the TWA crisis." Rafsanjani was in transit from a visit to Tunisia when the Israeli secret service intercepted a conversation between him and Iran's ambassador to Syria, Ali Akbar Mohtashamipour, a key figure behind Iran's ties to Hezbollah. Rafsanjani directed the ambassador to pressure Hezbollah to release the hostages.[21] Iranian Foreign Minister Ali Akbar Velayati did the same.[22] Even though the captives eventually were released as a result of the Iranian intervention, Washington refused to engage with Tehran. Ghorbanifar also tried courting the CIA, but none of these efforts bore fruit either. Distraught, Ghorbanifar was told by Adnan Khashoggi, a Saudi arms dealer, that the only way to connect with Washington was to go through Israel.[23]

Reports from the war front once again turned bleak: Baghdad had responded to the Iranian counterattack into Iraqi territory with increased use of chemical weapons and devastating missile attacks against major Iranian cities. Iran found itself forced to follow Khashoggi's advice.[24] It was Iran's last resort, but it was a matter of survival. The Rafsanjani camp believed that Iran needed Washington—without access to American arms and spare parts, the war could be lost, and without U.S. protection against the Soviet Union Iran could become a Soviet satellite. Having exhausted all other potential channels, Ghorbanifar went through Khashoggi to reach out to Tel Aviv, promising the Israelis that "if Iran wins this war, we shall not forget to thank those who helped us. . . . You will witness a dramatic change in Tehran's position towards Israel." The Israelis did not need any convincing. "We were no less eager than our contacts," Nimrodi explained.[25] The former Israeli military attaché to Iran envisioned "restoring the previous order . . . to see both countries join forces against their common enemies in the surrounding Arab world."[26] Israel had a duty to bring Iran out of its isolation, halt its support for terror, bring it back into a "geopolitical association with the West," and tilt the balance against Iraq, reasoned Kimche,

Nimrodi, and their Israeli associates.[27] But the Israelis never fully understood that Iran had no interest in Israel per se. Tehran's goal was to improve U.S.-Iranian relations, not Israeli-Iranian relations. Despite some common geostrategic goals, Iran sought only to use Israel to gain access to Washington.[28] "Israel is always the gate to America," a prominent reformist strategist explained. "I don't think anybody in the realm of imagination back then thought of a resumption of dialogue with Israel at all."[29]

Unaware of Iran's double-game, the Israelis proceeded with their plan to lure Iran back to the Western fold in order to balance the Arab and Iraqi threat and prevent the Soviets from getting a foothold in Iran. While Israel had its own incentives to patch up its relations with Tehran, Washington was a much tougher challenge. The United States was in the midst of a rapprochement with Saddam Hussein, and the humiliating memories of the Iranian hostage crisis were still fresh in American minds. But through Hezbollah, Iran did have something that the United States wanted—American hostages in Lebanon.[30]

This created a perfectly balanced triangular relationship—Washington wanted the release of the hostages, Tel Aviv wanted closer links to Iran, and Tehran wanted arms.[31] For Israel, the broader strategic aim of winning back Iran was more important than Hezbollah's hostage-takings in Lebanon or Iran's military needs. The causality was reversed—to reintegrate Iran into the Western camp, Israel was willing to boost Iran's military capabilities and resolve the Lebanese hostage situation.[32] But the plan couldn't even be tested unless tensions between the United States and Iran were lowered. So the first task was to win the blessing of Tel Aviv and then bring Washington into the plan. Nimrodi and Kimche approached Prime Minister Shimon Peres (elections had been held in 1984, and with the results virtually a draw, Labor and Likud decided to form a grand coalition), who consulted with Defense Minister Rabin and Foreign Minister Shamir, now head of the Likud after Begin's retirement. The three, nicknamed "Prime Ministers' Forum" in the Israeli press, approved the idea in the spring of 1985 on the condition that only captured or Israeli-made weapons could be sold to Iran; American weapons should be excluded, they insisted.[33]

Khashoggi and Ghorbanifar were instructed to contact the U.S. National Security Council, but National Security Advisor Robert "Bud" McFarlane wasn't impressed. He was just about to reject their request for arms and dialogue when Shimon Peres intervened and inquired about the possibility of engaging in secret cooperation with Iran. The Peres intervention bore fruit. McFarlane decided to test the Iranian connection through a third party that would bear full responsibility: Israel. While Israel was motivated by the periphery doctrine, the rivalry of the Cold War fueled the political minds of Washington. Political appointees in the Reagan administration such as Paul Wolfowitz, Robert McFarlane, and Richard Burt deemed the renewal of diplomatic ties with Iran as unrealistic, but they strongly believed that it was in Israel's and the United States' interest to nurture a replacement government that might renew this relationship.

As the war continued and casualties mounted, a cadre would emerge that could be nurtured to become a viable opposition element. Combined with the fact that the Soviet Union had stationed one hundred thousand soldiers on Iran's northern border, with periodic conduct of border exercises, Iran should have had a geostrategic concern regarding Soviet intentions, they reasoned. "However, that theory was created among ourselves and had no foundation in fact of contemporary events or intelligence material," McFarlane concluded in retrospect.[34] McFarlane was concerned that the Soviet Union's greater leverage over Iran would enable it to draw Tehran toward the Communist camp, particularly after the death of Khomeini. In a top-secret memorandum to U.S. Secretary of State George Shultz and Secretary of Defense Caspar Weinberger, McFarlane wrote that "the Soviet Union is better positioned than the U.S. to exploit and benefit from any power struggle that results in changes in the Iranian regime, as well as increasing socio-political pressures." He concluded that Washington's short-term goal should be to block Moscow's efforts to increase its influence in Iran, and the United States must avoid a situation in which Iran would feel that it had no choice but to turn to the Soviets.[35]

ARMS FOR HOSTAGES

After Peres's intervention, Reagan gave his approval to conduct a secret investigation of the proposed move and assigned it to Michael Ledeen, an American University professor who in Nimrodi's words was "known as a true and warm Zionist who often attended public events on behalf of Israel."[36] Asked by McFarlane to keep both the State Department and the CIA in the dark, Ledeen arranged a meeting with Shimon Peres in Tel Aviv on May 6, 1985.[37] Known today as one of Washington's most ardent opponents of any form of contacts with the Iranian regime, Ledeen belonged to the opposite camp back then. Ledeen told the Israeli prime minister exactly what he wanted to hear: America's lack of intelligence on Iran was deplorable and it needed Israel's assistance in establishing dialogue with Tehran. The Israeli prime minister "willingly granted the request," according to Nimrodi. "We have been approached by senior members of the Iranian regime, through middlemen, concerning sales of military equipment," Peres told Ledeen. The Israeli prime minister suggested that it might be useful to send a trial balloon to Tehran—one arms shipment, to test the intentions of the Iranians.[38] Even though the CIA was largely kept in the dark about the dealings with Iran, it supported the idea of reaching out to Iran to prevent it from falling into the Soviet Union's orbit and even recommended arms sales to Iran through a third country to strengthen Iranian moderates and improve U.S. intelligence on Iran.[39]

Kimche and McFarlane continued to plan the operation themselves. Assuring McFarlane that Rabin and Shamir were also on board, Kimche went on to say that the Iranians were confident that they could secure the release of American hostages in Lebanon.[40] This matter was high on McFarlane's mind because of pressure from Reagan himself. Still, Kimche warned McFarlane that the Iranians sooner or later would make a request for American arms.[41] On several points, McFarlane's and Kimche's versions differ.[42] Contrary to Kimche's testimony, McFarlane claimed to have left the meeting with Kimche "reserved and skeptical."[43] He believed that "Israeli interests and ours were not congruent" and suspected that the Israelis might have been seeking an opportunity to damage U.S.-Arab relations.[44]

After McFarlane briefed Reagan on the conversation, things moved quickly. McFarlane informed Kimche, Kimche updated Peres and Shamir, and Peres briefed Nimrodi and his team. On July 9, Ghorbanifar had arranged a major meeting in Hamburg with Hassan Karoubi, a close and trusted confidant of Khomeini who favored improved relations with Washington. As a cabinet member, Karoubi spent every Monday, Wednesday, and Saturday at Khomeini's house, Ghorbanifar told Kimche, Khashoggi, and Schwimmer.[45] The meeting with Karoubi started off tensely, but Karoubi knew exactly what to say to put the Israelis at ease. The first part of the meeting was spent analyzing the strategic situation in the region as well as Iran's internal situation. Karoubi did not conceal Iran's predicament. "America can help rescue Iran from its difficult position," he told the Israelis. "We are interested in cooperating with the West. We have common interests, and wish to be part of the West." A defeat in the war with Iraq would turn Iran into a Soviet satellite, Karoubi said, unless America and Israel discreetly intervened. He spoke of Iran and the West having a "common enemy—Soviet Union" and that the leftist elements in Iran had to be defeated. His request for American arms was unmistaken: "Our region, and yours, can expect a physical threat from the Soviet Union. We fear the Soviets and the Left in our country."[46]

Impressed with the clergyman, the Israelis offered their assistance. "We, too, wish to cooperate," Kimche replied. "We, too, would like to see a moderate government in Iran. . . . We [Israel] would like to serve as a bridge between Iran and the West."[47] Nimrodi then went on to describe how Iran's and Israel's common threats and enemies had brought the two countries closer in the past: "We have strived to strengthen Iran. I am not talking about strengthening a specific regime, but about helping build a strong, free and well-established Iran."[48] The conversation lasted four hours. Before they parted, Kimche asked Karoubi if he would tell his allies in Tehran about his meeting with the Israelis. "Yes," he replied. "But I don't intend to proclaim it on the streets." All in all, the meeting was a major breakthrough, and in a memorandum to Peres and Shamir Kimche recommended that the contact be maintained.[49]

The Iranian request for arms—one hundred TOW missiles to be specific—in return for Iranian pressure on Hezbollah to release four hostages did not go down well with Washington. Eager to salvage the transaction, Kimche flew to Washington on August 3 to meet with McFarlane with a new suggestion. The Israelis wanted to clarify Washington's intentions: was this a strategic operation aimed at building a new relationship with Iran, or solely a tactical move to win the release of U.S. hostages? Kimche inquired whether the United States would replenish Israeli missile arsenals if Israel were to go ahead and make a deal with the Iranians. The request was cleverly constructed to put the risk squarely on Israel, while forcing Washington to be willingly involved. McFarlane briefed the president and the cabinet on the new proposal. Key administration members opposed the deal, but the prospect of winning the release of the hostages was too tempting for Reagan. On August 6, 1985, the president gave the plan a green light, and the missiles were shipped off.[50] Even though the missiles went to the radical wing of the government—and not to the moderates as Ghorbanifar had promised—the arms-for-hostage operations continued unabated.[51] On September 15 the second shipment of missiles reached Iran. A few hours later, Benjamin Weir, an American hostage in Lebanon, was released. Reagan immediately called Peres to congratulate and thank him, and Peres in turn placed a call to Nimrodi to convey the same message.[52]

A second meeting with Karoubi took place on October 27, 1985, in Geneva. Ledeen attended the meeting to haggle directly with the Iranians over the number of missiles to be sold, and how many hostages would be released and when.[53] At first, the Iranian mullah requested the missiles for free in return for the release of the hostages, calculating that a compromise on this issue would make the Americans view Iran's other demands more favorably. The Iranian trump card was to offer Ledeen not only an end to Iranian-sponsored terror but also an invitation for an American delegation to visit Iran. "If you keep your promises and make the necessary moves toward officially renewing relations with the U.S.," the neoconservative professor replied, "we shall be prepared to make a fresh start with the revolutionary regime in Iran." At this point, the Israelis started to get nervous about Karoubi's exclusive focus on the future of U.S.-Iran relations and his neglect of Israel. Kimche intervened angrily and asked: "And where is Israel in all of this?" But Karoubi refused to make any commitments to Israel.[54] Ledeen left the meeting ecstatic, while the Israelis were disappointed.[55]

McFarlane didn't share Ledeen's enthusiasm. He expressed to Kimche his disappointment with the operations; after two arms shipments, only one American hostage had been released. This was partly the result of an embarrassing Israeli mistake. Not only had they shipped the wrong missiles, but the ones they had sent had the Star of David stamped on them. The Iranians felt cheated and insulted. Though Kimche shared some of McFarlane's concerns, he argued that the Iranians should be given a second chance because the matter was too important to be dropped at this stage. As they had done many times before, Ledeen and Lt. Col. Oliver North—a National Security Council staffer whose role in the affair would grow significantly over the next few months—sided with the Israelis and lobbied for the continuation of the operations.[56]

But McFarlane was skeptical. Shortly after the November meeting with Kimche, he handed Reagan his letter of resignation and recommended that the Israeli-Iranian operation be ended. Rather than establishing ties to Iranian moderates, the U.S. government had engaged in talks with arms merchants with little interest in seeking a political resolution to the U.S.-Iran estrangement, he argued. Unconvinced, Reagan instead sent McFarlane on December 7, 1985, to London to see Ghorbanifar and make a personal determination regarding the viability of any further dealings.[57]

McFarlane's exchange with Ghorbanifar did little to relieve his skepticism, and he returned to Washington only to repeat his recommendation that the operation be terminated. McFarlane resigned a few days later, but, sensing that the president wasn't finished with the Israeli-Iranian operation, he offered his assistance if it ever were to develop into a real political dialogue.[58] A few weeks later, on January 17, 1986, Reagan signed an intelligence finding that authorized the sale of American—not Israeli—arms to Iran. Neither the State Department nor the Pentagon was informed in advance of Reagan's unprecedented decision.[59] At this point, Kimche, Nimrodi, and Ledeen were also out of the picture. Ledeen was replaced by North, and Kimche by Amiram Nir, Peres's adviser on terrorism. According to Kimche, who held neither Nir nor North in high regard, this new team was far more focused on arms-for-hostages than on the original, geostrategic objective of reestablishing ties with Iran.[60]

The Israelis continued to push the United States to keep the Iranian channel alive, in spite of the Iranians' failure in delivering the hostages. Concerned that the failure to secure the release of all the hostages would prompt Reagan to put an end to the Iranian operation, Peres sent the president a letter on February 28, 1986, urging him to continue efforts to open up a dialogue with Iran for geopolitical reasons. "It is my firm conviction that the fundamental change we both seek as to the direction of the country in which we are dealing, holds promise not only for our two countries but for many others in the region and in the free world," Peres wrote.[61] He went on to argue that the United States should resolve the dispute in Lebanon through dialogue with Tehran in order to establish a "broader strategic relationship with Iran."[62] With or without the release of the American hostages, Peres was determined to resurrect the periphery partnership with Iran.

CHOCOLATE CAKE AND A BIBLE

Five months after resigning, McFarlane was contacted by his successor, John Poindexter, who told him that the Iranians had finally agreed to initiate a political dialogue and hold a high-level meeting in Tehran. The White House expected Rafsanjani, Prime Minister Mir Hussein Moussavi, or President Ali Khamenei to participate in the talks. The president wanted McFarlane to go. It was an offer he couldn't refuse.[63] Through the meetings in Tehran, the president sought to establish a correct relationship with Iran, end the Iraq-Iran war, and, last but not least, win the release of all American hostages in Lebanon.[64] Though McFarlane wanted to cut the Israelis out to reduce the risk of the operation, it simply wasn't a realistic option at this stage. Instead, he ended up coordinating the Tehran visit in detail with the Israelis.[65]

McFarlane left for Iran on May 25, 1986, together with retired CIA analyst George Cave, National Security Council staffer Howard Teicher, and a communications officer.[66] They first made a stop in Israel, where they met up with North, Nir, and Richard V. Secord, a retired United States Air Force major general. North took the opportunity to convince McFarlane to permit Nir to accompany them to Iran, insisting that a refusal would deeply offend the Israeli prime minister. McFarlane reluctantly agreed.[67] The Americans arrived at Tehran's Mehrabad airport at 9 a.m. on May 26 in a private American jet loaded with missiles and weaponry. Per North's suggestion, the Americans included as gifts a Bible with a handwritten verse from Reagan and a chocolate cake in the shape of a key—a symbolic opening of U.S.-Iran relations.

But to McFarlane's surprise—and contrary to the promises made by North and Ghorbanifar—two days passed without the American delegation having any meeting with a senior Iranian official. By the third day, at last, Mohammad Ali Hadi Najafabadi, the chairman of the Iranian Parliament's Foreign Affairs Committee and an adviser to Rafsanjani, appeared. Fluent in English, he had a self-assured manner that revealed both depth and breadth of knowledge. Finally, the discussions could begin. McFarlane and Najafabadi discussed their respective governments' views on the geopolitical situation in the region. Najafabadi explained that Iran needed to consolidate its revolution rather than support terrorism or continue the war. The former National Security Advisor, in turn, assured the Iranian official that Washington had no wish to roll back the revolution. "The governance and affairs of the government of Iran is your sovereign business," he said.[68] Conveying the U.S. government's tacit acceptance of the revolution as a fact was a critical point. Exactly two decades later, efforts to resolve the nuclear standoff between the United States and Iran faltered because Tehran was convinced that the George W. Bush administration would not accept the revolution and instead would insist on regime change.

McFarlane found "talking to [Najafabadi] heartening, for his words seemed to validate the original premise of our Iran undertaking—that there should have been sensible people in Tehran interested in ending the war, relieving their isolation, and restoring a measure of normalcy to relations with the West."[69] McFarlane also explained the American perspective on the Soviet threat against Iran, the Soviet occupation of Afghanistan, and Soviet ambitions to acquire a warm-water port on the Persian Gulf. He also addressed the Israeli issue. Was it impossible for Iran to see any legitimacy in the state of Israel, he asked? Najafabadi acknowledged the points made in regards to the Soviet Union but refused at first to answer any questions on Israel. He simply changed the subject when McFarlane brought it up again.

Later on, however, Najafabadi's answers softened a little. McFarlane quoted Najafabadi as saying, "'We are not prepared to address that at this time, but it ought to be on the agenda.' [It] implied passive acceptance of Israel as a state." Najafabadi's statements conspicuously lacked the Islamic regime's usual tirades against Israel. During several days of talks, Najafabadi never discussed the plight of the Palestinian people or the Palestinian issue itself. Apparently, the Palestinian conflict was not high on the Islamic Republic's agenda. When matters of Iran's security and geopolitical situation were at stake, the Islamic Republic comfortably put aside its ideology and rhetoric. "Najafabadi used Israel in language and wasn't shrill in any sense about Israel," McFarlane recalled.[70]

The serious discussions left McFarlane with the impression that there was "a basis for hope." There was sufficient absence of ideological zeal, and Rafsanjani seemed genuinely willing to make the talks succeed, McFarlane believed. As usual, the sticking point was the hostages. McFarlane drove a hard bargain and refused to deliver any of the missiles that had been brought to Tehran unless all of the hostages were released. His hard-line stance wasn't appreciated by Shimon Peres's representative, Nir. To McFarlane's great distress, Nir began conducting his own negotiations with the Iranians in the corridors of the hotel where they were meeting. While McFarlane was taking a tough stance, the Israeli agent informed the Iranians that McFarlane would settle for much less. He was wrong.[71]

At the end of the third day, Najafabadi summed up the Iranian position. Though the Iranians recognized the sincerity of the U.S. gesture, they believed it to be too soon, and the risks too great, for a U.S.-Iran rapprochement. Still, Rafsanjani would like to remain in contact, Najafabadi explained. On the hostages, Iran's final offer was to release two of them, but not all four. That wasn't enough for McFarlane, and the talks broke down. Later, he found out that the Iranians offered only two hostages because Peres's envoy had told them that this was McFarlane's bottom line. With his hopes dashed, a frustrated McFarlane left Iran empty-handed. But as the Americans were boarding the plane back to Washington, Cave reached an agreement with a member of the Iranian delegation that the channel should be kept open with Ghorbanifar as an intermediary. This "second channel" should, however, be void of "Israeli footprints," the Iranians insisted.[72]

THE *AL-SHIRAA* LEAK

For a few more months, Nir and North continued to lead the operation, resulting in additional arms shipments and hostage releases.[73] But as both the

United States and Iran recognized the need to have American and Iranian officials deal directly with each other, the "second channel" started to take shape. In mid-August, Secord met in Brussels with the Iranian official who had agreed with Cave that the communications should be kept alive. In mid-September, this Iranian official visited Washington in secret with the aim of gradually improving U.S.-Iranian relations. He informed the Americans that Khomeini's son had briefed his father in great detail about the talks and that the Iranians wanted dialogue with Washington; not just for arms, but for "broader reasons" as well.[74] To give the talks a push, Peres met with Reagan at the White House in September 1986, to ensure that the operation would proceed. Echoing the Iranian argument, the Israelis referred to the hostage situation as "a 'hurdle' that must be crossed en route to a broadened strategic relationship with the Iranian government."[75]

One of the Iranian proposals was the formation of a commission to meet in secret to discuss ways to gradually improve relations. "[The] Iranians already had selected four senior officials for their side, including representatives of all factions," Cave wrote a few years after the affair. This "demonstrated that there was a broad consensus in Iran for improving relations with the United States," the Iranians told Cave.[76] The secret commission met in Germany in October of that year and secured the release of hostage David Jacobsen and the delivery of five hundred TOW missiles to Iran.

But by November 6, 1986, internal infighting in Iran caught up with this channel. An associate of Ayatollah Ali Montazeri, a leftist ayatollah at odds with Rafsanjani, leaked details regarding McFarlane's trip to Iran to a Lebanese newspaper, *al-Shiraa*.[77] Failing to realize the repercussions of the leak, the members of the second channel reassembled in Geneva two days after the story broke. The Iranians were hoping that the talks would resume after the story had died down, even if Washington was unable to continue the arms shipments. A final meeting was held in Frankfurt on December 14, 1986, in which the Americans closed the dialogue for political reasons.[78] The affair had become a major scandal for the Reagan administration. The president was forced to confess on November 25 that despite the United States' own arms embargo and its efforts to stop other countries from selling arms to Iran, America had sold arms to Iran and transferred the money to the Contra guerrilla army that was fighting the Sandinista government of Nicaragua.[79] In a televised address to the nation, Reagan defended the operation and argued that "it's because of Iran's strategic importance and its influence in the Islamic world that we chose to probe for a better relationship between our countries."[80]

Both the Senate and the House commissioned investigations of the event, subpoenaing numerous U.S. officials to appear and testify. The blame game instantly began, causing a major rift between the United States and Israel.[81] On December 8, Shamir, now prime minister in the national unity government, "took note" of Reagan's notice that U.S. arms transfers to Iran were suspended but refused to pledge a halt in arms sales to Iran.[82] Two days later Peres said, "Arms sales to Iran were an American idea and Israel became involved only at Washington's request."[83] In January 1987, Peres defended Israel's actions by stating that it was exploring opportunities to moderate Iran. "Why don't we have the right to have a good look if there is a window of opportunity and see if there is a possibility for another future in Iran?" he told reporters.[84] Abba Eban, who headed an Israeli commission investigating that nation's involvement in the Iran affair, concluded that "it's our right to sell arms to Iran."[85] In an interview with the *Washington Post,* Shamir even urged Reagan to resume the contacts with Iran and reject the "guilt complex . . . [that] some Arab countries [were] trying to impose on Washington."[86] Further embarrassment to the United States and Israel was avoided because of Nir's mysterious death in a plane crash in Mexico the same week that he was scheduled to testify in the trial against North. At Nir's funeral in Israel, Rabin spoke of Nir's "mission to as-yet-unrevealed destinations on secret assignments and to secrets which he kept locked in his heart."[87]

The Iranians, for their part, vehemently denied having had any negotiations with the Israelis. "We have never negotiated with Israel . . . for arms purchases," Rafsanjani declared in late November. "If we find out that the weapons reaching us have come through Israel, we will not even use them in the warfronts."[88] Rafsanjani made it clear, though, that Iran was still willing to help free American hostages in Lebanon if Washington delivered weapons bought by the late Shah. Leftist elements in Iran demanded an investigation, but, sensing the damage that the revelation of Iranian-Israeli contacts would do to Iran's image in the Islamic world, Khomeini himself stepped in and put an end to the investigation requests.[89]

With or without an investigation, though, significant damage had already been done. The Arab states vented their anger at Washington for having supported Iran through Israel against Saddam Hussein.[90] For some states, Iran's fundamentalist ideology was potentially a greater threat than was Israel.[91] The affair put Arab-Iranian relations on a downward spiral.

Relations with Saudi Arabia almost became irreparable in 1987 after Saudi police shot dead 275 Iranian pilgrims during the annual *hajj* in Mecca.[92] Tehran's response was predictable—more denunciations of Israel and all Arab governments that were considering negotiations with the Jewish State. The following year Khamenei even lashed out against the PLO when it recognized Israel, arguing that "the partition of Palestine is not acceptable" and that a Palestinian nation can be set up only when "the Zionists are crushed and the lands they took returned."[93] But as the full extent of Iran's dealings with Israel came to light, Iranian denunciations of Israel rang increasingly hollow.

12

the dying gasp of the periphery doctrine

> Iran is Israel's best friend and we do not intend to change our position
> in relation to Tehran, because Khomeini's regime will not last forever.
>
> —Yitzhak Rabin, October 1987

Israel's strategic breather was coming to an end by 1987, a year after the Iran-Contra scandal broke. As Iraqi prospects for victory grew after the United States began providing Saddam Hussein with intelligence on Iranian troop movements, Tel Aviv concluded that a continuation of the war would be too risky and viewed a stalemate as the best possible outcome.[1] The guiding principle of Israel's policy continued to be to avoid any actions against Tehran that would jeopardize what Tel Aviv considered to be the inevitable return of Iran as a non-Arab, peripheral ally.[2] Even when it had become clear that Israel was helping Iranian radicals—and not the moderates—through its arms transfers the operations continued.[3]

The Iran-Contra affair wasn't an isolated incident. Contacts between Iran and Israel were frequent throughout the 1980s, all driven by the same forces—Iran's need for arms and Israel's hope of re-creating the Israeli-Iranian axis. The revolutionaries who broke into the U.S. embassy in Tehran in November 1979 found documents about the activities of Yitzhak Segev, Israel's last military attaché to Iran. The Iranians located Segev, and, more than a year before the Iran-Contra scandal broke, he received a phone call from Tehran. On the other side of the line were a certain Ayatollah Eskandari and a Mr. Khalili. Speaking to Segev in Persian, the ayatollah expressed an interest in cooperating with Israel.

The Iranians desperately needed American military equipment, and they offered in return Israeli soldiers who had been captured by Hezbollah in Lebanon. Eager to play a role in an Israeli-Iranian breakthrough, Segev immediately contacted the Israeli government and won its approval for meeting with the Iranians. Meetings were set up in Geneva, Madrid, and eventually in Israel itself, at Segev's residence outside Tel Aviv. Dressed in civilian clothes, the former Israeli military attaché even accompanied the Iranian clerics to the holy places in Jerusalem. There, in front of the Wailing Wall, Segev asked the Iranians about Khomeini's ideology and if Iran was really seeking to conquer Jerusalem. That goal, the Iranians replied with a smile, wouldn't be pursued in their lifetime. Nevertheless, Segev soon realized that the Iranians had no interest in relations with Israel. Rather, they just needed Israel's help in getting U.S. arms and spare parts. "They played games with me," Segev recalled. "After three meetings with them, nothing came of it because the soldiers were already dead," as he later came to find out.[4]

But Israel wasn't discouraged by these failures. Israel's worldview, which remained remarkably unaffected by the changing realities of Iran and by Israel's peace treaty with Egypt, was still dominated by the periphery doctrine—by the fear of Iraq and the promise of Iran.[5] Defense Minister Rabin often invoked the Iraqi threat to justify the need to reach out to Tehran. At a press conference in October 1987, he deplored skirmishes between the U.S. and Iranian navies in the Persian Gulf and told reporters "that the United States had been manipulated by Iraq into attacking Iran in the Persian Gulf War, and . . . that Israel had not changed its own long-standing tilt towards Iran."[6] He went on to reveal in the starkest possible terms Israel's unfazed view of Iran as a strategic partner. "Iran is Israel's best friend and we do not intend to change our position in relation to Tehran, because Khomeini's regime will not last forever."[7]

These were not empty words. Close advisers to Rabin testify that, in private, he often spoke of Iran with great nostalgia.[8] He told U.S. Ambassador Thomas Pickering on numerous occasions during his tenure in Israel between 1985 and 1988 that "the United States has to find a way to develop closer relationships with Iran." According to Pickering, "despite the then recent Revolution in Iran, he was very much interested in Iran and thought it was very important to develop a change in the relationship." Other prominent Israelis echoed these sentiments.[9]

But Israel was mistaken. All of its assumptions were resting on shaky ground: that the Iran of the Shah was the true Iran, that Iraq would always be a hostile state whereas Iran would never be a threat to Israel, and that the Soviet threat to Iran—in the midst of the Iraq-Iran war—would make Iran turn toward Israel.[10] To Tehran, Israel wasn't an asset in and of itself, it was a consumable good, a short-lived tactical relationship that could reduce the threat to Iran while safeguarding Iran's real strategic goal, regional leadership. "All these connections . . . with the Israelis used to be for spare parts. If there was no war, they would not have contacted us," Segev complained.[11]

In the Iran-Contra affair, the Iranian aim was to reestablish relations with Washington—not Israel. The entire operation, in which it engaged the Israelis while lambasting them publicly, reveals an inherent contradiction between Iran's short-term security needs and its long-term strategic imperatives. In the short term, even Islamic Iran needed Israel to balance the Arab threat. In the long term, however, Iran needed to befriend the Arabs by playing the anti-Israeli card to gain acceptance for Iran's leadership. Though Israel wasn't a threat to Iran, the religious leaders in Tehran believed that they couldn't succeed in their bid for regional leadership without taking a tough public stance on Israel, just as the Shah had reasoned before them. To this day, the Iranians insist that they never approached Israel for arms. Only through the open black market did Iran come across Israeli weaponry, Tehran adamantly maintains.[12] "[The Iranians] never brought us in the full picture of their calculations," maintained Eliezer Tsafrir, head of the Mossad in Iran and Iraq in the 1960s and '70s. "However ideological and Islamic, everything Iran was doing was nationalistic, and even similar to the Shah."[13]

On August 20, 1988, after months of intense negotiations, a cease-fire between Iraq and Iran was reached. Ayatollah Khomeini bitterly agreed to UN Security Council Resolution 598 demanding an immediate cease-fire—an act he likened to drinking a cup of poison—and the hostilities finally came to an end. After eight years of fighting, at a cost of several hundred billion dollars and more than a million casualties—most of them Iranians—and the devastation of the oil industries in both countries, the borders between the states remained unchanged.[14] But even the end of the war failed to change Israel's strategic view of Iran. Instead, the war had left Iran even more isolated and "therefore more likely than Iraq to appreciate the opportunities deriving from a renewed link with Israel," supporters of the periphery doctrine argued.[15] At the same time, the occupation of Gaza and the West Bank—where the Palestinian Intifada, which had broken out the previous winter, had significantly increased the cost of Israeli territorial aggrandizement—had become a major Israeli concern. Many Israeli leaders, including Rabin, realized that Israeli society was increasingly reluctant to pay the price for protracted conflict with the Arabs.[16] The war had also left Iraq with a larger and mightier army than ever. Israel's strategic breather had come to an end at a time when Iraq was at its peak militarily. "Iraq has built a very large army with over fifty divisions," Shimon Peres said on the eve of the cease-fire agreement. "The question is whether it will turn to re-habilitating its country or be tempted to recapture its standing in the Arab world [by attacking Israel]."[17] Combined with Israel's continued diplo-matic isolation, all these factors increased the sense of the peripheralists that Israel needed a strategic relationship with Iran.

But a new school of thought was also emerging in Israel, one that viewed Iraq—rather than Iran—as Israel's potential ally in the region. The periphery doctrine was beginning to collapse; the periphery was no longer a counterweight to the radical inner circle of Arab states but the perpetrator of radicalism. Some Israelis were coming to the realization that the Islamic Republic, and its rigid ideological opposition to Israel, could last much longer than they had originally expected. The inner circle, in the meantime, had become increasingly moderate. Both Egypt and Iraq, on the other hand, had gravitated toward the Western camp, Gens. Moshe Tamir and Uri Saguy and other supporters of this school pointed out. The peace treaty with Egypt was now eight years old and Saddam Hussein's Iraq, while not at all friendly toward Israel, had forged a tactical alliance with the West against Iran. And the Syrian threat to Israel had diminished considerably after the drubbing it had received from Israel during the Lebanon war. Conse-quently, the threat to Israel emanated from the Iranian periphery—either directly or via Hezbollah in Lebanon—and not from the Arab vicinity.[18] Tamir, who served as the director general of the Israeli Foreign Ministry at the time, even argued that Israel should rely on Iraq to counter the danger from Iran. "Iraq is an inseparable part of the large pragmatic Arab camp de-veloped to block the Iranian fundamentalist danger," he said.[19] Though the idea of Iran as a threat had few supporters in Israel, in a few years it would rapidly spread among the strategists in the Israeli Labor Party—not be-cause of any shift in Iran's ideology, but because of the dramatically chang-ing geopolitical map. But before it reached the higher levels of the Labor Party, Israel was given one last chance to test Iran.

On June 3, 1989, Ayatollah Khomeini died, bringing the moment of truth for those in Israel who believed that a succession struggle would bring Iranian moderates to power and end the Israeli-Iranian estrangement. Only days after Khomeini's death, Israeli government spokesman Avi Pazner said

that Israel wanted post-Khomeini Iran to renew formerly friendly ties rup-
tured by the revolution, and he expressed Israel's hopes for "an ensuing future improvement in relations."[20] In an interview with Israeli television,
Yossi Alpher, then an adviser to Rabin, pointed out once again the logic of
the periphery doctrine: Israel's real enemy was Iraq and other Arab states,
whereas Iran had every reason to be Israel's friend: "Iraq is getting stronger
every day by acquiring chemical and non-conventional arms that threaten
us. There is a reason to see to it that Iran can continue confronting and diverging the Iraqi forces. . . . Beyond that, Iran has oil, Iran has Jews and all
these are good reasons for renewal of connections with Iran, without any
relation to the governing regime."[21]

For those who believed that the ideological fanaticism of Khomeini lay
at the root of Iran's hostility toward Israel, the ayatollah's death raised expectations that a change in Israeli-Iranian relations was imminent. With
Khomeini gone from the Iranian political scene, and with Iraq remaining a
formidable threat to both countries, circumstances were ripe for a thaw in
relations, Tel Aviv reasoned. In November 1989, the Israeli Foreign Ministry
informed the U.S. State Department that Israel had resumed the purchase
of Iranian oil.[22] Israel had agreed to purchase two million barrels of oil for
$36 million, as part of a deal to secure Iranian help in winning the release of
three Israeli prisoners of war held in Lebanon.[23] Though the Iranian Foreign Ministry denied involvement, there was little doubt that contacts between Iran and Israel remained intact.[24] The matter was discussed in the
Israeli Knesset later, in February 1990, where Energy and Infrastructure
Minister Moshe Shahal revealed that the Israeli treasury made a $2.5 mil-
lion profit on the transaction.[25] Israel hoped that the oil deal could lead
to more, but for Iran it had more to do with economic desperation than
geopolitical calculations. Iran had emerged from the war with a broken
spirit and a broken economy. Though the revolution survived, Iran did not
win the war. Its dream of spreading the revolution had turned Iran into a
pariah—not a hegemon. "The way the Iraq-Iran war ended had a devastating effect on Iranian thinking. It was the most painful experience one
could ever have," according to a prominent reformist strategist in Iran.
"[It] led to the ascendance of pragmatism. It changed the question of cost-
benefit."[26]

RAFSANJANI GOES FOR DÉTENTE

Iran emerged from the Iraq-Iran war more isolated than ever. Its efforts to
export the revolution had put it at odds with its Arab neighbors while dev-

astating its national resources and global prestige.[27] As the Iranian regime realized that its policies had backfired, the debate in Iran quickly divided between two camps. On the one hand, hard-line revolutionaries argued that Iran was weak and needed to rearm "to defend the revolution." The other camp, led by Hashemi Rafsanjani, who had become president in 1989, argued that Iran must break out of its international isolation and that economic reconstruction should be the key priority, with only an incremental rebuilding of the military.[28] "Rafsanjani was much more interested in reconstruction efforts and pragmatic policies," explained Gary Sick, who served on the National Security Council during the Carter and Reagan administrations. "Things began to change, [and] 1988–89 was the dividing point where people began to look at things in a different sort of way."[29]

The Rafsanjani camp held that Iran should also mend ties with the Arab governments, because the investment in the Arab street had failed miserably in winning Iran a leadership role in the region. (The regime could never admit this publicly, though, because it contradicted the professed values of the revolution.) Between 1989 and 1992, Rafsanjani's "economy-first" camp edged its "isolationist" rivals out of power. To regain Iran's leadership position, however, the idea of exporting the revolution couldn't be abandoned. But instead of seeking to overthrow regional governments, Rafsanjani's approach was to export Iran's model by leading as an example of a modern, independent Islamic state. Iran needed to make its model attractive to Muslim nations by modernizing while still protecting society and Islam against "decadent" Western values.[30]

After Khomeini's death, the new leadership sought in a way to reestablish as much as possible the Shah's economic and—to some extent—politico-military ties to the West.[31] In the 1970s, when Iran's position was supported by the United States through Nixon's Twin Pillar policy, Tehran lacked the approval of the Arab states. Now Iran lacked both and needed to first curry favor with Washington. Improved relations with Washington were also necessary in order to rebuild the Iranian economy and become a model for other Muslim states. For one thing, Iranian officials believed they could borrow money to finance reconstruction because Iran's foreign debt stood at only $6 billion as a result of financing the war internally.

But Iran could receive foreign credit only if it moderated its foreign policy and avoided moves that would alarm the West. To clear the way for improved economic relations, Tehran tried to resolve outstanding disputes with its Arab neighbors and with the United States. Chief among the latter were the American hostages still held by pro-Iranian Lebanese groups.[32]

Iran's assistance to the United States in Lebanon came in the form of a direct reply to a call from President George H. W. Bush. In his inaugural address in 1989, Bush signaled to Iran that "Goodwill begets goodwill. Good faith can be a spiral that endlessly moves on." The Italian UN mediator in the hostage situation, Giandomenico Picco, courted Rafsanjani's support in winning the release of the hostages. At first, Rafsanjani was hesitant. Iran has "had no relations for some time with those holding the hostages," he told Picco. "These people are not easy to deal with." But realizing that Iran's efforts in Lebanon could lead to improved relations with Washington, Rafsanjani changed his mind. Iran successfully intervened and secured the release of the remaining hostages in the hope that the Americans would "halt their unreasonable animosity towards [Iran]."[33]

Iran's effort to improve relations with the West and the Arab regimes and end the violent export of the revolution created a new driving force for Iran's international outlook and conduct—the "de-ideologization" of Iran's foreign policy. "It was part of the natural evolution of our revolution," explained Mustafa Zahrani, a senior Iranian diplomat.[34] According to Javad Zarif, Iran's UN ambassador who played a critical role in the negotiations with the UN and the Lebanese hostage-takers, Iran's foreign policy "evolved into looking at states rather than the masses. That is why you see a steady improvement of relations between Iran and the Arab world [and] the Persian Gulf countries. [There was] an attempt by Iran to find a serious presence in the Islamic world [and] the non-aligned movement. Basically, Iran tried, after the war with Iraq, to redefine its position in the international community, in terms of being a regional power, [and] having good relations with other countries in the region."[35]

Iran lowered its rhetoric against the Arab countries of the Persian Gulf considerably and mustered a charm offensive to improve relations with the states of the Gulf Cooperation Council (GCC), with some initial success.[36] In a major victory for Iran, GCC member states began stating publicly that Iran should be included in any future regional security system.[37] At the same time, the rise of the reformist-minded Mikhail Gorbachev as the new leader of the Soviet Union had opened the way for significantly warmer relations between Iran and its traditional foe to the north. By 1989, no vestiges of the earlier difficulties between the two countries—Moscow's support for the Iranian Communist Party, its arming of Iraq, and its occupation of Afghanistan—remained.

But there were limits to Iran's outreach elsewhere as well. Though Iran helped secure the release of American hostages in Lebanon, Bush went back on his word and did not reciprocate the Iranian gesture. "When the hostages were all released, we didn't do anything," said Brent Scowcroft, Bush's National Security Advisor. Though the Bush administration recognized that Iran's ideological zeal had waned and that Tehran had "backed down a lot from the extreme days of Khomeini," the memories of Iran-Contra were enough to cause any American politician to shy away from Iran. "Picco says it was more our fault. Perhaps he is right," Scowcroft acknowledged. "Maybe it was the U.S.'s fault that [Picco] didn't succeed in connecting Iran and the U.S. At the time, Iran was more eager than the U.S. in warming up."[38] Similarly, Iran's relations with the Palestinians remained cool, including the emerging Palestinian Islamic organizations. Groups such as Hamas and the Islamic Jihad had also thrown their weight behind Iraq during the war.[39] Though Islamists, they were *Sunni* fundamentalists sprung from the virulently anti-Shia Egyptian Muslim Brotherhood. These groups had little regard for Iran in general, and for Shias in particular. Much to Israel's relief, Iran "didn't have any contacts with these groups back then."[40]

The tensions with the Palestinians also affected the debate between Rafsanjani and political rivals. The Iranian president and technocrats at the Iranian Foreign Ministry favored a policy of supporting whatever solution the Palestinians were willing to settle on, while the isolationists advocated a more activist line against Israel, just as they had done in the early 1980s.[41] Though Rafsanjani wanted to push for a more pragmatic policy, he had to pick his battles carefully. His outreach to the United States was risky enough; moving too fast on the Palestinian issue could jeopardize his entire presidency.

The end result was largely the continuation of the status quo. Iran's policy in practice (*siasat-e amali*) was to accept—but not support—the wishes of the Palestinians, including the now officially adopted two-state solution, while Iran's anti-Israel rhetoric remained intact though Tehran took no practical steps to act on it.[42] According to Mohsen Mirdamadi, a leading Iranian reformist and former member of the Foreign Relations Committee of the Iranian Parliament: "Our position was to respect whatever solution the Palestinians agreed to. If the Palestinians would agree to a two-state solution, we would not protest. We wouldn't support it, but neither would we object to it. But the policy of not objecting was in essence a policy of indirectly supporting it [a two-state solution]."[43]

But on August 2, 1990, Saddam Hussein once again put himself center stage in Iranian, American, and Israeli strategic calculations by embarking on yet another conquest of a neighboring state. Shortly thereafter, the Soviet Union collapsed and the Cold War ended with almost no blood being spilled. Overnight, the bipolar structure of the international system transformed into a unipolar composition, led by the United States. Geopolitical shifts, however, would ensure that Israel would see little benefit in post-Khomeini Iran's leaps toward pragmatism.

part two
the unipolar era

13

the new world order

Everything was going our way. All systems were go. And Iran
was a problem for us, but so what? We had everything else.

U.S. Ambassador Daniel Kurtzer, after Iraq's defeat in
the Persian Gulf War and the collapse of the Soviet Union

Between 1990 and 1992, the Middle East underwent two shocks of unprecedented magnitude—the defeat of Iraq in the Persian Gulf War and
the collapse of the Soviet Union. These geopolitical tsunamis significantly
changed the way Iran and Israel viewed each other. The common threats
that for decades had prompted the two states to cooperate and find common geostrategic interests—in spite of Iran's transformation into an Islamist anti-Zionist state—would no longer exist. While they both benefited
from these events, the uncertainty of a new world order brought with it new
dangers. As this new order in the Middle East was in the making, Tehran and
Tel Aviv soon found each other on opposite sides, even though Iran's revolutionary zeal was cooling. The disappearance of the Soviet empire and the
defanging of Iraq also freed up Iran's and Israel's own resources. Suddenly,
both states found themselves unchecked. Without an Iraq that could balance Iran, Tehran could soon become a threat, Israeli strategists began to argue. Once the dust had settled, the two former strategic allies were caught in
a vicious rivalry for the future order of the region. The Jewish State had the
most to lose from any changes in the regional order because of its strong ties
to Washington, which were largely based on Israel's role as a bulwark against
Soviet penetration in the Middle East. Iran, which had grown to detest the

isolation it found itself in, thought it could emerge the winner from these changes.

SADDAM STRIKES AGAIN

On August 2, 1990, almost a year after the fall of the Berlin Wall and the end of the Iron Curtain divide, Saddam Hussein invaded yet another neighbor, Kuwait, to take over Kuwait's oil fields. Within months, the George H. W. Bush administration carefully assembled a coalition of states under the UN flag and defeated the Iraqi army and restored Kuwait's ruling family, the House of Sabah. The Iraqi army was decimated. Iraq's annual military expenditure dropped from $26.4 billion in 1990 to $2 billion in 1991, and its armed forces, which numbered 1.4 million in 1990, dropped to 475,000 by the end of the war. But even though Iraq's defeat was monumental, it did not cease to be a vital military player in the region. With an army of approximately half a million men, Iraq could still pose a major threat to its immediate neighbors.

Saddam's foolish move brought with it many firsts. For the first time, a leading pan-Arab state went to war with another Arab state, poking a big hole in the idea of pan-Arabism. For the first time in decades, a much-weakened Soviet Union and the United States saw a conflict eye to eye, enabling the Security Council to authorize the use of force to repel an invading army. And for the first time, the United States went out of its way to attract Arab states to a regional coalition while keeping Israel at arm's length. In an effort to sabotage Bush's creation of an Arab anti-Iraq alliance, Saddam tried to link Iraq's occupation of Kuwait with Israel's control over Palestinian territory. In an effort to win sympathy on the Arab streets, Saddam offered to leave Kuwait if Israel relinquished its hold on Palestinian land. To avoid that linkage and the perception that Washington was leading a campaign against Islam, or that the conflict was between the West and the Arab world, Washington needed the inclusion of Arab states in the alliance. And the Arabs could be brought in only if Israel was excluded.

This new political dynamic—in which Israel was a liability rather than a strategic asset to the United States—was most worrisome to Tel Aviv, even though the destruction of Saddam's war machine greatly benefited Israel. Much to Israel's anger, both the United States and the United Kingdom used the promise of resolving the Arab-Israeli conflict as a carrot to convince the Arab states to join the anti-Iraq coalition. To make matters worse, William Waldegrave, British minister of state at the Foreign Office, stated in Parliament that, in the new Middle East order, Israel had ceased to matter. Waldegrave told the House of Commons that the United States should learn that a strategic alliance with Israel "was not particularly useful if it cannot be used in a crisis such as this. . . . [N]ow the U.S. knows that an alliance with Israel that is of no use for this situation is useless."[1]

Even when Saddam Hussein hurled thirty-four Scud missiles at Tel Aviv and other Israeli cities, in an obvious attempt to lure Israel into the war, the United States told Israel "in the strongest possible words" that it needed to keep itself out of the Iraq operation because Israeli retaliation would cause the collapse of Washington's anti-Iraq alliance.[2] For the government of Prime Minister Yitzhak Shamir, this was a very tough decision. Saddam's missile attacks damaged Israel's public morale; the country's otherwise lively and noisy capital quickly turned into a ghost town. Bush sent Undersecretary of State Lawrence Eagleburger to Israel to assure the leaders of the Jewish State that the United States was doing all it could to destroy the Iraqi missile launchers.

But neither the Israel Defense Forces nor the Ministry of Defense was convinced. Instead, a feeling prevailed among Israel's leaders that Washington was untrustworthy and that it could not be relied upon when it came to Israel's existence. Bad blood was created between Israel and the United States, according to Efraim Halevi, the former head of the Mossad. Washington's protection of Israel was ineffective, and the image that Israel was relying on the United States for protection was hard to stomach for ordinary Israelis.[3] Shamir's decision to accommodate the Americans was extremely unpopular, because it was believed that it "would cause irreparable damage to Israel's deterrent capabilities."[4] To make matters worse, people around Shamir felt that the United States did not reward Israel for, in their view, effectively enabling the coalition to remain intact by refusing to retaliate against Iraq. This new, tense relationship between Tel Aviv and Washington heightened Israeli fears of the changes the new world order could bring about.[5] For Iran, the war brought both danger and opportunities. Though the United States had failed to reciprocate Iran's goodwill measures in Lebanon, Saddam's invasion of Kuwait provided Iran with another opportunity to show that the United States could benefit from improved relations with Tehran. It also showed the Gulf Cooperation Council (GCC) states that they needed Iran to balance Iraq.[6] Iraq's aggression against a fellow Arab state was a moral victory for Tehran, as it demonstrated the Arabs' shortsightedness in previously supporting Iraq.[7]

Iran came out strongly against Iraq's invasion of Kuwait and used Saddam's aggression to remind the international community that Iraq—and not Iran—was the real threat to regional peace and security.[8] It adopted a policy of "positive neutrality," opposing Iraq's occupation and refusing to aid Saddam, while at the same time remaining outside the U.S. anti-Iraqi alliance. But "positive neutrality" was in essence a pro-American policy, even though Iran publicly criticized the United States for seeking to find a pretext to find a foothold in the Persian Gulf for its military—a fear that Iran had held since the time of the Shah.[9] "The Iraqis even came and begged for our support," explained Mahmoud Vaezi, Iran's deputy foreign minister at the time, "but we declared that our policy was neutral in the war, which in reality meant that it was a policy *against* Iraq."[10]

Behind the scenes, Iran communicated with the United States to avoid any misunderstandings, permitted the U.S. Air Force to use Iranian airspace, and denied Iraqi requests for support. On top of that, Iran kept a check on the refugee problem (millions of Iraqis fled to Iran and Turkey after the end of the war), refused to return Iraqi jets that Iraq had flown to Iran for safekeeping, and, perhaps most importantly, refrained from aiding the uprising of Iraq's Shia population against Saddam at the end of the war, a move that helped prevent Iraq from disintegrating into a sectarian civil war. These helpful steps even won Iran praise from U.S. Secretary of State James Baker.[11]

FRIENDS TURN TO FOES

The security environment in the Middle East changed dramatically as a result of the Persian Gulf War and the disintegration of the Soviet Union on December 31, 1991, which effectively ended the Cold War. As the bipolar international order transformed into a unipolar world led by the United States, the Middle East moved in a different direction. Out of the rumble, Iran and Israel emerged as the region's most powerful states in a Middle East that increasingly took on a bipolar nature. As powers rose and fell, new alliances were forged and new enmities created.

The disappearance of the Soviet bear from Iran's northern border led to a considerable warming in Tehran-Moscow relations.[12] Fearing Washington's increased maneuverability against Iran as a result of the end of the Cold War, Iran made ties with Moscow a priority. Russia was no longer a threat but a partner.[13] But in Afghanistan, the Soviet collapse brought new dangers for Iran. The Soviet withdrawal left in its wake a power vacuum filled by warring factions, which plundered the country and brought misery as great as the Soviet occupation. By the mid-1990s, this power vacuum was filled by the Taliban, supported by Pakistan and Saudi Arabia. The Taliban in turn provided a haven for al-Qaeda. These Sunni fundamentalists hated Iran with a passion, a point that did not pass unnoticed in Tel Aviv and Washington.[14] The al-Qaeda leadership declared early on that the world of Islam faces three great threats: Christians, Jews, and Shias.[15] Because the Taliban and al-Qaeda posed both a military and an ideological threat, Iran extended significant support to the anti-Taliban resistance throughout the 1990s. By the end of the decade, the Afghan threat was no longer a theoretical matter, as Taliban forces executed eleven Iranian diplomats in the northern Afghan city of Mazar-e Sharif, an incident that almost led to a full-scale war between Iran and the Taliban.

But as the Soviet threat to Iran vanished, the American threat grew only more ominous. In its war with Iraq, the United States had become a major power in the Persian Gulf—waters traditionally considered to be part of Iran's backyard. America was now inside Iran's sphere of influence with forces that could topple the regime in Tehran.[16] "The U.S. managed to portray Iran as a greater threat to the Arabs than even Israel," said Mohammad Reza Tajik, an adviser to former Iranian President Mohammad Khatami. "This had a crucial impact on our thinking. The U.S. sold more weapons to the Arabs as a result and became the hegemon of the Persian Gulf. Consequently, Iran came under direct U.S. threat."[17] Iran's rearmament program, which, according to British scholars Anoushiravan Ehteshami and Raymond Hinnebusch, was modest and defensive and cost only a fraction of what the Shah spent on arms, was partially in response to the perceived U.S. threat.[18]

Iraq, on the other hand, continued to figure as Iran's primary threat, in spite of its defeat at the hands of the U.S. Army. Though severely weakened, it was still seen as the only regional country able to threaten Iran's territorial integrity.[19] "I never had the confidence that [the Iraqis] would miss an opportunity to destroy Iran. And they gave me every reason to further believe that," explained Ambassador Javad Zarif, who led Iran's negotiations with Iraq both during and after the Iraq-Iran war.[20] The devastating psychological effect of the Iraq-Iran war and Saddam Hussein's continued reign in Baghdad left Iran simply with little choice but to focus on Iraq as a military threat. Many military strategists in Iran and Iraq believed that another confrontation was inevitable, with the marked difference that the next conflict would see the use of weapons of mass destruction at the very outset.[21] "We knew that as long as Saddam was in power, he would do all he could to seek revenge," said Deputy Foreign Minister Mahmoud Vaezi.[22] Both Iranian and Iraqi war colleges continued to plan against each other, and Iran's rearmament throughout the 1990s was primarily aimed at containing the Iraqi threat, a point that did not escape Israeli officials.

The Iraq-Iran war had revealed Iran's vulnerability to ballistic missiles, as Iraq had easily targeted the Iranian capital with Scuds fired from deep inside Iraqi territory. Determined to fix this hole in their defenses, the Iranians embarked on an ambitious program to develop long-range missiles, Israeli intelligence services found out in late 1994.[23] Soon after the Persian Gulf War Iran began to develop a ballistic missile based on the North Korean Nodong-1. The Shahab-III, as it was called, had a range of nine hundred miles and could reach Israel. Iran didn't successfully test-fire the missile until 1999, however, and, according to Israeli sources, it would take a few more years before the missile would be fully operational.[24] In spite of the range of the missiles, Tehran maintained that it had only defensive motives in mind. In the words of Mahmoud Sariolghalam, adviser to Iran's National Security Advisor Hassan Rowhani: "The perception has been that because Iran does not have any security partners . . . it is out on its own to defend itself [. . .] it is correct to say that Iran after the war never had an offensive strategy against any country. It was always defensive. The leadership learnt the hard way not to engage in war . . . the political and the economic and the social cost of engaging in a war is well understood, so it's always been a defensive strategy. The Shahab and the rest are [a] mechanism to maintain an infrastructure of deterrence."[25]

Around this time Iran also slowly restarted the Shah's nuclear energy program. Ayatollah Khomeini had suspended the program, arguing that nuclear weapons were "un-Islamic."[26] Still at an embryonic stage, the Iranian nuclear program lacked uranium centrifuges and much of the know-how to develop nuclear weapons—even if one assumes that weaponization was the Iranian goal. A comprehensive U.S. intelligence review from 2005 revealed that Iran would likely be able to manufacture the key ingredient for a nuclear weapon no sooner than 2015.[27] (The Iranian nuclear program accelerated in the late 1990s, and after two and a half years of intrusive inspections the International Atomic Energy Agency [IAEA] did not find evidence for an Iranian nuclear weapons program, but neither has it been able to confirm that the Iranian program is entirely peaceful.[28])

Even though Iran's missile program eventually would put Israel within its reach, Tehran continued to regard Israel as a nonthreat and a distant foe at most, just as it had in the 1980s. The Iranians did not worry about the military intentions of the Jewish State, even though Israel's capabilities—

which included an arsenal of missiles and F-15e fighters, not to mention several hundred nuclear weapons—were growing.[29] "There was a lot of rhetoric against Israel, but Iran never really saw Israel as a threat," explained a prominent Iranian political thinker.[30]

The setbacks Iran experienced during the Iraq-Iran war led it to moderate its political ambitions. Increasingly Iran viewed only the Caspian Sea and the Persian Gulf as Iran's security environment, rather than the entire Middle East. This put Israel outside of Iran's own definition of its sphere of influence. "I follow every single statement that an Iraqi leader makes," explained Zarif. "I follow every single statement that an American leader makes because I consider them in our national security environment. I don't necessarily see Israel in our national security environment."[31] Rather than a military threat, Israel was a political threat to Iran's interest and influence in the region.[32] "Israel has always been seen as a country that would try to sabotage Iran's position. After the collapse of the Soviet Union, many felt that Israel would try to create a base in the new central Asian republics against Iran. Initially, Tehran feared that Armenia would play this role, but it became Azerbaijan," said Ali Reza Alavi Tabar, a prominent Iranian reformist.[33] The Israeli game in the central Asian states, aimed at preventing Iran from spreading its influence north, meant that Tel Aviv was upping the ante, the Iranians believed.[34]

SECURITY IN IRAN'S BACKYARD

The defeat of Iraq and the need to create a new post-Saddam order in the region was a major opportunity for Iran to regain the role it had lost as a result of the excesses of the revolution and the damage from its war with Iraq. Convinced that its size and power destined it to be the preeminent state in the Persian Gulf, Tehran had much to gain and little to lose from any change in the region's order.[35] The path to this objective was clear—improved relations with the United States and the GCC states. Iran's policy of positive neutrality was warmly appreciated by the Arab sheikdoms of the Persian Gulf. Even Saudi Arabia, which Khomeini three years earlier had called an enemy of Islam, recognized Iran's new pragmatism in 1991 and extended an invitation to Rafsanjani to visit the Kingdom. Anti–status quo policies and ideological rigidity wouldn't bring Iran closer to its geopolitical goals, the leadership around Rafsanjani had concluded. Only months after the end of the Persian Gulf War, Iran and Saudi Arabia normalized their relations, in yet another sign that post-Khomeini Iran had shelved much of its revolutionary zeal.[36] For Tehran to so clearly contradict the decrees of Khomeini was, in the view of many experts, a clear sign that nationalism had defeated ideology in Iranian foreign policy–making.[37]

Rafsanjani coupled his outreach to Iran's Arab neighbors with a policy of "development first, rearmament second." Iran significantly cut its arms spending. Its military forces shrunk from 654,000 in 1988 to an average of 480,000 in the 1990–1999 period, and its military expenditure dwindled from $9.9 billion in 1990 to $5.3 billion in 1995. This wasn't mere demobilization following a war; it was a strategic decision made despite the lack of a final peace agreement between Iran and Iraq. As a result, Iran's armed forces were only slightly larger than those of Iraq *after* Saddam's defeat in the Persian Gulf War. Though Iran's new orientation did not escape the notice of decision-makers in Washington, they failed to appreciate the full extent of its new pragmatism.[38] Having found a foothold in the Persian Gulf, the Bush administration knew that its military presence in the region could continue only as long as the GCC states needed Washington to protect them from Iraq—and Iran. A significant warming of GCC-Iranian relations could jeopardize America's position in the Persian Gulf.[39]

But this did not dissuade Tehran from seeking a greater role in that region. Iran's leaders felt the time had arrived for Washington to recognize Iran's power and accept Iran as a regional leader. "It was the perfect time for Iran to reassert its position. The circumstances were in our favor," explained Alavi Tabar.[40] On the eve of Iraq's defeat, Rafsanjani said as much himself: "There is only one power that can provide the peace and stability of the Persian Gulf, and that is Iran's power."[41] Iran reached out to the GCC states in a bid to create a new inclusive security architecture in the Persian Gulf that would make the GCC less dependent on the United States.

The Iranians had already envisioned an opportunity to create such an order in the 1980s. At the insistence of Iran, UN Security Council Resolution 598, which put an end to the Iraq-Iran war, included an operative clause requesting the UN to consult *regional* states in efforts to enhance the security and stability of the area. In the spirit of that resolution, Iran emphasized the concepts of self-reliance and nonintervention by external powers, included in the GCC charter, to convince the Arabs that the security of the region should rest in the hands of regional states only (as Iran had done under the Shah). Iran was particularly concerned about Egypt and Syria's initiative, the GCC+2, which would make the security of the Persian Gulf "Arab" by including Egypt and Syria in the collective security arrangement but excluding Iran. Just as in the days of Nasser, Egypt under President

Hosni Mubarak sought an opportunity to penetrate the Persian Gulf region. "The Gulf states did not want to depend anymore on Iraq to counterbalance Iran, so we thought that what they were looking for was another Arab balancer, in other words Egypt and Syria, which would counterbalance Iran in nonstrategic conflicts," explained Nabil Fahmi, Egypt's ambassador to the United States.[42]

America, however, had a different order in mind. Having defended the Arabs against Saddam, the GCC states felt indebted to the United States and could do little but take Washington's wishes into consideration.[43] American pressure formed the options facing the GCC—to seek a Middle East order with Iran, or an Arab order with the United States. By offering the GCC states bilateral security deals, Washington preempted a common Persian Gulf security arrangement and managed to continue Iran's exclusion from regional decision-making. In the end the GCC states accepted these bilateral deals, and the Arab-Iranian honeymoon was effectively cut short.[44] Iran would soon realize that neither Washington nor Tel Aviv was eager to see Iran come in from the cold. But first, Israel had to sort out its own squabbles with America.

THE U.S.-ISRAELI SQUABBLE

For better or worse, the unipolar world put many of Israel's previous security assumptions into question. Undoubtedly, the collapse of the eastern front (Iraq) and the disappearance of the Soviet threat improved Israel's security environment. Suddenly, all conventional military threats against Israel almost completely evaporated.[45] This monumental geopolitical shift improved Israeli security in three ways. First, it put an end to Moscow's military support to Israel's Arab foes, particularly Syria, effectively eliminating the Arab military option. The Arabs no longer had a superpower to rely on. Most importantly, Iraq no longer constituted a realistic threat to Israel.[46] "There was no more eastern front, as they used to call it," Ehud Yaari of Israel television's Channel 2 explained.[47] Yitzhak Rabin, who was to become Israeli prime minister in 1992, summed up the implications of this development for Israel as follows: "Arab countries hostile to Israel can no longer rely on the Soviet umbrella that protected them in the past, whether militarily, politically, or economically."[48] Russia also lowered its political profile in the Israeli-Palestinian conflict, much to Tel Aviv's satisfaction.

Second, the fall of Communism opened the gates to the millions of Jews residing in the Soviet Union. Israel, always aware of its demographic war against the Palestinians, welcomed a huge influx of Russian Jews as a counter to the Palestinians, who had a higher birthrate than that of the Israelis.[49] In only a few years, more than one million Jews from the former Soviet Union immigrated to Israel.[50] Third, by invading Kuwait, Saddam killed pan-Arabism as a viable political and ideological force in the Arab world. "[The war] demonstrated politically that pan-Arabism was a myth," said Keith Weissman of the American Israel Public Affairs Committee.[51]

As the conventional military threats disappeared, Israel's focus turned to new threats: the internal threat posed by an increasingly rebellious Palestinian population living under occupation, the spread of weapons of mass destruction, and challenges to Israel's special relationship with Washington.[52] The most immediate threat was the Palestinian uprising—the Intifada. Israelis were taken aback by the Palestinian ability to continue resisting over such a long period of time (the Intifada broke out in December 1987 and continued, though with gradually decreasing intensity, at least up to the Gulf War in 1991). "It was quite disturbing to people. I think it shook the foundation of enough folks who were in the center that something needed to be done to change the dynamics of the Israel-Palestinian interaction," said Dan Kurtzer, U.S. Ambassador to Israel.[53] The cost of the occupation was becoming too high, and the disintegration of Palestinian society was in and of itself a danger. By virtue of the occupation, Israel was by default responsible for the problems in the Palestinian territories. The Palestinians were collapsing in the arms of Israel, in poverty and in total social disintegration, according to Yaari.[54] (Later, during talks between Israeli and Palestinian envoys in Norway that paved the way for the Oslo agreement, Israel's chief negotiator, Uri Savir, told his Palestinian counterpart Abu Ala that "the occupation is corrupting our youth. We want to free ourselves from it.")[55]

The other challenge was maintaining Israel's special relationship with Washington. Any shift in the regional order could undermine the Jewish State's strategic significance precisely because its position had been so favorable. During the Cold War, Israel played a key strategic role as a pro-Western outpost in a Middle East threatened by Soviet penetration. But with the Soviet Union gone, and U.S.-Arab relations at a peak, the Israeli alliance risked becoming obsolete to Washington. The Bush administration's promise to address the Palestinian issue immediately after the Persian Gulf War, and the Shamir government's resistance to making any territorial compromises, did not improve Israel's standing. The Gulf War showed Israel that the Soviet collapse had given Washington much more leeway with the region's Arab states, and that the demand for Israel's services as a reliable pro-Western ally in the muddy waters of Middle East politics had declined as a result. In many ways, Israel even became a liability to Washington.[56]

With U.S.-Arab relations already warming, a breakthrough in U.S.-Iranian ties could wipe out what little strategic significance Israel retained. Unlike Israel, Iran was strategically located right between the world's two largest reservoirs of oil and natural gas: the Persian Gulf and the Caspian Sea. Iran bordered the newly freed but landlocked central Asian states, which sat on major reserves of oil and natural gas and held the promise of becoming major markets for Western goods. With a population of more than sixty million, Iran itself offered a market that was ten times larger than that of Israel. As the Cold War ended, the Jewish State wrestled with the question of how to prove its strategic utility to the United States.[57]

Washington's eagerness for Middle East peacemaking after the Gulf War pushed U.S.-Israeli relations to a new low. The United States was at the apex of its power and needed to show the world that it would use its diplomatic muscle to resolve the Israeli-Palestinian issue once and for all. "It was time to seize the moment because . . . something potentially significant [was] stirring among the Arabs," Secretary of State Baker felt. The new attitude of the Arabs could convince Israel to opt for peace, he optimistically believed.[58] But Baker was in for a surprise. Shamir and Israel's Likud government were not in the mood to be convinced, nor were they excited about Washington's new confidence in Middle East peacemaking, suspecting that it was fueled by the Bush administration's debt to Syria and Egypt for their support in the Persian Gulf War. "There was a feeling that there was an inherent danger in this," explained Halevi, the former head of the Israeli Mossad. "The United States might feel a necessity to tilt towards the Arabs. . . . The conditions of peace would be such that it would not be acceptable to Israel."[59]

Though Shamir faced opposition at home, primarily from Labor's Rabin—who opposed the key tenets of neo-Revisionist Zionism by arguing that the dream of Greater Israel (*Eretz Israel*) had to be given up and that no military solution existed to the Palestinian problem—he continued to resist Washington's pressure. But Israel had few cards to play except stalling Washington's peace efforts and creating new facts on the ground. Since 1989, the Bush administration had been sparring with the Shamir government over its illegal settlements on occupied Palestinian territory. Though Shamir had assured Bush that these activities would be stopped, Israel did not keep its word, as Baker acknowledged. The squabble was often heated. At one point Baker even banned Israel Deputy Foreign Minister Benjamin Netanyahu from the State Department after Netanyahu had publicly accused the United States of "building its policy on a foundation of distortion and lies."[60]

In May 1991, Zalman Shoval, Israel's ambassador to the United States, said Israel would soon ask America for $10 billion in loan guarantees to help provide housing for the influx of Soviet immigrants. Though the request marked an escalation in Israeli aid requests, it also enabled the United States to link American aid to Israel's settlement policy. In September 1991, Israel formally made the request, only a month before a major U.S.-sponsored peace conference was scheduled to take place in Madrid. Bush resisted the Israeli request. He asked Congress to delay consideration of the request to avoid damaging Baker's effort to put together the conference. After months of battling over this issue with Israel and the pro-Israeli lobby in Washington—less than a year away from the 1992 presidential elections—Baker told Shoval on January 24, 1992, that the United States would accept existing settlements, but the loan guarantees would be granted only on condition that no new settlements be built. Bush clarified his position in very candid language in March of that year. "The choice is Israel's," he said. "She can determine whether she wants to take action which would permit the strong support of both the legislative and executive branches for these loan guarantees or not." But Israel refused to accept the American conditions and on March 17 Bush officially rejected Israel's request.[61] (After Rabin came into office later that year, the Bush administration agreed to give Israel the guarantees after all, with mild restrictions.)

Another sticking point was the question of negotiations with the Palestinian Liberation Organization (PLO). Though the United States was in no mood to forgive PLO leader Yasser Arafat for his embrace of Saddam during the Gulf War, it knew that a peace process without Arafat was a nonstarter. Shamir, on the other hand, used the principle of non-negotiation with terrorists as a justification for evading Washington's peace efforts altogether. During a heated telephone conversation between Bush and Shamir, Bush clarified that the United States was "not trying to force [Israel] to talk with the PLO. But we do wish there could be less delay in responding factually to us. . . . If you give us a positive response, then Israel and the U.S. can move forward together. If you don't respond, we have to interpret that you don't want to go forward. . . . I've just read the wire story quoting you about a confrontation with the United States. If you want that—fine." The tensions in U.S.-Israeli relations were fittingly summed up by Baker's brusque public message to Israel, "When you're serious about peace, call us." Clearly, U.S.-Israeli relations were at a low.[62]

By October 1991, Shamir had run out of excuses, and Washington managed to drag the Israelis to the peace summit in Madrid. Shamir had one condition, though: to avoid creating circumstances that would enable the international community to force Israel to go back to its 1967 borders, the Likud leader requested that the summit not be the permanent fixture that would be used to resolve the conflict. In other words, the conference would not be an ongoing event that would be convened to address the progress of the negotiations. Rather, it would meet only to initiate the talks, and then later, at the end of the negotiations, it would meet to recognize whatever outcome the negotiations had produced.[63] According to Kurtzer, what finally drove Shamir to Madrid was that Washington managed to convince the Likud leader that:

> On three levels Israel's position had changed so much for the better that the risks of entering a peace process were about as low as they could be. First, the global level in the fall of the Soviet Union, which literally coincided with Madrid. . . . Second, the regional upheaval, not only the defeat of Iraq in the war, but the process in which we mobilized a coalition that included Arab states that were prepared to join former Western colonial powers in repelling aggression by an Arab state. And third, the domestic factors. It must have been the third or fourth year of the first Intifada. The Palestinians clearly had not attained their objectives. They were clearly looking for a way to translate what was a failed militant strategy into some sort of a political process, and Israel, though more successful in stopping the violence at that period, had also failed to translate its successes into some kind of political victory.[64]

Bush had declared that all peoples of the region would have a say in the formation of the new order of the Middle East, and Baker worked extensively to ensure that regional states had a stake in the process so that it wouldn't be "easy to walk away from it." Washington's success in ensuring the participation of Israel, Syria, and the Palestinians alike reflected its new position of strength. Virtually every nation in the region was invited with one noted exception—Iran.[65]

MAKING PEACE IN MADRID

The Madrid conference was a celebration of America's new global position as the sole superpower. Though the Soviet Union was still a few months away from crumbling, the writing was on the wall. The great powers co-chaired the conference, but from the very outset it was clear who was calling the shots. The conference convened on October 30, 1991, with two separate yet parallel negotiating tracks, one bilateral and one multilateral. The bilateral track encompassed the first-ever direct talks between Israel and its immediate Arab neighbors, aimed at resolving the Israeli-Palestinian conflict and at finding peace between Israel and its Arab neighbors. The multilateral negotiations were meant to build the Middle East of the future. This track, which opened in Moscow in January 1992, focused on key issues that concerned the entire Middle East—water, environment, arms control, refugees, economic development, and, most importantly, regional security.

The invitations went out to a large number of countries. The main participants were the governments of Israel, Syria, Lebanon, and Jordan. (Per Israel's demand, the Palestinians wouldn't have a delegation of their own, but Palestinians who were not official PLO members could attend as part of a joint Jordanian-Palestinian delegation.) Egypt, the European Community, and the GCC states were also invited as participants, while the United Nations was invited to send an observer representing the secretary-general. Altogether forty-three nations participated in the multilateral talks, of which fifteen were regional states. At a time when Tehran believed that its opportunity had come to be accepted as a regional power and be included in Middle East decision-making, Washington dashed Iran's hopes by refusing to invite it.

In many ways, Washington failed to appreciate Iran's pragmatism, in particular Tehran's new position on Israel, in which Rafsanjani had declared that Iran would agree to any solution acceptable to the Palestinians. "We didn't see any readiness on their part to be part of a peace process with Israel," recalled Dennis Ross, special Middle East coordinator at the White House at the time. Washington failed to pick up on Iran's readiness because of the image of Iran as an inherently anti-American nation, formed by a decade of tensions between the two countries. As Ross put it: "Certain images get formed, and when they are formed, even when there are behaviors that seem to contradict the image, if there are other images at the same time that tend to confirm it, you give much more weight to those that tend to confirm it, and you dismiss those that should point you in a different direction. . . . The signals from Rafsanjani tended to be dismissed, but they were there. The behaviors that actually tended to fit with the traditional images [of Iran] were treated as if that was the real Iran."[66]

Others in the White House viewed Iran in the 1990s as more rather than less radical. The assassination of former Iranian Prime Minister Shahpour Bakhtiar in Paris in August 1991—reportedly by Iranian agents—showed that Iran was "irredeemable," because the murder took place while Iran was seeking improved relations with Washington, these elements argued. At a minimum, Iran's seemingly contradictory behavior raised the political cost of reaching out to Tehran.[67] And because Washington did not have any diplomatic relations with Iran, there was no interest in inviting states that could act like spoilers.[68] "Our relations [with Iran] were pretty bitter," Scowcroft recalled. "We were not at that time ready to include Iran."[69]

But there was another factor as well—Iran was simply viewed as irrelevant to the Israeli-Palestinian conflict. Iran's relations with and leverage over the Palestinians were considered insignificant precisely because of its lack of active involvement in the Palestinian cause.[70] "Iran simply had nothing to contribute. It had no leverage over the Arabs, so how could it help the peace process?" Scowcroft argued.[71] This view was held by the Israelis as well, who felt that Iran had little to offer on this matter. "Iran was irrelevant. It had no influence over the Palestinians, unlike Egypt and the Arab states, so its participation would have been unnecessary," an Israeli diplomat at the UN explained.[72] (A few years later, however, both Israel and the United States would blame the failure of the peace process on Iran's influence over the Palestinians.)

Iran wasn't just irrelevant to the Israeli-Palestinian conflict in the minds of Washington's decision-makers; it was irrelevant *period*. While Baker's team feared that Iran could act as spoiler to the conference if it was invited, they forgot to take into account Iran's ability to play a damaging role if it *wasn't* invited. At that unipolar moment, Washington simply did not see Iran as a power to be reckoned with—America's confidence was bordering on hubris. This was "America's moment in the Middle East," Kurtzer explained. "Everything was going our way. All systems were go. And Iran was a problem for us, but so what? We had everything else."[73]

Tehran reacted bitterly to Washington's snub. With or without influence over the Palestinians, Iran viewed itself as a major regional power and expected a seat at the table, particularly after the helpful role it felt it had played in gaining the release of hostages in Lebanon and indirectly aiding in the U.S.-led war against Iraq.[74] Madrid was, after all, not seen as just a conference on the Israeli-Palestinian conflict, but as the defining moment in forming the new Middle East order—one in which Tehran hoped to play a role commensurate with its geopolitical weight. The noninvitation deprived Iran of an opportunity to help shape the new order according to its own interests.[75]

To make matters worse, Syria's invitation to the conference threatened to break the Tehran-Damascus alliance and limit Iran's presence in and access to the Levant—a key strategic asset in which Iran had invested heavily.[76] This would be a major blow to Iran's influence and to its vision of its rightful position in the region.[77] (Iranian fears were not unfounded. Israel, concerned about Iran's support for Hezbollah guerrillas in Lebanon and increased Iranian power in the wake of Iraq's defeat in the Gulf War, called on Syria at Madrid to agree that Iran must be excluded from the framework and that Iranian-Syrian relations should be downgraded.[78]) "It definitely insulted Iran, there is no doubt about that," Iranian Deputy Foreign Minister Hadi Nejad-Hosseinian recalled.[79] Numerous Iranian officials told me that Tehran had been willing to participate in the talks and exert its influence and role provided it would not have to recognize Israel.[80] (Recognition of Israel was not requested of any of the conference's participants.) This fits well with Iran's other initiatives, because the conference was held while Iran was intensifying its efforts to reintegrate into the international community. "Getting into these bodies was exactly what Iran was aiming for at the time," Siamak Namazi of Atieh Bahar Consulting said.[81] A decade later Iran played a crucial role in the Bonn conference after the 2001 U.S. invasion of Afghanistan. This shows that Iran is eager to participate in such regional conferences when invited, said former Iranian President Mohammad Khatami's adviser Tajik. "Iran would have accepted an invitation to Madrid," he explained. "We accepted a role in the Bonn conference on Afghanistan and we wanted to participate in Madrid as well."[82]

The noninvitation to Madrid was in many ways the last straw for Rafsanjani's policy of détente with Washington. Already, Iran felt that its policy modifications and outreach had failed to be recognized and appreciated by the Bush administration. First, Washington chose to keep Saddam in power and let a good portion of the Iraqi Republican Guard remain intact to balance Iran.[83] "This was done on purpose," explained Col. Lawrence Wilkerson, former Secretary of State Colin Powell's chief of staff. "Just enough of the troops were kept not to be a threat to Iraq's neighbors, but well enough to balance Iran."[84] Second, Washington preempted the creation of an inclusive security architecture for the Persian Gulf. "It was the first time that Iran did a grand gesture. It sold on credit, [and] it got nothing in return," Namazi recalled. "[Iran] clearly felt that the policy of isolation would be in place no matter what it did."[85] Rafsanjani's goodwill gestures carried significant domestic political risk, and fewer and fewer officials around the Iranian president were willing to pay the cost of flirting with the United States. "The willingness to do positive work for America almost ended, because they never reciprocated. Whatever positive Iran did, the response was always more and more isolation," complained Masoud Eslami of the Iranian Foreign Ministry.[86]

Washington's failure to reciprocate Iranian gestures—even though Tehran's expectations may have been exaggerated—strengthened the hands of Iranian rejectionists, who argued that Washington would never come to terms with Iran voluntarily. Slowly Rafsanjani's policy of moderating Iran's foreign policy and drawing it closer to the Western bloc began to collapse.[87] Convinced that Washington wouldn't grant Iran its legitimate role in the region, Tehran concluded that it was left with no choice but to make America's nonrecognition as costly as possible by sabotaging its policies.[88] This conviction "prompted Iran to turn to Palestinian and Lebanese groups that shared the Iranian outlook," Tabar noted.[89] The Israeli-Palestinian issue was one of the few in which Iran could undermine the United States. Rafsanjani began adopting a sharper position on Israel and departed from his original line of accepting the wishes of the Palestinians.[90] In hindsight, Ross recognized that excluding Iran from Madrid was of greater significance than many thought at the time. "I think it's fair to say that we didn't look that closely at it, and in retrospect perhaps we should have . . . Iran just didn't get that much attention."[91]

As soon as it became clear that an invitation to the conference wasn't forthcoming, Iran's supreme leader, Ayatollah Seyyed Ali Khamenei, gave a green light to Ali Akbar Mohtashamipour—one of the cofounders of the Lebanese Hezbollah who during the 1980s had lobbied Ayatollah Khomeini to actively confront Israel—to organize a conference in opposition to Madrid.[92] This was a watershed moment, as Iran for the first time started to seriously reach out to rejectionist Palestinian groups, in spite of the Shia-Sunni divide and their enmity dating back to the Iraq-Iran war. Only a year earlier Iran had even reduced its financial support to Hezbollah in Lebanon.[93] Iran took the political lead against the Madrid conference, a position it wouldn't have taken had Washington invited it to participate, according to Ruholla K. Ramazani of the University of Virginia, the foremost expert on Iranian foreign policy.[94]

The rejectionist conference in Tehran coincided with the Madrid meeting and included militant Palestinian groups that, like Iran, saw U.S. mediation efforts as countering their interests.[95] Tehran ratcheted up its rhetoric against Israel and charged Arab governments that supported the peace process with treason, using its "Arab street" card to undermine the pro-Western Arab governments. It continued to refrain from confronting Israel directly, either conventionally or through the use of terror. There were still no terrorist acts against Israel with Iranian fingerprints, according to Israeli sources.[96] To Tehran's relief, the Madrid conference did not produce the breakthrough Washington had hoped for. The Shamir government was a reluctant participant from the outset and did little to make the negotiations succeed. As Madrid's failure became clear, hopes rose in the Rafsanjani camp that Washington would understand that change in the region couldn't take place without Tehran's cooperation. But before Rafsanjani could muster any new outreach to Washington, the Israeli Labor Party, recognizing the likely consequences of any new Middle East order for Tel Aviv's strategic standing, brought about a sharp shift in Israel's foreign policy.

14

trading enemies

We needed some new glue for the alliance [with America].
And the new glue . . . was radical Islam. And Iran was radical Islam.

—Efraim Inbar, Begin-Sadat Center

The Israeli public was exhausted when it went to the polls in June 1992. Several years of the Intifada, the Palestinian uprising that had begun in December 1987, had taken its toll on the Jewish State.[1] Israelis realized in increasing numbers that the occupation—which Israel had generally justified on security grounds—had become a security threat itself. "The occupation was no longer a routine that we could safely ignore. Israelis were worn out from the conflict and wanted peace, and peace of mind," wrote Uri Savir, who later negotiated the Oslo peace accord with the Palestine Liberation Organization (PLO).[2] Constantly at odds with each other, Likud and Labor presented two different perspectives on Israel's dilemma. Yitzhak Shamir and the Likud Party preferred the status quo—the Palestinians were a problem but it was impossible to make a deal with them. Israel would win neither peace nor security by compromising with the Arabs, they argued. Israel would be secure in the long run if it held on to the occupied territories and expanded its settlements. Even though Washington would protest, Israel would prevail if it remained firm, the Likud believed.

The Labor Party argued that some of the settlements could be sacrificed. Resources should be diverted from the settlement project to Israel itself to better absorb the influx of Soviet Jews. This was more important to Israel, because the Jewish State's primary security threat was no longer territorial—it was demographic. The Palestinians were quickly outgrowing Israel's Jewish population. Persian Gulf Arab states had evicted large numbers of Palestinian guest workers to avenge the PLO's support for Iraq in the war. Kuwait alone expelled three hundred thousand Palestinians. Many of them returned to the West Bank and Gaza, which further tilted the "battle of the bedrooms" in favor of the Palestinians.[3]

"We were facing the demographic bomb, the Palestinian womb," explained Dan Meridor, a prominent Likud politician who differed with his party on this point. "If we stayed from Jordan to the sea, in some years we may reach parity in numbers. This would be the end of the Zionist dream." The entire Jewish character of Israel was at stake—Israel had to either absorb the Palestinians and lose its "Jewishness" or go the South African route and give up democracy.[4] The first option would mean the end of the Zionist project, while the second option would kill Israel's democracy.[5] Israel also needed to repair its much-damaged relationship with the United States by showing greater flexibility, Labor argued. "The Madrid process had been launched and clearly the Shamir government wasn't going places with it. We needed to fix the relationship with the Bush/Baker administration, which had been spoiled by the Shamir/Sharon team," explained Itamar Rabinovich, a close adviser to Yitzhak Rabin.[6] The Labor leader astutely recognized that Israel couldn't stick to a static strategy while the environment around it underwent radical change. In the new international arena, Israel had to change the order of its priorities.

The June 1992 elections were in many ways a referendum on the two worldviews represented by Rabin and Shamir. As it turned out, the Israeli public sided with Rabin. Labor won a landslide victory and—for the first time in fifteen years—managed to completely exclude the Likud from power.[7] With the clear backing of the electorate, Rabin and Peres's Labor Party believed it could turn the dangers of the Intifada and Israel's troubled relations with Washington into an opportunity. Labor recognized that Israel's internal threats and external problems—particularly its falling grace in Washington—were closely linked. Addressing one without tackling the other would leave both unsolved.

This change in Israel's internal and external environment created a "new world"—a watershed moment for Israeli security that required drastic change.[8] The old order no longer existed, and Israel would have no future in the new order unless it could find a rationale for Washington to continue the strategic relationship.[9] Israel wasn't strong enough to reverse these trends—it could remain passive and watch its rivals lead the creation of a new order tilted in their favor, or it could take the initiative and shape a Middle East that suited Israeli interests. In this regional game, however, Israel's competition was no longer the Arabs—it was Iran. Israel was convinced that Iran, which emerged as one of the winners of the Persian Gulf War, would seek to impose its own order on the Middle East—particularly if it came to terms with America.[10] The fear was that Washington's continued focus on Iraq would disturb the regional balance and enable Iran to emerge as a political—and military—threat to Israel.[11] The sudden shift in Labor's view of Iran "stemmed from the fact that [Tehran] could aspire to [the] regional hegemony to which Israel aspires."[12] In this new rivalry for the future of the region, Labor viewed every Iranian gain as a loss for Israel.[13]

The only way out for Israel was to lead the re-creation of the balance of power in the Middle East to ensure that it would favor the Jewish State and grant it a central role in regional affairs.[14] Peres called the new regional design "the New Middle East."[15] In this Middle East, there would be a "regional community of nations, with a common market and elected centralized bodies, modeled on the European Community." Once the political disputes between Israel and the Arabs had been resolved, the economic ties between Israel and the Arabs would develop and Israel would emerge as the region's economic engine, producing goods for the 240-million-strong Arab market, Peres believed.[16] As the Hong Kong of the Middle East, Israel would achieve the same gross domestic product (GDP) per capita as the United States.[17] And by moving the economic center of the Middle East toward the Red Sea area and Israel, the Persian Gulf region (and Iran) would lose its strategic significance.[18] The position that couldn't be attained through military or political means—or by holding on to Palestinian territories—would be won through economic means, in Labor's vision.[19]

The strategy boiled down to two critical and mutually reinforcing components: make peace with the Palestinians and depict Iran as a threat to the region and the world. Circumstances were ripe for an accord with the Arabs. Washington wanted Israel to opt for peace and, in spite of the Intifada, the PLO was at its weakest point since its inception. At the time of Labor's peak, PLO leader Yasser Arafat was at his nadir. The Palestinian leadership had committed several decisive strategic mistakes in the preceding months: Arafat had supported Saddam's invasion of Kuwait, creating tensions not only with the United States but also with the Persian Gulf Arab states, which were the primary financiers of the PLO. Then, a few months later, the Palestinian leader supported a failed Communist coup in Russia, hoping that the would-be Communist rulers would renew Russia's support of the Palestinians.[20]

By the summer of 1993, the PLO was near collapse. It had failed to translate its tactical gains from the Intifada into political capital on the international scene. And with its financial support dried up, bankruptcy was just around the corner. In its hour of desperation, the PLO simply had to make a deal with Israel.[21] "If they didn't we would overrun them entirely," asserted Israel's former Mossad chief, Efraim Halevi.[22] Both the Palestinians and the Israelis agreed to peace precisely because the PLO was dying; the Palestinians were too weak to seek an alternative solution, and the Israelis were so strong that a better deal could hardly be found. It was better for Israel to save a weakened PLO than to destroy it, the Labor Party argued.[23] "The neighbors were weak, the Palestinians were broke, Syria had no backer, Egypt was out of the game, so we had a great window of opportunity to make peace," said Keith Weissman of the American Israel Public Affairs Committee (AIPAC). To Peres, it was nothing short of an opportunity to turn the tide of history.[24]

If Israel missed this opportunity, it would risk facing a radicalized Palestinian population in the future, possibly led by Hamas. Since the PLO's expulsion from Lebanon in the 1980s, it had started to lose ground in the West Bank and Gaza. Fundamentalist groups such as Hamas and Islamic Jihad had begun to fill the vacuum left by the PLO. By the 1990s, Hamas was beginning to challenge Arafat—reflecting the decay of Arab nationalism and the ascendancy of Islamic fundamentalism.[25] Ironically, Israel had supported Hamas at the beginning of the Intifada in order to weaken the PLO. But now it could no longer be indifferent to the shifting balance.[26] The choice was clear: make a deal with a weak PLO now or fight a strong Hamas in the future.[27] (Arafat faced a similar dilemma; either deal with the Labor Party in spite of the PLO's weakness or be sidestepped by Hamas and be a spectator in a future clash between Palestinian Islamists and Greater Israel supporters in the Likud.)[28]

This would be an unprecedented shift in Israel's geopolitical outlook. It completely contradicted the very heart of Israel's guiding strategy since the days of Ben-Gurion—the periphery doctrine. By seeking peace with the Arab states in Israel's vicinity and portraying the key peripheral state—Iran—as a threat, Rabin and Peres turned the periphery doctrine on its head. The shift was particularly astonishing because Peres and Rabin were the ones who only a few years earlier had led the efforts to improve relations between U.S. President Ronald Reagan and the Khomeini government in

Iran. Peres defended his new position by arguing that he, as a protégé of Ben-Gurion, hadn't changed. Rather, it was the world that had changed.[29] Instead of depending on the periphery to balance the Arabs, the weakness of the Arabs, the strength of the periphery, and the forces that pushed for the creation of a new order all put Israel and Iran on opposite sides in the new geopolitical equation. It was the final nail in the coffin of the doctrine of the periphery—now it was the Persian periphery that could pose a threat to the Jewish State, and not the Arab vicinity.[30] After all, the role Peres had in mind for Israel in the New Middle East came at the expense of Iran; in order for Israel to take center stage in the New Middle East, Iran would have to remain on the political fringe of the region and continue to be denied the role to which it believed it was entitled.[31] "There's no doubt that when the prospects for peace with the inner circle emerged, [the depiction of Iran as a threat] started," explained David Makovsky, an expert on Israeli foreign policy.[32]

The idea that the periphery could become a threat to Israel wasn't completely new. Rabin had begun to reassess the periphery doctrine already in late 1989, and he and Peres viewed a peace process with the Palestinians and a continuation of the periphery doctrine as mutually exclusive strategies. (Israel had faced this dilemma once before: a similar tradeoff between peace with a neighbor and an alliance with a periphery state had been made by Menachem Begin and Moshe Dayan when they chose to sacrifice Tel Aviv's relations with Ethiopia in order to make peace with Egypt in 1979.)[33] But the real wakeup call arose from the new generation of weapons, and it came when Saddam hit Israel with Scud missiles during the Persian Gulf War. Iraq, which, with Iran, always was considered part of the outer circle, suddenly had Israel within its reach. The Scud attacks "emphasized something that we were not aware of before—that there was a threat from over the horizon, from the periphery," explained Moshe Arens, Israel's minister of defense at the time.[34] If states that far away could hit Israel, the very concept of periphery lost its meaning.[35] The idea of befriending the periphery—which could be a threat—in order to weaken Israel's vicinity—which was too weak to pose a threat—lost much of its rationale, silencing the pro-periphery camp in Israel.[36]

These Israeli strategists had in late 1991 flooded Israeli newspapers close to the Labor Party with articles defying the traditional view of Iran as a strategic non-Arab ally and depicting it as Israel's greatest strategic threat. (Papers more skeptical of peacemaking with the Arabs were more cautious.)[37] For instance, the *Jerusalem Post* wrote in November 1991 that the "Iraqi decline has created a power vacuum that Iran, motivated by Pan-Islamic and hegemonic inclinations, was eager to fill. A massive Iranian military buildup complemented the newly-found political objectives. Both may be enhanced by a nuclear plan supported by India and China." As a result, the Israeli daily argued, "Iran looms as the next strategic challenge facing Israel. In a sense, Iran has become a mirror image of what Iraq hoped to become five years ago."[38]

Although nuances were deliberately lost in the rhetoric, the charges were based not on an existing Iranian threat but on the anticipation of a future Iranian threat. (Iran was decades away from a nuclear capability at the time, and its military spending was sharply decreasing.) Among Israel's policy elite, the campaign was led by Ephraim Sneh, a Labor member of the Knesset, Maj. Gen. Amos Gilad, and Uri Lubrani, the former Israeli envoy to Iran. "I was the one who first put it on the agenda of the Knesset. My argument was that Iran is a dangerous combination—a regime that wants our destruction that may get nuclear capacity," Sneh told me.[39] But initially, Iran hawks like Sneh fought an uphill battle, often finding their audience skeptical and unconvinced. Occasionally they were accused of being "panic-mongers and saber-rattlers interested in igniting wars beyond Israel's immediate borders."[40] Rabin was a skeptic at first. He didn't appreciate Sneh's efforts, asking him to tone down his rhetoric and refrain from making Iran a legislative focus.[41] But only a few months into his reign as prime minister—and two years before Iran became directly involved in Palestinian terror against Israel—Rabin's skepticism was replaced with passion and enthusiasm. The doctrinal shift was a reality.

Swiftly, a campaign was organized to convince the United States and the EU that Iran was a global threat. Peres and Rabin made sure that Israel's new fear of Iran wouldn't escape anyone's notice. By October 1992, they began echoing Iran's inflammatory rhetoric. Repeating their slogans at every opportunity, the Labor leaders adopted an unprecedented tone against Iran. Peres accused Iran of "fanning all the flames in the Middle East," implying that the failure to resolve the Israeli-Palestinian conflict was rooted in Iran's meddling rather than in the shortcomings of Israel and the Palestinians.[42] Rabin accused Iran of having "megalomaniac tendencies" and that it sought to become the "leading power in the region."[43] He told the Knesset in December 1992 that Israel's "struggle against murderous Islamic terror" was "meant to awaken the world which is lying in slumber" to the dangers of Shia fundamentalism. "Death is at our doorstep," Rabin concluded, even though only a few years earlier he'd called Iran a strategic ally.[44]

The Israeli shift was as intense as it was unexpected. "Suddenly this thing just appeared. They were all over with this; this was a campaign," recalled Gary Sick, who served on the National Security Council during the Carter and Reagan administrations.[45] Only days after the 1992 U.S. presidential elections, the Rabin government sought to convince the incoming Bill Clinton administration to focus not on Iraq as a menace, but on Iran. "Iran has to be identified as Enemy No. 1," Yossi Alpher, at the time an adviser to Rabin, told the *New York Times* four days after Clinton's election victory.[46] Rabin repeatedly presented this message to U.S. officials to pressure Washington to take action against Iran. "Iran as part of the threat became part of Israel's strategic presentation, because this was certainly the view that Rabin was presenting in Washington in the early 1990s," explained Robert Pelletreau, who served as assistant secretary of state for Near Eastern affairs at the time.[47] According to Israel Shahak, an Israeli academic and president of the Israeli League for Human and Civil Rights, Labor's strategy was "to push the U.S. and other Western powers into a confrontation with Iran." Israel couldn't confront Iran itself because it would risk turning the affair into an Israeli Islamic conflict. To forestall this danger, the Israeli message was that Iran wasn't a danger just to Israel, but to the entire Western world.[48]

Israel based its case on a number of factors. First and foremost, Israel accused Iran of seeking nuclear and chemical weapons.[49] Warning the international community that Iran would be armed with a nuclear bomb by 1999, Peres told France 3 television in October 1992 that "Iran is the greatest threat [to peace] and greatest problem in the Middle East . . . because it seeks the nuclear option while holding a highly dangerous stance of extreme religious militantism." You can't deter a fanatic, terrorist state with nuclear weapons, the Israeli foreign minister argued.[50] And if the nuclear-armed Shia theocracy acquired ballistic missiles as well, Iran would become a greater threat than the Palestinians.[51] (Israel wouldn't learn of the extent of the Iranian missile program until late 1994.)[52]

Second, the nature of the Iranian regime and its anti-Israel ideology was a threat in and of itself.[53] Coexistence with such an irredeemable regime was impossible. Iran was "insane," Peres and Rabin declared and added that Khomeinism was the only ideology left that believed that ends justified means.[54] "Khomeinism without Khomeini" was Rabin's mantra as he spoke of Israel's new security environment. The veteran Israeli politician, who "never missed an opportunity to blame Iran," argued that Khomeini's fundamentalist ideology continued to live on even after the ayatollah's death and that it had replaced Communism as an ideological threat to the West.[55] Rabin repeated his mantra on Khomeinism in "every single speech he gave when he traveled," Makovsky noted. "I think he said it a thousand times. He was really focused on Khomeinism."[56] And Iran, after all, did question Israel's right to exist.

Realizing that the mullahs were there to stay prompted Israeli decision-makers to view Iran as a "permanent enemy" because it called for Israel's destruction, even though such calls were far more frequent in the 1980s, when few in Tel Aviv worried about Iranian rhetoric and intentions.[57] An important difference was that Iran was no longer checked by Iraq. Israelis argued that rhetoric reflected intentions, and, having been freed from the chains of Iraq, Iran could acquire the capacity to turn intentions into policy.[58] Though it lacked such capacities at the time, Iran was still an existential threat and the "greatest risk Israel has ever faced" by virtue of its intentions, Peres maintained.[59] Israel's sudden change of heart raised eyebrows in the United States.[60]

The notion that Iran was the new threat to the region and to America's position in the Middle East was, as the *Washington Post* put it, "a controversial idea" with little credibility.[61] Though Israel referenced Iran's purchase of Chinese nuclear reactors as the wake-up call, the *New York Times* remained skeptical. "Why the Israelis waited until fairly recently to sound a strong alarm about Iran is a perplexity," it said. In the same article, Alpher and Sneh were quoted as linking Israel's wariness of Iran with the peace process and with the need for "sound relations with the new American Administration."[62] This would provide Israel with a "barrier between the crazy regimes and the sane regimes" of the Middle East.[63]

The Israeli campaign caught the Clinton administration off guard. Israel's advice did not fit Washington's agenda; the Clinton White House was focused on Iraq, not Iran. And contrary to the mid-1980s, Israel was now sending out feelers to Iraq while urging the United States to isolate Iran. "After the Iraq war, when it would make sense for us to talk to Tehran, the Israelis did not come and make the argument. Instead, they started to reach out to the Iraqis," said Martin Indyk, Clinton's special assistant for Near East and South Asian affairs at the National Security Council who later served as ambassador to Israel and as assistant secretary of state. Before joining the Clinton administration, he served as research director at AIPAC.

The feeling that the Peres-Rabin government exaggerated the Iranian threat was widespread inside the Clinton administration. Israel's campaign against Iran came at a time when Tehran was lowering its profile on the Palestinian issue, a fact recognized privately by decision-makers in both Tel

Aviv and Washington.[64] "At that time, there were Iranian attempts to rhetorically soften the radical language of Khomeini," Weissman of AIPAC explained. "No doubt about it, there was a famous Rafsanjani interview . . . where he said that if it's okay with the Palestinians, it's okay with us."[65] Still, very few officials took issue in public with Israel's change of heart. Former National Security Advisor Brent Scowcroft observed that many didn't even remember "Israel's sympathy towards Iran in the 1980s."[66]

The sudden Israeli turnabout on Iran fell on equally unconvinced Arab ears. In light of Israel's support for Iran during the Iraq-Iran war, it was hard for the Arabs to fathom the genuineness of Israel's new position. "For the Israelis to really fear Iran, that would have been consistent if they had taken that position vis-à-vis Khomeini," said Egypt's ambassador to the United States Nabil Fahmi. "The idea that they considered Iran to be sort of this threat is absurd."[67] The Arabs were also concerned about Israel's own intentions in the region. Peres's vision of a New Middle East instilled fear rather than hope in a lot of Arab states. It wasn't a vision of peace, but rather one of Arab submission and Israeli hegemony, these Arabs argued.[68] "Israel was too eager to materialize its new vision of the Middle East. It very much wanted to be part of the Middle East and show its utility to the Arab states," an Israeli diplomat explained. "But the eagerness made the Arabs suspect that the New Middle East was just a way for Israel to control them."[69]

Israel already pursued a policy of military hegemony over all nations that had the Jewish State within their reach.[70] The New Middle East would make Israel the economic hegemon of the region as well, the Arabs feared. And Israeli reassurances to the contrary fell on deaf ears. The Arabs misunderstood Israel, according to Shlomo Brom, a longtime advocate of Israeli-Palestinian peace: "It was a classic case of misperception. Peres said that we want to help our neighbors because we believe that it will create a reality of peace. What can we contribute? We can contribute the technological advantage and so forth. He said this quite naïvely, with no special pretensions. But it was perceived completely wrongly."[71]

THE IRANIAN THREAT—REAL OR IMAGINED?

But however passionately Peres and Rabin spoke of the Iranian threat, the numbers weren't on their side.[72] The skepticism that met their accusation was rooted in a rather simple fact—no one believed that Iran overnight had turned into a major threat to the region. Though Iraq's demise had benefited Tehran, it had also led to an unprecedented buildup of the armies of the Gulf Cooperation Council (GCC) states. Saudi Arabia in particular stood out. Its military spending dwarfed that of Iran. The Saudis spent more than $40 billion on arms in 1991, at a time when Iran's military expenditure stood at $6.7 billion. Iran's aging military was less of a threat to the Arabs than the Arabs' sophisticated U.S.-built weaponry was to Iran.[73] Israel itself did not let the optimism for peace reduce its military budget. On the contrary, the threat portrayal of Iran helped justify Israel's military expansion.[74] With a military budget of $8.7 billion in 1992, Israel, with a population of four million, outspent Iran, with a population of sixty million. (Rafsanjani cut Iran's military spending from $6.7 billion in 1991 to $4.2 billion in 1992, according to the U.S. State Department.)[75] During his very first meeting with Clinton, Rabin changed Israel's annual arms request from tactical F-16s to modified F15-e's that could reach Iran.[76] Israel ordered twenty-five of these, for $85 million each.[77]

Iran hadn't changed; everyone else had. Iran was more prominent on the Israeli radar not because it had become more antagonistic toward Israel but because all previous threats had more or less evaporated. There were simply no other conventional military threats left.[78] "Nothing special happened with Iran, but because Iraq was removed, Iran started to play a greater role in the threat perception of Israel," Brom recalled.[79] The defeat of Iraq and the disappearance of the dreaded "eastern front" caused Israel's eyes to turn to Iran. "Iran became the major threat because the eastern front disintegrated. There was no longer that coalition that always presented an existential threat because of the expeditionary forces from Iraq and the long-range missiles that Iraq has. After 1991, that front disintegrated," said Ranaan Gissin, who was a spokesperson for Ariel Sharon when he was Israel's prime minister.[80] Even lobbyists supporting Israel recognized that "not much" had changed with Iran during the five short years when Rabin went from calling Tehran a geostrategic friend to his warnings of the Persian menace.[81] And few failed to notice that Israel seemed more concerned about the Iranian threat to the GCC Arab states than were the Arabs themselves. Saudi Arabia even declared Iran a nonthreat.[82] "Peres's usage of that tool was more smokescreen than reality," recalled Egyptian ambassador Fahmi.[83] Though Iran looked bigger than before, the decline of other powers hardly made Iran a greater threat in and of itself. "Was Iran an imminent or greater threat in 1991?" asked Barry Rubin, director of the Global Research in International Affairs Center in Jerusalem. "The answer is, not so much."[84] Even the asymmetrical threat Iran could pose was limited at the time. Iran was active with Hezbollah in Lebanon but it had no presence in the Palestinian territories, explained Efraim Halevi, who served as the deputy director of the Mossad at the time.[85] A few years later, this changed. By 1995, Iran was a major backer of Palestinian rejectionist groups. But in 1992, when Rabin and Peres launched their campaign against Iran, Israeli alarmism regarding Iran preceded the Iranian threat.

Some Israelis say that Israel needs an existential threat. It could be a country, like Iran; an ideology, like Islamic fundamentalism; or at other times it could be a tactic—terrorism. "You have to recognize that we Israelis need an existential threat. It is part of the way we view the world. If we can find more than one, that would be preferable, but we will settle for one," an Israeli Iran expert explained to me. This phenomenon is deeply rooted in the Jewish experience. After centuries of persecution, a Holocaust that almost wiped out the entire Jewish population in Europe, and fifty years of statehood punctuated by frequent wars, such thinking is understandable. When facing an existential threat, countries tend to work from worst-case scenarios. Everything that happens is then judged against that worse-case scenario. "When you are always prepared for the worst, you can pass off subpar performances as the best thing that ever happened," the Iran expert joked.[86] Many officials in the Israeli Ministry of Defense, however, see great dangers with this emphasis on worst-case scenarios. But few express their criticisms openly.

Brom is an exception. "In many cases, you can see how [planning for worst-case scenarios] leads to self-fulfilling prophecies. That is my debate with many Israelis," he told me in his small, spartan office at the Jaffee Center for Strategic Studies in Tel Aviv. "It's much easier to give worst-case scenarios. It usually serves the personal interest of the planner. Because if you are giving the worst-case prophecy, then when it is not realized, everyone is happy. No one remembers it. But when it is realized, you can always say, 'I told you so.'" He laughed as he said this, but I got the feeling that his levelheadedness had not been popular at the Israel Defense Forces. He had been part of the Israeli intelligence apparatus when it systematically overestimated, and at times exaggerated, Iran's nuclear capabilities. "Remember," he said mockingly, "the Iranians are always five to seven years from the bomb. Time passes but they're always five to seven years from the bomb."[87]

The Rabin-Peres campaign against Iran was initially as controversial in Israel as it was in the United States. The Israeli military sharply rejected the assessment of Israel's political leadership. The Israeli head of military intelligence, Gen. Uri Saguy, stated publicly that Iran wasn't a threat because its military program was aimed at its immediate neighbors and not at Israel.

"To be sure, this country calls for a holy war against us, but its armament policy isn't tied to us, and would be the same even if we did not exist," Saguy told reporters. Saguy received public backing from Gen. Ehud Barak, the Israeli chief of staff who went on to become prime minister. The real threat to Israel was Iraq, Barak argued. Focusing on Iran at a time when it couldn't pose a threat to Israel was counterproductive. "We should, therefore, not create a climate of hysteria by setting ourselves up as Iran's main target," Barak declared.[88]

In spite of Iraq's defeat, many in the Israeli military continued to worry about Saddam's chemical and nuclear weapons program. "Iran wasn't an immediate threat. Iran was never an immediate threat. Iraq was, however," Gen. Amnon Lipkin-Shahak explained.[89] Israeli academics and security experts were equally critical. Israel Shahak pointed out that the Labor government depicted Iran as a threat at the height of Iran's weakness. "Let me observe that when (as plenty of other evidence shows) Israel after the Gulf War decided that Iran was its enemy number one, the latter was still exhausted after the lengthy war with Iraq and hadn't yet begun its nuclearization," he wrote.[90] Shai Feldman of the Jaffee Center for Strategic Studies wrote that Israel's need for a new "boogey man" lay behind the exaggeration of Iran's military power.[91] Anoushiravan Ehteshami and Raymond Hinnebusch argued that Peres and Rabin turned Iran into a modern day Golem—a mythical figure of fear and loathing in Israeli folklore.[92] The Israeli leadership had applied a "political-strategic concept" that failed to distinguish between Iranian rhetoric and the reality of Iran's defensive military needs, wrote Ehud Sprinzak of the Hebrew University of Jerusalem.[93] Others outside government pointed out that Iran's strategy was defensive, and that its armed forces served as a deterrent. "At the most [Iran] projects threats to reply to other threats, but not threats in the meaning of initiating one and offensive aims at other countries, including Israel," Ephraim Kam of the Jaffee Center said.[94]

But Rabin and Peres's sudden campaign against Iran made political and strategic sense for Israel, the Labor Party believed, precisely because it went hand in hand with Israel's efforts to make peace with its immediate Arab neighbors and to reinvigorate its strategic relationship with Washington.[95] Even though Iran was not a credible threat at the time, its relative rise in power after Iraq's defeat could make it one in the future. Israel could not face down both a rising Iran and a vengeful Arab pact at the same time. Of the two, Iran was more likely to be a challenge, so Israel should use the opportunity to make peace with the Arabs before Iran actually did become a threat. The window of opportunity to follow this course would exist only for another seven years, Rabin predicted in 1992.[96] "Let's do a deal [with the Arabs] before the Iranians come with whatever the Iranians will come with. Create a situation that doesn't allow the Iranians room to intervene," Rabin reasoned, according to Ehud Yaari of Israeli television's Channel 2.[97]

The Arabs themselves would be more inclined to finally make peace with Israel if they felt more threatened by Iran's fundamentalist government than by Israel's nuclear arsenal and occupation of Palestinian territory. Though Arab-Persian divisions were not as strong as Israel's quarrel with the Arabs, pro-Western Arab governments could be receptive to the argument, the Labor Party reasoned. After all, the Arabs' Iraqi buffer against Iran had been crushed. In the new geopolitical map of the region, the Arabs and the Israelis had "a common threat in Iran and fundamentalism," according to U.S. diplomat Dennis Ross.[98] The Labor leadership believed that Arab fears of Iran should be used as leverage to get them to put aside their demand for Israel to quit the Palestinian territories. The idea that the Arabs would make peace with Israel only if they were faced with an even greater threat was not new. In the early 1980s, when Washington was adamant about defeating Khomeini's Iran, the Reagan administration had unsuccessfully sought to sell the idea to a reluctant Likud government. The aim was to achieve a "strategic consensus" between Israel and its "moderate" Arab neighbors. "The holy grail of U.S. policy in the region has always been to get the Arabs to forget about the Arab-Israeli conflict and to focus instead on some other threat," noted former National Security Council member Sick.[99]

Unlike the Likud government, the Labor Party embraced the idea unreservedly. Peres called Iran the greatest threat to the Arabs and argued that Saudi Arabia's unprecedented arming spree was rooted in Arab fears of Shia Iran—not Arab fears of Israel. "The clouds that hang on the skies of the Middle East are fundamentalist clouds and not Israeli ones," Peres told a gathering in Milan in November 1993.[100] To lure the Arabs to Israel's side, Peres argued that Saudi Arabia could receive Israeli assistance against Iran via the Red Sea.[101] A few years later, while on a groundbreaking trip to Qatar in the Persian Gulf, Peres told reporters that "the Arab countries are aware that Iran, violence and extremism are the enemies of both Israel and the Arabs. Iran constitutes a direct threat and is the main enemy of development and progress, not only to Israel, but also to the Arab world."[102] The Labor Party stressed the Iranian threat to the Arabs even more passionately in private discussions with Arab officials.[103]

But Israel's potential Arab peace partners were not the only ones who needed convincing. For decades Israelis had viewed the Arabs as their mortal enemies. More than two generations of Israeli children had grown up learning that Yasser Arafat and the PLO were terrorists who sought the destruction of the Jewish State. Five years of the Intifada did not soften this view. Even though most Israelis yearned for peace, convincing the public that Arafat and the Palestinians were no longer terrorists but partners for peace was a monumental task. Just as Labor had done with the Arab states, it needed to present the threat of a more ominous danger looming on the horizon to convince a skeptical Israeli public to accept this dramatic strategic shift.[104] "Rabin played the Iranian threat more than it was deserved in order to sell the peace process," noted Efraim Inbar of the conservative Begin-Sadat Center in Jerusalem.[105] Rabin asked rhetorically what the real threat to Israel was—the weak Palestinians or the rising Iranians? "We need to reach a peace agreement before the Iranians have a nuclear missile capability that could reshape the balance of power in the region," he told Israeli voters.[106] The heightening of fears regarding Iran "served a political purpose," said Indyk. "It sent the signal that the threat is no longer the Palestinians or the Arabs, therefore we need to make peace with the inner circle."[107] Iran became "a convenient argument" in the Israeli domestic discourse, used by the Labor Party to induce Israeli public opinion to favor bold steps for peace with the neighboring Arabs.[108] "[For instance], if you want to argue for a quick deal with Syria, [then] you say that 'because Iran is so and so, we need to de-link Syria from Iran,'" Yaari explained.[109] Perhaps most importantly, the alarmism over Iran reinforced the message that Washington needed Israel. The strategic significance Israel had enjoyed during the Cold War could be regained through the common threat of Iran and Islamic fundamentalism—instead of being a friendly bulwark against Soviet expansionism, Israel would now be a friendly bulwark against Iran's regional ambitions in a unipolar world.[110] "There was a feeling in Israel that because of the end of the Cold War, relations with the U.S. were cooling and we needed some new glue for the alliance," Inbar said. "And the new glue . . . was radical Islam. And Iran was radical Islam."[111]

DUAL CONTAINMENT

It didn't take long before the new glue started to stick. Only a few months into Clinton's first term—and only eight months after the Rabin-Peres government embarked on a campaign to isolate Iran—Washington adopted the policy of Dual Containment.[112] On May 18, 1993, in his new capacity as special assistant for Near East and South Asian affairs at the National Security Council, Indyk outlined the policy in an address at the Washington Institute for Near East Policy, a pro-Israeli think tank that Indyk helped found in 1985. It was a major policy declaration, originally slated to be given by National Security Advisor Anthony Lake himself.[113] The policy was a major shift in America's approach to the region. Traditionally, Washington sought to balance Iran and Iraq against each other to maintain a degree of stability. Now, Indyk argued, America's strength had reached such levels that it did not need to balance the two against each other—it could balance both without relying on either. "We don't need to rely on one to balance the other," Indyk declared. Iraq was under debilitating UN sanctions, Iran was still recuperating from the Iraq-Iran war, and the United States was the predominant power in the Persian Gulf with the "means to counter both the Iraqi and Iranian regimes."[114] Iran was too weak to pose a major threat to the United States, Indyk argued, but unless it was contained it could benefit from Iraq's weakness and create problems for Washington's regional policies. An exclusive focus on the Iraqi threat could lead to dangerous consequences if "the balance of power in the gulf [tilts] in favor of Iran."[115] According to Kenneth Pollack, who then served as an Iran analyst with the CIA, the policy was "designed to reassure Israel that the U.S. would keep Iran in check while Jerusalem embarked on the risky process of peacemaking."[116]

While winning praise in Tel Aviv, the new policy met with heavy criticism in Washington. Foreign policy experts inside the Beltway found the Israeli focus of the new policy disturbing. The Israeli origin of Dual Containment "was pretty much accepted in Washington," according to Assistant Secretary of State Pelletreau, even though in public administration officials conceded only that the policy was "influenced or stimulated" by Israeli thinking.[117] The harshest critics maintained that the Israeli tilt of the policy produced undesirable consequences for American interests. "It was a nutty idea," Scowcroft complained. It was simply "crazy" to try to balance both Iran and Iraq with American power, he said.[118] Privately, many officials in the Clinton administration agreed, because Dual Containment "stuck your enemies into the same corner," they were then compelled to cooperate with each other against the United States. "The way the policy was articulated during the Clinton administration didn't make a lot of sense to a lot of people," a senior State Department official admitted.[119] But as Israel's campaign began to win traction in the White House, the Labor Party soon found out that worst-case scenarios were not the only path to self-fulfilling prophecies. As Washington and Tel Aviv turned their focus to Tehran, the ayatollahs responded in kind by putting aside their enmity toward Sunni Islamists in the Palestinian territories.

15

from cold peace to cold war

Wherever you look, you find the evil hand of Iran in this region.

—U.S. Secretary of State Warren Christopher, March 10, 1995

The Labor Party's campaign to isolate Iran took Tehran by surprise. The Iranians thought Israel would continue to dismiss Iran's usual tirades against the Jewish State, just as it had in the 1980s. The unspoken understanding between the two was still valid as far as the Iranians were concerned: Iran would remain nothing more than an armchair critic; it would continue to issue colorful diatribes against Israel while paying lip service to the Palestinian cause. Israel, in turn, would turn a deaf ear to Iran's rhetoric and remember that Tehran's slogans did not reflect Iran's real policy. But Rabin and Peres's offensive indicated that times had changed. Slowly, Tehran began to realize that Israel was becoming its key rival in the formation of a new Middle East order. To the Iranians, no Israeli accusation revealed Israel's real objectives more than its claim that Iran wanted to establish hegemony over the Middle East.

Even though Iran was in no position to challenge or replace the United States as the undisputed power in the region—America had become a de facto power in the region through its military presence in the Gulf Cooperation Council (GCC) countries—Iran's rising power and the quest for a new order certainly fueled Tehran's appetite for a political and economic role that likely would come at the expense of Israel's position. Iran's isolation was unnatural, unjust, and untenable, the Iranian clergy reasoned.[1] The failure of the 1991 Madrid conference should have taught Washington a valuable lesson—that no major change in the region could take place without Iran's cooperation. "There is no doubt that Iran wanted and felt that it was its right to play the role of a regional power," explained Hadi Nejad-Hosseinian, who served in the cabinet of Iran President Hashemi Rafsanjani in the 1990s. "We should be the greatest power in the region and play a role accordingly. We have the potential and we should actualize it."[2] Whether America and Israel liked it or not, they had no choice but to recognize the reality of Iran's power and influence, Tehran argued. "Iran *is* a regional power. Iran *can* solve the Armenia-Azerbaijan problem. Iran should be part of the Shanghai Conference. Iran is part of ECO [Economic Cooperation Organization], [and] Iran should be part of the GCC," argued Abbas Maleki, who served as deputy foreign minister at the time.[3]

But leadership wasn't the same as hegemony, Tehran maintained. Iran was aiming for the middle ground between remaining voiceless on regional matters and seeking hegemony. In that middle ground, Iran would no longer be isolated, and it could reclaim its role as a natural competitor for preeminence in the Middle East.[4] The concept of role (*naqsh*), in the minds of the Iranians, wasn't a means for domination in an offensive way, but rather an indication of *inclusion* for defensive purposes. *Naqsh* is what "makes other actors listen to you and consult with you" so that you can "inhibit processes if they harm your interest," explained Mahmoud Sariolghalam, an adviser to Iran's former National Security Advisor Hassan Rowhani.[5] Listening to the U.S.-educated Sariolghalam in his posh Tehran office, designed to resemble Iran's ancient pre-Islamic palaces, I found it difficult not to be struck by how little things had changed. The more the Islamic Republic's foreign policy was presented as different from that of the Shah, the more it resembled it at its core. Achieving and sustaining a position of preeminence in the Persian Gulf—based on Iran's inclusion in all decisions of relevance to the region—was the guiding principle of the Iranian monarch's foreign policy. The means had changed dramatically. The ideology had shifted astonishingly. But the end goal remained remarkably similar.

Neither the changes nor the similarities of Iran's behavior had passed unnoticed in Israel. Even the need for political inclusion for defensive purposes was recognized by many Israeli strategists. "The meaning of domination—striving for regional domination—isn't striving for territorial expansion, which the Iranians don't put among their goals," said Ephraim Kam of the Jaffee Center for Strategic Studies at Tel Aviv University. "It is more of a need to influence what happens in their region, and first of all, the

Persian Gulf region, which is the most critical region to Iran. There lies the threat against them. That's the area through which the flow of oil passes, which is key to the Iranian economy. That's where the Americans are."[6]

But it mattered little whether Iran's real beef was with Washington or with Tel Aviv, even if the position Iran felt it was entitled to in the region did not contradict the role Israel needed to play to salvage its special relationship with Washington. Iran and Israel were two of the few countries in the region that were powerful enough to shape the new Middle East order. This alone put the two non-Arab powerhouses on a collision course. Israel recognized this reality first, but the Iranians were quick to pick up on it.

Iran believed that Israel needed to create an international coalition to contain and prevent Iran from becoming a regional leader.[7] "We didn't feel a greater threat from Israel," explained Amir Mohebian, political editor of *Resalat,* a conservative daily newspaper in Iran, "but they felt it from us since our situation had improved. Israel felt that Iran's chains had been ripped, that Iran was rising."[8] This competition for power in the region tossed Iran and Israel against each other, Tehran believed. "This rivalry is natural, because Iran and Israel are the two power poles in the Middle East," Nejad-Hosseinian explained. "None of the other nations in the region can match us."[9] Much like Israel, Iran viewed its rivalry with Israel in zero-sum terms. Every gain Iran made came at the expense of Israel, and vice versa.[10] Advances in Israel's standing, as well as improvements in Arab-Israeli ties, would make it all the more difficult for Iran to achieve its political goals.[11] Said Nejad-Hosseinian: "Unfortunately, some Arab countries such as Qatar had established relations and trade with Israel. This was a danger to Iran. If all the countries of the region were to follow suit, the struggle against Israel would lose supporters and Israel would become normal to the peoples of the region. From Iran's perspective, the stronger Israel's influence in the Arab countries became, the greater Israel's potential to threaten Iran would become."[12]

With the counter-Madrid conference, Iran began to reach out to Palestinian rejectionist groups with which it historically had poor relations. Like the PLO, Hamas had supported Saddam Hussein during the Iraq-Iran war. As an ideological offspring of the Sunni activists in the Egyptian Muslim Brotherhood, this Palestinian group had little in common with Iran's Shia clerics. Overcoming these differences was not an easy task. Even though Israel's Labor government was targeting Iran, as long as an Israeli-Palestinian deal was out of reach Tehran was reluctant to act too openly against Israel. But all of this changed on September 13, 1993.

FROM COLD PEACE TO COLD WAR

Far away, under the cover of the Institute for Applied Social Science in the Norwegian capital of Oslo, Israelis and Palestinians had been negotiating a peace treaty in complete secrecy since January 1993. The idea for such negotiations had first been brought to Shimon Peres in late 1992 by Yossi Beilin, Peres's close adviser and protégé. By August 19, 1993, a historic agreement was reached based on the principle of "land for peace"—by returning occupied land to the Palestinians, Israel would obtain peace. News of the meeting was leaked to the press on August 27, and less than three weeks later, with much fanfare, the Declaration of Principles was signed by Israeli Foreign Minister Shimon Peres and PLO official Mahmoud Abbas (Abu Mazen) at a White House ceremony. The deal was symbolically concluded with a historic handshake between Yasser Arafat and Yitzhak Rabin—the two former enemies. Against all odds, and in complete secrecy, the Israelis and Palestinians had succeeded in brokering a peace deal that could push Iran to the fringes of regional politics in a way that Madrid never could. Iran reacted swiftly and harshly. It elevated opposition to Israel into high policy by increasing its rhetorical opposition to Israel and announcing in the hard-line newspaper *Ettelaat* that Iran would offer limitless support to the opponents of the Oslo agreement.[13] Almost overnight, the cold peace that reigned between Israel and Iran in the 1980s turned into a cold war.[14]

A day after the ceremonies on the White House lawn, Rafsanjani accused Arafat of having "committed treason against the Palestinian people." Oslo was "a treacherous step" that would lead to "the crippling result of divisions within the Islamic nations of the world"; the leaders of the PLO and Jordan had betrayed their own peoples by having sat down with the leaders of Israel, the Iranian president charged.[15] Though calls for Israel's destruction had been made in the past, their frequency increased as Iran's policy on Israel hardened.[16] In March 1994, a slight majority of Iran's 270 parliamentarians signed a statement "stressing the need for the annihilation of Israel from the world map," arguing that the Palestinian issue wouldn't be settled except through armed struggle against Israel.[17]

Peace between the Arabs and the Israelis wasn't a threat to Iran per se. Only when combined with the Israeli-American effort to isolate Iran—depict it as a threat and exclude it from regional decision-making—did peace make Tehran nervous. Israel was seeking to use a demonized image of Iran to further Arab willingness to make peace with the Jewish State, the Iranians feared.[18] If Oslo was successful, and the Arabs rushed to make peace with Israel, Iran would be left in a state of prolonged isolation, Rafsanjani feared.[19] In the new Israel-centric order that would be created, Israel would lead while Tehran would be prevented from "playing a role equal to its capacity and power."[20] And what originally would be a political threat could, down the road, lead to a military threat. "If the Arabs were to get closer to Israel, Iran would become even more isolated. And then Israel would be in a position to turn itself into a major problem for Iran," explained Masoud Eslami of the Iranian Foreign Ministry. Simply put, Iran would be subjugated to Israeli hegemony, the "old idea of the Jews dominating the region from the Nile to Euphrates," the Iranians feared.[21] But if Iran was included in the political process, an entirely different picture could emerge, the Iranians maintained. "We would have been more inclined to support, and cooperate with, the peace efforts if we were given an active and participatory role from the outset, instead of them creating the entire plan and then expect us to simply go along with it," Ali Reza Alavi Tabar, a prominent Iranian reformist, argued.[22]

The Rafsanjani government, which prior to Madrid had reduced Iran's profile on the Palestinian issue and signaled that it wouldn't stand in the way of a peace agreement, would have been willing to go along with an Israeli-Palestinian accord if America had accepted Iran's leading role in the region in return and ended the policy of isolating Tehran. By being included in the political process, Iran could both ensure that the peace treaty wouldn't undermine Iran's interests and demonstrate its ability to be a positive and stabilizing force in the region.[23] "We can play a very positive role when we are included," Alavi Tabar insisted. "Look how we helped resolve the conflict between Armenia and Azerbaijan. We provided humanitarian aid to both sides, as well as heating oil that was sorely needed in the middle of the cold winter there. . . . We can play a positive role in the entire Middle East."[24]

"A DIFFERENT BALL GAME"

For the first time, Iran began to translate its anti-Israel rhetoric into operational policy. Contrary to the dictum of Ayatollah Khomeini, Iran would now become a front-line state against Israel, because if Oslo failed, so would the efforts to create a new regional order on the back of Iran's isolation. Ironically, Iran's support for Hezbollah had in the preceding years waned considerably because of Rafsanjani's new foreign policy orientation, making many Shia leaders in Lebanon feel abandoned by Iran.[25] Now, however, Tehran's focus turned back to Hezbollah and other Islamist groups. Iran's

vocal stand against Israel and the United States would strengthen its standing with the Arab masses, Tehran reasoned, which in turn would make it
more difficult for Israel to form an Arab-Israeli front against Iran.[26] Just as
it had done at the beginning of the revolution, Iran appealed to the Arab
street to undermine pro-Western Arab governments from below by making
them look soft on Israel. The aim was to "create a situation in which the Israelis couldn't reach the deal," explained an Iranian political figure. "Because the more messy the situation, the better off we are, because it wins us
time."[27]

Iran intensified its efforts to overcome differences with radical Palestinian groups. Oslo helped create a marriage of convenience between Iran and
Islamic Jihad, but it would still take a few more years before relations with
Hamas began to thaw.[28] Though it was a slow process that did not lead to
any concrete actions until early 1994, it was still very significant, because
Iran's relations with and access to Palestinian groups had been minimal up
until then.[29] Iran walked a fine line. On the one hand it wanted to declare its
support for the rejectionist groups as openly as possible to draw the disgruntled Arab street to its side. "We are supporting those who are struggling
for their rights, regardless of whether they are from Hamas or belong to
other groups," Iran's Foreign Minister Ali Akbar Velayati declared as he accused the PLO of not representing the wishes of the Palestinian people.[30]
On the other hand, it had to avoid any hint of supporting these groups militarily, since that could make Iran a target.

In spite of Velayati's denials, Israeli intelligence pinned the blame on
Iran for a spree of mid-1994 terror attacks targeting Israeli interests worldwide. On July 18, 1994, a bomb blew up the headquarters of the Argentine-
Israeli Mutual Association (AMIA) in Buenos Aires. Eighty-six civilians
were killed and more than three hundred wounded in what was the worst
terrorist attack to date in Argentine history. Nobody has been convicted of
the attack, but few in Israel doubt who the culprits are—Iran and Lebanon's
Hezbollah.

Two years earlier, on March 17, 1992, a bomb had destroyed the Israeli
embassy in Buenos Aires, killing 29 people. Though other groups had
claimed responsibility for this bombing, Israel still suspected a Hezbollah
link. According to Israeli accounts, these terror attacks were retaliations for
Israeli operations in South Lebanon. Israeli forces had assassinated the
leader of Hezbollah, Sheikh Abbas Mussawi, and his family a month before
the embassy bombing. Three months before the AMIA attack, Israel had
bombed a Hezbollah camp deep inside Lebanon and kidnapped Lebanese

Shia leader Mustafa Dirani in an attempt to extract information on a missing Israeli soldier. "There is no doubt that the [embassy] bombing was connected to the Mussawi operation and that the government at the time was unaware of possible consequences for Jews abroad," said Avinoam Bar-Yosef, the director general of the Jewish People Policy Planning Institute, a Jerusalem think tank affiliated with the Jewish Agency for Israel and the Israeli government.[31] Itamar Rabinovich, former adviser to Rabin and Israeli ambassador to the United States, concurred. "One was a response to the killing of Abbas Mussawi in Lebanon, one was a response to an attack on a Hezbollah camp deep in Lebanon."[32]

Whether Iran was behind the AMIA bombings or not, and whether they were retaliations or acts of aggression, the perception in Israel was that Tehran had turned to terror. The prophecy had been fulfilled. The Iranian threat that Peres and Rabin invoked to convince the Israeli public to agree to territorial concessions to Palestinians had become a reality. "This was the first time [that] there was a clear Iranian fingerprint," Israel's Gen. Amnon Lipkin-Shahak said. "Suddenly we saw more and more indirect Iranian involvement in what was going on inside Israel."[33] This created an entirely new dynamic in Israeli-Iranian relations. Iran was no longer a distant and potential foe. Through Hezbollah, Iran was a border state.[34] And through the Palestinian groups, Iran was now inside of Israel or at least inside Israeli-occupied territory. The idea of making peace with the Arab vicinity to confront the Persian periphery had failed, because the periphery had penetrated the vicinity.[35] Israeli intelligence indicated that Iran was pushing Palestinian groups to take up an armed struggle against Israel and the Oslo process.[36]

By attacking Israeli interests on this large scale, Iran had raised the stakes, Israel believed. Iran's days as an armchair critic of Israel were over. Every action Israel took against Hezbollah or the Palestinians, and every effort to turn Peres's vision of a New Middle East into reality could now be met by a terror attack sponsored by Tehran. "Well, this is a different ball game," Rabinovich explained. "If you cannot act against Hezbollah in Lebanon without an Israeli embassy being blown up or Jewish community center being blown up in Buenos Aires, this gives you pause. This is a different equation."[37]

Radical voices wanted Israel to respond in kind. The Iranian Mujahedin-e Khalq Organization (MKO), a Marxist-Islamist terror organization that, since its fallout with Khomeini in 1981, had waged a terror campaign against the Iranian government from its bases in Iraq, approached several

Israeli officials in early 1995 and offered assistance against Tehran. (Funded by Saddam Hussein and listed on the U.S. State Department's terrorist list since 1992, the MKO had killed numerous Iranian officials and civilians through terror bombings.[38]) In return, the group wanted Israel to wage a lobbying campaign in Washington to remove MKO from the State Department's terrorist list. The official Israeli response was to reject any ties to the MKO while expressing support for the idea that Iran should be isolated.[39]

But others wanted to go further. Ephraim Sneh, the hard-line Labor Member of Parliament who had pushed Rabin and Peres to take a confrontational line against Iran back in 1992, flirted with the MKO and sought to win support for it in Israel, even though prominent Iran experts in Israel advised him against it.[40] According to a renowned Israeli military commentator, the pro-MKO camp in Israel argued that "The Iranians do have a real opposition. It's very easy, very cheap to support it. If a bus explodes here, why not arrange an explosion in Tehran? . . . [The Iranians] are supporting and pushing suicide bombings, car explosions. Why not do it indirectly the same way, and tell them that this is a sword with two edges?"[41]

But cooler heads prevailed. Even though the MKO continued to court the Israeli government, Tel Aviv refrained from escalating tensions with Tehran any further by entering into a public relationship with the MKO. Israel's own position could also be compromised if it openly supported an anti-Tehran terror group while pressing the world to take action against Iran because of its alleged involvement in terror. Still, the Labor government left the door to the MKO half open. It permitted the MKO to use two Israeli satellites to beam its TV broadcasts into Iran.[42]

By 1994, Iranian actions against Israel seemed to justify the Rabin government's previous allegations of the Iranian threat. The threat was non-conventional, however, since Tehran still lacked an offensive conventional military capability that could reach the Jewish State. (Ironically, the land-for-peace formula embedded in the Oslo accords only increased Israel's appetite for arms. Israel's military expenditure stood at $8.6 billion in 1990, which was less than that of Iran, but by 1995—at the height of the peace process—Israel's military spending had increased to $9.4 billion. From 1992 on, Israel spent from $1.8 billion to $4.2 billion per year more on arms than did Iran.)[43] Privately, the Israelis recognized that despite Iran's support of Palestinian rejectionist groups such as Hamas and the Islamic Jihad, which in the spring of 1994 began engaging in a series of terror bombings in Israel, Iran wasn't the root of the terror that Israel endured. Discussing the matter with his close associates, Rabin himself identified the suffering of the Palestinian people in the occupied territories, and not Iran, as the driving force of the terror.[44] "Whatever Iran was doing against Israel through terror," said David Menashri, a Tel Aviv University professor, "the Palestinians did a better job at it themselves."[45] In fact, the spring 1994 terror bombings were a direct response to the attack by an extremist Jewish settler on Muslim worshipers at the Ibrahimi Mosque in Hebron, in which twenty-nine Palestinians were killed.

This posed a significant political problem for the Rabin government. If Israel put the blame squarely on the Palestinians, either directly on Arafat or indirectly on him by holding him responsible for not preventing the terror, it would undermine the very basis of the peace process—the idea that the Palestinians were partners in peace and not enemies. Pursuing peace with the Palestinians was next to impossible if Israel simultaneously accused them of committing terror. Iran, however, was a convenient—and partially responsible—target. Playing up the Iranian threat in Israel's domestic rhetoric, the Labor Party believed, wasn't necessarily very aggressive conduct, particularly because the party believed that there was some truth to the allegation. Though exaggerated, "the threat was real, it wasn't invented," Rabinovich told me.[46] And the exaggeration of the threat reinforced Israel's other objectives—it undermined any warm-up in U.S.-Iran relations, it compelled Washington to take stronger measures against Iran, it turned many pro-Western Arab states against Iran, and it became "the greatest threat to [Iran's] goal of regional dominance."[47] If Israel hadn't painted Iran as the main threat to peace and stability in the region and beyond, the international community and the United States would not have sought to contain and isolate it.[48]

To the opponents of the peace process in Israel, however, this was cynical politics. The Labor Party "preferred to focus on Iran rather than the latent threat of the Palestinians," complained Efraim Inbar of the conservative Begin-Sadat Center in Jerusalem.[49] But as long as the peace process progressed and the terror could be contained, these voices were overshadowed by the successes of the Labor government in the international arena. As Rabin and Peres had predicted, the Oslo process helped to end Israel's isolation. After the signing of the accords, Israel established diplomatic relations with a record number of states, including several Arab governments.[50] The normalization of relations with heavyweights China and India was the most radical change in Israel's international status since 1948 and boosted its bid to retain strategic significance in the Middle East—and in Washington.[51]

ISRAEL TARGETS U.S.-IRAN RELATIONS

The Israeli-U.S.-Iranian triangle had shifted remarkably in just a few years. In the 1980s, Israel was the unlikely defender of and apologist for Iran in Washington, taking great risks to pressure the Reagan administration to open up channels of communication with Iran. Now, Israel did the opposite. Israel wanted the United States to put Iran under economic and political siege.[52] Shimon Peres's New Middle East and the American policy of Dual Containment that went into effect in 1993 after more than a year of Israeli pressure would all but write Iran's isolation into law.[53]

A few voices questioned the wisdom of this at the time. After all, if Iran was a threat to Israel by virtue of its ideology, capabilities, and nuclear program, wouldn't Israeli interests be better served by seeking to influence Iran's behavior through a U.S.-Iran dialogue, rather than by working diligently to prevent such a dialogue from taking place? With Washington's strength at its peak, could Israel not have used its ties to the United States to compel Iran to shift gears on Israel? Would that not have been a more effective route than to intensify Iran's isolation? Within the Israeli Foreign Ministry, there was a minority who posed these questions and argued that talks between Tehran and Washington could be used to Israel's advantage. Tehran would be forced to moderate its tone and conduct in order to win the cooperation of Washington, the reasoning went.[54]

But the prevailing view in the Israeli government was that a U.S.-Iran dialogue would not benefit Israel because Iran was interested only in reducing tensions with Washington—not with Israel.[55] "What the Iranians want is to have the U.S. recognize them as a regional superpower in the Middle East," Israeli Gen. Amos Gilad argued.[56] Just as it did in the Iran-Contra affair and the Lebanese hostage negotiations with Washington in the early 1990s, Iran would try to cut Israel out of the deal because Israel itself couldn't offer Tehran anything it needed.[57] Any indication of Iran moderating its behavior toward Israel would be nothing but a tactical maneuver with no strategic implications, aimed solely at reducing U.S. pressure on Tehran.[58] "They are only interested in pretending to be opening [talks] with us at times when they think that maybe they can have some sort of a deal with the Americans. That's all. They are not interested in Israel per se," argued Ehud Yaari, a veteran Israeli television journalist.[59] As soon as the U.S.

pressure eased, Iran would betray the Jewish State, Israel believed.[60] Once that happened, it would be very difficult for Israel to compel Washington to reinstate the pressure. So negotiations were nothing short of a slippery slope, and Israel could quickly lose control of them.[61] And even worse, if the Iranians didn't betray Israel, the United States could. Putting aside ideology and rhetoric, Iran and the United States shared many common interests in the region. Both were hostile to Iraq, both needed stability in the Persian Gulf, both cherished the free flow of oil, and both opposed—to varying degrees—the growing Taliban guerilla movement in Afghanistan and the Afghan drug-trafficking. Israel feared that these common interests between Iran and the United States would in a U.S.-Iran dialogue overshadow Israel's concerns with Iran and leave Israel alone in facing its Persian rival.[62]

This was particularly true if U.S.-Iran relations were put in a global context, in which Washington needed to maintain some influence over Iran and its gas and oil reserves in order to keep the United States' future geopolitical rival—China—in check. "A small state is always worried that a global ally will make a deal in which it takes a global view of the deal and forget about local details that for a local actor are very important," Rabinovich explained.[63] Apprehension that Washington would "sell Israel out" and pursue its own interests in a U.S.-Iran dialogue weighed heavily on the minds of Israeli strategists.[64] Because Israel viewed a U.S.-Iran dialogue as a greater threat than that of Iran itself, the optimal strategy was to prevent a dialogue from materializing in the first place.[65] This provided the American Israel Public Affairs Committee (AIPAC), the most potent pro-Israeli lobby group in the United States, with a new cause to rally around.

AIPAC—THE KING OF LOBBIES

Founded in 1953, the American Israel Public Affairs Committee describes itself as "America's Pro-Israel Lobby." With more than one hundred thousand members nationwide, it has consistently been ranked by *Fortune* magazine as one of the most powerful lobbies in the United States.[66] Lobbying the U.S. government on issues and legislation "to ensure that the U.S.-Israel relationship is strong so that both countries can work together" and following the motto that it is better to be feared than loved, AIPAC efficiency, sophistication, and ruthlessness have left in awe friends and foes alike. But the peace process posed a major challenge to the organization.

For decades, AIPAC had worked to torpedo U.S.-Arab arms deals, soften Washington's stance on opposition to Israeli settlements in the occupied territories, prevent any peace deal from being forced on Israel, pressure the United States not to recognize the PLO as a legitimate organization, and pursue a pro-Israeli—and often pro-Likud—tilt in Washington's Middle East policies. AIPAC deliberately took a harsher position on these issues than the Israeli government, not only because it was dominated by individuals who felt closer to the Likud than to Labor, but also to give the Israeli government maximum maneuverability in Washington. "AIPAC represents the hawkish end of strategic Israeli thinking, and they do so consciously," former Mossad chief Yossi Alpher explained. Their job is to give Israel maximum leverage to maneuver, and to do that, they take the hawkish point of view.[67] The peace process, however, deprived AIPAC of its key rallying call—the Arab and Palestinian threat to Israel's existence. Now the Palestinians were peace partners, not enemies, and Israel would benefit from the United States aiding them economically. This was a difficult reality for AIPAC to come to terms with. As an organization, a critical part of its raison d'être was threatened.

Labor's approach to the Palestinians ensured that the lobby's relations with Rabin would start off on a tense footing. Rabin had always had a problematic relationship with American Jewish organizations, partly because of his secular inclinations and upbringing, but mainly because of what he perceived as repeated attempts by American Jewish leaders to sideline Israel's government (particularly its Labor governments) by approaching the U.S. administration on Israel's behalf. Lobbying the administration should be off-limits to AIPAC, he insisted, whereas Capitol Hill was fair game,[68] "He felt that the community had become too big of a part of the bilateral [U.S.-Israel] relationship," explained Jess Hordes, director of the Anti-Defamation League in Washington, D.C.[69] Early in his tenure as Israel's prime minister, Rabin gave AIPAC a very clear message—you won't be Likudniks on my watch.[70] He reiterated this message in a meeting with the Conference of Presidents of Major American Jewish Organizations that same year.[71]

Needless to say, Rabin's tough stance added new friction to an already tense relationship. "He wasn't the ultimate diplomat," Hordes recalled.[72] What helped soothe relations was Iran. Israel's new push against Iran provided AIPAC with an opportunity to reinvent itself in the Oslo era, when its traditional function of countering Arab influence in Washington had become obsolete.[73] "AIPAC made Iran a major issue since they didn't have any other issue to champion," said Shai Feldman of the Jaffee Center for Strategic Studies in Tel Aviv. "The U.S. was in favor of the peace process, so what would they push for?"[74] AIPAC needed a new issue, and Israel needed help in turning Washington against Iran. It was a win-win situation.

By mid-1994, Israel and AIPAC turned the full force of their diplomatic and lobby power against Iran. Rabin's advisers requested that he ask the West to impose "some potent economic sanctions against Iran."[75] This wasn't an easy task, because even though Iran wasn't a popular country in the United States, it wasn't considered a threat. But whatever challenges lay ahead, they could be resolved with AIPAC's help.[76] Rabin held a teleconference with U.S. Jewish leaders in September 1994 to coordinate the strategy. His message was clear—Iran was the greatest threat to Middle East peace. "Behind [the Palestinian rejectionists] there is an Islamic country, Iran, that in addition tries to develop in the coming seven to fifteen years nuclear weapons and ground-to-ground missiles that can reach every part of the Middle East," he said.[77]

Knowing the Clinton administration's commitment to the peace process, Rabin used the Oslo agreement as a hook. "You guys got to do something about the Iranians, because they are killing us," Israel told the Clinton administration, according to Ken Pollack, who served in the Clinton White House, suggesting that Tel Aviv couldn't pursue peace with the Arab inner circle unless the United States adopted a tougher line on Iran on the periphery.[78] At the behest of the Israeli government, AIPAC drafted and circulated a seventy-four-page paper in Washington arguing that Iran was a threat not only to Israel, but also to the United States and the West.[79] "The pro-Israeli community turned strongly against Iran, influencing U.S. policy on Iran in an almost emotional way," former National Security Advisor Brent Scowcroft recalled.[80]

In late 1994, Rabin accused North Korea of having supplied Iran with Scud ground-to-ground missiles with a range of three hundred miles—much less than the distance between Iran and Israel.[81] A month later, citing unnamed American and Israeli officials, the New York Times reported that Iran's alleged nuclear weapons program was ahead of schedule and could result in a preemptive Israeli strike against its reactors.[82] Iran responded by issuing a stern warning to Israel. "Should Israel commit such a blunder, we will teach her a lesson not to ever attempt another aggression against Iran," Iran Speaker of the Parliament Ali Akbar Nateq Noori told Iran News.[83]

But these Iranian statements only played into the hands of Israel, whose efforts to portray Iran as a threat benefited from Tehran's tough talk. The Iranian rhetoric aside, what eventually made Israel successful was the Clinton White House's peace-process-centric policy. Washington had invested heavily in Oslo and in the creation of a new order in the Middle East. The Clinton administration was willing to go to great lengths to convince the Is-

raelis and Palestinians to remain on the path of peace, even if it meant escalating tensions with Iran. According to Pollack, "It was simply a matter of,
'What do we need to do to get you guys to move down this road, tell us what
you require and we'll do it.' And look, we didn't like Iran anyway."[84]

By October 1994, Washington started to adopt the Israeli line on Iran.
In response to Israeli pressure—and not to Iranian actions—Washington's
rhetoric on Iran began to mirror Israel's talking points.[85] U.S. Secretary of
State Warren Christopher told an audience at Georgetown University in
October 1994 that "Iran is the world's most significant sponsor of terrorism
and the most ardent opponent of the Middle East peace process. The international community has been far too tolerant of Iran's outlaw behavior. . . .
The evidence is overwhelming: Iran is intent on projecting terror and extremism across the Middle East and beyond. Only a concerted international
effort can stop it."[86]

Months later, Christopher went on to declare that "wherever you look,
you find the evil hand of Iran in this region,"[87] while former Assistant Secretary of State Martin Indyk defined Iran as a threat to Israel, Arabs, and the
West—a position that Washington had refused to take only two years earlier.[88] The Clinton administration told the Israelis that "the peace process
was another insulator against Iran. Because if we were successful in bringing the Arabs into the orbit of peace-making, then the Iranian influence on
inter-Arab politics would be further marginalized."[89] This was exactly what
Israel had been telling Washington for the last two years. Washington's recy-
cling of Israel's argument back to Tel Aviv reflected the success of Rabin and
Peres's campaign against Iran. Washington's turnaround was a direct result
of Israel's pressure, because the United States reacted to Iranian actions only
when Israel threatened not to proceed with the peace process, according to
Pollack.[90]

But neither America's adoption of the Israeli line on Iran nor Dual
Containment was sufficient. Having achieved these goals, Israel raised the
bar and requested additional pressure on Iran.[91] After all, while the Clinton
administration had adopted Israel's rhetoric and hard stance on Iran in the
political sphere, U.S.-Iran trade remained unaffected by Dual Containment. Trade between the two countries totaled $3.8 billion in 1994, with an
additional $1.2 billion in goods sold by U.S. companies through foreign
subsidiaries, making the United States one of Iran's largest trading partners.[92] This inconsistency was brought to AIPAC's attention by Helmut
Kohl, the German chancellor, who at a meeting with AIPAC in 1994 defended Germany's trade with Iran by pointing out Washington's own exten-

sive trade relations with Tehran. "We looked at the figures, and he was right," Keith Weissman of AIPAC explained. "Basically, more American money was being sent to Iran than any other country. That's what got us [AIPAC] interested in the economic side of it."[93] (Remarkably, throughout the 1990s, Israel never passed any laws prohibiting Iranian-Israeli trade.)[94] AIPAC organized a campaign to bridge the gap between Washington's political and economic approach to Iran. Together with the Israeli government, it pressured the Clinton administration to lead by example, because American efforts to shut down Russian and European trade with Iran would fail unless America's political and economic policies were aligned. "The right, AIPAC, the Israelis were all screaming for new sanctions," Pollack explained, adding that the Clinton administration saw Iran only through the prism of the Israeli-Palestinian conflict.[95]

The campaign did not win much traction until the Rafsanjani government offered the American oil company Conoco a lucrative oil deal in 1995. In the midst of the Israeli campaign to impose sanctions on Iran, Rafsanjani made one last effort to improve relations with the United States. The repeated snubs from the United States had cost Rafsanjani dearly at home, but now the Iranians followed a double policy. On the one hand, they courted Washington when possible, and on the other hand, they supported Palestinian Islamists and took the lead against Israel in the Islamic world to strengthen Iran's appeal in the Arab street. This would make it more difficult to exclude Iran from regional affairs in the future, Tehran reasoned, because it would make Iran an even more potent spoiler.[96] Because a direct political rapprochement with the United States remained unlikely, Rafsanjani chose to use Iran's economic ties with Washington to create areas of common interest that could later pave the way for a political rapprochement.[97] American investments in Iran's ailing oil industry would be a win-win solution, Rafsanjani figured.

In his attempts to expand Iran's economic relations with the international community, Rafsanjani had for years fought to reopen Iran's oil industry to foreign companies. The symbolism of this move was significant. The oil industry had played a central role in the Iranian revolution and in the country's economic and political development earlier in the twentieth century. Iran opened bidding for production agreements for two of its offshore oil fields to international companies in 1994. The first oil contract after the revolution, worth $1 billion, was expected to go to the French-owned Total. However, after having negotiated with Conoco, Iran announced on March 6, 1995, that the contract would go to the Americans.[98] The deal was approved by Ayatollah Ali Khamenei himself and was intended as an olive branch to Washington, the Iranians say. To ensure the blessing of the White House, Conoco had kept the U.S. government closely informed of its negotiations. The State Department had repeatedly reassured Conoco that the White House would approve the deal.[99]

For AIPAC, the Conoco deal "was a coincidence and a convenient target."[100] The organization went into high gear to use the Iranian offer not only to scuttle the Conoco deal, but also to put an end to all U.S.-Iran trade. In a report that it released on April 2, 1995, titled "Comprehensive U.S. Sanctions Against Iran: A Plan for Action," AIPAC argued that Iran must be punished for its actions against Israel. "Iran's leaders reject the existence of Israel. Moreover, Iran views the peace process as an American attempt to legalize Israel's occupation of Palestinian, Muslim lands," it said.[101] Pressured by Congress, AIPAC, and the Israelis, President Clinton swiftly scrapped the deal by issuing two executive orders that effectively prohibited all trade with Iran.[102]

The decision was announced on April 30 by Clinton in a speech before the World Jewish Congress.[103] A day later, Christopher told journalists that the controversial decision was motivated by Iran's "repugnant behavior"— Tehran still sponsored terrorism, opposed the Middle East peace process, and was trying to acquire nuclear weapons, he argued.[104] But in reality, targeting the Conoco deal—which was a result of Tehran's eagerness to improve relations with the United States—was "a major demonstration of [American] support for Israel."[105] Immediately, speculation in the U.S. media began on "where U.S. foreign policy ends and Israeli interests begin."[106]

By now, the Clinton administration viewed Tehran as an implacable foe and Iranian olive branches as self-serving.[107] Taking an uncompromising stance on the Iranian threat "was the point of departure" of the Clinton White House, said Dennis Ross, former special Middle East coordinator under Clinton. "We weren't interested in creating a new opening towards Iran. We were interested in containing what we saw as a threat."[108] To further justify the decision, U.S. officials speaking on condition of anonymity told the *Los Angeles Times* on May 9, 1995, that Iranian officials trained two Palestinian suicide bombers who killed twenty-one Israelis earlier that year. In what was the first American allegation directly linking Iran to specific terrorist attacks aimed at thwarting the Oslo agreement, these unnamed U.S. officials also accused Iran of sending financial aid to the families of the suicide bombers.[109] The next day, Peres told the *Jerusalem Post* that the greatest threat to Israel came from fundamentalists armed with nuclear weapons. "What's the greatest threat—the old Syrian tanks or Iran's nuclear reactors?" he asked.[110] Politically, the decision to scuttle the Conoco deal had no cost. With AIPAC and Israel lobbying against accepting Iranian olive branches, and with no major political campaign in favor of a U.S.-Iran rapprochement, changing course on Iran had no political downside. (Conoco's efforts to reverse the decision were hopelessly unsuccessful.) "From a political standpoint, nobody pays a price to be tough on Iran," Ross commented.[111]

But the initial sanctions weren't enough. Though Clinton had with the stroke of a pen eliminated billions of dollars worth of U.S.-Iran trade through two executive orders, he could easily lift the orders and reinstate the trade. If sanctions were imposed by Congress, however, the president's—any president's—maneuverability would be limited. On its own initiative, AIPAC revised a bill that Senator Alfonse D'Amato of New York had introduced with the help of the Israelis in early 1995 and then convinced D'Amato to reintroduce it in 1996—with AIPAC's proposed changes.[112]

AIPAC launched a formidable lobbying campaign and managed to win extensive support for the bill—the Iran Libya Sanctions Act (ILSA)—on Capitol Hill.[113] ILSA went beyond the executive orders that President Clinton had promulgated sixteen months earlier, because it targeted both American and non-American companies that invested $40 million or more in the Iranian oil and gas sector. The official aim of the bill was to deny Iran and Libya revenues that could be used to finance international terrorism and limit the flow of resources necessary to obtain weapons of mass destruction.[114] The Clinton administration balked. Robert Pelletreau, assistant secretary of state at the time, testified in Congress against the bill, arguing that extraterritorial sanctions would be counterproductive by alienating countries whose cooperation the United States needed to cripple the Iranian regime. "We want to isolate the Iranians, not become isolated ourselves," he told the House International Relations Committee.[115] But Clinton was no match for AIPAC's influence in Congress. The bill passed the House of Representatives 415 votes to 0 and was reluctantly signed into law by the president in August 1996.[116]

Though AIPAC's efforts had helped eliminate billions of dollars worth of trade with Iran, the pro-Israel lobby felt that ILSA actually should be welcomed by American businesses because it primarily targeted foreign companies. "We promulgated ILSA . . . to level the playing field," explained Weissman of AIPAC. "We wanted to show that we were not penalizing

American business for foreign policy reasons. . . . But nobody [in the business community] liked it. Maybe it was naïve of us." Much of corporate America was infuriated by the bill. Even though the ILSA sanctions targeted foreign companies, they still posed a danger to American companies because of the potential threat of countersanctions by European and Asian governments. To make matters worse, even though it pressed for U.S. sanctions, Israel itself continued to purchase Iranian goods through third countries. "There were many times over the years that a few of the things Israel did vis-à-vis Iran admittedly allowed people to perceive that we [the United States] were harder-line than they [Israel] were," Weissman admitted.[117]

These contradictions aside, ILSA was a major success for AIPAC and Israel—not as a result of forcing a change in Iranian foreign policy, because it never did. In retrospect, Indyk admits that ILSA "was counterproductive to our efforts to try to change Iranian behavior because it split us from our allies, the Europeans."[118] Rather, the success of ILSA lay in the almost irremovable political obstacle it created to any effort at improving U.S.-Iran relations   a critical objective of Israel as a result of its fear that a dialogue between Washington and Tehran would come at the expense of Israel's strategic role. "We were against it [U.S.-Iran dialogue] . . . because the interest of the U.S. did not coincide with ours," Israeli Deputy Defense minister Sneh admitted.[119]

16

with likud, the periphery
doctrine returns

> The Likud tended to be more open to the idea [that] maybe there
> are residual elements in the revolutionary regime [in Iran] that see
> things geopolitically the same way as it was during the Shah's time.
>
> —Dore Gold, former Israeli UN ambassador, October 28, 2004

In spite of Israel's rhetoric about mad mullahs and the irredeemable ideology of the Islamists, many Israelis understood the strategic calculus behind Iran's opposition to the peace process. Both Washington and Tel Aviv recognized that the peace process and Israel's diplomatic efforts to form a new order in the Middle East were damaging to Iran's strategic position.[1] The new dividing lines of the Middle East would no longer be Islam vs. the Arab-Persian split, as Iran preferred it, but rather between those within the Oslo process and those outside of it.[2] And peace with the Palestinians could lead to peace with Syria, which would in turn incline the Arab world in Israel's favor and further diminish Iran's influence in the region. As a result, Iran had a strategic interest in countering the peace efforts, the Israelis reckoned.[3] "Imagine that there would have been a deal between Israel and Syria in 1993, which was quite close, and Iran found itself without the Syrian ally and without access to Lebanon and loses its Lebanon base, and Israel and the Palestinians reduce tensions," explained Itamar Rabinovich, who advised former Prime Minister Itzak Rabin and also served as Israeli ambassador to the United States. "Iranian policy in the Middle East loses many of its assets and sources. It therefore begins to develop an interest in undermining the peace process, and one of the main methods to undermine the peace process is the work of fundamentalist Palestinian groups."[4]

Not only was Iran in danger of losing its alliance with Syria, but the peace process would also "cement the U.S. military presence in the region, a role Iran sees as a threat to its goal of regional dominance," the Washington Institute for Near East Policy wrote.[5] "I always felt that they [the Iranians] felt threatened for geostrategic reasons," Keith Weissman of the American Israel Public Affairs Committee (AIPAC) recalled. "Look, the Arabs would have gotten more confident because they would have felt that the Israelis would back them up now [against Iran], as well as the Americans."[6]

In spite of Iran's obvious fear of isolation, Washington did not predict that Iran would turn against the peace process in the way that it did. According to Martin Indyk, former U.S. assistant secretary of state, the United States feared that Iran and Iraq would form an axis to balance the United States and defeat efforts to isolate them. "We were much more focused, at the time, on a break-out strategy in which our Dual Containment would lead [Iran] to a rapprochement with Iraq," he explained. The idea that Iran would turn to terror wasn't something Washington considered likely, even though the accusation of Iranian support for terror was used to justify Iran's isolation. "What the Iranians did was to outsmart us by taking on the peace process. And they became very aggressive supporters of Palestinian terrorism and not just Hezbollah."[7]

In time, Washington began to understand the critical strategic flaw in its policy of Dual Containment— by rejecting Iranian overtures and aiming to create a new order in the Middle East based on Tehran's exclusion, the United States was giving Iran strong incentives to sabotage the weakest link in the policy, the fragile Israeli-Palestinian talks. According to Indyk, the Iranians "had every incentive to oppose [the peace process]. Our strategy was to, on one hand, use the engine of peacemaking to transform the region and on the other hand contain the [Iranians] through sanctions and isolation. The two were symbiotic. The more we succeeded in making peace, the more isolated [they] would become. The more we succeeded in containing [the Iranians], the more possible it would be to make peace. So they had an incentive to do us in on the peace process in order to defeat our policy of containment and isolation. And therefore, they took aim at the peace process."[8]

Though Washington did not expect Iran to remain passive as the new Middle East order was being built, it underestimated Tehran's ability to affect the process. "There was no expectation that they would sit idly by, because we knew they couldn't afford to," explained Daniel Kurtzer, former U.S. ambassador to Israel.[9] But toward the end of 1995, it was becoming clear that terrorism could derail the entire Israeli-Palestinian project.

YIGAL KILLS YITZHAK

On November 4, 1995, terrorism struck Israel again, but from unexpected quarters. Yigal Amir, an Israeli right-wing extremist, shot and killed Prime Minister Rabin in a parking lot adjacent to Tel Aviv's Kings of Israel Square. Rabin had attended a peace rally in support of the Oslo accord and was just about to enter his car when the assassin struck. Israel was in shock; the government in Tehran rejoiced. The hard-line newspaper *Jomhuri Eslami* wrote that "across the world, free nations agree with Moslems in rejoicing over the slaying of this bloodthirsty Zionist even though their governments mourn or send condolences," while the English-language *Kayhan International* said, "No one should mourn Rabin, who brought blood, tears and darkness in the life of hundreds and thousands."[10] The speaker of the Iranian parliament, Ali Akbar Nateq-Nouri, said that Rabin paid in his own coin: "We condemn terrorist acts, but Zionists should have known when they opened the door to terrorism that they themselves would be victims to the plots they hatch for others."[11]

The assassination of Rabin sparked a new round of public spats between Tehran and Tel Aviv. The Iranians felt emboldened—without Rabin, the peace process was in jeopardy. Iran's supreme leader, Ayatollah Ali Khamenei, told Tehran radio that "the government and the people of Iran believe that the existence of Israel is false and artificial. In fact, there is no nation called Israel, rather Zionist leaders, acting solely on racism, have gathered some people from around the world and set up a made-to-order state in order to occupy Palestine."[12]

The Israelis responded by intensifying their efforts to isolate Iran and depict it as a global threat. On February 15, 1996, Israel Foreign Minister Ehud Barak told members of the UN Security Council that Iran would be able to produce nuclear weapons within eight years.[13] Just as Iran sought to hinder Israeli-Arab relations, Israel sought to prevent Iran from using its trade with the EU to escape isolation. "You must really stop flirting with the Iranians," Prime Minister Shimon Peres told France 2 Television in March 1996. "Iran is the center of terrorism, fundamentalism and subversion . . . [and] is in my view more dangerous than Nazism, because Hitler did not possess a nuclear bomb, whereas the Iranians are trying to perfect a nuclear option."[14]

Though the Labor Party chose the path of Oslo, it was becoming increasingly clear by 1996 that it had achieved precious little peace. The Israeli public, which in 1992 handed Labor a resounding election victory, felt uneasy about the peace process and was gravitating toward Likud's anti-Oslo platform. Then, in the spring of 1996, terrorism dealt another devastating blow to Peres and his party. Between February 25 and March 4, four major terrorist attacks hit the cities of Tel Aviv, Jerusalem, and Ashkelon, killing fifty-nine Israeli civilians. Peres immediately placed the blame on Tehran, arguing that the Iranians were seeking to topple his government. "They are doing whatever they can to bring an end to peace and bring an end to the government that goes for peace . . . we have evidence they are pressing upon [Islamic] Jihad and other subversive organizations to act against Israel before the elections," he said.[15] (Hamas, however, publicly claimed responsibility and gave the reason for the bombings as vengeance for the Israeli assassination of Yehya Ayyash, a high-ranking Hamas operative.)

To this day, Peres believes that the four terrorist attacks were ordered by the Iranians to damage the prospects for peace, according to Weissman. "It's not an unreasonable assertion, really, that the Iranians understood that by electing [Binyamin "Bibi"] Netanyahu, you would slow down the peace process. And that is what happened."[16] (However, Israel has not presented any hard evidence to back this claim.)

FROM OSLO BACK TO THE PERIPHERY DOCTRINE

Maj. Gen. Amos Gilad is the archetype of a tough-talking Israeli general who despises nuance and loathes the idea of having to revisit what his critics consider to be his often inaccurate assumptions about his "enemies." In the 1990s no one pushed more for a one-dimensional Iranian threat depiction within the Israeli Ministry of Defense than he did, as head of the military's National Intelligence Assessment. His obsession with Iran verged on what his critics describe as "Iran-mania."[17] "Amos Gilad made the Iran missiles a personal vendetta," explained an Israeli military officer who worked closely with Gilad, adding that he "always thought in apocalyptic terms without any appreciation for nuance."[18] Together with Knesset member Ephraim Sneh, Gilad was successful in putting Iran on the Israeli radar and in convincing the Labor Party to pursue an aggressive policy on Iran.

But Gilad met his match in Netanyahu. On May 30, 1996, the U.S.-educated head of the Likud Party defeated the incumbent Peres by a razor-thin margin in an election that became a referendum on the peace process. Only 15,000 votes separated the two.[19] The Netanyahu victory marked the beginning of the end of the Oslo process and paved the way for a brief thaw in Israeli-Iranian relations. Even prior to the 1996 elections, in response to internal criticism of Labor's Iran policy Rabin had formed a committee to present recommendations on how to approach any Iranian threat. Many in Israel saw the Iranian escalation against Israel after 1994 as a direct result of the Peres-Rabin government's campaign against Iran. The Labor government's rhetoric was exaggerated and self-defeating and had unnecessarily put Israel on Iran's radar.[20] The rhetoric was "liable to become a self-fulfilling prophecy," recalled Yossi Alpher, a former Mossad official and senior adviser to Prime Minister Ehud Barak. "The more we talk about a possible Iranian nuclear attack on Israel, the more Iran will worry about us and the more likely that there will be some uncontrolled escalation."[21]

These critics called for a policy that would avoid saying things that could feed into Iranian fears and produce Iranian bluster. After all, Iran could pose a challenge to Israel, but it wasn't an existential threat. Even with the deployment of Fajr rockets in Lebanon, Iran's ability to inflict damage on Israel was limited and vastly inferior to Israel's capabilities.[22] Israel knew that Iran did not possess weapons of mass destruction and that it was highly unlikely to initiate a conventional war with Israel.[23] Even though Israeli intelligence discovered the existence of an Iranian missile program in late 1994, there was widespread recognition in Israel that Iran's armament, missile program, and potential nuclear program were not aimed at Israel.[24] "Remember, [the Iranians] may talk about us, but we are not their real first or even second strategic concerns or reason for developing nuclear weapons," Alpher continued.[25]

Labor's committee was an interministerial team consisting of representatives of the Mossad, the Foreign Ministry, the Defense Ministry, and the Israeli National Security Council. It was led by Gen. David Ivry, Israel's former ambassador to the United States (who had led Israel's raids on the Iraqi nuclear reactor in 1981). Shmuel Limone, an Iran expert at the Ministry of Defense, served as its secretary.[26] Other key members were Oded Eran, one of Israel's most prominent diplomats; Uri Lubrani, the Israeli envoy to Iran in the 1970s; and David Menashri, a professor at Tel Aviv University who was Israel's most prominent expert on Iran (and himself an Iranian Jew).[27]

Though Labor's aggressive campaign had succeeded in putting international pressure on Iran, the committee argued that Israel had little to gain by making Iran an enemy of Israel. Labor's inflammatory rhetoric had only attracted Iran's attention and strengthened Iran's perception of an Israeli threat, which in turn had made Israel less rather than more secure. Within the committee, Eran and Menashri favored opening up channels of communication with Iran, a proposition that Lubrani in particular strongly opposed on the grounds that he believed the regime in Tehran was doomed to fall.[28] In the end, the Peres-Rabin government ignored the committee's recommendations and continued its aggressive stance toward Iran.

The incoming Netanyahu government was more receptive to the committee's findings. The Likud prime minister immediately requested an intelligence assessment of Israel's security environment from both the Mossad and military intelligence. The debate between these agencies was the same as in the 1980s—did Iran or Iraq constitute the greatest threat to Israel? And could Iran be relied on to balance Iraq?[29] Only weeks into Netanyahu's term, the assessments were ready. The Likud prime minister invited the military and the Mossad to a full cabinet meeting to make their cases. Gilad represented the military, and Uzi Arad, the director of intelligence of the Mossad, argued on behalf of the intelligence services. Although the debate was heated and passionate—as were all cabinet discussions in the Netanyahu government—the outcome was unprecedented. Gilad argued that Iran had replaced Iraq as an existential threat to Israel. First, he said, the Iranian regime was hostile to Israel and was determined to destroy the Jewish State. Gilad dismissed the notion that moderates would get the upper hand in Iran and argued for the opposite scenario. "I presented a tough line that claimed that Iran would be dominated by the conservatives. . . . This was at the level of strategic intentions," the major general explained.

Second, he said, the Iranian capabilities had grown, particularly through Tehran's missile program. Gilad asserted that the Iranians would have Israel within reach of their missiles by 1999. The third component was Iran's nuclear development program. The National Intelligence Assessment concluded that Iran would have a nuclear device by 2005. "Even one primitive device is enough to destroy Israel," Gilad maintained. Finally, he maintained that Iran opposed the peace process and had developed a terror threat against Israel through its support for Islamic Jihad, Hamas, and Hezbollah. "Altogether, it seemed that ideologically and strategically, Iran [was] determined to destroy Israel," Gilad concluded.[30]

Arad presented a radically different perspective. He argued that Iran's rearmament was defensive and primarily aimed at deterring Saddam Hussein. Iran needed to rearm as a result of the natural continuation of its enmity with the Arab states; after all, Iran and Iraq had yet to sign a conclusive peace treaty. Furthermore, Iran was in debt, the internal political situation was unstable, and oil prices were low. All of this reduced Iran's ability to pose a threat, Arad argued, whereas Iraq—with its existing Scud missiles, of which thirty-four had been fired at Israel during the Persian Gulf War—

was a proven danger.[31] In fact, the Arabs' perception of Iran as a threat could give life to the periphery doctrine again, leading to an Israeli-Iranian realignment to counter the common Arab threat.

The heart of Arad's argument was that Israel had a choice: it could either make itself Iran's number-one enemy by continuing Peres and Rabin's belligerent rhetoric, or ease off the pressure and allow the Iranians to feel a greater threat from other regional actors. "There are enough bad guys around them; we don't have to single out ourselves as the enemy," the argument read.[32] Yet, Israel should remain cautious and pursue a policy of wait and see because Iran's ambitions could go beyond its legitimate defense needs.[33] Most importantly, Israel should avoid falling into a pattern of escalation with Iran prompted by the previous rhetoric of the Labor Party. "We needed to tone down," said Shlomo Brom of the Jaffee Center for Strategic Studies and a member of the original Iran committee.[34]

Netanyahu listened carefully as the two sides fought it out. Gilad spoke with great confidence, knowing very well that no prime minister had ever dismissed the findings of the military's National Intelligence Assessment. And with the Israeli tendency to embrace doomsday scenarios and treat nuanced and slightly optimistic assessments with great suspicion, the odds were on his side. But Netanyahu's response left Gilad baffled. In an unprecedented move, the prime minister rejected the National Intelligence Assessment and adopted Arad's recommendation of reducing tensions with Iran.[35] Netanyahu's dismissal of his assessment was a major blow to Gilad, and to this day he manages to disguise his bitterness only by pointing out the many mistakes of his rivals. "One of the most important organizations in Israel, I don't want to mention their name because I am ashamed to mention them," he said dismissively, "said that in 2005, everyone would be happy because the regime in Iran would fall."[36] Even though the doomsday scenario Gilad predicted never came true, he insisted that the intensified enmity between Iran and Israel has proven him right. "It was a great intelligence achievement," he told me with unmasked content. To his credit, in 2001 Iran successfully tested its Shahab-3 missiles, which can reach Israel— only two years later than Gilad had predicted. But contrary to his assessment, Iran has not used the missiles to destroy Israel.

NETANYAHU ENDS THE TEHRAN TIRADES

Much to Gilad's frustration, Netanyahu focused on PLO leader Yasser Arafat and the Palestinian threat instead of on Iran, and he put a complete end to Israel's confrontational rhetoric against Tehran. It was a major policy shift that affected all levels of Israel's planning vis-à-vis Iran. "Until the Netanyahu government, there was a proliferation of Israeli statements trying to deter Iran, warning Iran, the long arm of the Israeli air force, etc. That was stopped, to his credit, by Netanyahu," said Ehud Yaari of Israel's Channel 2.[37] According to Dore Gold, who served as Netanyahu's UN ambassador, the new Israeli prime minister wanted to avoid the mistakes of his predecessor. "There was a sense that perhaps some of the rhetoric of the previous Peres government might have damaged certain relationships in the region. For example, by talking about the new Middle East and Israel having an economic role," he said.[38] Several of Netanyahu's advisers went so far as to argue that Israel and Iran shared mutual interests, beyond the disagreements between them.[39] Israeli media sympathetic to the Likud government's shift on Iran argued that the previous Labor government was to blame for the escalation with Iran, citing Israeli envoy Lubrani's efforts to convince the Clinton administration to finance a coup d'état. The publication of the Labor initiative had "caused huge damage to Israel," unnamed Israeli intelligence officials told Israel's Channel 2. "If in the past the United States was the great Satan and Israel the small Satan, then today the Iranians regard Israel as the Satan that sits inside the brain of the big Satan and activates it."[40] The Netanyahu government viewed these statements as counterproductive and sought to avoid such entanglement with the Iranians. "He [Netanyahu] didn't want to use rhetoric that would just antagonize them [the Iranians] for no reason," said Gold, who also served as foreign policy adviser to Netanyahu.[41]

But Netanyahu went beyond just lowering the rhetoric. He tried to reach an understanding with Iran through the help of prominent Iranian Jews, he stopped Israeli attacks on Iran within international organizations, he arranged for meetings between Iranian and Israeli representatives at European think tanks, and he encouraged Israeli parliamentarians to reach out to their Iranian counterparts at meetings of the Inter-Parliamentarian Union. As usual, the Iranians later denied having participated in meetings with the Israelis.[42]

At one point, Netanyahu even sought Kazakh and Russian mediation between Iran and Israel. In December 1996, Kazakhstan's oil minister, Nurlen Balgimbaev, who enjoyed excellent ties with Tehran, visited Israel for medical treatment and was approached about arranging a dialogue with Iran to discuss ways to reduce tensions between the two countries.[43] But there was little the Kazakhs could do to melt the ice between Iran and Israel. The Likud government also tried to alleviate Iranian and Arab fears that Israel was seeking a hegemonic role in the region or that the struggle against Islamic fundamentalism—initiated by Rabin and Peres—was a war on Islam itself. During a flight between Jerusalem and Cairo, Gold showed Netanyahu an article written on this topic by Fawaz Gerges, an Arab-American professor, and convinced the Likud leader to publicly denounce the idea that a civilizational clash was in the making.

A few weeks later, on July 10, 1996, Netanyahu made the rejection in his address to the U.S. Congress. "Nor, I must say, do we have a quarrel with Islam," he said. "We do not subscribe to the idea that Islam has replaced communism as the new rival of the West."[44] The statement was carefully designed to signal a departure from the Rabin-Peres emphasis on regional rather than internal threats to Israel. "We thought that we could get some mileage that a Likud prime minister would say that Islam is not the enemy," Gold explained.[45]

But Netanyahu's shift on Iran was motivated by more than just an attempt to delete Israel from Iran's radar. First of all, he recognized that it was terrorism against Israeli civilians that had sealed his election victory and turned the Israeli public against Labor. Once in power, Netanyahu feared that a continuation of the terror could defeat him just as it had defeated Peres.[46] By lowering Israel's rhetoric on Iran, Netanyahu sought to avoid any unnecessary provocation against Iran that he believed could lead to more terrorist attacks with unpredictable political consequences.

Secondly, at a strategic level, Netanyahu ideologically opposed the Oslo process and did not conceal his mistrust of the Palestinians. He believed that because peace with the Arabs remained unlikely, Israeli security was best achieved by forging alliances with the Middle East's non-Arab states— that is, a return to the doctrine of the periphery. "We have to forget the 'new Middle East,' there is no such thing," Netanyahu told aides, according to the Israeli daily *Maariv*.[47] Not only was Peres's vision of a New Middle East inherently flawed, the policy of demonizing Iran countered Israel's national interest in two critical ways. On the one hand, Israel was investing heavily in a partner—Arafat—whom the Likud believed was bound to betray Israel and seek its destruction. The Netanyahu government believed that Arafat ultimately would never conclude a peace treaty with Israel and was negotiating only to win time and strengthen his own position.[48] "For Peres, Arafat was a partner who had veered off the Oslo road because of Iran's support of Hamas. The problem is there [with Iran], not with Arafat," Gold explained. "We had a total mirror image. We said [that] Arafat is the problem."[49]

On the other hand, Israel was coupling its investment in the Palestinians with a policy that turned a key periphery state—Iran—against Israel. Peres's belligerent rhetoric reduced the chances of reviving the Iranian-Israeli entente. Because the Likud saw a durable agreement with Arafat as next to impossible, it believed that the Labor strategy would leave Israel a double loser—without peace and without a periphery to balance the Arabs. Israel's hard-line prime minister needed to keep the Iran option alive precisely because he didn't believe in a peace with the Palestinians. "The Likud tended to be more open to the idea [that] maybe there are residual elements in the revolutionary regime [in Iran] that see things geopolitically the same way as it was during the Shah's time," Gold explained.[50] So even as the Likud under Netanyahu was pressuring the United States, the EU, and Russia to prevent Iran from developing weapon programs that could put Israel within Tehran's reach, the Netanyahu government was also trying to revive its periphery alliance with Iran, viewing it as a preferable strategy to that of putting its trust in the Palestinian leadership.[51]

Thirdly, from a domestic political perspective, Netanyahu aimed to turn the Israeli public against the Oslo process and end the land-for-peace formula. But he couldn't direct Israel's anger toward Arafat and the Palestinians if Iran was seen as the source of the terror.[52] "Blaming the Iranians for Palestinian terrorism would be counterproductive to his message that terror was coming from the Palestinians," Weissman of AIPAC explained.[53] Just as the idea of an Iranian threat served Peres and Rabin's desire to convince the Israeli public to support reconciliation with the Arabs, that idea undermined Netanyahu's efforts to convince Israelis to oppose that very same reconciliation. Iran's role in the peace process wasn't a concern to Netanyahu, Gold explained. "It wasn't part of the discussion. Our concern was Arafat," he said.[54] To the Likud government, Rabin and Peres had played politics with Israel's security by targeting Iran and keeping silent about states such as Saudi Arabia, which donated far more money to Hamas than Iran did.[55]

Finally, but most importantly, Netanyahu shared Peres and Rabin's fear of the implications of a U.S.-Iran dialogue. But there was a new twist to it now. If Iran and the United States would resume relations *while Iranian-Israeli relations remained hostile,* then Israel would certainly be left out in the cold.[56] "The U.S. has many things to talk to Iran about: drugs, Iraq, weapons of mass destruction. Why would it talk to Iran about Israel?" Gilad asked rhetorically.[57] The initial signals sent to Iran when the Likud Party blamed Labor for the tensions with Iran were motivated by Washington's inability to get Europe to join its efforts to isolate Iran, a senior source in the prime minister's office told Israeli radio. The Likud government believed that the era of Dual Containment was over and feared that the United States would open relations with Iran. Israel had to reduce tensions with Iran to prepare itself for such a scenario. The lower the tensions were with Iran, the more the negative repercussions of improved U.S.-Iran relations could be minimized.[58] Just like Labor, Likud's strategy was to oppose U.S.-Iran relations as long as it could, but Likud wanted Israel to be able to swiftly reposition itself if a political breakthrough between Iran and the United States was in the making. Once a U.S.-Iran dialogue was inevitable, Israel would be in a better position to influence the talks by making itself a part of the process.

Netanyahu's efforts to open up to Iran did not mean that Israel would reduce the pressure on Iran in other areas. Israel continued to lobby the United States to pressure Russia not to cooperate with Iran in the nuclear field; pro-Israeli groups in Washington continued to lobby for economic sanctions; and Israel continued to seek Iran's international isolation.[59] Israel was also careful not to repeat the mistake of the Iran-Contra scandal; any Iranian warm-up to the West had to include a change in Israeli-Iranian relations. If Iran wanted to improve relations with the United States, there should be no other way to do it than through Israel.

Iran, for its part, lowered its profile and involvement against Oslo as soon the Israeli-Palestinian talks began to stall. As long as the peace process wasn't going anywhere, it didn't threaten Iran and there was no need for Tehran to act against it. The Iranians couldn't admit it publicly, but Netanyahu's election victory was privately welcomed in Tehran precisely because Likud was less eager to push for a new Middle East based on Iran's prolonged isolation.[60] Though suspicious, the clerical regime was at the same time curious to see what the Likud government's maneuvers could lead to. Tehran wasn't interested in resuming relations with Israel, but it welcomed opportunities to reduce tensions between the two.[61] "There were talks that the Netanyahu team wanted to patch up relations with Iran and that they opposed the thesis that an Iranian-Israeli enmity was inevitable," recalled Mohsen Mirdamadi, a member of the Iranian Parliament's foreign relations committee.[62]

The Iranians pushed Lebanon's Hezbollah to agree to a cease-fire with Israel in April 1996. (That month, Israel had conducted a sixteen-day military blitz against Hezbollah in Lebanon dubbed "Operation Grapes of Wrath." Though no one won the war, Israel failed to appreciably damage Hezbollah, which led to the cease-fire agreement. Iranian Foreign Minister Ali Akbar Velayati launched a nine-day intense diplomatic drive that resulted in a truce between Hezbollah and Israel, as well as the release of several hostages.[63]) The Iranians proposed several specific quids pro quo to Israel, including reducing support to Hezbollah in return for an end to Israeli pressure on Russia to halt its nuclear cooperation with Iran.[64] The Iranian deputy foreign minister also indicated that Tehran would be willing to assist in the search for the missing Israeli pilot Ron Arad, an Israeli Air Force weapon systems officer who was captured by the Lebanese Shi'ite militia Amal in 1986 and whom the Israelis believe ended up in Iran.[65] In a rare move, Israel publicly praised Iran's efforts in winning the release of the hostages and the remains of Israeli soldiers killed in Lebanon. "As a goodwill gesture I want to thank everyone who dealt in this humanitarian deed—in Lebanon, in Syria and in Iran . . . and I want to ask them to continue in their efforts," Israeli Defense Minister Yitzhak Mordechai told reporters.[66]

But as was the case many times before, Iran coveted good relations with Washington, not with Tel Aviv. Various Track-II and Track-I½ channels (informal diplomatic channels often involving academic scholars, retired civil and military officials, public figures, and social activists) established in 1996 convinced the Netanyahu government that Tehran wanted to have its cake and eat it too. It wanted to improve relations with the West, but it wasn't going to give up its anti-Israeli stance, because that lent Iran legitimacy in the Arab world. Its quids pro quo were all tactical maneuvers aimed at reducing American pressure on Iran and not on improving relations with Israel. In the end, Netanyahu's efforts amounted to nothing but a brief Israeli-Iranian spring thaw. For Iran, however, Likud's political agenda and opposition to Oslo were good enough. The Iranians preferred Likud over Labor for the same reason that Likud blamed the Palestinians and not Iran: An Israel that didn't pursue a peace based on Iran's isolation wouldn't need to turn Washington and the international community against Iran. "In Iran, the perception was that Likud wasn't serious about peace [with the Palestinians], so they did not need a scapegoat," an Iranian political strategist told me bluntly. "Labor, however, needed a scapegoat."[67]

17

khatami's détente

The American civilization is worthy of respect. When we appreciate the roots of this civilization, its significance becomes even more apparent.

—Iran President Mohammad Khatami, January 7, 1998

As we cheer today's game between American and Iranian athletes, I hope it can be another step toward ending the estrangement between our nations.

—President Bill Clinton (statement before World Cup soccer game between Iran and the United States), June 21, 1998

Iran had what some consider a second revolution on May 23, 1997. Defying Tehran's political and religious establishment, the Iranian people used what little room they had to send a clear signal to the ruling regime: Change must come! Turning out in massive numbers, they went to the polls and elected an unknown librarian, Seyyed Mohammad Khatami, as their next president. Khatami ran on a platform of rule of law, democracy, improved relations with the outside world, and an inclusive political system. Thanks to a record turnout of women and youth, Khatami won a landslide victory over his conservative opponent. The reformists, as his political allies soon were to be called, took former President Akbar Hashemi Rafsanjani's pragmatic streak to entirely new levels. Not only would efforts to moderate Iran's internal and external policies continue, they would significantly intensify in spite of tough resistance from conservative elements in the regime. Khatami's record on internal reform may be disputed, but few question the warm-up in relations with the West and the Arab world that his presidency brought.[1] But much like in the early 1990s, Iran's relationship with Israel was a different story.

Curiosity about Iran's unlikely new leader soon turned into infatuation—in the Arab world and beyond. The Arab-Iranian thaw culminated at the Organization of the Islamic Conference (OIC) in December 1997 in Tehran, where Iran's Arab neighbors participated with high-level delegations. Perhaps the most important guests were Crown Prince Abdullah of Saudi Arabia and PLO leader Yasser Arafat, who hadn't set foot on Iranian soil since 1980. Iran's new attitude toward its neighbors and the international community was evident from the outset. In his opening remarks Khatami reassured Iran's Arab neighbors of Tehran's peaceful intentions and its acceptance of the Arab regimes—the highest-level indication that the export of the Iranian revolution had come to an end.[2] The Saudi crown prince responded in kind: "With the immortal achievements credited to the Muslim people of Iran, and their invaluable contributions throughout our glorious Islamic history, it is no wonder that Teheran, the capital of the Islamic Republic of Iran, is hosting this important Islamic gathering; it is quite natural for the leadership of this Muslim country to be quite aware of its duties and responsibilities towards the Islamic Nation at this critical juncture in our common history."[3]

The recognition Iran had sought from the Arab states finally seemed to have arrived. In March 1996, as the Israeli-Palestinian peace process was stalling, then-President Rafsanjani had met with Arafat in Islamabad, Pakistan, to reduce tensions between Iran and the Arab camp.[4] Later that year, the Rafsanjani government toned down its rhetoric against the Palestinian leader. There were no more condemnations of Arafat's pursuit of a two-state solution, even though Tehran continued to voice skepticism about the peace process. Tehran's shift was partly a result of Arafat's clampdown on Islamic militants in the Palestinian territories. By strengthening his control over Gaza and the West Bank, the Palestinian leader had signaled that, as Egyptian Ambassador to the United States Nabil Fahmi put it, "You can play all you want on the Lebanese border, but if you are going to play inside Palestinian politics, you are going to get hurt." The Iranians got the message. Supporting Palestinian rejectionists would no longer come without a cost.[5] But more importantly, as Israel itself turned against the peace process and Arab-Israeli tensions rose, Iran had to soften its stance to capitalize on this golden opportunity to mend fences with the Arab governments.

The Arab League had recommended that all its members freeze the normalization of ties with Israel until the Netanyahu government returned to the Oslo process. The Iranians warmly welcomed the decision, and only weeks after Khatami's election Arafat indicated that the reformist winds in Iran had opened up new opportunities between the Palestinian National Authority and Iran.[6] Just as a sense of threat from Iran helped bring the Arabs closer to Israel, Arab frustration with Israel pushed them closer to Iran.[7] Tehran spared little time in showcasing that it didn't pose a threat to its Arab neighbors and that Israel's demonization of Iran served only to divert attention from what Tehran called Washington and Tel Aviv's own menacing policies.[8] Rather than Iran being a threat to moderate Arab states, it was now Israel's turn to once again be seen as an enemy to the Muslim states of the region. In a sharp indication of how swiftly the tables had turned in the Middle East, the Saudi and Iranian foreign ministers jointly condemned Israel. "There is an agreement that Israel's policies are obstructing security and stability in the Middle East," Saudi Foreign Minister Prince Saud al-Faisal told reporters in November 1997.[9]

Khatami's détente wasn't limited to the Arabs. EU-Iranian relations blossomed under Khatami and frustrated American and Israeli attempts to isolate Tehran. The most significant hurdle to improved EU-Iranian relations—Ayatollah Khomeini's 1989 fatwa (an Islamic legal pronouncement) against British author Salman Rushdie—was resolved in the fall of 1998 through negotiations between Iranian Foreign Minister Kamal Kharrazi and his British counterpart, Robin Cook. Iran publicly vowed not to implement Khomeini's fatwa, describing it as the late ayatollah's personal view and not the policy of the Iranian state. "The government of the Islamic Republic of Iran has no intention, nor is it going to take any action whatsoever to threaten the life of the author of *The Satanic Verses* or anybody associated with his work, nor will it assist or encourage anybody to do so," Kharrazi told Cook. The triumph of national interest over ideology couldn't have been clearer.[10]

Khatami's outreach also extended to the United States. Only four months after taking office, the new Iranian president granted an interview to Iranian-born CNN correspondent Christiane Amanpour, who left Iran right after the revolution. In carefully prepared remarks, Khatami tried to reach out directly to the American people and address the outstanding issues between Washington and Tehran, including terrorism: "We believe in the holy Quran that said: slaying of one innocent person is tantamount to the slaying of all humanity. How could such a religion, and those who claim to be its followers, get involved in the assassination of innocent individuals and the slaughter of innocent human beings? We categorically reject all these allegations. . . . Terrorism should be condemned in all its forms and manifestations; assassins must be condemned. Terrorism is useless anyway and we condemn it categorically."[11]

Khatami went on to express regret for the 1979 embassy takeover in Iran and distanced himself from the burning of the U.S. flag—a common scene at hard-line rallies in Iran. Both the flag burning and Iran's anti-American slogans must be viewed in the larger context of the "wall of mistrust" that existed between the United States and Iran, Khatami said. Even though he called for more respectful language, Khatami insisted that these slogans were not meant to insult the American people. Rather, the statements served to express the desire by Iranians "to terminate a mode of relationship between Iran and America."[12]

Washington was quick to respond. Martin Indyk, who by then was serving as U.S. ambassador to Israel, told reporters that Washington would welcome dialogue with Iran and that it recognized Iran's Islamic government. Months earlier, Indyk already had declared the Clinton administration's interest in talking with Iran. "The United States has made it clear repeatedly that we have nothing against an Islamic government in Iran," Indyk said. "We are ready for a dialogue with the government of Iran."[13] The Clinton administration soon became infatuated with Khatami and the idea of finally putting an end to the two-decade enmity between the two countries.[14] Both private and public signals were sent between the two capitals, indicating that a breakthrough might be in the offing.

Three of Washington's signals were particularly noteworthy. In a groundbreaking speech by Secretary of State Madeleine Albright, the United States issued an indirect apology for the CIA coup against Iran's democratically elected prime minister, Mohammed Mossadeq, in 1953 and proposed a road map for a U.S.-Iran rapprochement. Clinton issued the other signals himself. During a press conference he expressed understanding for Iranian resentment of the West. "I think it is important to recognize, however, that Iran, because of its enormous geopolitical importance over time, has been the subject of quite a lot of abuse from various Western countries."[15] And on the eve of the U.S.-Iran soccer game at the World Cup in France on June 21, 1998, Clinton took the opportunity to reciprocate Khatami's move and reach out directly to the soccer-crazy Iranians. Right before the start of the game, his prerecorded statement was aired worldwide: "As we cheer today's game between American and Iranian athletes, I hope it can be another step toward ending the estrangement between our nations. I am pleased that over the last year, President Khatami and I have both worked to encourage more people-to-people exchanges, and to help our citizens develop a better understanding of each other's rich civilizations."

But neither soccer diplomacy nor eased visa restrictions nor softer rhetoric managed to thaw relations between the two countries. Ironically, the economic sanctions and the heightened rhetoric that the Clinton White House had put in place during its first term turned out to be the most difficult stumbling block to a rapprochement. While Tehran and Washington's failure lay primarily in miscommunication, missed signals, and Iranian overconfidence, at every step Israel and the pro-Israeli lobby continued to put political obstacles in the path of Iran and the United States.[16] Clinton's outreach to Iran worried supporters of Israel in the United States, particularly the American Israel Public Affairs Committee (AIPAC), which had made containment of Iran a priority and which lobbied against dialogue with Iran.[17] To make its disapproval clear to Washington, the Israeli Foreign Ministry instructed its diplomats to boycott conferences in the United States addressed by Iranian officials.[18]

PERIPHERY PLUS

Washington and Europe's excitement over the reform movement in Iran never reached Israel. Netanyahu's numerous efforts to open up to Rafsanjani had borne little fruit even though Iran lowered its rhetoric and its profile in the Israeli-Palestinian conflict. By 1997, in spite of the Khatami victory, the Netanyahu government grew disenchanted with its Iran strategy, particularly because Iran's missile and nuclear program continued to progress. Though Israel recognized that these missiles were not operational, the Likud began to lose faith in a modus vivendi with the clergy in Iran.[19]

Instead, by early 1997 Netanyahu started to use the same language and rhetoric against Iran as his predecessors did. He reversed his previous decision and indicated that Iran was more dangerous than Iraq because it "has global ambitions. It has an ideology."[20] He told Jewish-American leaders that his government would "let the Russian government know in no uncertain terms" about Israel's opposition to Russia's alleged assistance to Iran's ballistic missile program.[21] He also accused Iran of trying to develop missiles that could reach the United States. "We believe Iran is intent on developing ballistic missiles, first to reach Israel, then to reach Europe, then to reach a range of 10,000 kilometers [6,000 miles]—meaning reaching the Eastern Seaboard of the United States," he said.[22] Even though the Iranian missile program was still embryonic, it posed a new type of a challenge for Israel. Unlike missiles from Syria—a country Israel could easily retaliate against—the new missile threat was located near the operational limits of the Israeli Air Force.[23]

Israel's alarmist rhetoric was only mildly affected by Khatami's election. Only days after the landslide victory of the reformists, Israeli Foreign Minister David Levy warned Iran that if it did not change its ways it could face an international coalition like the force that battled Iraq in 1991.[24] The Israeli focus on the alleged Iranian missile threat was initially met by skepticism in Washington. Given that Iran did not possess any long-range missiles at the time, and given Netanyahu's silence on Iran for more than nine months while he emphasized the Iraqi threat, the Israeli shift raised many eyebrows in the Clinton administration. The Americans had already grown frustrated with Netanyahu's unwillingness to move the peace process forward and feared that the missile threat was a diversionary tactic. "Some in the Clinton administration thought that his focus on the Iranian missile issue was a way of changing the channel from the problematic aspects of Oslo," recalled David Makovsky of the think tank Washington Institute for Near East Policy.[25]

The American suspicions were not unfounded—the Israeli right had traditionally sought to turn Washington's focus away from the Palestinian conflict. "For everybody it was convenient that Iran becomes a major issue for the West because in that way we sort of submerged into a wider issue and relegated to a secondary status our problem with the Palestinians," explained Shlomo Ben-Ami, Prime Minister Ehud Barak's Moroccan-born foreign minister.[26] But Netanyahu did not budge, warning the United States that the "entire global economy would be held hostage by Iran" if Tehran got its hands on ballistic missiles, and that Iran was scheming to dominate the region and become a world power.[27] "This sounds fantastic but Iran wants to be a world power with a world ideology of fundamentalist domination, seeing the West as its great enemy," he told reporters in November 1997.[28]

Netanyahu's failed outreach to the Rafsanjani government led Israel to conclude that Iran's hostility would remain intact regardless of the nature of its regime, turning Iranian capabilities into a threat in and of themselves. Since Iran continued to question Israel's right to exist, Israel felt it had no choice but to be cautious about Iran's power, even if Iran's actions did not match its rhetoric. Tel Aviv reckoned that it had no other option but to affect Iran's ability to act on its harsh language against Israel by frustrating Iran's missile and nuclear program. "Moderation in Iran does not mean that it will stop its nuclear program," explained Ranaan Gissin, former Prime Minister Ariel Sharon's spokesperson. "Even if the regime changes, this small group [of fundamentalists] will still have an impact on Iran. Also, I don't see any country really stopping its nuclear program unless forced to. . . . By their own volition, they will never stop, even if the regime changes."[29]

This left Israel with a major dilemma. The failed outreach to Iran, and Likud's unwillingness to pursue peace with the Palestinians, put Israel in a situation in which both the inner circle and the periphery—which because of technological progress was inching ever closer to Israel—had become threats. Even though the failure to win Iran back finally silenced the periphery veterans whose faith in an Iranian-Israeli entente had been unshaken by the 1979 revolution, periphery thinking remained strong in the Israeli psyche and manifested itself through a new interpretation.[30]

Now that Israel was convinced that it could make peace with neither the Arab vicinity nor the Persian periphery, the logic of the doctrine of the periphery dictated that Israel needed to balance both the Arabs and Iran by allying with friendly states *beyond* the periphery. "Look, there is the old periphery and the new periphery," Knesset member Ephraim Sneh, a major proponent of this view, told me. "The old periphery was aimed to outflank the Arab enemies of Israel. That was the case of Iran at that time. Now we should have a new periphery to outflank Iran." In 1996 Sneh wrote in his book *Israel After the Year 2000* about the need to weaken Iran by investing in what he called "the new periphery."[31] In this "periphery-plus" strategy, the new periphery consisted of both old and new periphery states. Turkey was the most important "old periphery" state, which like Iran was Muslim but non-Arab. India was the most important new periphery state—it was the new Iran. It was a majority non-Muslim, non-Arab country on the outer periphery of the Middle East that essentially replaced Iran in the Likud's strategic outlook. Other new periphery states were found in the Caucasus and in the central Asian republics.[32]

The emerging Israeli-Turkish-Indian connection was hardly unexpected. It marked the logical evolution of a pair of strategic relationships that had charted similar trajectories for the better part of the 1990s.[33] In fact, in the view of many Israeli strategists, it remained a mystery to the Jewish State why it took India so long before it recognized the common Indian-Israeli trajectory. "There was always a thinking," noted Yossi Alpher, an adviser to Barak and a former Mossad official, "that 'what's wrong with the Indians?' Why are they trying to be leaders of the Non-Aligned Movement that is full of hostile Muslims when we are their natural allies?"[34] Though strategic ties to India and Turkey served many purposes, weakening Iran was the most critical one for the Jewish State.[35]

The greatest danger Iran posed to Israel after 1996 was its ability to emerge as a regional power that could challenge Tel Aviv's military and nuclear monopoly and limit the Jewish State's military and political maneuverability.[36] It wasn't necessarily an Iranian nuclear attack per se that topped Israel's list of concerns. Not only did Iran lack the capability, but even when its missile program became operational Iran wouldn't be able to destroy Israel without causing its own destruction because of Israel's second-strike capability. Through its German-made nuclear submarines, Israel would be able to retaliate against a nuclear attack from Iran, giving Israel a formidable deterrence. "Whatever measure they have, they can't destroy Israel's capability to respond," Gissin said.[37] But a rising Iran could at a minimum challenge the perception of Israel's military superiority and the maneuverability Israel enjoyed by virtue of this perception. "It would endanger the image that we are a superpower that can't be defeated," Gen. Amos Gilad argued.[38]

This would empower organizations such as Hezbollah, which would feel that they could act under the protection of an Iranian umbrella.[39] Israel's retaliation options would be significantly limited if escalation against Hezbollah could lead to a response from a self-assured Iran. "If others have [a nuclear bomb], they will deter Israel, chain our hands, and prevent any kind of retaliation. This is very important," Gilad noted.[40] Under those circumstances, Israel could be forced to accept territorial concessions that it otherwise could avoid. "It will give [the Arabs] the power of nuclear blackmail. I don't want the Israeli-Palestinian negotiations to be held under the shadow of the Iranian nuclear bomb," Sneh explained.[41]

These fears did not mean, however, that Israel would refuse to reach out to Iran occasionally even though it held little hope for a breakthrough with the Khatami government. In October 1997, Foreign Minister Ariel Sharon sought to repay an old Israeli financial debt to Iran dating from the Pahlavi era via Russia and through the help of the Israel-Arab Friendship Association, an organization that sought to improve Israeli-Iranian relations by accepting Iran's role and aspirations in the region. "If Israel gives Iran the standing of regional power, there could be an integration of interests," Yehoshua Meiri, the head of the association, told the *Jerusalem Post*.[42] Sharon calculated that settling the debt would help ease tensions with Iran and open up a channel to the Khatami government. He was supported by elements in the Israeli intelligence community who argued that talks with Iran were both necessary and possible.

The Defense Ministry, however, opposed the Sharon deal and argued that increasing Iran's cash flow would be tantamount to directly helping Israel's biggest enemy acquire long-range missiles and a nuclear capability. Pointing to the contradiction in opening up to Iran while working toward Tehran's international isolation, Ministry of Defense officials argued that "it would be a serious mistake to give the money back to the Iranians. . . . It is inconceivable that on the one hand Netanyahu should declare that Iran is our number one enemy and that his men should try to convince various countries to join the U.S. embargo, while on the other hand a senior minister should initiate a move to return the money. We are simply making fools of ourselves."[43] After all, Israel had made itself a major stumbling block preventing a U.S.-Iran rapprochement.[44]

The contradiction between Israel's own policies on Iran and what it requested of Washington had already caused some irritation in America. For example, the American pistachio industry was outraged that the Israeli market was flooded by Iranian pistachios at the expense of pistachios produced in California.[45] Though the volume of this trade was negligible—$185 million in 1997 and $360 million in 1998—its symbolic value was significant because Israel had successfully pressured Washington to cut all its trade with Iran.[46] It was later revealed that Israeli companies had traded not only nuts and other commercial goods with Iran, but also chemicals and military equipment.[47] The Iranians, in turn, did not let ideology stand in their way. "A thief has stolen our money, why would we care about their ideology?" Deputy Foreign Minister Hadi Nejad-Hosseinian argued.[48]

Preliminary negotiations regarding the debt—which was estimated at close to $2 billion, including interest—started, but were later stopped per Netanyahu's instructions.[49] (The case later went to arbitration at the International Court of Justice in The Hague and remains unresolved.) Israel's failure to mend fences with Rafsanjani, its conviction that Iran would be hostile to Israel no matter what, its military doctrine that dictated that Iranian capabilities must be stymied, and its fear that the Clinton administration might sacrifice Israeli interests to cut a deal with Khatami prompted Israel to dismiss Iran's changing attitude toward Israel under Khatami.

IRAN'S NEW ISRAEL POLICY

Khatami's pragmatism wasn't limited to the United States, the EU, and the Arabs. The rise of the reformists in Iran intensified Tehran's efforts to reintegrate itself into the entire international community.[50] This affected Iran's stance on Israel as well. Iran's policy and, most importantly, its posture on Israel significantly modified during Khatami's tenure.[51] As its investment in improved relations with the Arab governments started to pay off, Iran's need for the Arab street diminished, as did its need to antagonize Israel and oppose the peace process.[52] The stronger Iran's relations with the Arabs and the EU grew, the more insulated Iran became from Israeli-Palestinian developments.

After the success of the OIC meeting in Tehran in 1997, the Khatami government believed that its relations with the region had grown sufficiently strong for Iran to withstand the consequences of an Israeli-Palestinian agreement. In short, the peace process was no longer a threat to Iran's standing in the region.[53] The first step was to tone down Iran's rhetoric. Even though many of the reformists were more ardent opponents of the Israeli state than were their conservative counterparts, and even though they recognized that Iran's hard-line stance had been necessary to counter the dangers of the Oslo process in 1994–1995, they still believed that Iran's vocal and visible opposition to the peace process had damaged the country's image and complicated the decontainment process.[54]

Israel and America's efforts to create a new order for the region at Iran's expense could be countered without supporting Palestinian terrorist groups and pushing Iran into a deeper conflict with the West, the reformists maintained. Khatami's outspoken interior minister, Abdullah Nuri, went so far as to break an old taboo in the Islamic Republic by openly discussing alternative solutions to the Palestinian issue to that proposed by Khomeini himself: "As the Arab countries do not opt for war, with what political, economic or military power do we want to fight Israel? What do Iranians gain from such an attitude, except being blamed for supporting terrorism? Today, the Palestinians have a government, that we recognize, and they are in charge of deciding on behalf of their own people. The current situation is not ideal, but we must come to terms with realities and avoid being a bowl warmer than the soup."[55]

The use of terror as a political tool was too costly and immoral, the reformists argued, pointing out that Iran itself was a key victim of terror.[56] Rafsanjani's terror weapon had also enabled Israel to further undermine U.S.-Iran relations, they said.[57] During his interview with CNN, Khatami condemned terrorism against Israelis, though he cautioned that support for liberation movements was a different matter. "Supporting peoples who fight for the liberation of their land is not, in my opinion, supporting terrorism. It is, in fact, supporting those who are engaged in combating state terrorism," Khatami told CNN.[58] Then, in a remarkable shift back to the early policy of Rafsanjani, Khatami did not rule out the possibility of an Israeli state in historical Palestine.[59] Khatami's statement wasn't for Western audiences only—a month earlier, the soft-spoken Iranian president had argued in his address to the OIC that a two-state solution was acceptable.

With Iran feeling that it once again had the upper hand in the Israeli-Iranian rivalry—the peace process was failing while Iran was gaining recognition in the region—Tehran wanted to consolidate its gain by easing tensions with Israel and compelling it not to undermine a U.S.-Iran rapprochement.[60] "There was an interest in demonstrating [to Israel] that we would be happy with a just resolution to the conflict," a Khatami adviser recalled.[61] At quasi-official talks with Americans hosted by a Scandinavian think tank, Iranian Foreign Ministry officials and academics revealed that "the debate on Israel has exploded" and that Iran had no choice but to go along with a two-state solution. "It would be very difficult for Iran to do anything but accept it," they explained, hinting to their American interlocutors that the Iranian government had come to terms with the idea that Israel was a fact in the region.[62]

In that debate, the arguments of Nuri had played a decisive role. "What kind of logic is it," he asked, "that everyone has the right to speak and decide on Palestine and on [the faith of] the Palestinians, but the Palestinians themselves do not have such a right? Why should we claim the right to impose our views on them?" he asked. Many of the reformists in Khatami's camp were ardent opponents of the Jewish State, yet they felt that the heavy burden of the Palestinian issue needed to be lifted from Iran's shoulders.[63] "We didn't want to be more Catholic than the pope," Iran former Deputy Foreign Minister Abbas Maleki explained. "When the Palestinians want to negotiate, why should Iran insist on non-negotiations?"[64] The debate revealed that the Palestinian issue was increasingly seen as a nationalist cause and not a religious matter, as Khomeini wanted to see it.

Though Khatami never publicly repeated these arguments, Iran slowly shifted back to its pre-Oslo position on the Palestinian issue. It would accept but not necessarily actively support whatever solution the Palestinian people agreed to, while maintaining the right to criticize any deal it deemed unjust (but without taking any concrete actions against it).[65] "We would not interfere in the peace process, but we would express our opinions. We have a right to express views, but that is not the same as interference in the peace process. We would accept the Palestinian position, without supporting it," explained Mohammad Reza Dehshiri of the Iranian Foreign Ministry.[66] Sticking to the tradition of Iranian foreign policy, Tehran remained highly critical of Israel, and the Khatami government continued to refuse recognition of the Jewish State while vocally supporting the Palestinian cause. But instead of calling for Israel's destruction, Khatami tried to get the international community to focus on the "threat" of Israel's undeclared nuclear weapons arsenal and urged human rights organizations to condemn Israeli actions in the occupied territories.[67] Privately, Iranian officials told European and American officials that nothing in the revolution made a two-state solution unacceptable to Iran.[68] Despite Iran's previous rhetoric, they said, Tehran did not seek the destruction of Israel and pointed to the fact that Khatami himself had never questioned Israel's right to exist.

This policy shift was repeatedly mentioned by Iranian officials—and at times directly to Israeli officials. According to the Israeli newspaper *Yediot Aharonot*, Iran's ambassador to the United Nations Educational, Scientific and Cultural Organization (UNESCO), Ahmad Jalali, met secretly with Israeli Chief Rabbi Eliahu Bakshi-Doron at a conference in Morocco in February 1998. Bakshi-Doron, who emigrated to Israel from Iran, was reportedly told by Jalali that "Iran is not Iraq and would never attack Israel."[69] Earlier that month *Yediot Aharonot* reported that Iran Vice President Massumeh Ebtekar had told the newspaper at the World Economic Forum in Davos, Switzerland, that Iran was reconsidering its Israel policy and that it would welcome dialogue with Israel on nonpolitical matters.[70] Ebtekar later denied having been interviewed by the Israeli newspaper and reiterated that Iran wouldn't recognize the Jewish State.[71] (As an eighteen-year-old student in 1979, Ebtekar acted as a translator during the U.S. embassy takeover in Iran and was nicknamed "Sister Mary" by the U.S. media. Like many of her fellow hostage-takers, she had turned reformist in the mid-1990s.)

A year later, the Israeli daily *Haaretz* reported that Iran had, via the British government, approached the Israelis with a request to negotiate a missile treaty. The unconfirmed report said that the Iranians reassured the Israelis that its arms buildup wasn't directed against Israel but against other countries perceived as regional threats, primarily Iraq.[72] Though the Iranians insisted that they never spoke to Israeli officials or newspapers, they often took the opportunity to clarify Iran's position on Israel in public interviews. Addressing Hooshang Amirahmadi of the American Iranian Council, Iran's UN Ambassador Javad Zarif spelled out Iran's new position:

Amirahmadi: The general impression is that Iran's official policy is working toward the destruction of Israel.

Zarif: Iran does not officially recognize Israel. That is not tantamount to taking any action against it. Iran has made it very clear that it does not seek hostility or conflict with anyone. Iran has made that very clear in the most general terms and in the most categorical terms that we do not seek hostility. At the same time, we have not been shy in stating our position that we do not recognize Israel. That is a policy position that we have adopted. We believe that that position is not incompatible with accepting whatever solution the Palestinians come up with, that is, whatever they decide will be their decision. If it will bring stability and security to the region, then everybody would welcome it.

Amirahmadi: Two nations, two states. Is that an acceptable solution?

Zarif: If it is acceptable to the Palestinian people, we have nothing against it.

Amirahmadi: So you do see some territories called Israel as legitimate?

Zarif: The problem is the continued occupation of Palestinian territory. Once that problem is resolved, and how it is resolved depends on the Palestinians and Israelis, then it's a different story. . . . But that is not up to us to decide. It's up to the people who live in that territory to decide. We can only present our analysis and even venture to provide suggestions of what can be positive, what can be conducive to security and peace.

Amirahmadi: And your policy is not to destroy the Israeli society?

Zarif: Our policy is not to destroy any society.[73]

Lost in the translation was the most critical aspect of Khatami's Israel policy. By recognizing a two-state solution, Iran would grant Israel indirect recognition. Few in the West paid attention to this subtle but crucial shift. This frustrated the Khatami government immensely, which came to view the oversight as yet another indication of Washington's inflexibility toward Iran.[74]

BARAK SEES ONLY LEBANON

Despite receiving "strategic signals from Khatami that a policy review was in place," periphery-plus thinking prompted the Netanyahu government to focus on Iran as a potential threat.[75] The same neglect of Iranian signals occurred under Netanyahu's successor, the Labor Party's Ehud Barak. The most decorated soldier in Israel Defense Forces (IDF) history, Barak had as chief of staff of the IDF criticized Yitzhak Rabin and Shimon Peres's line on Iran as counterproductive.[76] The real threat was Iraq, he had said back in 1993, and he carried that view with him to some extent when he defeated Netanyahu at the polls on May 17, 1999.

As power shifted back to the Labor Party, ending the Lebanon occupation and addressing the Palestinian and Syrian issues became Israel's top priority once again, while Iran was downgraded to a lesser problem. "Iran wasn't really on our agenda," Ben-Ami told me. "In those two years, I think the agenda zeroed in on these two particular questions, the Palestinians and Syrians. I don't remember one cabinet meeting—the reduced cabinet meeting, the so-called defense–foreign policy cabinet—where Iran was an issue."[77] Still, Iran slowly crept back into Israel's radar for three key reasons.

Iran's relations with Hezbollah had suffered a setback after Iran's failed efforts to reach out to the United States in the early 1990s. Rafsanjani's moderate outlook and eagerness to broker a deal with Washington irritated many hard-line elements in the Lebanese organization. A sense of abandonment spread in the Bekaa Valley as Iran lessened its involvement with Hezbollah.[78] But the Madrid conference and the Oslo process reversed Hezbollah's fortunes. Lacking solid relations with the Palestinian Sunni organizations, Iran needed Hezbollah to counter Israel's spreading influence. Through Lebanon's Shia fighters, Iran could both gather intelligence as well as inflict a devastating cost on the Jewish State for its pressure on the United States to act against Iran. And most importantly, with Hezbollah Iran did not need advanced ballistic missiles to reach Israel. "Hezbollah was the long arm of Iran," Ben-Ami explained, and the militants had effectively turned Iran into a border state. "Their essential policy was disrupting the peace process, and the best way to disrupting the peace process was harassing the Israeli forces in Lebanon."

Many Israelis saw Iran's involvement with Hezbollah as far more ominous than its contacts with Palestinian rejectionists. Without the Iranian-Hezbollah link, Israeli-Iranian relations could take a turn for the better, the argument went. "The sticking point is not the Palestinians, or the regime, but Hezbollah," said Gen. Amnon Lipkin-Shahak, who succeeded Ehud Barak as the fifteenth Chief of the General Staff in 1995.[79] Not only did Iran arm Hezbollah with thousands of rockets and missiles that could hit most of northern Israel, Iran also directed the Lebanese organization to prepare an infrastructure to carry out acts of terrorism inside Israel, argued Ami Ayalon, the director of the Israeli secret service Shin Bet.[80] As the cost and un-popularity of the occupation of southern Lebanon skyrocketed, Israel increasingly felt that Lebanon had turned into a trap. Rather than providing Israel with security, the occupation offered Iran an opportunity to check-mate Israel. "We felt that we were being taken hostage," Ben-Ami recalled.[81]

Second, the Israeli invasion of Lebanon had given Iran an opportunity to affect the Israeli-Palestinian conflict indirectly through its influence in Lebanon. Iran's ties to Hezbollah made it a more potent spoiler, a fact the Barak government couldn't afford to neglect as it prepared to relaunch the peace process. Israel was already noticing Iran's interest in using Hezbollah to penetrate the Palestinian areas, and the Barak government was concerned that Iran would intensify its anti-Israeli policies once the peace process was back on track. "Iran was an enemy of the peace process," Ben-Ami noted. "It wasn't interested in a peace agreement between Israel and the Arab world, probably because this would have isolated Iran even further."[82]

Finally, like so many times before, the Clinton administration's interest in Khatami fueled concerns that Washington would cut a deal with Tehran and leave Israel stranded.[83] Even though such a scenario was unlikely, the Israeli government wasn't willing to take the risk. "When you start negotiations, you know when they begin [but] you don't always know where they will end," former head of the Mossad Efraim Halevi told me. "There is a fear that the United States might make concessions that Israel wouldn't like it to make."[84] Clearly, talks with Iran would not occur without America paying a price, without making some sort of compromise to win concessions from the Iranians. More than anything, Israel feared that Washington would accept the legitimacy of the Iranian regime and its unique position in the region, which would come at Israel's expense. Such a deal would mean that the Iranians "could have a relative freedom of action, that America would take them off the list of countries that support terrorism [and] . . . that they could have a regional role."[85] Iran would end up changing very little of its regional policies because it valued relations only with Washington, not with Israel. As long as Israel was excluded from the deal, there would be insufficient pressure to address Israel's concerns with Iran, that is, Iran's support for Hezbollah and Palestinian rejectionist groups, its missile program, and its alleged nuclear weapons program. Or, even worse, the Iranians sought talks only to reduce the American pressure, the Israelis feared. "It was all nice smiles," said Dan Meridor of the Netanyahu government. "They wanted to talk just to run away from the American pressure. . . . It was a trick."[86]

Consequently, so long as prospects for U.S.-Iranian relations looked dim, Israel was better off isolating Iran than accommodating it. The status quo, with a hostile Iran that was unable to pose a real threat to the Jewish State, was preferred to a situation in which a U.S.-Iranian understanding would leave Israel facing Iran alone while Tehran would use its new-won friendship with Washington to develop its military capabilities unchecked. "It was very well understood that they will not give up their nuclear research program just because of the blue eyes of President Clinton," Ben-Ami commented. "They would ask for compensation, and the compensation might have been something that wasn't very palatable to Israel." Moreover, even if Iran recognized a two-state solution, Tehran could still go back to a more ideological stance against Israel once it attained a position of strength. Just as Israel had always insisted on direct recognition by Arab states as a quid pro quo for successful negotiations, so did it insist on direct recognition from Iran to ensure that Iran's foreign policy wouldn't re-radicalize.

But with the Clinton administration signaling a growing eagerness to talk to Iran, Israel was getting nervous. Some in Israel's foreign policy circles argued that continued opposition to a development that seemed inevitable would only further weaken Israel's standing. A new reality had emerged that Israel couldn't ignore. "Until now, Israel rejected every possible contact between the United States and Iran," said David Menashri, Israel's most prominent expert on Iran and a supporter of Israeli-Iranian contacts while serving on the Israeli Iran committee. Now, he said, "I am not sure that we can oppose the process."[87]

After the Iranian parliamentary elections in February 2000, when the reformists claimed a majority in the Iranian Majlis (legislative body), Israel's Justice Minister Yossi Beilin, a key architect of the Oslo process, argued with tacit support from the Israeli Foreign Ministry that Israel should reassess its relations with Iran.[88] "The Iran of President Khatami and Iran after the elections is a country with far more nuances and far more complexity than we have become accustomed to see," Beilin wrote in *Haaretz*. "We should examine our attitude toward Iran."[89] But the Barak government's determination to resolve the Israeli-Palestinian issue once and for all made it difficult for Israel to give Iran issue the attention it required. At no point did Barak put the idea of encouraging a U.S.-Iran dialogue on the cabinet's agenda. In retrospect, Foreign Minister Ben-Ami believed that this was a mistake. Pushing for a U.S.-Iran dialogue "would have been a good thing to do" to serve Israel's interest because, as the Israeli prime minister said himself, the Iranians will never make peace with the little Satan before having first made up with the great Satan.[90]

But instead of pushing for a U.S.-Iran dialogue, soon after he took office in 1999 Barak altered the status of Iran from enemy to threat as preparation for the withdrawal of Israeli troops from southern Lebanon in May 2000. Rejecting the idea of Iran as an enemy signaled that Israel didn't view Iran as an inevitable and eternal threat. "The current Israeli position holds that Israel does not have a conflict with the Iranian people, the state of Iran or with Islam," Israeli diplomats declared. The shift had been worked out by the Iran committee, which had been making calls for a conciliatory policy ever since the Rabin government.[91]

The decision was triggered by the Clinton administration's "infatuation" with the idea that Khatami would become an Iranian version of Mikhail Gorbachev, the leader of the Soviet Union until its collapse in 1991. The Israelis did not want to be locked out of a potential dialogue, and at the same time they did not want to seem to beat the war drum when the United States was pursuing dialogue.[92] To sweeten the signal further, Israel "unofficially" condemned a terrorist attack against a close adviser to Khatami in the hope that it would help strengthen moderate forces in Iran.[93] But Barak was never serious about reaching out to Iran. After all, Iran was still developing the Shahab-III missile, which Israel argued was a clear indication of Iranian nuclear weapons ambitions.[94] Instead, David Levy, who served as foreign minister to both Netanyahu and Barak, later revealed that Israel had turned down efforts from Iran to open secret-channel talks. "After cautious reviewing and weighing the implications of these talks," the Barak government determined that "things were not ripe" and rejected the Iranian overtures.[95] (As usual, the Iranians denied ever having made such overtures, accusing Israel of fabricating these stories to undermine Iran's status in the Islamic world.)[96]

On April 17, 2000, Barak did what few Israeli prime ministers before him had dared to do—he began a withdrawal from occupied Arab lands in southern Lebanon, calculating that the cost of holding on to the territory was greater than the perception that Israel had been defeated. The withdrawal took a little more than a month to complete and was widely supported by the Israeli public. (Lebanon and Syria insist that Israel still occupies a strip of Lebanese land called the Shebaa Farms. Israel, with support from the UN, claims that the Shebaa Farms is Syrian land, not Lebanese.) Barak chose to complete the withdrawal before final-status negotiations with the Palestinians resumed so that Iran and Hezbollah wouldn't be able to undermine the peace talks, and to minimize Iran's ability to reduce Israel's maneuverability. "By disengaging from there under UN auspices, we left them [the Iranians] with no platform to pursue that particular policy," Ben-Ami noted.[97]

Officially, the Iranians declared victory and pointed to the withdrawal as evidence of the usefulness of violent resistance against Israel. Supreme leader Ayatollah Ali Khamenei said on May 25 that "this victory revealed that the solution to the bullying and atrocities of the usurper Zionists is only in the logic of resistance, Jihad and devotion."[98] A week later, he added that the events in Lebanon "could recur, and occur in Palestine itself. . . . [I]t is possible that in several years['] time sections of occupied Palestine, and ultimately the entire occupied Palestine, will be returned to the Palestinian people."[99] But privately, the Iranians knew that the victory had a flip side. Iran's influence over Israel was based on the assistance it gave to Hezbollah.

The Lebanese organization's raison d'être, in turn, was the struggle against Israel's occupation. The occupation also gave a rationale for Iran's strategic ties in the Levant. Without Israel's occupation, much of this could fall apart. If Hezbollah failed to transform itself successfully from a guerrilla resistance into a political movement, Iran could lose its influence in Lebanon, which in turn could weaken the Iranian-Syrian axis. The withdrawal also deprived Syria of one of its main bargaining chips against Israel, fuelling speculation that Damascus might provoke a conflict with Israel. Khatami felt that an Israeli reentry into Lebanon could pose a greater danger to Hezbollah's future and urged Syria to show restraint. He told Syria's president Hafez al-Assad that after the "historic victory over the Zionists," Hezbollah must keep a "humble and low profile" in order not to damage the "high moral standing" it had gained.[100]

CAMP DAVID II AND THE AL-AQSA INTIFADA

Immediately after the withdrawal from Lebanon, Barak turned his focus to the Palestinians, aiming to resolve the conflict once and for all. The decorated Israeli soldier believed that the Israeli public would be most prone to accept concessions to the Palestinians if the peace deal was conclusive—all outstanding issues had to be resolved and a complete end to the conflict had to be agreed upon. With great enthusiasm, but little preparation, the White House hosted the Palestinians and the Israelis at Camp David on July 11 with the hope of reaching a final solution to the conflict. President Clinton had his own sense of urgency—his presidency was coming to its end and brokering a final settlement would seal his legacy.

Though Israel accused Iran of beefing up its support for Palestinian re-jectionist groups in order to sabotage the talks, Iran kept a relatively low profile during Camp David. As usual, it criticized the talks and questioned Washington's claims of impartiality, but there was a sea change in Iran's ap-proach compared with its behavior back in 1994–1995.[101] "I don't recall that there was much [Iranian activity] at all," Halevi said.[102] Two forces pushed Iran to lower its profile. First, Iran had significantly insulated itself from Israeli-Palestinian developments by improving relations with its im-mediate neighbors and with Europe. Iran did not consider the Camp David II talks much of a strategic threat to its standing, making active Iranian op-position to the deal unnecessary. Iran's reaction to the al-Aqsa Intifada fur-ther demonstrated that Iran's approach to the Israel-Palestine conflict was motivated more by strategic considerations than by ideology. If ideology or the plight of the Palestinians drove Iran's Israel policy, Tehran's reaction to the suppression of the Intifada would likely have been much harsher.

Second, Israel's withdrawal from Lebanon had limited Iran's ability to undermine the talks. Iran needed time to recover from the withdrawal and find new channels to reach the Palestinian rejectionists. "I think they were really taken aback by the withdrawal from Lebanon, and they needed to re-deploy their efforts to make them more efficient," Ben-Ami said. "Once we left Lebanon, they went into a situation that they didn't know before. For the first time, they don't have an instrument to disrupt negotiations be-tween Israel and the Palestinians." According to Ben-Ami, had Israel not withdrawn from Lebanon, Iran might have used Hezbollah to create havoc in the region. Depriving Iran of that card to play—in addition to satisfying a strong desire for withdrawal among the Israeli electorate—was one of the main reasons for withdrawing from Lebanon.[103]

After two weeks of intense negotiations, the Camp David talks ended with no agreement in sight. Both Barak and Clinton were now faced with a legacy of failure rather than one of triumph. To divert attention from their own failures, they needed to find a culprit.[104] The blame game began im-mediately after the breakdown of the talks; because Iran had kept a rela-tively low profile, both Israel and the United States instead pinned full re-sponsibility for the failure on Yasser Arafat and the PLO, even though all the parties had agreed beforehand that no side would be blamed if the talks failed. Washington feared that the breakdown could cost Barak his prime ministership and bring back into power the anti-Oslo Likud Party. These fears were heightened by the Al-Aqsa Intifada, which erupted two months after the Camp David fiasco.[105]

On September 28, the Israeli opposition leader Ariel Sharon visited the Temple Mount in the Old City of Jerusalem. Sharon's visit had been officially approved by the Barak government in advance, in spite of warnings from peace activists and some officials that it could lead to riots. His visit was condemned by the Palestinians as a provocation and an incursion, and, sure enough, it sparked a new Intifada. The following day, after Friday prayers, riots broke out in Jerusalem, during which several Palestinians were shot dead. Though few blamed Iran, Tehran felt vindicated by Washington and Tel Aviv's failure. "Iran couldn't have been happier," said Yoram Schweitzer, an Israeli intelligence expert at the Jaffee Center for Strategic Studies.[106] The considerable souring of relations between Israel and the surrounding Arab states, particularly the decisions of Egypt and Jordan to recall their ambassadors, was also welcomed by Iran.[107]

As in the past, Tehran sought to capitalize on the tensions between Israel and the Arabs by calling for the Muslim world to unite against Israel, calling the Jewish State "that malignant tumor, that evil tree," and depicting it as a "threat to all the Muslim world, even to those governments who think that their connection with the usurper Zionist government is in their interests."[108] But compared with the mid-1990s, Iran's rhetorical attacks on Israel were less frequent and, with a few noticeable exceptions, less geared toward Arab audiences. The Arab governments had been won—the Intifada and the election victory of Ariel Sharon in early 2001 boosted Iran's reconciliation with the Arab states, including those that had signed peace treaties with Israel.[109] Openings even occurred with Arafat's Fatah movement, bringing Iran closer to secular Palestinian groups as well.[110] Now, Tehran sought to muster international public opinion against Israel by, for instance, calling for a "war crimes tribunal to handle Israeli 'crimes' in the occupied territories," and for the UN Security Council to send international observers to prevent an escalation of the violence.[111]

But while Israel accused Iran of funding Palestinian terror, the Palestinians themselves complained about empty Iranian promises.[112] Clearly, Iran's rhetoric still conveyed a sense of Iranian obligation toward the Palestinians. Iran's supreme leader told the head of Hamas that "the holy war for Palestine is for the honor of Islam and Muslims, and we will continue our firm support for the Palestinian people despite all the political and economic pressure, and that the issue of Jerusalem was "not a Palestinian problem, but one for all Moslems."[113] But it was easier for Iran to offer rhetorical rather than practical support. The Iranian slogans were rarely followed up with concrete actions, even after the outbreak of the second Intifada. While the Iranians took the lead in making grandiose speeches about the Palestinian cause, they seldom tried to live up to the standards they set in their statements. European diplomats in contact with representatives of Islamic Jihad and Hamas who visited Iran after the Intifada broke out reported that both groups were utterly disappointed with their Iranian hosts. Tehran provided them with neither money nor weapons. A joke in the streets of Tehran reflected Iran's pretense: "Why aren't there any stones left to stone the adulteress? Per the order of the Supreme Leader, all the stones have been shipped to Palestine as Iran's contribution to the Intifada."[114]

18

betrayal in afghanistan

> States like these [Iran, Iraq, and North Korea], and their
> terrorist allies, constitute an axis of evil.
>
> —President George W. Bush (State of the Union Address),
> January 29, 2002

The entire world was holding its breath as America suffered through "indecision 2000." For Israel and Iran, the outcome of the six-week presidential election dispute could become the single most important factor determining the future of the Middle East. In both capitals, it was thought that if Al Gore and Joe Lieberman won, they would continue the Clinton administration's Middle East policies: strong support for Israel and the Middle East peace process, along with significant pressure to sanction and isolate Iran (even though Clinton, toward the end of his presidency, sought to reach out to Iran). Rightly or wrongly, the Iranians believed that Clinton's greatest mistake was that he let Israel dominate America's foreign policy in the Middle East and that he unnecessarily linked Iran's long-standing but resolvable problems with the United States to Iran's bitter rivalry with Israel.[1]

It was thought that a George Bush–Dick Cheney White House, on the other hand, could bring back the foreign policy approach of the elder George Bush—pressure on Israel to withdraw from Palestinian territories, greater sensitivity to the interests of Washington's Arab allies, and an energy policy that wouldn't cut off American oil businesses from major markets such as Iran. After all, Dick Cheney, George W. Bush's vice-presidential running mate, had as the CEO of the American energy service company Halliburton severely criticized the Clinton administration's economic sanctions on Iran. There was little doubt who Israel and Iran rooted for as they anxiously watched the ballots in Florida being counted and recounted.

On December 9, the U.S. Supreme Court approved the machine recount in Florida that gave Bush the victory in that state—and nationwide. Despite having lost the national popular vote by more than half a million votes, Bush won the electoral vote and became the first president since Benjamin Harrison in 1888 to be elected despite receiving a minority of the popular vote. Immediately, fears spread in Israel that Washington would soften its stand on Iran, ease Clinton's economic sanctions, and narrow its efforts to block Tehran's nuclear program.[2]

The Israelis had reason for concern. Shortly after the elections, American oil executives met with Iran Foreign Minister Kamal Kharrazi in New York, and Bush's nominee for secretary of state, Gen. Colin Powell, told the Senate Foreign Relations Committee during his confirmation hearing that Washington should bring more nuance to its Iran policy.[3] Clearly, Powell wanted to change course in the Middle East, but Iran wasn't necessarily high on the Bush administration's foreign policy agenda.[4] If anything, Iran was once again overshadowed by the Israeli-Palestinian conflict. On Bush's inauguration day, President Bill Clinton called Powell to discuss the Middle East. What was supposed to be a brief conversation about what went wrong with the peace process and how it could be put back on track turned into a forty-minute discussion that almost caused the incoming secretary of state to arrive late to the inauguration ceremony. Clinton squarely blamed PLO leader Yasser Arafat for the failure to reach peace and hardly ever mentioned Iran—in spite of Israel's attempts to paint Tehran as a key spoiler of the peace process. Much like his predecessor, Powell believed that a solution to the Israeli-Palestinian problem would create an opening to Iran, and not the other way around. And even if he wanted to open up to Iran, Powell believed that he would have a harder time selling the idea of a U.S.-Iran dialogue to the pro-Israel lobby in the United States than to the Israeli government itself.[5]

While Israel was preparing for its worst-case scenario—the Labor Party's Ephraim Sneh, who now served as Prime Minister Ehud Barak's deputy defense minister, said that "if indeed the U.S. adopts a conciliatory approach to Iran . . . the implications are that we will need to face this threat alone"—Israel's allies in Washington were gearing up for a fight.[6] The Iran Libya Sanctions Act (ILSA) was due to expire in August 2001, and the powerful pro-Israel lobbying organization American Israel Public Affairs Committee (AIPAC) feared that the Bush administration would try to terminate it. Instead of waiting for Bush and Powell to make their move, AIPAC took advantage of the disorganization in the White House that followed the election conflict.

"Indecision 2000" had deprived the Bush administration of more than six badly needed weeks to organize the administration and fill key posts in the State Department and elsewhere. More than three months into his presidency, Bush still had not found many of the people who would head his government agencies, including those who would be responsible for policies on Iran. AIPAC's machinery, however, was in great shape. The pro-Israel lobby began laying the groundwork for ILSA's renewal on Capitol Hill, and by mid-March—before Bush had even formulated a position on ILSA—AIPAC had gathered more than three hundred cosponsors in the House (the bill needed only 218 votes to pass). Though the sanctions had failed to change Iran's foreign policy, AIPAC still hailed ILSA as a great success. AIPAC Executive Director Howard Kohr urged the House International Relations Committee to renew ILSA because it had "met the test and proven its effectiveness over time" and because "Iranian behavior demands it."[7] The pro-Israeli Washington Institute for Near East Policy argued that ILSA's renewal would help Iran's "real moderates" and hurt the "so-called moderates" around President Mohammad Khatami, who shared the "anti-Israel policies set by Iran's hard-line clerical leadership."[8] The Bush administration was quickly outmaneuvered; through its preemptive work on Capitol Hill, AIPAC checkmated Bush and saw the sanctions bill pass with overwhelming numbers in both chambers. Still, cautious optimism characterized Iran's approach to the United States during the first months of the Bush administration, and a lull reigned in the war of words between Tehran and Tel Aviv.[9] All that was to change on the morning of September 11, 2001.

SEPTEMBER 11

On September 11, 2001, America discovered that the real Islamic threat did not lay in Shia Iran—as Israel had insisted since 1991—but in extremist elements in the Sunni world. Nineteen extremists loyal to Osama bin Laden, the founder and leader of the Sunni al-Qaeda terrorist organization that was sheltered by the Taliban government in Afghanistan (which was itself supported and funded by Saudi Arabia and Pakistan), hijacked four jet airliners and flew one into each of the two towers of the World Trade Center in New York, one into the Pentagon in Washington, D.C., and one into a field in rural Pennsylvania. The world didn't change on that day, but America did—and Washington's response to the cataclysmic terror attack would eventually bring more turmoil to the Arab and Muslim world. That evening Powell ordered a small group of his top staffers to work through the night to produce a strategy for assembling an international coalition to take out Osama bin Laden. The plan became the blueprint for the diplomatic strategy around "Operation Enduring Freedom"—America's war against the Taliban and al-Qaeda in Afghanistan.[10] To win against the Taliban, the United States needed more than overall international support—it needed the specific support of Iran, Afghanistan's neighbor and a bitter enemy of the Taliban.

Throughout the 1990s, Iran had been the primary sponsor of the Northern Alliance, a group of anti-Taliban forces led by the legendary guerrilla fighter Ahmed Shah Massoud. Together with Russia and India, Iran had armed and funded the Northern Alliance at a time when the United States was turning a blind eye to the Taliban's human rights violations and its support for terror. Having a staunchly anti-Iranian and anti-Shia government in Afghanistan hardly undermined the Clinton administration's overarching goal of isolating Iran. That policy came back to haunt America a few years later. But now, the Iranians were eager to offer their help to Washington and show America the strategic benefits of cooperation with Iran. "The Iranians had real contacts with important players in Afghanistan and were prepared to use their influence in constructive ways in coordination with the United States," recalled Flynt Leverett, then senior director for Middle East affairs in the National Security Council.[11] The plan that had been prepared by Powell called for cooperation with Iran that would be used as a platform for persuading Tehran to terminate its involvement with anti-Israeli terrorist groups in return for a positive strategic relationship with Washington.[12]

The plan incensed Israel. Suddenly, much like after the end of the Cold War, events in the Middle East risked making Israel a burden rather than an asset to the United States, while giving Iran a chance to prove its value to America. If a U.S.-Iran dialogue was initiated, there would be "a lot of concern in Israel," Yossi Alpher, an adviser to Barak and a former Mossad official, told me. "Where are we [Israel] in this dialogue? Will the U.S. consult with us about our needs and fears? Will we be part of some package deal with Iran and if so, what part?"[13] Alpher's comment reflected Israelis' inherent fear about their relations with the United States: would the United States protect Israel's interests in geostrategic conflicts in which the interests of the two allies were not necessarily aligned? More specifically, Israel feared that a U.S.-Iran rapprochement wouldn't entail Iranian missile disarmament or Iranian recognition of the Jewish State. American geopolitical interests, they thought—particularly the need to contain China's rise by controlling Beijing's access to energy through Iran—could prompt Washington to sacrifice its commitments to Israel.

A flare-up in Israeli-Iranian tensions that neither the Camp David talks nor the Al-Aqsa Intifada managed to ignite erupted as a result of September 11 precisely because an earth-shattering event shook the foundations of the status quo in the Middle East and forced all states to reassess their position and role in the post-9/11 era. With Britain as the go-between, Washington courted Iran while it kept Israel at arm's length. And just as the British government had done in 1991 regarding the Persian Gulf War, Britain Foreign Secretary Jack Straw suggested that Israel was partly to blame. In a statement that the Israelis called an "obscenity" and a "stab in the back," Straw implied that terrorism and the festering Israeli-Palestinian dispute might be linked to the 9/11 attacks.[14]

Israel and U.S. neoconservatives, who had found their way back to the corridors of power after Bush's election, had a different plan in mind. America should put all the actors it accused of supporting terror on notice—particularly Iran and the Palestinian Authority. In a letter signed by forty-one prominent neoconservatives, including William Kristol, Richard Perle, and Charles Krauthammer, Bush was urged to target not only al-Qaeda, but also Hezbollah and demand that Iran and Syria immediately cease all military, financial, and political support for that organization. If they refused to comply, Bush should "consider appropriate measures of retaliation against these known state sponsors of terrorism."[15] Starting a war with Iran and Syria could overstretch the United States, but it would also put America and Israel on the same side in the war and increase—rather than decrease—the United States' need for Israel.

At first, the neoconservatives made only modest progress. As the United States was beginning its military operations in Afghanistan, State Department and National Security Council officials began meeting secretly with Iranian diplomats in Paris and Geneva in October 2001, under the sponsorship of Lakhdar Brahimi, head of the United Nations Assistance Mission in Afghanistan.[16] The contacts were initiated by Ambassador James Dobbins, the Bush administration's special envoy for Afghanistan. Fully supported by Powell, Dobbins told Brahimi that he would like to meet with the Iranians, and within a few days officials from the Iranian Foreign Ministry contacted Dobbins to offer their assistance. In the initial meetings German and Italian delegations also attended to provide Iran and the United States political cover. Their attendance gave the talks, which soon were dubbed the Geneva Channel, a multilateral appearance. In reality, however, the discussions were bilateral and the highest-level contacts between officials of the two countries since the Iran-Contra scandal.

The talks progressed better than expected. The discussions focused on "how to effectively unseat the Taliban and, once the Taliban was gone, how to stand up an Afghan government," and the Iranians gave extensive assistance to the United States in the war, unaware of what was about to unfold after the success in Afghanistan.[17] The Iranian diplomats impressed their American and European counterparts tremendously with their knowledge and expertise about Afghanistan and the Taliban. And Iran's help was not negligible. The Iranians offered their air bases to the United States, they offered to perform search-and-rescue missions for downed American pilots, they served as a bridge between the Northern Alliance and the United States in the fight against the Taliban, and on occasion they even used U.S. information to find and kill fleeing al-Qaeda leaders.[18]

Though Dobbins's mandate was limited to talks on Afghanistan, a tight-knit group around Powell had prepared a secret comprehensive package of carrots on a stick to offer the Iranians. Unlike the Pentagon, the State Department favored a strategic opening to Iran, not just tactical discussions. The American diplomats realized that the cooperation over Afghanistan could be extended to cover al-Qaeda and other terrorist organizations. The United States and Iran could expand their intelligence-sharing cooperation and coordinate more robust border sweeps to capture al-Qaeda fighters who were fleeing into Pakistan and Iran. Ryan Crocker, a member of the American negotiating team who was charged with discussing general issues, knew about the package. Crocker, along with like-minded colleagues at the State Department, was ready to implement Powell's proposal at the drop of a hat—if only the president would approve it. But hard-liners in the White House worked strenuously to prevent Bush from going along with it. "[Vice President] Cheney and [Secretary of Defense Donald] Rumsfeld were always there to sabotage our cooperation in Afghanistan if it got too far," Wilkerson said.[19]

Nowhere was the common interest of the United States and Iran more clear than during the Bonn Conference of December 2001, at which a number of prominent Afghans and representatives from various countries, including the United States and Iran, met under UN auspices in the capital of Germany to decide on a plan for governing Afghanistan. The United States and Iran had carefully laid the groundwork for the conference weeks in advance. Iran's political clout with the various warring Afghan groups proved to be crucial. It was Iran's influence over the Afghans and not America's threats and promises that moved the negotiations forward. It was also the Iranian delegation—and not Dobbins—that pointed out that the draft of the Bonn Declaration contained no language on democracy or any commitment on behalf of Afghanistan to help fight international terrorism. Curiously enough, Dobbins's instructions contained nothing about democracy.

By the last night of the conference, an interim constitution had been agreed upon and all other issues had been resolved except the toughest one—who was to govern Afghanistan? The Northern Alliance insisted that, as the winner of the war, the spoils should be theirs. Though they represented about 40 percent of the country, they wanted to occupy eighteen of the twenty-four ministries. Around 2 a.m., Dobbins gathered the Afghan parties, the Iranians, the Russians, the Indians, the Germans, and Brahimi of the UN to resolve this final sticking point. For two hours the different delegations took turns trying to convince Yunus Qanooni, the representative of the Northern Alliance, to accept a lower number of ministries, but to no avail. Finally, the Iranian lead negotiator—Javad Zarif—took the Afghan delegate aside and began whispering to him in Persian. A few minutes later, they returned to the table and the Afghan conceded. "Okay, I give up," he said. "The other factions can have two more ministries." This was a critical turning point, because the efforts by other states to convince Qanooni had all failed. "It wasn't until Zarif took him aside that it was settled," Dobbins admitted in retrospect. "We might have had a situation like we had in Iraq, where we were never able to settle on a single leader and government." The next morning, the historic Bonn agreement was signed. America hadn't only won the war, but, thanks to Iran, it had also won the peace.[20]

For the Iranians, this was a moment of triumph. Not only had a major enemy of Iran—the Taliban—been defeated, Iran had also demonstrated how it could help stabilize the region and how America could benefit from a better relationship with Tehran. Hinting at Iran's willingness to expand the discussions to include other areas, Zarif at one point told Crocker jokingly that now that the Afghan issue had been resolved, perhaps it was time to address the nuclear dispute that divided the two countries. Without hesitation, Crocker put the ball back in Zarif's court and asked if he should pull up his instructions on that file, indicating that the State Department had already prepared talking points on the matter. Zarif, however, did not have authority to go beyond Afghanistan at that time even though the Iranians treated the discussions as a strategic opening.[21] "It was consistent with their behavior that they wanted strategic talks," Dobbins explained, while pointing out that the Iranians didn't reveal their full intent until much later.[22]

The Iranian dilemma was that the agenda for the discussions—Afghanistan, the nuclear issue, terrorism—included only *American* concerns. Iran's concerns with U.S. policies were nowhere to be found. While Iran's supreme leader Ayatollah Khamenei and President Khatami fully supported the Afghan talks and the idea of a strategic opening to Washington, broader talks would have to include Iranian as well as American concerns, they insisted.[23] For the State Department and for National Security Advisor Condoleezza Rice, this wasn't a problem. Both wanted to explore a greater opening with Iran, but they were hindered by some in the White House who were passionately anti-Iranian.[24] "I saw no glimmer of interest outside of State" for a strategic discussion with the Iranians, Dobbins recalled. In spite of Iran's central aid to the United States in Afghanistan, there was no real receptivity to Iranian goodwill measures in the Bush White House. It was 1991 all over again: There was no appreciation for Iran's strategic interest in a stable Middle East and the possibility that Tehran wanted to patch up relations with the United States. Not even Iran's pledge at the Tokyo donor conference in January 2002 to offer Afghanistan $500 million—by far the largest pledge by any country at the conference, including the United States—impressed hard-liners in the Bush White House.

Iran's offer to help rebuild the Afghan army—under U.S. leadership—in order to strengthen the Afghan government vis-à-vis the various warlords who still controlled parts of the country also fell on deaf ears. "We're prepared to house, pay, clothe, arm, and train up to twenty thousand troops in a broader program under your leadership," the Iranians told Dobbins during one of the meetings in Geneva. Dobbins pointed out that if Iran and the United States shared the responsibility of training the troops, they would end up working with two different doctrines. The Iranian commander, who had accompanied the Iranian delegation to discuss the offer with Dobbins, just laughed and said, "Don't worry, we're still using the manuals you left behind in 1979." There would be no problems with the loyalty of the troops either, he explained, because Iran was still paying for the Afghan troops the United States was using to mop up Taliban and al-Qaeda elements on the Afghan-Pakistan border. "Are you having any difficulty with their loyalty?" the commander asked Dobbins rhetorically.[25]

Dobbins returned to Washington to brief key administration officials on the unprecedented Iranian offer, which he concluded was intended as a friendly gesture. He first briefed Powell, who then set up a briefing with Rice. She concurred that the offer should be explored, and a third meeting was set up with Powell, Rice, and Rumsfeld. This time, however, Dobbins ran into a brick wall. Throughout the entire meeting Rumsfeld did not utter a word. Staring intently at Dobbins, he took a few notes but never showed any real interest in the proposal. Right there, the proposal died. "To my knowledge, there was never a response," Dobbins said. "There was a disposition not to take Iranian offers seriously and not to give them any broader meaning." Moreover, Dobbins, argued, the administration's disinterest in a broader strategic opening was "because Washington largely focused on Iran's behavior towards Israel" rather than on its behavior toward America.[26]

Israel was alarmed by Washington's cooperation with Iran. In an unusually harsh rebuke of Bush, Israeli Prime Minister Ariel Sharon publicly suggested that Bush was acting like 1937–1940 British Prime Minister Neville Chamberlain, selling out Israel the way Chamberlain had sold out the Czechs by refusing to confront Adolf Hitler.[27] Tensions between the United States and Israel already had begun before September 11. Powell had developed a new Middle East initiative envisioning Jerusalem as a shared capital between Israel and a Palestinian state—a noticeable departure from previous American positions on the Israeli-Palestinian conflict. For Likud, an undivided Jerusalem as Israel's eternal capital was a non-negotiable red line. The Bush administration's new policy threatened to transform Sharon from an American ally into an unyielding obstacle. Sharon's personal attack on Bush did little to ease the tensions. The comments incensed the thin-skinned American president, and White House press secretary Ari Fleischer called Sharon's remarks "unacceptable."[28]

The Israeli-American tensions had not escaped Iran. The Khatami government felt increasingly confident that the gridlock in the Israeli-Iranian-American triangle could be broken in Iran's favor. Valiollah Shojapurian, an Iranian lawmaker belonging to the reformist camp, credited Khatami's policy of détente and warned of Israel's anger at Iran's success. "This international approval of Iran has terribly angered our staunch enemy Israel but it has given us a new opportunity to rebuild our international ties," he told *Aftab-e Yazd*, an Iranian daily.[29]

Neoconservatives in Washington and the Israeli government tirelessly sought ways to put a halt to the U.S.-Iranian cooperation. Through various means they tried to shut down the Geneva Channel and preempt any possibility that Bush would commit a Nixon-goes-to-China with Iran—that is, reach out and befriend a major U.S. foe. One approach was to manipulate the Iranians into closing the channel themselves. The idea was to encourage or provoke a radical ayatollah into criticizing the talks as a way of currying favor with Iranian extremists, which would in turn force the supreme leader to back out of the channel. Ironically, neoconservatives who had played a leading role in the Iran-Contra scandal now attempted to sabotage the very political breakthrough they had fought for fifteen years earlier. After having been shunned from government for more than a decade, Michael Ledeen, the neoconservative friend of Israel former Prime Minister Shimon Peres who in the 1980s sought a U.S.-Iran dialogue together with the Israelis— and who was believed at one time by the CIA to be "an agent of influence of a foreign government"—found his way back into the corridors of power after the Bush election in 2000.[30] His access to the president was through Bush's top adviser, Karl Rove, with whom he met periodically.[31] As the Freedom Scholar at the American Enterprise Institute, Ledeen began writing a weekly column for *National Review* in 2000 in which he repeatedly argued for targeting Iran. Ledeen expressed his dissatisfaction with the slow pace of Washington's march against Iran by concluding his articles with "Faster, please. Faster."[32]

The collapse of the Soviet Union and defeat of Iraq in the 1991 Persian Gulf War had led to Ledeen's 180-degree turn. Just as Israel did, he now saw Iran as a rival that needed to be isolated and weakened rather than as a potential ally with whom to engage and strengthen. In December 2001, Ledeen, who now served as a consultant to Undersecretary of Defense Douglas Feith, organized a meeting in Rome with his old friend of Iran-Contra infamy, Manuchehr Ghorbanifar, the Iranian charlatan and arms dealer deemed a "serial fabricator" by the CIA. As a student of the Italian fascist movement, Ledeen enjoyed extensive contacts within the Italian intelligence service and also invited Nicolo Pollari, the head of Italy's military intelligence agency, SISMI, and Italy's Minister of Defense Antonio Martino.[33] Also attending were several exiled Iranians; Larry Franklin, a Defense Intelligence Agency Iran analyst who would later plead guilty to spying for Israel in 2005 and who is currently serving a thirteen-year prison sentence; and Harold Rhode, a Middle East expert who played a key role in the Iran-Contra scandal.[34] Franklin and Rhode were part of a small, tight-knit group of neoconservative hard-liners on Iran favoring regime change in Tehran and were determined to put an end to Powell's diplomacy. Later on, their policy network at the Pentagon would include the Office of Special

Plans, an alternative intelligence shop led by Douglas Feith that provided the American intelligence apparatus with inaccurate information that helped pave the way for the war with Iraq.[35]

The meetings were organized in Europe because Ghorbanifar couldn't obtain a U.S. visa following his past encounters with the CIA. Ledeen carefully kept the State Department and the CIA in the dark about the sensitive meeting, contrary to standard protocol regarding contact with foreign government intelligence agencies. But word quickly reached U.S. Ambassador to Italy Mel Sembler, as well as the CIA station chief in Rome, and the matter soon reached the highest levels of the Bush administration. After an intervention by CIA Director George Tenet himself, Feith and Ledeen were ordered to cease all contacts with Ghorbanifar and his entourage.[36] But the damage had been done. The Iranians had gotten word of the meetings and were infuriated that high-level U.S. officials would meet with Ghorbanifar and other Iranian exiles who by now had turned against the clerical regime. But whatever damage Ledeen and Ghorbanifar managed to inflict on the Geneva Channel, it was nothing compared to what was about to unfold.

KARINE A AND THE "AXIS OF EVIL"

On January 3, 2002, Israel intercepted the ship *Karine A* in international waters in the Red Sea. Captained by a member of the Palestinian navy, the ship contained Katyusha rockets, mortars, rifles, machine guns, sniper rifles, ammunition, anti-tank mines, and other explosives. The Israelis contended that the ship had come from the Iranian island of Kish. Because most of the weapons were still in their factory wrappings and clearly marked as having been produced in Iran, the Israelis argued that the conclusion was obvious: Iran was attempting to arm Arafat's Palestinian Authority in violation of the Palestinian Authority's agreements with Israel. This was the smoking gun the Israelis needed to halt the U.S.-Iran dialogue and put an end to Washington's pressure on Israel to deal with the Palestinians.[37] It was a heaven-sent gift for Sharon, and it conveniently coincided with the visit to Israel of Gen. Anthony Zinni, Bush's new envoy to the Middle East. To many, it was almost too good to be true—so good that even Israel's allies began questioning the validity of the story. The normal route for Iranian shipments to its proxies went through Damascus and Lebanon—by air, they argued, and not by boat around the Arabian Peninsula, where the Israeli navy was known to patrol.

The Iranians denied having any connection to the ship, but no denials could dent the image of Sharon inspecting the ship and its Iranian-produced arms. Washington accepted the Israeli side of the story and described the Israeli evidence as "compelling." To the Bush administration, any doubt that may have existed about Iran's continued ties to terrorism was removed.[38] This was a major setback for proponents of dialogue with Iran such as Powell. "It put Powell back on his heel about what was possible to achieve with the Iranians," Wilkerson said.

In Iran, President Khatami was taken off guard. He ordered a meeting of the Iranian National Security Council to learn who was behind the shipment. Khatami was well aware that rogue elements existed within the Iranian government who at every turn sought to undermine his détente with the United States. But no one on the council admitted to having knowledge of the shipment. Through the Geneva Channel, the Iranians immediately contacted Dobbins and informed him of Khatami's meeting with the council. The Iranian diplomats were instructed to request from the United States evidence about the shipment's origins so that authorities in Tehran could act on it. At the same time, the Khatami government sent a message to Washington through the Swiss embassy in Tehran, denying any involvement in the affair. It repeated the request for information from the United States and offered to give Washington any information Iran might uncover. But neither the message to Dobbins nor the memo sent via the Swiss was taken seriously by the Bush administration. Washington never provided Tehran with any evidence for the Israeli claim, but it did respond to Tehran a few weeks later and asserted that the information it had was reliable and sufficient, effectively dismissing Tehran's denial.[39]

To the ever-suspicious Iranians, the entire affair was bogus. It served one purpose only, they believed: to undermine the Geneva Channel. "In a matter of a few days, a policy of cooperation was transformed into a policy of confrontation," Zarif said. "*Karine A* continues to be a mystery that happened at an exactly opportune moment for those who wanted to prevent U.S.-Iran engagement."[40] In retrospect, even some Bush administration officials have begun to question the affair. Some speculate that it was staged by the Israelis. Others argue that rogue elements in Iran may have been behind it. But no one in the Bush administration pursued the matter further; once the U.S. intelligence service corroborated the Israeli account, it became sacrosanct. "But subsequently, we have all pondered on whether it was a hoax or not," Wilkerson admitted.[41]

Quite apart from speculation about the origin and details of the *Karine A,* few question the effect it had on Washington's approach to Tehran. Within a few days, Pentagon officials made a flurry of accusations against

Iran, charging it with providing safe haven to fleeing al-Qaeda fighters in order to use them against the United States in post-Taliban Afghanistan. But the accusations rested on shaky grounds. Per the request of the United States, Iran had increased its troop strength on the Afghan border, and it had brought a dossier to UN Secretary-General Kofi Annan on 290 al-Qaeda members whom Iran had detained. Many of these detainees were later repatriated to Saudi Arabia, Afghanistan, and other Arab and European countries. "I wasn't aware of any intelligence supporting that charge," recalled Dobbins. "I certainly would have seen it had there been any such intelligence. Nobody told me they were harboring al-Qaeda."[42]

Then, on January 29, 2002, in Bush's first State of the Union address, he lumped Iran together with Iraq and North Korea as dangerous and threatening states that formed an "Axis of Evil." Whether Iran was included in the axis for rhetorical reasons or whether Bush believed that Iran, Iraq, and North Korea were collaborating, one thing is certain: the *Karine A* incident contributed directly to Iran's membership in Bush's club of evils.[43] Tehran was shocked. Khatami's policy of détente and the help Iran provided the United States in Afghanistan was for naught. Having seen his domestic agenda fall apart, Khatami's international standing was now also given a blow. He had stuck out his neck and argued against hard-liners in Tehran, whose skepticism about America's trustworthiness appeared to have been proven right.[44] "'Axis of Evil' was a fiasco for the Khatami government," said Farideh Farhi, an Iran expert at Hawaii University. "That was used by the hard-liners, who said: If you give in, if you help from a position of weakness, then you get negative results."[45]

Ironically, Iran had called the United States the Great Satan for more than two decades by the time Bush referred to Iran as evil. Clearly, both states had made use of their share of excessive and counterproductive rhetoric. But there are few examples where such an undiplomatic statement was made at such a sensitive time—just weeks after Iran had proved itself an indispensable ally in Afghanistan. Hard-liners in Tehran, as well as some members of the Iranian delegation negotiating with the Americans, argued that Iran shouldn't have offered the United States help without exacting a price up front. "Iran made a mistake not to link its assistance in Afghanistan to American help in other areas and by just hoping that the U.S. would reciprocate," Zarif argued. Some of these diplomats were later forced to pay for the fiasco with their careers, making others in Iran's foreign policy circles think twice before extending a hand of friendship to the Bush administration.

Tehran's immediate reaction to the Axis of Evil speech was to close down the Geneva Channel in protest. Washington had yet again failed to reciprocate Iranian goodwill, and had instead punished Iran for its support, the Iranians reasoned.[46] In their last meeting with Dobbins, the Iranians protested the Axis of Evil comment. Dobbins explained that the United States still had many disagreements with Tehran, including the Israeli-Palestinian conflict, and that the cooperation in Afghanistan, while very helpful, did not change that reality. On most issues, the United States and Iran were still at odds, he pointed out. The Iranian response crystallized the opportunity that the Axis of Evil comment likely had squandered. "We would have liked to have discussed those matters too," the Iranians said, unveiling to Dobbins Tehran's intentions of using the channel and the cooperation on Afghanistan to resolve outstanding issues between the United States and Iran.[47] For the Iranians, it was particularly bewildering to be lumped with Saddam Hussein, Iran's bitter enemy.[48]

But Bush's comments didn't spark anger in Tehran alone. The speech, and the term, was heavily criticized in the United States as well—including by U.S. officials (though they seldom made their criticism public until after they had left office). Dobbins felt that it was "ludicrous" and "ridiculous" to suggest that Iran, Iraq, and North Korea formed an axis. "It was a bit like suggesting that the Soviet Union and Nazi Germany should be treated equally after Germany had invaded the Soviet Union," he told the New America Foundation in August 2006.[49] He warned Rice that the speech could induce Iran to retaliate by destabilizing Afghanistan. But Rice was unmoved by the warning and dismissed Afghanistan and Iran as relatively unimportant. The United States had greater plans in mind, she told Dobbins, and neither Iran nor Afghanistan mattered much in the greater picture.[50] Powell's staff echoed Dobbins's concerns, but the secretary of state "didn't see a major problem with it [the speech]."[51]

The *Karine A* story gave new life to Israel's long-standing campaign to have the international community declare Iran a state sponsor of terror.[52] Peres ordered the publication of a "black book" for distribution around the world. "This black book will reveal all the facts concerning the actions of the ayatollahs' regime against Israel," he said. "It will contain all the calls from Iranian leaders for the destruction of Israel, as well as details on its nuclear programme aimed at achieving this aim."[53] Iran, in turn, called for the United Nations to set up a criminal court to try Israeli officials for war crimes.[54] Soon, the rhetoric spilled over into direct threats. Israel threatened to attack Iran's nuclear installations at Bushehr, and the Iranians responded by threatening to attack Israel with ballistic missiles if Israel violated Iranian sovereignty.[55]

At one point, the rhetoric became so aggressive that both Washington and Israeli generals intervened to defuse tensions. In February 2006, Washington asked Sharon to soften his tone toward Iran.[56] That same month, the head of Israel's National Security Council, Gen. Uzi Dayan, reminded his colleagues in Tel Aviv that Iran had to be depicted as a global threat, not just a threat to Israel. Iran is "not an enemy for Israel," Dayan told Israel's army radio. "We shouldn't threaten Iran—from our point of view Iran is not an enemy—but we should make sure that Iran does not manage to procure weapons of mass destruction."[57] But in spite of the Axis of Evil speech and Israel's efforts to isolate Iran, Tehran never turned against America in Afghanistan. By the time the Iranians stopped showing up for the Geneva meetings, the major obstacles in Afghanistan in the fight against the Taliban and in setting up the new Afghan government had already been overcome. But soon the Iranians would need to find their way back to Geneva, because shortly after the Afghan war they realized that hard-liners in Washington had all along been planning to extend the war to Iran's western neighbor—Iraq.

19

snatching defeat from
the jaws of victory

If humility is the strength of the weak,
then hubris is the weakness of the strong.

—Mardy Grothe

I think it is a huge mistake not to open a channel [to Iran].

—Leading Israeli military commentator (on Israel's failure
to capitalize on Iran's outreach), October 17, 2004

It was September 2000, a year before the explosive 9/11 terrorist attacks. But Dick Cheney, Donald Rumsfeld, Paul Wolfowitz, Florida Governor Jeb Bush, and Cheney aide I. Lewis Libby already had their collective eye on Iraq as they gathered at the neoconservative think tank Project for the New American Century in Washington, D.C.[1] Under the auspices of this organization, they drafted a document stating their vision of America's role in the Middle East, which included an attack on Iraq. Called "Rebuilding America's Defenses: Strategies, Forces and Resources for a New Century," their report argued that the United States must have a permanent military presence in the Persian Gulf, and that although "the unresolved conflict with Iraq provides the immediate justification [for an Iraqi invasion], the need for a substantial American force presence in the Gulf transcends the issue of the regime of Saddam Hussein."[2] Their report was made public and distributed widely within the Beltway. The move against Iraq was on. Many have speculated that America went to war with Iraq primarily to serve Israeli interests.

The pro-Israel lobby pushed the Bush administration into invading Iraq after 9/11 for Israel's security, the argument goes. In reality, Israel became a staunch supporter of the war only once it realized that Washington had set its mind on attacking Iraq, come what may.[3]

Israel arguably had good reasons to support an American invasion of Iraq. Saddam's survival and potential capability of producing weapons of mass destruction (WMD) stood in the way of Israel's primary objective: to drastically reshape the political map of the Middle East by locking in the balance of power in Israel's favor. If the Americans were successful in Iraq, the reasoning went, Iraq could become the next Egypt—a mighty and populous Arab state whose dependence on the United States would force it to make peace with Israel. If Iraq added its name to the Arab states that recognized Israel, then Israel's regional enemies—Iran and Syria—would find themselves further isolated and weakened.

A U.S. invasion of Iraq would also enable Israel to revive its contacts with the Iraqi Kurds. The Barzani clan, with whom the Israelis enjoyed long and fruitful cooperation in the 1960s and 1970s, was still a major force in Kurdish politics. With its support, Israel could use Iraqi Kurdistan for intelligence gathering and infiltration of northwestern Iran, just as Iran was using Lebanon's southern border to do the same in Israel. In fact, in September 2006 the BBC obtained evidence that, subsequent to the U.S. conquest of Iraq, the Israelis started giving military training to Kurds in northern Iraq, close to the Iranian border. The Israeli newspaper *Yediot Aharonot* had reported the same back in December 2005.[4] But as problematic as Iraq potentially could be, Israel no longer perceived Iraq as its primary threat. Since the late 1990s, when Iran began its ballistic missile program in earnest, Iran had topped Israel's list of regional threats. Contrary to common perceptions, Israel originally opposed the Iraq war.

In early 2002 the Israeli government began to suspect that the United States might attack Iraq. This would be a mistake, Israel reasoned, because Iraq was the wrong threat; energy should not be wasted on a secondary enemy when the real threat—Iran—was ignored. A wave of Israeli officials, both military and civilian, traveled to Washington to lodge their opposition. Israel's message was clear: Iraq was needed to balance the real enemy. In February 2002, Binyamin Ben-Eliezer of the Labor Party visited Washington to persuade the Bush administration that Iran was "the real strategic threat" and that America must "deal with it diplomatically or militarily, or both." If Washington did not, Ben-Eliezer threatened, "Israel will have to do it alone."[5] Other Israelis rejected the neoconservative argument that the fall of Saddam and the emergence of an Iraqi democracy would spark a popular uprising in Iran against the mullahs.

But once they concluded that the minds of the neoconservatives in the administration were set and that President Bush would go to war with Iraq no matter what, Israel changed its tactics. By late spring 2002, a new wave of Israelis approached the White House. "It was the most curious thing I ever saw," recalled Lawrence Wilkerson, Secretary of State Colin Powell's chief of staff. The message of the second wave was rather different: Iraq was a threat, they argued, as they provided new intelligence to back up their sudden change of heart. But so was Iran, they said, and Washington should not stop at invading Iraq. Iran should be the real target, but the Iranian threat could not be addressed unless Iraq was first neutralized. The government of Prime Minister Ariel Sharon saw the invasion of Iraq as a necessary step to a follow-up war against Iran. In early November 2002, Sharon revealed the Israeli objective when he urged Washington to invade Iran "the day after" Iraq was crushed.[6]

For the very same reasons, Iran opposed the war. True, Saddam's intentions toward Iran remained hostile, but his army, decimated by the U.S.-led coalition in the Persian Gulf War, was vastly weakened; also, the Iraqi economy was in tatters and Saddam's hands were tied after a decade of UN sanctions and international isolation. In the short term, Iraq posed little threat to Iran. The danger of a hostile but powerless Saddam was preferable to the danger posed by the installation of a pro-Western client government in Iraq with hostile intentions against Tehran and backed by Western arms. A Baghdad regime with a Western tilt would complete America's encirclement of Iran, strategists in Tehran feared: To Iran's south, pro-American Arab states had outsourced their security to Washington and legitimized America's military presence in the Persian Gulf. To the north, U.S. troops were present in Azerbaijan and the central Asian republics. To the southeast, Pakistan had emerged as a key American ally in the global war on terror, even though it had been the creator and primary backer of the Taliban regime in Afghanistan. And with the defeat of the Taliban, American troops roamed Iran's eastern border as well. Tehran, which shares an eight-hundred-mile border with Iraq, feared that a successful U.S. conquest of Iraq would make Iran an indefensible target in the Bush administration's plan to transform the Middle East. Statements from Washington's neoconservative think tanks and institutes did nothing to reassure them. For example, one administration preinvasion joke went, "Everyone wants to go to Baghdad. Real men want to go to Tehran."[7]

Though few in Tehran wanted to burn their fingers by trying to reach out to Washington again, the neoconservative war drums in early 2002 worried the Iranians enough to muster another try. The clerics still held a few valuable cards that they hoped to play to tip the Washington debate in favor of the State Department and those favoring dialogue. One of these cards was Iran's superior intelligence on and familiarity with Iraq. Thanks to the eight-year war in the 1980s, the Iranians, unlike the Americans, understood the complex Iraqi tribal social networks and knew how to navigate them. Washington would need such knowledge, Tehran figured, which would give the Iranians some leverage over the neoconservatives. Without a channel of communication, misunderstandings could occur, which would benefit Iran's regional rivals, including Israel and the Sunni Arab states. Iraqi opposition groups with close ties to Tehran—both Shia organizations and Kurdish factions led by Jalal Talabani (who would later become Iraq's president)—also pressured the Iranians to aid the Americans. After all, the Iranians needed a channel to understand and influence American decisions on Iraq, and the Americans needed Iran to not complicate America's plans. So by late spring 2002, the Geneva Channel was resurrected after the State Department approached the Iranians.

Because of their experience from the previous discussions on Afghanistan, Iran wanted to expand the group to include the other major powers. The United States opposed that format, because it would include Russia and France, two states that vehemently opposed military action against Iraq. The solution was to use the format for the previous talks on Afghanistan, while conducting discussions on Iraq on the sidelines.[8] On the Iranian side, the talks were headed by senior political figures, including UN Ambassador Javad Zarif. His counterpart on the American side was Ambassador Zalmay Khalilzad, an Afghan-American who spoke fluent Persian and enjoyed close ties to President Bush. The talks lacked the cooperative spirit they enjoyed during the Afghan war but continued nonetheless out of mutual necessity.[9] Some of the Iranian negotiators felt that Khalilzad had a chip on his shoulder. They believed that this man who spoke English with an Afghan accent sought to compensate for his immigrant status by taking excessively hawkish positions in the negotiations.

Iran's balancing act was a delicate one. Balancing the fear that a successful U.S. operation would leave Iran encircled and the next vulnerable target was the fact that, if he survived, Saddam would be emboldened and an even greater threat. In addition, a successful war but unsuccessful reconstruction effort could lead to Iraq's disintegration, with considerable spillover effects: The Kurds in the north of Iraq could declare independence, in turn motivating similar calls from Iran's Kurdish minority, who numbered six million (almost 10 percent of the population). And a power vacuum could suck Turkey, Saudi Arabia, Syria, and Iran into the Iraqi arena against their wishes. So, despite the fact that Tehran opposed the American war against Iraq, once it was clear that it was going to happen, Iran concluded that moderate support for the American effort was the lesser of two evils.[10]

As soon as the U.S.-Iran talks restarted, neoconservatives in Washington began undermining them. A little more than a decade earlier, Michael Ledeen and the Israelis were on the other side of the debate. Ledeen argued forcefully on the op-ed pages of the *New York Times* in July 1988—just as the Iraq-Iran war had ended—that the United States must open talks with Iran: "The United States, which should have been exploring improved relations with Iran before . . . should now seize the opportunity to do so. To wait might suggest to even pro-Western Iranians that a refusal to seek better relations is based on an anti-Iran animus rather than objections to specific Iranian action. Those Iranians who have been calling for better relations with the West have clearly been gathering strength. . . . Among the advocates of such improved relations are two leading candidates to succeed Ayatollah Ruhollah Khomeini: Ayatollah Hojatolislam Rafsanjani and the Ayatollah Hussein Ali Montazeri."[11]

Now, Ledeen and the Israelis sought to prevent Rafsanjani or any other Iranian official from talking to the Americans. In June 2002, only weeks after the Geneva Channel had been revived, Ledeen organized a second meeting in Rome with Pentagon officials and Ghorbanifar. This time Ledeen made sure that the meeting was an open secret, and soon the Senate Select Committee on Intelligence was apprised of it. In the summer of 2003, *Newsweek* disclosed the Ghorbanifar-Ledeen-Pentagon dealings. Ghorbanifar himself told American journalist Laura Rozen that he had held more than fifty meetings with Ledeen after 9/11 and provided him with more than "4,000 to 5,000 pages of sensitive documents" concerning Iran, Iraq, and the Middle East.[12]

Although the Pentagon dismissed the meetings as "chance encounters," the revelation that such high-level American officials had been involved in talks with Iranian opposition elements made a U.S.-Iran breakthrough even more difficult to achieve. But Ledeen's efforts failed to incite the Iranians to close the Geneva Channel. The contacts continued, and, according to Kenneth Pollack of the Brookings Institute, Iran ended up playing a very helpful role in the Iraqi invasion, particularly in the reconstruction phase immediately following the Iraqi army's collapse. Among other things, Iran instructed its influential Shia proxy groups in Iraq after the war to participate in reconstruction rather than resist the American occupation. And when Iran could have created havoc for the United States, it chose not to. "If the Iranians wanted to create chaos in Iraq [after Saddam's fall], they could have easily done so in the darkest days after the war, and the United States was fortunate that they did not," Pollack wrote.[13]

AN OFFER WASHINGTON COULDN'T REFUSE

Defeating Iraq militarily turned out to be the cakewalk the neoconservatives had predicted. On April 9, 2003, only three weeks into the invasion, U.S. forces moved into Baghdad. The Iraqi capital was formally occupied by U.S. forces, and the Saddam era was officially over. The swiftness with which the United States defeated the strongest standing Arab army—which the Iranians had failed to defeat after eight bloody years of warfare—sent shivers down the spines of America's foes in the region and beyond. Even Washington hawks themselves were surprised by the ease with which Saddam's Republican Guards were destroyed. In Tehran, the clergy faced a new and grim reality. America's encirclement of Iran was now complete. During their twenty-four-year reign, the clerics had seldom felt so vulnerable. Only days before Bush declared "Mission Accomplished" on the USS *Abraham Lincoln* on May 1, Tehran felt it had to make one last attempt at reaching out to the United States. Figuring that the regime's very existence was at stake, the Iranians put everything on the table—Hezbollah; the Israeli-Palestinian conflict, including Hamas and Islamic Jihad; and Iran's nuclear program.

The Iranians prepared a comprehensive proposal, spelling out the contours of a potential grand bargain between the two countries addressing all points of contention between them. The first draft of the proposal was written by Sadegh Kharrazi, the nephew of the Iranian foreign minister and Iran's ambassador to France. The draft then went to Iran's supreme leader for approval, who asked Iran UN Ambassador Zarif to review it and make final edits before it was sent to the Americans. Only a closed circle of decision-makers in Tehran was aware of and involved in preparing the proposal—Foreign Minister Kamal Kharrazi, President Mohammad Khatami, UN Ambassador Zarif, Ambassador to France Kharrazi, and Ayatollah Ali

Khamanei. In addition, the Iranians consulted Tim Guldimann, the Swiss ambassador to Iran, who eventually would deliver the proposal to Washington.

The proposal stunned the Americans. Not only was it authoritative—it had the approval of the supreme leader—but its contents were astonishing as well. (See Appendix A.) "The Iranians acknowledged that WMD and support for terror were serious causes of concern for us, and they were willing to negotiate," said Flynt Leverett, who served as senior director for Middle East affairs at the National Security Council at the time. "The message had been approved by all the highest levels of authority."[14] The Iranians were putting all their cards on the table, declaring what they wanted from the United States and what they were willing to offer in return.[15] "That letter went to the Americans to say that we are ready to talk, we are ready to address our issues," said Mohammad Hossein Adeli, who was then a deputy foreign minister in Iran.[16]

In a dialogue of "mutual respect," the Iranians offered to end their support to Hamas and Islamic Jihad—Iran's ideological brethren in the struggle against the Jewish State—and pressure them to cease attacks on Israel. On Hezbollah, Iran's own brainchild and its most reliable partner in the Arab world, the clerics offered to support the disarmament of the Lebanese militia and transform it into a purely political party. On the nuclear issue, the proposal offered to open up completely the Iranian nuclear program to intrusive international inspections in order to alleviate any fears of Iranian weaponization. The Iranians would sign the Additional Protocol to the Non-Proliferation Treaty, and they also offered extensive American involvement in the program as a further guarantee and goodwill gesture. On terrorism, Tehran offered full cooperation against all terrorist organizations—above all, al-Qaeda. On Iraq, Iran would work actively with the United States to support political stabilization and establishment of democratic institutions and—most importantly—a nonreligious government.

Perhaps most surprising of all, the Iranians offered to accept the Beirut Declaration of the Arab League—that is, the Saudi peace plan from March 2002, in which the Arab states offered to make peace collectively with Israel, recognizing and normalizing relations with the Jewish State in return for Israeli agreement to withdraw from all occupied territories and accept a fully independent Palestinian state; an equal division of Jerusalem; and an equitable resolution of the Palestinian refugee problem. Through this step, Iran would formally recognize the two-state solution and consider itself at peace with Israel. This was an unprecedented concession by Tehran. Only a year earlier, hard-liners in Tehran had dismissed the Saudi initiative, arguing that an Israeli return to the pre-1967 borders would be an unjust solution for the Palestinians.[17]

In return, the Iranians had both tactical and strategic demands. At the tactical level, they wanted members of the Iranian terrorist organization based in Iraq, the Mujahedin-e Khalq Organization (MKO), handed over to them in return for the al-Qaeda operatives the Iranians held. The Iranians were not keen on handing over the al-Qaeda operatives unless the United States changed its attitude toward Iran. Tehran would risk making itself a key target of al-Qaeda if it handed the operatives over to the United States, and, unless the United States agreed to reciprocate, the Iranians would be left facing the wrath of the Sunni terrorist organization all by themselves. Moreover, Iran treated the al-Qaeda prisoners as a valuable bargaining chip. It would be unwise to give it up without securing a countermeasure from the United States. Exchanging MKO and al-Qaeda terrorists would be a suitable transaction in the spirit of the war on terror, the clerics reasoned, and it would demonstrate Washington's intention not to use terrorist groups to topple the ayatollahs.

After all, the MKO had been included on the State Department's terrorist list under different names since 1992. In a speech to the UN Bush had even referred to Saddam's support for the MKO as evidence of his ties to terrorists. "Iraq continues to shelter and support terrorist organizations that direct violence against Iran," he told the UN General Assembly on September 12, 2002.[18] Its terrorist status notwithstanding, the MKO had strong supporters in Washington and Tel Aviv. In August 2002, the MKO played a role in revealing the progress of Iran's nuclear program. Much indicates that the intelligence the MKO disclosed originated in Israel. The Israeli intelligence services, which were adamant about not appearing to be the driving force behind U.S. pressure on Iran over the nuclear issue, had first approached the son of the Shah with the information. The heir to the Iranian throne had declined to make the news public, however, leaving the Israelis with few other options than to seek out the MKO.[19] In the White House, the Iranian terrorists were protected by Rumsfeld, Cheney, and the other neoconservatives, who saw the MKO as a potential asset in an effort to destabilize the Iranian regime.[20] After the U.S. invasion, the secretary of defense had decided, much like Saddam himself had done, to use the MKO fighters to keep the Iraqi population in check. He let the MKO keep their weapons and ordered them to man checkpoints in southern Iraq alongside U.S. troops. When Powell argued that the United States could not cozy up to a terrorist organization in the midst of America's own war on terror, Rumsfeld replied that he did not have enough troops to disarm the MKO.[21]

The hawkish defense secretary's position on the MKO was an open secret in Washington. In late May 2003, ABC News reported that the Pentagon was calling for the overthrow of the Iranian regime by "using all available points of pressure on the Iranian regime, including backing armed Iranian dissidents and employing the services of the Mujahedin-e Khalq."[22] (Though Powell finally managed to close the MKO's offices in downtown Washington, D.C., in August 2003, the group is still active in the United States and Iraq. In January 2004, members organized a major fundraiser at Washington's MCI Center, with Richard Perle, a key figure in neoconservative circles, as one of the key speakers. The MKO's spokesperson and top lobbyist, Ali Reza Jafarzadeh, has since found employment as a terrorism expert for the Fox News network.)

At the strategic level, the Iranians wanted to reach a long-term understanding with the United States by putting a halt to hostile American behavior, such as the "Axis of Evil" rhetoric and interference in Iran's domestic affairs; ending all U.S. sanctions; respecting Iranian national interests in Iraq and supporting Iranian demands for war reparations; respecting Iran's right to full access to nuclear, biological, and chemical technology; and finally, recognizing Iran's legitimate security interests in the region. The document also spelled out a procedure for step-by-step negotiations toward a mutually acceptable agreement.[23]

Getting the proposal to the United States was a major operation. As the caretaker of U.S. interests in Iran, the Swiss ambassador in Iran, Tim Guldimann, served as the go-between when the two countries needed to communicate. The channel was set up in 1990, right before the first Persian Gulf War, because Washington recognized that it needed to communicate with Iran to avoid potential misunderstandings during the war. The Americans had sought out the Swiss and given them very strict directions about the channel. Information was to be strictly conveyed—in both directions—without any interpretation by the Swiss. The Swiss embassy in Tehran would send Iranian messages to the Swiss embassy in Washington via the Swiss Foreign Ministry, which in turn would deliver it to the U.S. State Department.[24]

The Iranians, well aware of the infighting and turf wars that characterized the Bush administration, apparently feared that the proposal might not reach the White House if it was sent to the State Department. Even if Powell received it, there was no guarantee that he could bring it to Bush's attention, given the tensions that existed between Powell and White House officials. Another channel was needed besides the State Department; someone who had direct access to the president. Guldimann, whose frequent briefings of U.S. officials in Washington regarding events in Iran were much appreciated, had the answer—Representative Bob Ney of Ohio.

The powerful Republican chairman of the House Administration Committee was an unusual lawmaker. He was the only Persian-speaking member of Congress, having learned the language from his Iranian roommates at Ohio State University. After college, he spent a year in the southern Iranian city of Shiraz as an English teacher. As the revolution swept Iran, Ney returned to the United States and embarked on a career in politics, where his experience in Iran often came in handy. His knowledge and expertise on Iran had won him the respect of lawmakers and White House officials alike.[25]

In early May 2003, Guldimann visited Washington and briefed Ney personally on the proposal. The Swiss diplomat gave the congressman a copy of the two-page proposal, which included an outline of Iranian and American aims and a proposed procedure on how to advance the negotiations, as well as an eleven-page account by Guldimann of his conversations with Iranian officials. Guldimann's account clarified Tehran's position and the authenticity of the proposal. A few days earlier, on May 4, Guldimann had faxed the proposal to the State Department—together with a one-page cover letter detailing Tehran's intentions with the proposal and its authenticity. Another copy was sent to the U.S. ambassador in Geneva, Kevin Moley. "I got the clear impression that there is a strong will of the regime to tackle the problem with the U.S. now and to try it with this initiative," Guldimann wrote in the cover letter. (See Appendix C.)

Ney, who had advocated U.S.-Iran dialogue since Khatami became president in 1997, quickly realized that the document could create a major breakthrough in U.S.-Iran relations and aid America's war against al-Qaeda. "This is it," he told me at the time with unveiled excitement. "This is the one that will make it happen." He promptly sent a staffer to hand-deliver the document to Karl Rove, the president's senior adviser, whom Ney had known since his college years. Within a few hours, Rove called Ney to verify the authenticity of the proposal, assuring the Ohio lawmaker that he would deliver the "intriguing" document directly to the president. The first step of the operation had been successfully completed—the proposal had reached the highest levels of the U.S. government. Washington's response, however, would surprise everyone, including the Swiss.

HUBRIS

For many in the State Department, the proposal was a no-brainer. Iran offered major concessions in return for an end to the sanctions policy sponsored by the pro-Israel American Israel Public Affairs Committee (AIPAC), which probably had cost the United States more diplomatically than it did Iran economically. More importantly, the offer was authentic and had the approval of the highest level of authority in Iran, a fact the State Department recognized.[26] Powell and his deputy, Richard Armitage, favored a positive response to the Iranians. Together with National Security Advisor Condoleezza Rice, they approached the president about the proposal, but instead of instigating a lively debate on the details of a potential American response, Cheney and Rumsfeld quickly put the matter to an end. Their argument was simple but devastating. "We don't speak to evil," they said.[27] Even if Powell and his allies had put up a fight, they probably would not have succeeded. "The State Department knew it had no chance at the interagency level of arguing the case for it successfully," Leverett said. "They weren't going to waste Powell's rapidly diminishing capital on something that unlikely." Not even a single interagency meeting was set up to discuss the proposal.[28] "In the end," Wilkerson said, in a harsh reference to the neoconservatives led by Cheney and Rumsfeld, "the secret cabal got what it wanted: no negotiations with Tehran."[29]

The Iranian offer came at a time when the United States was seemingly at the height of its power. Iraq had been defeated just weeks earlier, and though some saw it as just a slogan, the Bush administration seemed to really believe it: Freedom was on the march. Just as in 1991, when the United States chose not to invite Iran to the Madrid conference, negotiating with the Iranians was low on the White House's agenda. Hard-liners in the Pentagon and the vice president's office interpreted the Iranian proposal—probably correctly—as a sign of weakness. Iran could have made this offer —one that blatantly countered its official ideology—only because it was weak and desperate, they argued. These officials opposed a deal with Iran no matter what the ayatollahs offered, because, they said, America could get what it wanted for free by simply removing the regime in Tehran. If, on the other hand, talks were initiated and America accepted Iran's assistance, Washington would be put in the awkward situation of owing the ayatollahs.[30] Why talk to Iran when you could simply dictate terms from a position of strength? After all, the swift success in Iraq showed that taking on Iran would not be too complicated. Only a month earlier, Undersecretary of

Defense for Policy Douglas Feith had briefed Defense and State Department officials on how the war in Iraq could be continued into Iran and Syria in order to replace the regimes there. The plans were quite extensive and far-reaching. "It was much more than just a contingency plan," Wilkerson recalled.[31] But just saying no to the Iranians was not enough. The Beltway hawks apparently wanted to add insult to injury.

Instead of simply rejecting the Iranian offer, the Bush administration decided to punish the Swiss for having delivered the proposal in the first place. Only a few days after its delivery, Washington rebuked Guldimann and the Swiss government for having overstepped its diplomatic mandate. "It was the most shameful thing," Wilkerson confessed. But the message to Tehran was clear—not only would the Bush administration refuse Iran the courtesy of a reply, it would punish those who sought to convey messages between the two.[32]

An opportunity for a major breakthrough had been willfully wasted. Many former Bush administration officials admit that the nonresponse was a mistake. The proposal came at an opportune time. Tehran did not have a functioning nuclear program, and they were not swimming in oil revenues from soaring energy demand. "At the time, the Iranians were not spinning centrifuges, they were not enriching uranium," Leverett said in an interview. Paul R. Pillar, former national intelligence officer for the Near East and South Asia, characterized it as a "missed opportunity," and Richard Haass, head of policy planning at the State Department at the time and now head of the Council on Foreign Relations, pointed out that the proposal was at least worth exploring. "To use an oil analogy, we could have drilled a dry hole," he said. "But I didn't see what we had to lose."[33] To those in the administration opposed to the neoconservative agenda, it was difficult to fathom how such an opportunity could have been dismissed. "In my mind it was one of those things you throw up in the air and say, 'I can't believe we did this,'" Wilkerson said.[34]

(Later, in February 2007, Secretary of State Condoleezza Rice was pressed by the House International Relations Committee on the Iranian grand-bargain proposal and was asked if the United States had missed a major opportunity. Contradicting an earlier interview with National Public Radio, in which she acknowledged having seen the proposal, Rice now told lawmakers that she could not recall ever having received it. "I just don't remember ever seeing any such thing," she said dismissively about the Iranian proposal. Fearing that the United States would end up having to negotiate with Iran, a possible motivation for Rice's about-face may have been to avoid having the outcome of any potential negotiations with Iran in 2007 be compared to what the United States could have achieved in 2003, when the country was in a far stronger position.)[35]

The proposal was not an isolated incident. Iranian diplomats in Europe and elsewhere were sending similar signals to the United States in the spring of 2003. Iran's envoys to Sweden and Britain also began sending signals that the regime was ready to negotiate a deal, using back channels other than the Swiss Foreign Ministry.[36] And in Geneva, much to the irritation of the neoconservatives, the discussions between Zarif and Khalilzad continued. On May 3, before Tehran realized that its proposal to the White House would be rebuffed, Zarif and Khalilzad met to discuss developments in Iraq. The Pentagon had warned Khalilzad about rumors of an imminent attack by al-Qaeda against U.S. forces in the Persian Gulf. Khalilzad was instructed to request Iran's help in drawing information from the al-Qaeda operatives held in Iranian captivity to shed light on the rumors. The information could be invaluable in preventing a potentially disastrous attack on U.S. forces. But Khalilzad had no authority to offer anything in return, particularly not the return of the MKO terrorists in Iraq. Seeking to break the stalemate in the discussions, Zarif offered a compromise: If Washington gave Iran the names of the MKO fighters in Iraq, Iran would give the United States the names of the al-Qaeda operatives in Iranian captivity.[37] The proposal fell on deaf ears, but the two diplomats agreed to meet again on May 25 to discuss this and other matters further.

Only a few weeks before Guldimann delivered the Iranian document to Washington, the Iranians made a similar offer to Israel in Athens. In an effort to signal the Jewish State that Iran was ready to come to an understanding with it, Gen. Mohsen Rezai, the former commander of the Iranian Revolutionary Guards, addressed a group of American, Israeli, and Palestinian officials and semiofficials at a meeting sponsored by an American university.[38]

In an unprecedented move, Rezai engaged in a question-and-answer session with the Israelis and discussed a bold proposal of a strategic realignment of U.S.-Iranian relations.[39] The gist of Rezai's plan was to work out a modus vivendi regarding the Israeli-Iranian standoff; the two states would respect each other's spheres of influence and stay out of each other's hair. If the United States and Israel reversed its isolation policy of Iran, Tehran would modify its behavior on several key issues, including Israel.[40] Iran would significantly moderate its position on the Israeli-Palestinian conflict by adopting a "Malaysian" or "Pakistani" profile, that is, it would be an Islamic state that would not recognize Israel, would occasionally criticize Israel, but would completely avoid confronting or challenging the Jewish State, either directly or via proxies.[41] Iran would also pressure groups such as Hezbollah to refrain from provoking Israel. In return, Israel would cease to oppose a U.S.-Iran rapprochement and would recognize Iran's role in the region, while the United States would end its policy of isolating Iran and accommodate a key Iranian role in the security of the Persian Gulf. For Iran, this was a way to slowly decouple U.S.-Iran relations from the Israeli-Iranian rivalry. "In the first year of the revolution, we didn't recognize Israel, yet we had diplomatic relations with the U.S.," said an official at the Iranian Foreign Ministry. "And when necessary, Israel could trade with Iran via the United States. This would be a temporary solution since we cannot recognize Israel at this time. . . . Israel would in practice be able to reach its goals, and Iran would in practice not oppose Israel's policies in the region."[42]

Support for the Pakistani/Malaysian model was particularly strong in the Iranian Foreign Ministry, in parts of the military establishment, and in the president's office, and it was also endorsed by former President Rafsanjani.[43] It also enjoyed the reluctant support of Ayatollah Khamenei, and this explained why Iranian diplomats on numerous occasions, including at a dinner on Capitol Hill attended by Zarif and several U.S. lawmakers, repeated the call for Iran's inclusion in regional decision-making in return for Iranian passivity on Israel.[44] The Iranians also communicated the gist of the Pakistani/Malaysian model to members of the Washington foreign policy community, who confirmed Iran's willingness to bargain on sensitive issues such as Iran's support to Hezbollah, Islamic Jihad, and Hamas, and even on Iran's human rights record.[45]

The Israelis were intrigued by the presentation. In a respectful and cordial tone they engaged the general whose aid and advice to Hezbollah had caused Israel so much pain and suffering in Lebanon. Many of the details of the proposal were not new—the Israelis had heard the same message delivered by official and unofficial representatives of Tehran in other meetings. But as the Israelis heard more and more Iranians repeat the same message, confidence grew that Tehran was serious. It wasn't just empty talk. The consistency of the message made it "more clear that it was a policy. Not a strategic policy, but a policy," explained one of Israel's foremost authorities on defense and security matters. "If I were a decision-maker, I would say, 'Let us move to quiet contacts.'"[46]

But the neoconservatives in Washington and hard-liners in the Israeli government did not want any "quiet contacts." The victory in Iraq and the rebuffing of the Iranian proposal energized them, and they redoubled their efforts to convince the White House to target Iran. "The liberation of Iraq was the first great battle for the future of the Middle East," wrote William Kristol, a leading neoconservative and the founder of the Project for the New American Century, in the *Weekly Standard,* in early May. "The next great battle—not, we hope, a military battle—will be for Iran. We are already in a death struggle with Iran over the future of Iraq."[47] Arguing that success in Iraq would "spell the death knell for the Iranian revolution," Kristol joined other neoconservatives in promoting the notion of a domino effect. As Iraq became a democracy, other dictatorships in the Middle East would either follow suit or perish under the weight of the demands of their own peoples. "Popular discontent in Iran tends to heat up when U.S. soldiers get close to the Islamic Republic," wrote Reuel Marc Gerecht of the American Enterprise Institute (AEI) in the same magazine.[48]

A confrontation with Iran was within reach, but before Washington could increase the heat on Iran the diplomatic option needed to be completely blocked. On May 6, at an AEI conference, Israeli-born Middle East specialist Meyrav Wurmser (whose husband currently serves as a senior adviser to Cheney) spelled out the next target of the neoconservatives: Khalilzad's discussions with Zarif in Geneva. "Our fight against Iraq was only one battle in a long war," Wurmser said. "It would be ill-conceived to think that we can deal with Iraq alone. . . . We must move on, and faster. . . . It was a grave error to send [Khalilzad] to secret meetings with representatives of the Iranian government in recent weeks. Rather than coming as victors who should be feared and respected rather than loved, we are still engaged in old diplomacy, in the kind of politics that led to the attacks of Sep. 11."[49]

Six days later, on May 12, a terrorist attack in Riyadh, killing eight Americans and twenty-six Saudis, provided the neoconservatives with the impetus to put an end to Khalilzad's diplomacy. Within days, fingers were pointed at Iran. Rumsfeld declared that the operation seemed to have been ordered by al-Qaeda in Iran. On May 15, David Martin of CBS News reported that the Pentagon had evidence that the attacks in Saudi Arabia "were planned and directed by senior al-Qaeda operatives who have found safe haven in Iran." But no such evidence existed. Although phone calls had been detected between al-Qaeda operatives in Saudi Arabia and Iran, there was no evidence that these activities were undertaken with the Iranian government's approval or knowledge. "The Iran experts agreed that, even if al-

Qaeda had come in and out of Iran, it didn't mean the Iranian government was complicit," Wilkerson said. "There were parts of Iran where the government would not know what was going on."[50]

The next meeting in Geneva was scheduled for May 25, but by May 14 the Iranians suspected that Washington might cancel the talks. Iran's ambassador to Afghanistan reported to Tehran that the Americans would be a no-show for the meeting, even though Washington had yet to formally cancel it. As a result, Zarif never traveled to Tehran from New York to receive instructions for the meeting. (As Iran's UN ambassador, Zarif was based in New York and had to travel to Iran both before and after every Geneva session to receive instructions and brief Tehran on the deliberations. Because of the sensitivity of the matter, all briefings and instructions were conducted orally, many of them directly with Iran's supreme leader.)[51] A few days before the scheduled meeting, Washington sent a message to Tehran via the Swiss—whose services were needed once more—that the Geneva Channel had been closed. The neoconservative hawks had scored yet another victory, but the battle for Iran was far from over.

The diplomats at the State Department were down, but they were not out. In 2003, just as in 1996, when AIPAC moved ahead with congressional sanctions to ensure that President Clinton would not be able to reverse them (since only Congress can undo congressionally mandated sanctions), Congress could once again limit the president's maneuverability. The newly created alliance between AIPAC and evangelical Christian Republicans on Capitol Hill turned out to be particularly helpful for this cause. Senator Sam Brownback, an ambitious second-term evangelical Republican from Kansas, had in the early spring of 2003 taken the lead in the Senate in undermining any U.S.-Iran dialogue. Knowing Powell's inclination to seek a dialogue with Iran and a grand bargain, Brownback worked to place political obstacles in Powell's path.

On April 8, Brownback introduced a controversial amendment to the 2004 Foreign Relations Authorization Act authorizing $50 million a year to aid Iranian opposition activists. The amendment was a simple recycling of ideas proposed in June 2002 by Pentagon staffers in the Bush administration's Iran policy review discussions. Though the Pentagon staffers' efforts had failed, Brownback gave new life to their ideas in the Senate. By introducing an amendment that would extend financial support to Iranian opposition groups—similar to American funding of the opposition group Iraqi National Congress, led by Ahmad Chalabi—Washington would take a decisive step toward making regime change in Iran official U.S. policy. Once this happened, prospects for a U.S.-Iran dialogue or a grand bargain would effectively be eliminated.

The amendment sought to create an Iran Democracy Foundation that in turn would disperse $50 million to various Iranian opposition groups and satellite TV channels in the United States. Only a week earlier, at a private briefing on Capitol Hill organized by the Iranian Jewish Public Affairs Committee,[52] Reza Pahlavi, the son of the late Shah and a supporter of Brownback, had urged Hill staffers to support the idea of funding the Iranian opposition. The Persian prince reassured staffers that any concerns about the money tainting the opposition groups could be resolved by creating "a degree of separation" between Congress and the Iranian recipients. The Iran Democracy Foundation would do just that. In fact, the language in the amendment closely resembled that used in the Iraq Liberation Act passed by Congress in 1998, which made regime change in Iraq official U.S. policy and paved the way for the Iraq war of 2003 by effectively eliminating all diplomatic options. AIPAC immediately came out in support of the amendment.[53]

Pahlavi's links to Israel and pro-Israeli forces in Washington were not new. In the early 1980s he had approached then–Defense Minister Sharon with a plan to overthrow the clerics. But with the rise of the neoconservatives in the Bush administration, Pahlavi had a new excuse to reconnect with his old friends. Just as he needed the pro-Israeli groups to get his message across to Beltway decision-makers, AIPAC and the neoconservatives benefited from giving their agenda an Iranian face. "There is a pact emerging between hawks in the administration, Jewish groups and Iranian supporters of Reza Pahlavi to push for regime change," Pooya Dayanim, president of the Iranian Jewish Public Affairs Committee in Los Angeles, told the Jewish magazine *The Forward*.

Though Pahlavi met with the board of the hawkish Jewish Institute for National Security Affairs, Sharon, former Prime Minister Benjamin Netanyahu, and Israel's Iranian-born president, Moshe Katsav, he failed to impress his audience.[54] His political savvy did not match his enthusiasm. For instance, Pahlavi pushed to address the annual AIPAC conference in May 2003 in Washington, but AIPAC officials had to convince the son of the Shah that too close an association with the pro-Israel lobby might not go down too well with his own base—the Iranian diaspora in the United States.[55]

But Pahlavi's help and suggestions for the creation of the Iran Democracy Foundation were welcomed. Brownback's amendment became the perfect vehicle for Pentagon hawks to prevent Bush from acting on the Iranian grand-bargain proposal. Ironically, in spite of the Kansas senator's condemnation of the Iranian government's support of terror, he apparently did not apply the same benchmark to himself. When the French authorities arrested MKO leader Maryam Rajavi in June 2003 in Paris, Brownback immediately tried to help the Iranian militants. Even though the MKO was funded by Saddam Hussein, as Bush himself had acknowledged, and even though it was on the State Department's list of terrorist organizations and was responsible for the deaths of several Americans, Brownback sent a letter to France Ambassador Jean-David Levitte, urging that no action be taken against Rajavi. France should not do the "dirty work of the Islamic Republic of Iran" by empowering "a terrorist regime over a group of its own people who are protesting for freedom," he wrote.[56] But the Kansas senator's efforts to help the terrorist-listed organization were for naught.

Brownback's initial push for the amendment also failed, partly because the intended opposition groups failed to come across as competent and credible. At a briefing on Capitol Hill, Reza Pahlavi left Hill staffers confused and unconvinced when he spoke of America in the "we" form. Pahlavi praised the U.S. efforts in Iraq and pointed out the moral superiority of the American army. "We [America] have taken casualties that we would have avoided had we not tried to avoid civilian deaths on their [Iraqi] side," he told the perplexed staffers, who first thought that perhaps a small contingency of Iranian soldiers loyal to Reza Pahlavi had fought alongside American marines as they entered Baghdad. Though he failed to pass his amendment, Brownback arguably attained his key goal: complicating U.S.-Iran relations and hindering the State Department from pushing the White House toward exploring further dialogue with Tehran. For Israel, continuous U.S.-Iran tensions helped keep the military option open and hope alive that, after Baghdad, real men would go to Tehran.

Meanwhile, in Tehran, the American nonresponse was perceived as an insult. Now it was Iran complaining about the difficulty of dealing with an ideological regime—the Bush administration. "These people in Washington don't see the world for what it is; they only see what they want to see," an Iranian reformist told me. "We used to suffer from the same mindset after the Revolution, but we learned very quickly the dangers of an ideological foreign policy. We paid a very high price for our initial mistakes."[57] Washington's handling of the Iranian proposal strengthened Iran's belief that dealing with the United States from a position of weakness would not work.

Offering support to America in Iraq or compromises was futile because Washington would demand complete submission from Iran when it believed it had plenty of maneuverability and other options to choose from. The Bush administration would agree to deal with Iran on an equal basis, the clerics reasoned, only if it were deprived of all other options.

Just as in the 1991–1993 period, after Iran was shunned from the Madrid conference and the United States intensified its efforts to isolate Iran following Iran's help in the first Persian Gulf War, Washington's decision strengthened the hands of those in Tehran who argued that America could be compelled to come to the negotiating table only if a cost was imposed on it when it did not come to the table. The balance in Iran thus tilted in favor of the hard-liners, and, as before, the diplomats involved in the opening to the United States paid a price for their risk-taking. "The failure is not just for the idea, but also for the group who were pursuing the idea," Seyyed Mohammad Hossein Adeli said.[58] (As Iran's ambassador to Britain, Adeli was later fired by Iran's new hard-line president, Mahmoud Ahmadinejad.) Just as the first Bush administration had done in 1991, the current Bush administration reasoned that the United States did not need to negotiate with Iran; America was too strong and too awesome, Iran too weak and too fragile. It was hubris again.

The Israeli hawks, in turn, believed that Iran's outreach was an attempt to buy time in order to strengthen itself against the American threat, which had grown perilous after the defeat of Saddam in Iraq. Both the Barak and Sharon governments rejected Iran's outreach on the grounds that Iran did not have an interest in Israel, but was only seeking to improve relations with the United States, after which it would continue to counter Israel.[59] According to Knesset member Ephraim Sneh, who refused to believe that Iran was willing to soften its stand on Israel, dialogue with Tehran was "totally baseless, totally futile." It would only provide Iran with another chance to escape American justice. The Iranians will never change their stance on Israel, he believed, so the only option is to replace the regime. "The regime in Tehran, they don't accept the legitimacy of the Jewish State in this part of the world," he told me at his Tel Aviv office. "When this is the case, what should I talk to them [about]—the terms of my execution?"[60] Why should the United States negotiate with Tehran and permit the ayatollahs to survive, when America had the strength to end it once and for all, the Israeli hawks argued. But other voices in Israel were more cautious and at times regretted having missed what could have been an opportunity and an opening. "I think it is a huge mistake not to open a channel," a leading Israeli military commentator said. "Not in order to solve everything, but [for] both sides to understand each other better. Both sides will understand the red lines [through dialogue]."[61]

Just as before, the complexity of regional politics revealed that few victories are long-lasting in the Middle East. Only months after the defeat of Saddam, an insurgency erupted that yet again turned the tables for Iran and the United States. While Tehran's influence began to rise, because of its ties to the Shias in the south and the Kurds in the north, Washington's maneuverability began to shrink. The Bush administration had painted itself into a corner by undermining its own credibility and all but convincing the Iranians that America's end goal—regardless of its short-term cooperation with Tehran—was the destruction of the Islamic Republic. The glee on Deputy Oil Minister Hadi Nejad-Hosseinian's face was obvious when he explained how the United States had inadvertently strengthened Iran. Washington had helped transform Iran into a regional power by defeating Saddam and the Taliban, all the while getting itself bogged down in Mesopotamia. "Iraq couldn't have turned out better for us," he told me, smiling.[62]

part three
looking ahead

20

facing the future, facing reality

Who dominates the Middle East—Iran or the United States?
—Former German Foreign Minister Joschka Fischer, May 29, 2006

Since the end of the Cold War, Israel and Iran's rivalry has stood in the way of many of America's strategic objectives in the Middle East. Both states have undermined U.S. policies that they deemed beneficial to the other. Iran worked against the Middle East peace process to prevent the United States from creating what Tehran feared would be an Israel-centric Middle East order based on Iran's prolonged isolation. Israel, in turn, opposed talks between the United States and Iran, fearing that a U.S.-Iran rapprochement would grant Iran strategic significance in Washington at Israel's expense precisely because Iran was a powerful country that shared many global interests with the United States, in spite of their conflicting ideologies.[1]

The United States could benefit from a powerful Iran serving as a buffer against Chinese access to Persian Gulf and Caspian Basin energy resources, just as Iran had served as a buffer against the Soviet Union before the collapse of Communism. Israel feared a strong, missile-equipped, and potentially nuclearized Iran that neither it nor Washington would be able to influence much.[2] While many in Israel felt that the Jewish State couldn't compete with Iran at the strategic level—in terms of being of value to the United States—others argued that Israel's special relationship with the United States wasn't based on strategic interests to begin with. The special relationship is "based on a kind of affinity," explained Shlomo Brom of the Jaffee Center for Strategic Studies. "It is based on the fact that a large sector in the U.S. population support Israel: the Jews, the Christian Right, and others. It is based on common values."[3]

Neither Israel nor Iran—nor indeed the entire Middle East—has overcome the geopolitical earthquake that shook the region after the collapse of the Soviet Union. Israel and Iran's fear that the creation of a new order in the region would benefit the other is acute precisely because the Middle East lacks a geopolitical basis for its frail order. The recurring process of establishing a new and stable balance brings to the surface and intensifies regional rivalries. Not only has the Soviet collapse yet to be absorbed, but the full consequences of America's defeat of the Taliban and Iraq are still to be known. To make matters worse, Washington has sought to establish an order that contradicts the natural balance by seeking to contain and isolate Iran, one of the most powerful countries of the region. Even if an artificial order could be established based on the exclusion of a regional giant like Iran, it won't be able to stand on its own legs and will last for only as long as the United States is willing to invest in its upkeep. The price, however, is becoming increasingly onerous for the United States.

The conflict between Iran and Israel wasn't sparked by an ideological difference, nor is it ideological fervor that keeps it alive today. Certainly, this does not mean that the ideologies of these states are irrelevant; at a minimum, the rhetoric they produce makes a political accommodation more difficult. Anti-Zionist views are held by most, if not all, Iranian officials. But the impact of the ideological orientation of these leaders on Iran's foreign policy is a different matter altogether. The major transformations of Israeli-Iranian relations have all coincided with geopolitical rather than ideological shifts. The Shah began distancing himself from Israel after Iran had become so strong that it could neutralize the Arab threat and befriend the Arab states from a position of strength. At that point, Iran increasingly viewed its relationship with Israel as a burden rather than an asset. The Shah's failure to win Arab support for his leadership position, partly a result of his close ties to Israel, prompted the revolutionaries to seek a different formula to bridge the Arab-Persian divide—political Islam. That orientation intensified Tehran's need to oppose Israel, even though clandestine security ties with the Jewish State continued.

The most dramatic turn for the worse in Israeli-Iranian relations came in the early 1990s, with the end of the Cold War and the defeat of Iraq in the Persian Gulf War. Ironically, Iran's ideological zeal was sharply declining in those years. While Iranian foreign policy has always had an ideological component, ideology has been translated into operational policy in relation to Israel only when coupled with a strategic interest, as was the case in the post–Cold War era.[4] "The Israelis are against Iran having an important, or number-one, role in the region. As a result, they are against Iran's development," explained Mohsen Mirdamadi, who headed the Foreign Relations Committee in the Iranian Parliament in the late 1990s. "So this is a strategic conflict we have with Israel. And if we were looking at it ideologically, we would still oppose Israel."[5]

When Iran's ideological and strategic interests collided, as they did in the 1980s, strategic considerations consistently prevailed. For the Iranians, this is not a contradiction but a simple fact of life. Ideology is not an absolute for the rulers in Tehran. Former President Hashemi Rafsanjani admitted as much at a Friday prayer sermon. "We have made inappropriate measures or never made any measures. And we have delayed making decisions. Our ideology is flexible. We can choose expediency on the basis of Islam."[6] On another occasion, Rafsanjani rejected the notion that Iranian foreign policy should be based on ideological principles in which the state would have to act according to its duties (vazifeh) under Islam, regardless of the consequences it would suffer. "To put the country in jeopardy on the ground that we are acting on [an] Islamic basis is not at all Islamic."[7] According to former Deputy Foreign Minister Abbas Maleki, Iran's foreign policy has long ceased to be ideological. "Ideology means that we must have pro-Muslims policies in all of the world. Yes, we claim that we are pro-Muslims in all of the world . . . but we didn't support Chechen Muslims. If ideology was the first motivator for Iranian foreign policy, Iran must do that. But Iran didn't."[8] As much as the Iranian leaders may have wanted to pursue their ideological goals, no force in Iran's foreign policy is as dominant as geopolitical considerations.[9]

In spite of Israel's rhetoric to the contrary, many high-level decision-makers in Tel Aviv recognize this and contend that Iran's ambitions are independent of the Islamist nature of its ruling regime. "What had been for the Shah an ambition built on nationalism was for his successors a parallel ambition built on an Islamist radicalism that often simply served as a thin disguise for nationalism," argued Barry Rubin, director of the Global Research in International Affairs (GLORIA) Center in Jerusalem. The Iranian endgame, as the Israelis see it, has not differed much from the time of the Shah.[10] "The Persians want hegemony! They always have, they always will," an old Iran hand in Israel told me bluntly.

When one scratches the surface, even Iran's President Mahmoud Ahmadinejad's venomous outbursts against Israel turn out to have strategic motivations. Ahmadinejad did something few Iranian leaders had done before him—he questioned the Holocaust. (The previous president, Mohammad Khatami, had carefully avoided these excesses.) "Today, they have created a myth in the name of Holocaust and consider it to be above God, religion and the prophets," Ahmadinejad told a crowd in the fall of 2005 in the southeastern Iranian region of Zahedan. "If you [Europeans] committed this big crime, then why should the oppressed Palestinian nation pay the price?" he continued. "You [Europeans] have to pay the compensation yourself." Immediately, the president of the UN Security Council issued a statement denouncing the Iranian president's comments. The Europeans, not surprisingly, were infuriated and threatened to join the United States in taking a much harsher position against Iran. The swift international backlash took Tehran by surprise, sparking an intense internal debate within the government. The statements angered Iran's nuclear negotiators, who had been conducting delicate talks with the Europeans since 2003 over Iran's nuclear program. The rhetoric undermined their fine-tuned balancing act that sought simultaneously to avoid referral to the Security Council and to defend Iran's right to uranium enrichment, they maintained.

The camp around Ahmadinejad forcefully argued that Iran should enlarge the conflict and make Israel a critical and visible part of the international debate on Iran's nuclear program. Viewing it in isolation only benefited the West. By expanding the scope of the debate, Iran would find the necessary levers to defend its position. At a minimum, the Ahmadinejad camp argued, a cost should be imposed on Israel for having made the Iranian nuclear program a subject of grave international concern and for having convinced Washington to adopt a very hawkish policy on the matter. Ahmadinejad's opponents in the more moderate camp agreed on the necessity of putting Israel on the defensive and enlarging the debate, but they strongly differed as to the best way to achieve those objectives. According to a senior Iranian official, people close to Ahmadinejad favored putting into question issues Israel had managed to settle over the past two decades: Israel's legitimacy and right to exist, the reality of the Holocaust, and the right of European Jews to remain in the heart of the Middle East. Such an approach, they argued, would resonate with the discontented Arab street and reveal the impotence of the pro-U.S. Arab regimes, which would be in equal parts pressured and embarrassed.

Just as Iran had done in the early 1980s, it again sought to neutralize the pro-Western Arab governments in the region by playing to the Arab street. If the nuclear standoff was framed as an American-Israeli assault on an Islamic Iran that stood up for the Palestinians, it would be next to impossible for Arab governments—however much they disliked Tehran—to publicly oppose Iran because that would make them appear to be siding with Israel. This was an old Iranian trick; the Israelis are well familiar with it, though they have little with which to counter it. "In my view this remains, even with this nuclear thing, the main purpose of Ahmadinejad's incendiary rhetoric," explained Shlomo Ben-Ami, Israel's former foreign minister. "If the discourse in the Middle East is an Arab discourse, Iran is isolated. If it is an Islamic discourse, then Iran is in a leading position. And always with the view of protecting Iran and the Iranian revolution, which is why they tried all the time to oppose the peace process."[11]

More moderate voices in Tehran strongly opposed this approach because of the difficulties they predicted it would cause for Iran's nuclear diplomacy. They favored Khatami's tactic of invoking the suffering of the Palestinian people and Israel's unwillingness to make territorial concessions, but avoiding hot-button issues such as Israel's right to exist or the Holocaust. Taking the rhetoric to such levels, they argued, could backfire and turn key countries like Russia and China against Iran. Part of this debate played out publicly in the pages of Iran's press. *Sharq*, a reformist daily that Ahmadinejad later shut down for criticizing him too openly, published an editorial blasting the Iranian president's Holocaust denial. The commentary focused on two arguments—the Holocaust wasn't Iran's issue; and rather than turning the table on Tehran's enemies, Ahmadinejad's statement would only make things worse for Iran.[12]

What was conspicuously absent from the internal debate in Tehran, however, was the ideological motivations and factors that Iran publicly invoked to justify its stance on Israel. Neither the honor of Islam nor the suffering of the Palestinian people figured in the deliberations. Rather, both the terms of the debate and its outcome were of a purely strategic nature. Both camps aimed at giving Iran the initiative in the confrontation with the United States and Israel to avoid suffering the fate of Iraq, where from 1991 until the 2003 invasion Washington remained largely in firm control of events. Though the regime didn't reach a consensus on how to resolve the matter, all Iranian officials were forbidden by Ayatollah Khamenei to repeat the venomous Holocaust remarks for the time being—much to Ahmadinejad's frustration.

That decision still holds. When Ahmadinejad visited New York to address the UN General Assembly in September 2006, Western journalists challenged him on the Holocaust issue. But rather than repeating his earlier remarks, Ahmadinejad turned the question into a different debate: Whether the Palestinians should pay for the crimes of Nazi Germany, and why debating the Holocaust is a crime in some European states. "If this event happened, where did it happen?" Ahmadinejad asked CNN's Anderson Cooper. "The 'where' is the main question. And it wasn't in Palestine. [So] why is the Holocaust used as a pretext to occupy the Palestinian lands?" He then went on to call for more research into the topic as he completely avoided acknowledging the reality of the Holocaust or repeating his previous characterization of it as a myth.[13] But even without repeating his earlier remarks, Ahmadinejad showed how easily he could undermine his moderate rivals in Tehran by infuriating Western audiences.

NUCLEAR AYATOLLAHS?

The standoff over Iran's nuclear program must also be addressed in this context. Just as the Israeli-Iranian enmity isn't driven by ideological differences between the two, neither is it solely caused by a sense of threat in Israel arising from Iran's nuclear activities. Certainly Israel has legitimate concerns about Iranian nuclear plans, but these worries cannot in and of themselves explain why Israeli-Iranian relations took a turn for the worse in 1992—three years after Israel discovered that Iran had restarted its nuclear program—nor why those concerns were temporarily put to rest by Netanyahu in 1996 when he tried to reach out to Iran. "Israel didn't really pay any attention to [the Iranian nuclear program] until the peace process," explained Keith Weissman of the American Israel Public Affairs Committee (AIPAC).[14] At that time, the program was at an embryonic stage. Iran didn't have any uranium centrifuges and it lacked much of the know-how to develop nuclear weapons—and it still does.

According to a comprehensive U.S. intelligence review, in 2005 Iran was about a decade away from manufacturing the key ingredient for a nuclear weapon.[15] Furthermore, according to several Israeli decision-makers, the Labor Party exaggerated the Iranian threat for political reasons. Though a distant threat did exist, Prime Minister Yitzhak Rabin overplayed it to sell the land-for-peace formula to the Israeli public, a former adviser to Rabin explained.[16] After all, Israel's behavior did not square with the idea that it faced an existential threat from Iran. If it did, one would expect Israel to explore all avenues to neutralize that threat, including a U.S.-Iran dialogue. Instead, Israel worked strenuously to prevent any such dialogue from taking place.

The Shah started Iran's nuclear program back in the 1970s. Iran produced more oil then than it does today, and its domestic consumption was much lower in those days. Still, President Gerald Ford offered Tehran the chance to buy a U.S.-built reprocessing facility for extracting plutonium from nuclear reactor fuel. Through that offer, Iran would master the complete nuclear fuel cycle, which also would grant it the know-how to produce material for a nuclear bomb. But Washington wanted to go even further. In 1975, Secretary of State Henry Kissinger developed a negotiating strategy for the sale of nuclear energy equipment to Iran projected to bring American business more than $6 billion in revenue. Dick Cheney, Paul Wolfowitz, and Donald Rumsfeld all held key national security posts in the Ford administration. More than a quarter century later, however, the same individuals were in the forefront of a campaign seeking to deny Iran access to that same technology, arguing that a country with Iran's oil wealth would seek the technology for military purposes only.[17]

Though Iran is still years away from having the capability and material to build a nuclear bomb, the standoff has reached a critical point because of Iran's efforts to master uranium enrichment. According to Israel, once Iran learns how to enrich uranium in large quantities and to high degrees, it will have passed a "point of no return." Iran will have acquired the necessary know-how, after which it will be next to impossible to stop Tehran from going nuclear. But there are many problems with this analysis. For one, Iran—unlike Israel—has signed the Non-Proliferation Treaty (NPT), and the majority of the parties to the treaty believe that Iran has a right to uranium enrichment under Article IV of the NPT, which guarantees all states "the inalienable right . . . to develop research, production and use of nuclear energy for peaceful purposes without discrimination." Denying Iran that right would change the terms of the treaty, which many nuclear have-nots are reluctant to go along with unless the nuclear-haves live up to their commitment under Article VI of the treaty and begin dismantling their nuclear arsenals.[18] Second, according to some nonproliferation experts, the concept of a point of no return is an arbitrary measure used for political purposes. "The 'point of no return' concept is not a valid one, and the voices in America and in Israel using it to push for a quick solution are misleading," said Jon Wolfsthal, a former senior Energy Department official. "This is a made-up term by those who want immediate action."[19]

Immediate action is precisely what the Israelis have been calling for. "Every day that passes brings the Iranians closer to building a bomb," Israel's Foreign Minister Tzipi Livni said in the summer of 2006. "The world cannot afford a nuclear Iran."[20] The pro-Israel lobby in Washington took a characteristically more hawkish position than the Israeli government itself. "The parallels of the geo-political climate of March 5, 1933, and that of March 5, 2006, are stunning in their likeness; eerie in their implication," AIPAC Executive Director Howard Kohr told five thousand AIPAC supporters at their annual banquet in Washington in March 2006. Before Kohr's speech, the audience was shown a series of video clips comparing Adolf Hitler's rise to power with Ahmadinejad's tenure as Iran's president.[21] The Israelis have put a tremendous amount of pressure on the Bush administration to act. They played a key role in convincing Washington to adopt a zero-enrichment policy, meaning that Iran must be completely denied any enrichment technology. Even a small pilot-scale program would be unacceptable, because Iran could still learn how to master the technology from such a program, the Israelis maintained. Whenever the Bush administration hinted at warming up to a compromise, the Israelis sounded the alarm bells.

For instance, when the Bush administration expressed support for a proposal that would permit Iran to continue its nuclear development as long as enrichment took place in Russia, AIPAC came out strongly against the Bush administration.[22] At a briefing on Capitol Hill, a senior Israeli diplomat was asked what kind of inspections regime would make the Israelis feel comfortable with an Iranian *civilian* nuclear program. Without hesitation the diplomat replied, "None." Instead, he explained, the only guarantee acceptable to Israel was "the debilitation of Iran's industrial base." If the United States doesn't take quick action on Iran, the Israelis said, the Jewish State "may have to go it alone," hinting that it might try to destroy Iran's nuclear facilities itself.

The prospect of an Israeli assault on Iran's nuclear installations created a major headache for the White House, because the United States would be automatically blamed for such action—regardless of whether President Bush had given the Israelis a green light or not. And since Israel itself does not have the military capability to successfully take out Iran's program through air strikes, the veiled threats coming out of Tel Aviv were likely aimed at pressuring Washington not to moderate its stance, by warning it about the consequences of an Israeli assault on Iran: a major escalation of the violence in the region that would pose a serious danger to U.S. security, given Washington's increasingly vulnerable position in Iraq. Whether it liked it or not, Washington would get sucked into the ensuing mess.

Ironically, Tehran might not be pursuing a nuclear weapon itself, but the capability to be able to go nuclear in case it faces an imminent threat.

(For Iran to possess such a capability, however, is still seen as a major problem by Western powers.) International Atomic Energy Agency (IAEA) Executive Director Mohamed ElBaradei has suggested that Iran's preferred option is to have the capability to make weapons without having to do so. ElBaradei said the Iranians know that mastering uranium enrichment is "a deterrent" in and of itself and that "they don't need a weapon; [enrichment] sends a message." The IAEA director qualified his comments on the *NewsHour with Jim Lehrer* on March 18, 2004: "Well, what I mean is . . . if you have an enrichment program or a reprocessing program, which means that you can produce uranium . . . you are really sending a message that we know how to do it, should we decide to make a weapon. We don't need . . . to develop a weapon, but I am telling you—you know, the world, my neighbors, that I can do it."[23]

The Iranians are well aware that a decision to weaponize would likely weaken rather than advance Iran's strategic position. As long as the Middle East is kept as free as possible from nuclear weapons, Iran will enjoy a conventional superiority vis-à-vis its neighbors because of its size and resources. However, if Iran weaponizes, it will risk sparking a nuclear arms race that may lead small states such as Bahrain and Kuwait to opt for a nuclear capability as well. In such a Middle East, Iran would lose its conventional superiority and find itself at strategic parity with states less than one-twentieth its size. This is partly why Iran joined with another populous regional state—Egypt—to keep the Middle East a nuclear-free zone back in the 1970s. As large states, Iran and Egypt would have the least to gain and the most to lose by going nuclear. As a small state, Israel would have the most to gain. (The Israelis disagree with this analysis and assume that Iran will seek to obtain a nuclear weapon no matter what.)[24]

Furthermore, Tehran believes that it has effective deterrence capabilities against almost all states in the region, including Israel, and wouldn't need nuclear weapons to dissuade the Jewish State from attacking Iran. "From the government's perspective, weapons of mass destruction would not constitute a deterrence against Israel. We have other deterrences that work better," Iran's UN Ambassador Javad Zarif explained, hinting at Iran's asymmetric capabilities in Lebanon.[25] (The effectiveness of this deterrence was demonstrated during the Israeli-Hezbollah war in the summer of 2006.) The only threat against which Iran lacks an effective deterrence is the United States (though Iran does have a partial deterrent in the form of influence over Shia militias in Iraq, which could badly hurt the already-failing U.S. occupation there). But if relations with the United States could be patched up, Iran could perhaps also be deprived of one of the key motivators for attaining nuclear weapons.

A DETERRABLE TEHRAN?

Israel's fear of a nuclear Iran is understandable, even though Israel does not believe that Iran would necessarily use the doomsday weapon against it.[26] That would surely lead to Iran's own destruction: Iranian civilian and military leaders are well aware of Israel's arsenal of two hundred nuclear warheads and its second-strike capability through its three nuclear-equipped Dolphin submarines. And contrary to the depiction of the Iranians as "mad mullahs," most strategic thinkers in Israel recognize that the Iranian government is extremist and radical—but rational.

In fact, Iran is a more potent adversary of Israel precisely because it is *not* irrational and careless. Iran has acted with greater savvy and caution than have many of Israel's traditional foes. Whereas Saddam was careless and adventurous, and committed strategic blunders by attacking Iran in 1980 and Kuwait in 1990, Tehran has operated according to completely different principles. Even under the most ideological days of the Iranian revolution, Iran was never reckless or completely insensitive to its losses.[27] "People here respect the Iranians and the Iranian regime. They take them as very serious, calculating players," said Ehud Yaari, a veteran Israeli television journalist.[28] Efraim Halevi, the former Mossad boss, concurred. "I don't think they are irrational, I think they are very rational. To label them as irrational is escaping from reality and it gives you kind of an escape clause," he said.[29] As long as the other side is rational, an Israeli deterrent capacity against an Iranian nuclear threat has a strong chance of succeeding precisely because the Iranians know the price of attacking Israel, according to Reuven Pedatzur, director of the Galili Center for Strategy and National Security and a fighter pilot in the Israeli Air Force reserves.[30]

Iran's rationality may also be the reason why thus far it has not shared chemical or biological weapons with any of its Arab proxies such as Hezbollah, and why a nuclear Iran likely would not share nuclear weapons with terrorist groups. Israel has signaled Iran that it would retaliate against any nuclear attack on Israel by hitting Iran—regardless of who attacked Israel. Tehran has fully grasped the meaning of the signal—if any of Iran's proxies attacked Israel with a nuclear warhead, Israel would destroy Iran. But even without this stern warning, Iran would be unlikely to share the doomsday weapon with its proxies precisely because those groups would cease to be proxies if they acquired such a powerful weapon. Iran's ambition, after all, is to become the region's undisputed power; given its tendency to view all other actors as potential competitors, it's hardly likely Tehran would undermine its goal by sharing the sensitive technology. Judging from Tehran's past behavior, the Iranian leadership is too Machiavellian to commit such an irrevocable and devastating mistake.

The minority view in Israel, dubbed the Beginist view, is advocated by people like Deputy Defense Minister Ephraim Sneh, Knesset member Uzi Landau, and Gen. Amos Gilad. They argue that the preemptive doctrine of Menachem Begin—who destroyed Iraq's nuclear facility by bombing Osirak in 1981—must guide Israel's approach to Iran. The states in the Middle East are irrational and suicidal, according to this school of thought, and, as a result, no stable deterrent option is available.[31] Israel cannot afford to take any risks with such enemies. The only viable defense is to ensure that these countries do not gain access to nuclear technology to begin with by preemptively destroying their nuclear facilities.

Advocates of this line often point to a statement made by Rafsanjani in early 2002, in which he discussed how Israel's smaller territory would make it more vulnerable to a nuclear attack, hinting—the Beginists say—that Iran believes it can win a nuclear war with Israel. (Rafsanjani later accused Israel of distorting his statement.)[32] In the end, the Beginists have had a greater impact on Israel's rhetoric and portrayal of the conflict than on its actual policy regarding Iran. After all, if Iran is an irrational and suicidal state, then why hasn't it committed suicide yet? For the last twenty-seven years, the Islamic Republic seems to have declined every opportunity to destroy itself. In fact, the clerics in Tehran are probably more powerful now than ever before. Given the Iranian government's many internal problems and its unpopularity at home and abroad, it is difficult to see how the clerics could have achieved this success had they been irrational.

Nevertheless, it is not surprising that many in Israel have drawn the conclusion that Tehran is irrational because that is arguably what the clerics want Iran's enemies to believe. But behind their often contradictory behavior lies a single, carefully calculated policy. Iran uses this contradiction to conceal its interests and make itself appear irrational and unpredictable. It has been called "simulated irrationality."[33] "We should not be calculable and predictable to them [Iran's enemies]," Amir Mohebian, an influential conservative strategist, explained. "The U.S. could not mess with Imam [Khomeini] because he wasn't calculable. . . . Saddam's fall was because he was calculable; they knew that even if he had weapons of mass destruction he would not dare use them."[34]

This line of thinking is not limited to the conservative camp in Iran. According to an adviser to the Iranian National Security Advisor, it is rooted in Iran's experience during the nineteenth and twentieth centuries, when the country's openness enabled foreign powers to manipulate it in order to exploit its natural resources and render it dependent on the West. The Iranian government believes that "you have to maintain a calculated distance with foreigners," the adviser explained. "You don't let them understand how you're running your affairs. And that's why I think there is an intention out there to confuse. That is why they would let so many contradictory policies be aired by different institutions. That's fine. That buys [Iran] security [because] we know what we are doing."[35] Iran may have fooled many in Israel with this strategy, but it has also contributed to the enormous lack of trust between Iran and the outside world, which in turn has made it all the more difficult to find a solution to Iran's problems with the United States and the international community.

Whether Iran is rational or not, suicidal or not, or even if it is intent on attacking Israel or not, a nuclear Iran would still pose a problem for Israel because of its impact on Israel's strategic maneuverability. The real danger to Israel of a nuclear-capable Iran is twofold. First, an Iran that does not have nuclear weapons—but that can build them—will significantly damage Israel's ability to deter militant Palestinian and Lebanese organizations. It will damage the image of Israel as the sole nuclear-armed state in the region and undercut the myth of its invincibility. That image is "the most powerful stabilizer of the peace. It's our deterrence," Gilad told me. Such an Iranian deterrence capability would undermine Israel's military supremacy and prevent it from dictating the parameters of peace and pursuing unilateral peace plans. "We cannot afford a nuclear bomb in the hands of our enemies, period. They don't have to use it; the fact that they have it is enough," Sneh argued. A nuclear Iran could force Israel to accept territorial compromises with its neighbors to deprive Tehran of points of hostility that it could use against the Jewish State. Israel simply would not be able to afford a nuclear rivalry with Iran and continued territorial disputes with the Arabs at the same time. Second, the deterrence and power Iran would gain by mastering the fuel cycle could compel Washington to cut a deal with Tehran in which Iran would be recognized as a regional power and gain strategic significance in the Middle East at the expense of Israel.

WASHINGTON'S OPTIONS: BETWEEN A ROCK AND A HARD PLACE

When it comes to Iran and the Israeli-Iranian rivalry, conventional wisdom says that Washington does not have any good options. But some are worse than others. Some are built on fancy theories that have little connection to reality, similar to Israel's insistence on remaining loyal to the periphery doctrine in the 1980s even after Khomeini had seized power in Iran. The Israelis' worldview was based on rather simplistic assumptions about the mechanisms of international relations that failed to take into account Iran's conflicting interests. On the one hand, Israel believed that the Arab-Israeli rift was so deep that no real peace with the Arabs was achievable (in spite of its agreement with Egypt at Camp David I); on the other hand, it assumed that Iran reasoned along the same lines that Israel did. Iran would always be at odds with its Arab neighbors because of the Arab-Persian rift, Israel assumed, making it a natural and long-lasting ally of Israel regardless of the wishes of the rulers of Tehran. Geostrategic realities would simply leave Tehran with no other options.[36] Based on these assumptions, a notion was formed about what Iran's behavior *should* be. When Iran's behavior did not conform to this notion, the validity of the assumptions underlying it wasn't questioned. Rather, Iran's behavior was deemed irrational and temporary. Sooner or later it would "come to its senses."

This same divorced-from-reality outlook has characterized the Bush administration's approach to the Middle East since September 11. One fantasy in which the Bush White House has invested much energy and hope is regime-change in Iran, which itself is based on the idea that with a different regime ruling Tehran, the problems between the United States and Iran, as well as Israel and Iran, would more or less automatically be resolved. "The moment the [Islamic] regime is gone, the [Israeli-Iranian] relationship will change 180 degrees," Sneh maintained.[37] Mindful of the close relationship Israel and the Shah enjoyed, it is easy to reach this dubious conclusion. But there is much disagreement in Israel about this point. Some, like Menashe Amir, the legendary director of Radio Israel's Persian service, see the religious zeal of the Iranian leadership as the sole cause of the enmity. "Today, Iran is against Israel due to religious reasons," he told me in his Jerusalem office, which is decorated with Iranian artifacts and paintings. "Future Iranian regimes won't have that problem."[38]

Others argue that a change in individual leadership or regime in Tehran would not affect Iran's nuclear drive. A secular and democratic government in Tehran may actually be more inclined to acquire a nuclear bomb, Ariel Sharon's spokesperson Ranaan Gissin maintained, or, at a minimum, it will be under popular pressure to continue the program at the same pace.[39] Israel "cannot be confident that reform in Iran will eliminate the strategic threat to Israel," said Uzi Arad, former director of intelligence for the Mossad and currently a professor at the Interdisciplinary Center in Herzliya.[40] Moreover, there is no guarantee that a democratic Iran would be any more stable or any less radical than the current regime. "If a change in the regime is possible, then the threat is there. It will be an unstable situation and continue to be an unstable regime," Israel's Gen. Amnon Lipkin-Shahak explained. Just as the Shah's regime was replaced by a radical government, a weak democratic regime in Iran could face the same fate.[41] Gilad, in turn, dismissed the entire discussion as useless and academic because, in his view, the regime in Iran isn't likely to fall. "I exclude any possibility for regime change," he asserted.[42] As problematic as the ayatollahs have been, the nature of the clerical regime is not the root of the Israeli-Iranian or the U.S.-Iranian enmity. After all, it was geopolitical changes that sparked the Israeli-Iranian rivalry after the end of the Cold War, not the ideology or nature of Iran's leadership. Just as the Islamic Revolution did not end Iran's quest for primacy (in fact, it initially intensified it), there is little to suggest that a secular Iran would be less inclined to seek preeminence and more prone to accept a timid role in regional affairs.

THE FAILURE OF CONTAINMENT—THE LEBANON WAR OF 2006

Another failed policy is containment—the idea that the solution to the conflict lies in containing and weakening Iran. This policy has not only failed, it has backfired and made a bad situation worse by making Iran stronger—and angrier. The last attempt to weaken Iran—the 2006 summer war in Lebanon—exemplifies this point. Though Israel did not expect the July 12 Hezbollah border attack and kidnapping of its soldiers, the Jewish State had planned and prepared for war against Hezbollah for more than two years. In 2005, a senior Israeli army officer began giving off-the-record PowerPoint presentations to American diplomats, journalists, and think tanks, setting out in frightening detail the plan for the expected operation. "Of all of Israel's wars since 1948, this was the one for which Israel was most prepared," Professor Gerald Steinberg of Bar Ilan University explained.[43] At first, everything went as planned. As Washington gave Israel's war its blessing and support—Secretary of State Condoleezza Rice referred to the fighting as the "birth pangs of a new Middle East"—Israel Defense Forces Chief of

Staff Dan Halutz and a crowd of officers gathered hundreds of feet below-ground in the command bunker of the Israeli Air Force in Tel Aviv to monitor the developments. Late on the night of July 12, the first reports came in. Fifty-four missile launchers had been destroyed by Israel's jet fighters, which were returning to base. Relieved, Halutz called Prime Minister Ehud Olmert at his residence in Jerusalem. "All the long-range rockets have been destroyed," Halutz proudly declared. But he didn't stop there. After a short pause, he added: "We've won the war."[44]

In the meantime, as neoconservatives in Washington were urging the Bush administration not only to support the war but to join it as well, decision-makers in Tehran were trembling. Both Hezbollah and Iran were surprised by the scale of Israel's response to the raid. "We expected Israel's response to the taking hostage of the two soldiers to be at most a day or two of shelling or a few limited attacks of specific places," the deputy secretary general of Hezbollah, Sheikh Naim Kassem, later told reporters.[45] Iranian intelligence had warned Tehran's political leaders that Israel had plans to attack Lebanon later, in October 2006, but they had no indication that the scale of the war would be this large or that it would begin as early as July.[46] "This was God's gift to Israel," Nasser Hadian, a reformist strategist, said. "Hezbollah gave them the golden opportunity to attack."[47]

The Iranian fear was that Washington and Israel were paving the way for a military confrontation with Iran by first taking out Hezbollah—Iran's first line of defense. This was more than a proxy war, Tehran feared; it was the prelude to a final showdown. Pundits in the United States speculated that Iran had triggered the conflict to take attention away from the Iranian nuclear standoff, but in Tehran the feeling was that "one of Iran's cards had been unnecessarily wasted" by Hezbollah's foolish attack against Israel. The conventional wisdom in Tehran was that a direct confrontation between the Lebanese militants and the Israeli army would likely work to Hezbollah's disadvantage.[48] "Israel and the U.S. knew that as long as Hamas and Hezbollah were there, confronting Iran would be costly," Mohsen Rezai, Secretary of the Expediency Discernment Council of Iran, told the Iranian newspaper *Baztab*. "So, to deal with Iran, they first want to eliminate forces close to Iran that are in Lebanon and Palestine."[49] On this point, the Israelis and Iranians didn't seem to disagree. For years, the Israelis had been worried about Hezbollah's military buildup; with its deployment of thousands of missiles and rockets, the Shia guerrilla group could hit large parts of northern Israel. Through Hezbollah, the Iranians were gaining a deterrent capability and leverage that was unacceptable to Israel. In the minds of the Israelis, the fighting in Lebanon was not just about Hezbollah; it was also about Iran. "To some degree, one of the aims of this war is to make sure in Tehran, when they look at the pictures of Beirut, they also think about Tehran," Steinberg told the Council on Foreign relations in an interview.[50]

But neither Israel's hopes, nor Tehran's fears, came true. After some initial successes, the Israelis were stunned at Hezbollah's powerful response, including its firing of thousands of Katyusha rockets into northern Israel. Rather than facing an amateur militia, the Israelis soon realized that they were fighting a well-trained and well-equipped guerilla army. Hezbollah even used a Chinese-made C-807 missile against an Israeli warship off Lebanon's coast, catching the Israelis off guard and disabling the ship. Israeli intelligence had failed to fully discover before the war what Hezbollah was hiding in its arsenals.[51] The Lebanese fought a high-tech war, and they paid as much attention to the media battle as they did to the fighting on the ground. Trained and equipped by the Iranians, Hezbollah fighters cracked the codes of Israeli radio communications, intercepting reports on the casualties they had inflicted. Whenever an Israeli soldier was killed, Hezbollah confirmed it by listening to the Israeli radio and then sent the reports immediately to its satellite TV station, Al-Manar, which broadcast the news live. Thus Arab audiences knew the names of Israeli casualties and where they had been killed well before the Israeli army had a chance to inform the soldiers' families. The psychological impact of this on the Israelis—who had grown accustomed to superiority over the armies of their Arab neighbors—was devastating.

As the war progressed, Israeli tactical miscalculations and strategic shortsightedness changed the situation on the ground—as well as public opinion in Israel. At the outset, the vast majority of the Israeli public supported the war. It was seen as a defensive and necessary war to finally put an end to Hezbollah's border attacks. However, the initial euphoria of the Israeli leadership—and the Israeli public—soon turned to despair. After a few weeks of hard fighting with no clear gains for the Israel Defense Forces, polls showed that 63 percent of Israelis believed that Olmert should resign. And 74 percent wanted the inexperienced Moroccan-born defense minister, Amir Perez, to step down as well.[52] The battle cry that at the beginning of the war read "Let Israel win!" had by the third week turned into "We will settle for a draw." By the end of the war, after thirty-four days, Israelis half-jokingly said that what was important wasn't whether Israel had won or lost, but that it had played the game. Rather than strengthening and reinforcing the image of Israel's invincible deterrence, the war that was to weaken Iran only made Israel itself more vulnerable. Even though Hezbollah took a beating (as did Lebanon in general; the more than one thousand casualties overwhelmingly were civilians, and the country's infrastructure was systematically bombed by Israel from the first days of the war), its strategic capability wasn't significantly damaged, and its political strength within the complicated Lebanese sectarian mix may have been enhanced. Israel was under just as much threat after the war as before.

Even the Iranians were surprised by the outcome—and by Hezbollah's fighting power. The fear, and to some extent the expectation, had been that Israel would destroy Iran's Lebanese ally, after which "the entire regional calculus would change in Iran's disfavor."[53] Instead, Iran's—and even more so Hezbollah's—stock in the Arab street rose to unprecedented levels, Israel and the United States were weakened, and pro-Western Arab governments found themselves squeezed between their disgruntled populations and a White House that showed little consideration for the interests and wishes of its allies. Saudi Arabia, Egypt, and Jordan, three key U.S. allies whose regimes would have much to lose from Iran's rise, took the unusual step in the early days of the war of chastising Hezbollah for having started the war. Never before had an Arab government so publicly denounced an Arab group fighting Israel.[54] The Saudi calculation was that, by offering political coverage for other countries to condemn Hezbollah, America would rein in the Israelis. But the Saudi move backfired. The Bush administration worked to prolong the war rather than shorten it, embarrassing the Saudi leadership by revealing its lack of influence over the Bush White House.[55] At the same time, popular support for Hezbollah was so strong in Saudi Arabia, Jordan, and Egypt that their leaders were quickly forced to change their anti-Hezbollah line. To add insult to injury, not only did Israel's move strengthen Iran, it benefited further from Washington's weakening of Iran's Arab rivals.

Containment has also failed even when circumstances were far more favorable for the United States. Washington and Tel Aviv currently face a radically different situation compared to 1993, when containment was first put in place through the peace process. At that time Washington stood at the apex of its power. The Soviet Union had collapsed, and, in the "New World Order" that was forming, the United States was the world's sole superpower. Diplomatically, Washington's stock was equally high. Then–Secretary of State James Baker had marshaled a broad coalition—including numerous Arab states—to expel Saddam Hussein from Kuwait, and he had kept his word that Arab cooperation against Iraq would lead to a push for Israeli-

Palestinian peacemaking. Iran, on the other hand, was weak. It was still recuperating from the Iraq-Iran war, and its relations with the Arab states and
Europe remained frosty. Still, isolating Iran proved far more difficult than
Washington had envisioned. Despite its extensive efforts, the policy of containing Iran proved a huge failure.

Today, the tables have turned. Washington's credibility is at an all-time
low. The invasion and occupation of Iraq has weakened the United States
both militarily and diplomatically. Israel's war with Hezbollah has done little to buy it new friends in the Arab world, and the pro-Western Arab governments' impotence in influencing Washington has increased the rift
between these regimes and their peoples. In spite of their undeniable economic successes, the Arab states of the Persian Gulf are weakened, because
their security is directly tied to the strength of the United States.

Iran, on the other hand, has gained strength. The Bush administration
has expedited Iran's emergence as a key power in the Middle East by swiping
its immediate rivals—Afghanistan's Taliban and Iraq's Saddam Hussein—
off the geopolitical chessboard. No regional power can balance and contain
Iran without extensive U.S. support—and as the cost of this policy in-
creases, its sustainability becomes questionable. Sooner or later, containment will break down and the United States will be forced to either integrate
or confront Iran. Increasingly Washington's—and Israel's—best option
seems to be to bite the bullet and find some accommodation with Tehran,
because the cost of not talking to Iran is steadily increasing. Opportunities
to negotiate with Iran from a position of strength in the last five years have
all been squandered by the neoconservatives, who, like Israel, did not want
any U.S.-Iran talks at all. As a result, future talks may have to start from a
point that is more favorable to Tehran than to Washington and Tel Aviv.

THE NONEXISTENT MILITARY SOLUTION

Military action against Iran would be extremely risky, and even if it were to
succeed the costs would be staggering. Top officers in the U.S. Army and
Marine Corps, as well as many conservatives in the U.S. national security
elite, warn that a U.S. attack on Iran would be potentially catastrophic for
the U.S. position in Iraq and the region generally, given Iran's asymmetric
counterstrike capabilities. Israel, on the other hand, cannot take on Iran by
itself. The Israeli Air Force still lacks the capability to take out all of Iran's
known nuclear facilities. Unlike the Iraqi program, Iran's nuclear facilities
are spread throughout the country. In addition, the distance to Iran is far
greater, and the Israelis cannot reach Iran without air refueling. More im-

portantly, U.S. war plans involve targeting not only the nuclear plants but also much of the infrastructure related to the nuclear program. The United States is able to destroy these points, but Israel is not. A rash and unsuccessful military campaign could turn the political momentum in Iran's favor and undermine efforts to stop Tehran. Furthermore, with approximately twenty-five thousand Iranian Jews still living in Iran, military confrontation could jeopardize the security of this ancient community, a move the Jewish State would be reluctant to take. And even though Israel has lobbied the United States to deal with Iran in a decisive manner, pro-Israeli groups in Washington are wary of pushing the United States too hard, lest they be seen by the American public as pressing America to go to war for Israel's sake. Jewish organizations in the United States have already quietly asked the White House not to cite Israel's security as a top rationale for a possible showdown with Iran, fearing a backlash from the American public.[56]

A POSSIBLE WAY OUT—REGIONAL INTEGRATION AND COLLECTIVE SECURITY

The one policy that hasn't been seriously pursued is regional integration through dialogue and engagement. This policy would be based on the recognition that, like China, Iran is a country that the United States cannot contain indefinitely, that Iran becomes more antagonistic when excluded, and that the United States can better influence Iran by helping it integrate into the world's political and economic structure rather than by keeping it out. This approach is also favored by leading Iranian human rights activists, who believe it will facilitate internal political reform as well. And what the Iranians are asking for is, in essence, an end to a policy that has cost the United States a lot and won it little.

Beyond being the least costly policy option, there are indications that the policy has a fair chance of succeeding. Both imperial and Islamic Iran have had ingrained in them the notion that Iran's size, population, educational level, and natural resources have made the country destined to obtain regional preeminence and that it should play a leadership role reflective of its geopolitical weight. This has been—and continues to be—the main driving force of Iranian foreign policy both during the era of the Shah and after the 1979 Islamic Revolution. Revolutionary Iran initially aspired to be the leader of the entire Islamic world. The Shah's aspirations for Iran's role far exceeded the Middle East geographically; he dreamed of establishing Iran as the preeminent naval power in the Indian Ocean basin.

However, since the end of the Iraq-Iran war Tehran has gradually reduced its aspirations and the definition of its national security environment to encompass only the Persian Gulf and the Caspian Sea and not the greater Middle East.[57] Within this area Iran wants to be second to none, and its foreign policy has radicalized when regional or outside powers have sought to isolate and contain it. According to Murad Saghafi, a secular reformist with close family ties to the late Ayatollah Khomeini, Iran would accept a U.S. rapprochement that safeguarded Iran's regional interests. "If they say, Iran has a place in the world, we don't want to attack Iran, let's make Iran a leading gas producer, [Iran] will say yes," Saghafi said.[58]

But even though revolutionary Iran hasn't hesitated to sacrifice its ideological objectives for the sake of state and regime survival, are there any guarantees that it would become more pragmatic once it could pursue its ideological objectives without sacrificing its strategic position? Would ideology continue to be a secondary motivator of its foreign policy, or would it come to the forefront? In short, would a more powerful Iran also be a more *radical* Iran? It is impossible to make such predictions with complete accuracy. But a review of Iran's past behavior indicates that a more powerful and integrated Iran is also a more moderate Iran. Its behavior after Likud's victory in 1996 is a case in point. As Iran's power rose and it improved its relations with the Arab states, the EU, and the Organization of Islamic Conferences and successfully countered American efforts to isolate it, its position on the Israeli-Palestinian issue tempered. Iran did not use its rising power to intensify its anti-Israel policies. Iran may have realized that it couldn't exclude Israel from regional decision-making (just as Israel failed to exclude Iran) and that in the long run it did not need to isolate Israel in order to achieve its leadership objectives.

A new U.S. approach could turn its Iran foreign policy into a force for stability by accommodating legitimate Iranian security objectives in return for Iranian concessions on various regional and international issues, as well as significant Iranian policy modifications, including Iran's acceptance of U.S. global leadership and an end to its hostilities against Israel. As Iran itself had suggested in its 2003 proposal to Washington, Tehran would have to accept Israel as a fact in the region and respect a two-state solution to the Israel-Palestine conflict. Joschka Fischer, Germany's former foreign minister, urged the United States to adopt this approach in an opinion piece in the *Washington Post* in May 2006. "Iran's alternatives should be no less than recognition and security or total isolation," he wrote.[59] Such an order would better reflect the region's natural balance, which in turn would make it more stable and less costly to sustain for the United States.

This idea also enjoys support in Israel among moderate elements, who recognize that a winner-take-all approach will in the long run probably leave Israel in a weaker position. Ben-Ami, Israel's former foreign minister, argued in the pages of *Haaretz* that "the question today is not when Iran will have nuclear power, but how to integrate it into a policy of regional stability before it obtains such power. Iran is not driven by an obsession to destroy Israel, but by its determination to preserve its regime and establish itself as a strategic regional power, vis-à-vis both Israel and the Sunni Arab states. . . . The answer to the Iranian threat is a policy of detente, which would change the Iranian elite's pattern of conduct."[60] Ben-Ami went on to point out that this is first and foremost an American responsibility, but that the Bush administration—like Israel—has been more interested in fighting "evil" than in pursuing conflict resolution. A U.S.-Iran dialogue is absolutely necessary, Ben-Ami argued, even though it would lead to serious compromises for Washington and Tel Aviv, such as recognizing Iran's regional importance. Unlike his predecessors in the Labor Party, Ben-Ami pointed out that alleviating the Iranian threat would aid the Israeli-Palestinian peace process, and that seeking to exaggerate the threat to scare the Arabs and the Israeli public to the negotiating table would be damaging to Israel in the long run.

What Ben-Ami put forward is that the Israeli-Palestinian conflict cannot be resolved unless the geopolitical context in which it transpires is addressed. Many have argued that the Israeli-Palestinian issue is the key to resolving all problems in the Middle East. Colin Powell, for instance, believed that Israel-Palestine peace would pave the way for an accommodation with Iran. The key, however, may lie in the other direction. Though the conflict between Israelis and Palestinians touches everyone and everything in the region in a profoundly emotional way, it is not a conflict that sets the geopolitical balance. Neither is it driven by geopolitical factors. Rather, it is the geopolitical *imbalance* in the region that renders that conflict all the more unsolvable. Unless the underlying conflicts in the region are addressed, any process seeking to resolve the Israeli-Palestinian dispute will be hostage to geopolitical rivalries. It will be a pawn in the competition between Israel and Iran for the future order of the region, as it was in the mid-1990s. These issues are clearly linked, whether they are treated as such or not.

Though only Washington can lead the process of reintegrating Iran into the regional order, significant steps are also needed from Israel to make this policy successful. Thoroughly convinced that its Arab neighbors would destroy Israel if they could, the Jewish State seeks survival through military domination.[61] The Israelis hold on to a concept referred to as their strategic, or military, edge. The hostile intentions of its neighbors are immutable, the Israeli leadership has generally believed, making it discount the impact that its actions have on their objectives.[62] And because of Israel's smaller population and geographic size, the standard doctrine holds, it has no choice but to seek to be stronger than its neighbors at all times, because "if any one of our enemies has the capability to eliminate us, they will," as Shmuel Bar, a veteran of the Israeli intelligence community, put it.[63] Most Israelis dismiss the idea that Israel can affect Iran's objectives and motives. "They are dedicated to their dreams, and their dream is to destroy Israel. . . . Nothing will change their mind. They are only flexible about the timetable," Israel's Gen. Gilad maintained.[64] If intentions are immutable, then Israel has no choice but to ensure the weakness of its neighbors. As long as Israel's neighbors are kept weak, their intentions will be irrelevant. "In this region, we have to consider every weapon as if it is directed toward Israel," Deputy Defense Minister Sneh argued. "This is the assumption that should lead us in everything that we are doing. We are living in a dangerous, unstable region, and we have to live according to worst-case scenarios all the time."[65]

The emphasis on worst-case scenarios is, to a great degree, a result of overcompensation by the intelligence apparatus for the mistake Israel committed on the eve of the 1973 Yom Kippur war, when it grossly underestimated Arab capabilities while overstating its own abilities. The result was that a complacent Israel was stunned by a well-coordinated Egyptian and Syrian surprise attack that inflicted enormous Israeli losses in the first days of the war, nearly leading to a catastrophic defeat, before Israel regained its balance and went on the offensive. "The correction to this is an overcorrection, by far. Today, the prevailing culture, or I would say the mindset of the intelligence . . . is to attribute to the enemy almost infinite power and completely underestimate what our strength means to them," said Shmuel Limone of the Ministry of Defense.[66] This doomsday mindset tends to lead to self-fulfilling prophecies, materializing the worst-case scenarios rather than preventing them from arising.[67] In addition, the emphasis on hostile propaganda from Israel's foes, which in the case of Iran is abundant, tends to make Israel either miss positive signals or dismiss them as deception tactics.[68] Taken to the next step, the policy dictates that Israel take preemptive action against any state or organization that is about to acquire capabilities that could give it parity. According to David Ivry, former Israeli ambassador to the United States, preemption is an old Israeli policy. "Our tradition states, 'He who arises to kill you, arise earlier and kill him first.' The phrase 'arise earlier' contains the entire doctrine."[69]

In April 2004 Prime Minister Ariel Sharon received a comprehensive national security report—Project Daniel—which argued that Israel has an inherent right to preemption because, it concluded, Arab and Iranian leaders are irrational and do not value self-preservation. This undermines the effectiveness of Israel's deterrence and necessitates complete Israeli military domination and the avoidance of parity at all cost. In this view, anything less than overwhelming Israeli superiority will constitute an existential threat to the Jewish State.[70] As a result, Israel must constantly seek to outgun its neighbors by preempting any would-be challengers. As the countries of the region progress, Israel must outrace them. It cannot afford to lose its lead, because if the neighbors gain the military upper hand they will destroy Israel. This doctrine shows why democratization in Iran may be insufficient to fundamentally change the Israeli-Iranian rivalry. Even a democratic Iran would be considered a threat to Israel if it could challenge Israel's military superiority—nuclear or conventional.[71] "It's become the only way we believe we can firmly establish a presence in the region. In a sense it is a form of domination," an Israeli analyst admitted. "But it's not hegemonic. We do not want to be or think we can be the dominant cultural force. It is existence through domination." But it's domination nevertheless.

While integration remains the only policy that can stabilize the region, it cannot succeed unless the Israeli-Iranian rivalry is tamed, which in turn requires significant changes in both Iranian and Israeli foreign and security policies. At a minimum, Iran must accept the two-state solution and reduce its regional ambitions by settling for a role that doesn't outstrip its resources. Clearly, Iran cannot expect to gain a prominent role as a rightful force for stability in the region if it continues to view asymmetric military capabilities as a legitimate political tool. Israel, on the other hand, must amend its military outlook because its belief that it must dominate the region militarily will likely put it on a collision course with Tehran regardless of Iran's ideology, political structure, or policies. Relinquishing this military doctrine will likely also facilitate peacemaking between Israel and its Arab neighbors.

The clash between Iran's regional ambitions and Israel's insistence on strategic dominance will continue to fuel instability and undermine Washington's interests in the region unless America recognizes that neither stability nor democracy can be achieved without ending the balancing game and genuinely seeking a Middle East that integrates the legitimate aspirations of all states, including Iran. So far, the Bush administration has remained steadfast in resisting such a shift. Somewhere along the way, America became so weakened by the failure in Iraq that the Israeli-Iranian rivalry was overshadowed by Washington's own fears that Iran would successfully challenge America's regional domination. In his State of the Union address on January 10, 2007, Bush accused Iran of destabilizing Iraq and supporting Shia militias killing American soldiers there, while neglecting the fact that Sunni insurgents—supported by elements in Jordan and Saudi Arabia— were responsible for more than 90 percent of American casualties in Iraq. Desperate to hold on to America's regional hegemony, Bush signaled that Iran would be confronted and isolated even more aggressively by the United States through the creation of an anti-Iran alliance consisting of Arab states and Israel; that is, balance-of-power politics would continue to guide America. But even if Washington were to stabilize Iraq and salvage U.S. hegemony in the Middle East, the balancing game would ensure that the eight-hundred-pound gorilla—the Israeli-Iranian rivalry—would continue to remain unaddressed and hidden behind slogans of democracy and freedom, while rendering stability and security in the Middle East an ever so hopeless dream.

CHAPTER 1 **Introduction**

Epigraphs: "Ahmadinejad Says Iran Ready for 'Final Nuclear Step,'" AFP, November 16, 2006; Victor Ostrovsky, *By Way of Deception* (New York: St. Martin's, 1990), 330; Samuel Segev, *The Iranian Triangle* (New York: Free Press, 1988), 249.

1   Ahmadinejad's statement has generally been mistranslated to read, "Wipe Israel off the map." Ahmadinejad never used the word "Israel" but rather the "occupying regime of Jerusalem," which is a reference to the Israeli regime and not necessarily to the country. Moreover, the hard-line Iranian president misquoted Ayatollah Khomeini in his speech. The father of the Iranian revolution had used the phrase "Sahneh roozgar," which means "scene of time," though for years the term was incorrectly translated by the Iranian government to mean "map." Ahmadinejad, however, said "*Safheh* roozgar," which means "pages of time," or "pages of history." No one noticed the change, and news agencies stuck with the standard—but incorrect—translation. The significant issue is that both phrases refer to time rather than place, making it incorrect to translate it as "wiping *Israel* off the *map.*" As a result, Ahmadinejad "was not threatening an Iranian-initiated war to remove Israeli control over Jerusalem" but was rather "expressing a vague wish for the future," according to Jonathan Steele of the *Guardian*. See Jonathan Steele, "Lost in Translation," *Guardian,* June 14, 2006; and Ethan Bronner and Nazila Fathi, "Just How Far Did They Go, Those Words Against Israel?" *New York Times,* June 11, 2006.

2   "Israel Focuses on the Threat Beyond the Periphery," *New York Times,* November 8, 1992.

3   Seymour M. Hersh, "The Iran Plans," *New Yorker,* April 17, 2006. The White House denied the allegations made in the story.

4   Barbara Demick, "Iran Remains Home to Jewish Enclave," *Knight-Ridder,* September 30, 1997.

5   In 1979 Iran's Jewish community numbered approximately eighty thousand.

6   Norman Cohn, *Cosmos, Chaos, and the World to Come* (New Haven: Yale University Press, 2001).

7   Paul Kriwaczek, *In Search of Zarathustra* (New York: Vintage Books, 2002), 184–185. The henotheistic nature of pre-exilic Judaism is exemplified in the First Commandment, "I am the Lord your God; you shall have no other gods before me."

8   Larry Derfner, "See No Evil, Hear No Evil," *Jerusalem Post,* September 28, 2006.

9   Barbara Demick, "Iran: Life of Jews Living in Iran," Sephardic Studies, http://www.sephardicstudies.org/iran.html.

10 Frances Harrison, "Iran's Proud but Discreet Jews," BBC, September 22, 2006. "Ahmadinejad didn't do anything to the Jews so far. Despite everything he says in the media about the Holocaust and Israel, the Jews don't feel any pressure and most of the adults want to stay there," another Iranian Jew told the *Jerusalem Post.*

11 Ewen MacAskill, Simon Tisdall, and Robert Tait, "Iran's Jews Learn to Live with Ahmadinejad," *Guardian*, June 27, 2006.

12 Sadeq Saba, "Iran Jews Express Holocaust Shock," BBC, February 11, 2006.

13 John R. Bradley, "Iranian Jews Wary of Becoming Scapegoats," *Washington Times*, March 21, 2006. Later in January 2007, Khatami gave an interview to the Israeli newspaper *Yediot Aharonot*, in which he criticized Ahmadinejad for holding a conference in Tehran questioning the Holocaust. "I strongly condemn the holding of this conference," he said on the sidelines of the annual World Economic Forum in Davos, Switzerland. "The Holocaust against the Jewish people was one of the most grave acts against humanity in our time. There is no doubt that it happened." "Khatami Slams Controversial Holocaust Conference," AFP, January 26, 2007.

14 "Iranian Jews Shaping Israeli Policy," *Jane's Islamic Analysis*, October 1, 2006.

15 Orly Halpern, "Cramped in Ashdod, Cheering for Iran," *Jerusalem Post*, June 11, 2006. Orly Halpern, "Immigrant Moves Back 'Home' to Teheran," *Jerusalem Post*, November 3, 2006.

16 "It doesn't mean people are lying," he added. "They are just dealing with you with a different character." Michael Slackman, "The Fine Art of Hiding What You Mean to Say," *New York Times*, August 6, 2006.

17 Interview with Shmuel Bar, Tel Aviv, October 18, 2004.

18 Interview with Ehud Yaari, Jerusalem, October 24, 2004.

19 Interview with Mustafa Zahrani of the Iranian Foreign Ministry, New York, February 26, 2004.

20 William Kristol, "It's Our War—Bush Should Go to Jerusalem—and the U.S. Should Confront Iran," *Weekly Standard*, July 24, 2006.

21 James Bamford, "Iran: The Next War," *Rolling Stone Magazine*, July 24, 2006.

22 Michael Ledeen, "The Same War," *National Review Online*, July 13, 2006.

23 John Gibson, "Iran Attacking Israel Is Really Attack on U.S.," *Fox News*, July 13, 2006.

24 Brian Knowlton, "Rice Says Israel May Need to Prolong Offensive," *International Herald Tribune*, July 16, 2006.

CHAPTER 2 **An Alliance of Necessity**

1 UN Special Committee on Palestine, Recommendations to the General Assembly, September 3, 1947.

2 Resolution 181 was adopted by a vote of thirty-three to thirteen, with ten abstentions. Both the United States and the Soviet Union supported it.

3 R. K. Ramazani, "Iran and the Arab-Israeli Conflict," *Middle East Journal* 3 (1978): 414–415.

4 Sohrab Sobhani, *The Pragmatic Entente: Israeli-Iranian Relations, 1948–1988* (New York: Praeger, 1989), 23. (Mohammad Mossadeq had been elected Iran's prime minister in 1951 by a vote of seventy-nine to twelve by the Iranian parliament. The landslide victory left the Shah with no other option but to assent to the Parliament's vote, in spite of his differences with the charismatic Mossadeq. The Iranian prime minister was later overthrown by a coup organized by the CIA and the British intelligence, strengthening the Shah's grip on power.)

5 Ibid., 3, 34.

6 Robert Reppa, *Israel and Iran—Bilateral Relationships and Effect on the Indian Ocean Basin* (New York: Praeger, 1974), 91.

7   Ramazani, "Iran and the Arab-Israeli Conflict," 415.

8   "Nasserism," which maintained that the West sought the suppression of the Arab masses and that the Arab-Israeli conflict was an instrument for Western intrusion in the Middle East, had become a powerful force in the Middle East by advocating anti-Colonialism and pan-Arab socialism.

9   Sobhani, *Pragmatic Entente,* 18.

10 Interview with former Iranian intelligence officer, Washington, D.C., March 14, 2004.

11 Phone interview with Ambassador Fereydoun Hoveyda, former head of the Permanent Mission of Iran to the UN, Washington, D.C., March 3, 2004. Samuel Segev, *The Iranian Triangle* (New York: Free Press, 1988), 62. In the early 1970s, the Shah offered Palestine Liberation Organization (PLO) head Yassir Arafat a more pro-Arab position on Israel in return for an end to the PLO's support for the Iranian opposition. Later in the 1960s, the support of Arafat and the PLO—a major flag-bearer of pan-Arabism—for Iranian opposition and separatist groups further fueled Iranian opposition to pan-Arabism. The PLO opened its training camps to Iranian opposition elements that waged a military campaign against the Shah's regime, in hope that a change of regime in Tehran would bring Iran into the pro-Arab camp. (Interview with former Iranian diplomat under the Shah, Washington, D.C., April 2, 2004.)

12 Segev, *Iranian Triangle,* 35–36.

13 In 1954 Sultan Sanandaji, a low-level Iranian diplomat at the Iranian embassy in London, had approached an Israeli diplomat at the Israeli embassy in London, First Secretary Mordechai Gazit, and offered Israel access to Iranian energy sources. Sanandaji's proposal quickly led to a diplomatic frenzy involving the highest levels of government in both Iran and Israel. Later that year, Yisrael Koslov, a representative of Israeli Prime Minister Levi Eshkol, finalized the deal during a secret visit to Tehran. Segev, *Iranian Triangle,* 40.

14 Ibid., 60–61, 39–41. A second pipeline from Eilat to Israel's Mediterranean port of Ashkelon was constructed after the 1967 war, during which the Suez Canal was closed down yet again. The Eilat Ashkelon pipeline provided Israel with a steady supply of oil for its refineries and its growing domestic consumption. Its capacity was around 400,000 barrels per day in 1970, with plans of increasing it to 1.2 million barrels per day by 1980. Declassified Memorandum of Conversation between Pete Wolgast of Esso and Warren Clark of the U.S. Department of State, October 8, 1970. This document and the other government documents referenced here are available at the National Security Archives.

15 Declassified correspondence between Foggy Bottom and U.S. embassy in Tehran, February 13, 1969.

16 Interview with Deputy Minister M. Vakilzadeh, Washington, D.C., February 28, 2004.

17 Interview with former Iranian Minister of Agriculture A. A. Ahmadi, and his deputy, M. Vakilzadeh, Washington, D.C., February 28, 2004.

18 Gary Sick, *October Surprise* (New York: Random House, 1991), 60.

19 Sobhani, *Pragmatic Entente,* xviii–xxii.

20 Ramazani, "Iran and the Arab-Israeli Conflict," 416.

21 Interview with Charles Naas, former U.S. deputy ambassador to Iran in the 1970s, Washington, D.C., March 8, 2004.

22 Interview with Naas, March 8, 2004.

23 Sobhani, *Pragmatic Entente,* 128.

24 Interview with Gholam-Reza Afkhami, an advisor to the Mohammad Reza Shah, Washington, D.C., March 5, 2004.

25 Sobhani, *Pragmatic Entente,* 109.

26 Ramazani, "Iran and the Arab-Israeli Conflict," 427.

27 Sobhani, *Pragmatic Entente,* 27.

28 Nader Entessar, "Israel and Iran's National Security," *Journal of South Asian and Middle Eastern Studies* 4 (2004): 1–2; Segev, *Iranian Triangle,* 43.

29 Interview with former Iranian ambassador under the Shah, Washington, D.C., April 2, 2004. These accusations were categorically denied by Eliezer Tsafrir, who served as the head of the Mossad in Iran and Iraq in the 1960s and 1970s. Interview, Tel Aviv, October 16, 2004.

30 Interview with former Iranian intelligence officer, Washington, D.C., March 14, 2004.

31 Interview with former Iranian diplomat stationed in Israel, Tehran, August 12, 2004.

32 Declassified telegram from the U.S. embassy in Tel Aviv, December 7, 1970.

33 Sick, *October Surprise,* 61.

34 Behrouz Souresrafil, *Khomeini and Israel* (London: Researchers, 1988), 32.

35 Sobhani, *Pragmatic Entente,* 114; Segev, *Iranian Triangle,* 42.

36 Interview with former Iranian ambassador, Washington, D.C., April 2, 2004.

37 Interview with former senior Israeli diplomat stationed in Tehran, Tel Aviv, October 31, 2004.

38 Declassified Memorandum of Conversation, U.S. embassy in Tehran, Andrew Killgore, Political Counselor, October 14, 1972.

39 R. K. Ramazani, *Iran's Foreign Policy 1941–1973* (Charlottesville: University Press of Virginia, 1975), 404.

40 Seyed Assadollah Athari, "Iranian-Egyptian Relations," *Discourse: An Iranian Quarterly* 2 (2001): 51.

41 Ramazani, *Iran's Foreign Policy,* 321. When, as part of the resolution of the Cuban missile crisis in 1962, the Soviet Union ceased its propaganda attacks on Iran in return for an Iranian pledge not to permit U.S. missile bases on its soil, Cairo's role in confronting and provoking Iran grew. Using the Shah's relations with Israel as a pretext, Nasser challenged Iran's role in the region, depicted Iran as an oppressor of Arab peoples, and accused Tehran of seeking to colonize Arab lands—the same charges Egypt leveled against Israel. Ramazani, "Iran and the Arab-Israeli Conflict," 416.

42 Interview with former Iranian intelligence officer, Washington, D.C., March 14, 2004.

43 Ibid. The intelligence sharing also included assessments of developments in the Arab world, though the Iranians often mistrusted the Israeli intelligence and suspected that the Israelis shared only intelligence of poorer quality. Interview with former Iranian diplomat stationed in Israel, Tehran, August 12, 2004.

CHAPTER 3 Rise of Israel, Rise of Iran

Epigraph: Walter Isaacson, *Kissinger: A Biography* (New York: Touchstone, 1992), 563.

1 Interview with former Iranian Ambassador to Denmark and Greece, Washington, D.C., April 2, 2004.

2 Interview with Charles Naas, Washington, D.C., March 8, 2004.

3 Interview with former Iranian deputy UN Ambassador Mehdi Ehsassi, Tehran, August 3, 2004.

4 Interview with Alinaghi Alikhani, former minister of finance under the Shah, Washington, D.C., April 7, 2004.

5 Samuel Segev, *The Iranian Triangle* (New York: Free Press, 1988), 70.

6 *Borba* (Yugoslavia), November 1967.

7 Declassified memorandum from State Department official and the chargé d'affaires at the U.S. embassy in Tehran, November 10, 1970.

8 Conversation on April 27, 1971, between Iran's top diplomat in Tel Aviv and a political officer at the U.S. embassy. The conversation is summarized in a confidential memo found in the U.S. embassy in Tehran during the 1979–1981 hostage crisis. The memo was subsequently published by Iran's revolutionary government. It is available at the National Security Archive in Washington, D.C.

9 Seyed Assadollah Athari, "Iranian-Egyptian Relations," *Discourse: An Iranian Quarterly* 2 (2001): 51. Phone interview with Ambassador Fereydoun Hoveyda, former head of the Permanent Mission of Iran to the UN, Washington, D.C., March 3, 2004. Athari, "Iranian-Egyptian relations," 51–52. Interview with Henry Precht, former Iran desk officer at the U.S. Department of State, Washington, D.C., March 3, 2004.

10 Phone interview with Fereydoun Hoveyda, March 3, 2004.

11 Interview with former Iranian diplomat under the Shah, Washington, D.C., April 2, 2004.

12 R. K. Ramazani, "Iran and the Arab-Israeli Conflict," *Middle East Journal* 3 (1978): 418.

13 Athari, "Iranian-Egyptian Relations," 51–52.

14 Interview with Gholam-Reza Afkhami, an adviser to the Mohammad Reza Shah, Washington, D.C., March 5, 2004. Iranian diplomats in New York were instructed by the Shah to assist the Egyptians in creating ties with U.S. lawmakers and leaders of the Jewish-American community to facilitate Egypt's transition to the pro-Western camp. Phone interview with Fereydoun Hoveyda, March 3, 2004.

15 Ramazani, "Iran and the Arab-Israeli Conflict," 418.

16 Asadollah Alam, *The Shah and I*, ed. Alinaghi Alikhani (New York: St. Martin's, 1991), 152.

17 Phone interview with Fereydoun Hoveyda, March 3, 2004.

18 Interview, Tel Aviv, October 31, 2004.

19 Alam, *The Shah and I*, 179–180. The confidential meeting was arranged by the Shah's Court Marshall, Asadollah Alam, without the knowledge of the Iranian Foreign Minister.

20 Henry Paolucci, *Iran, Israel and the United States* (New York: Griffon House, 1991), 10.

21 Interview with former Iranian deputy UN Ambassador Mehdi Ehsassi, Tehran, August 3, 2004.

22 Interview with Alinaghi Alikhani, April 7, 2004.

23 Interview with a former deputy commander in chief of the Iranian navy, March 16, 2004.

24 Segev, *Iranian Triangle*, 77–78.

25 Interview with former Iranian intelligence officer, Washington, D.C., March 14, 2004.

26 Interview with a former deputy commander in chief of the Iranian Navy, March 16, 2004.

27 Sohrab Sobhani, *The Pragmatic Entente: Israeli-Iranian Relations, 1948–1988* (New York: Praeger, 1989), 73.

28 Alam, *The Shah and I*, 82, 129, 170. Though tensions existed between Iran and other Arab states, Iran did not feel any direct military threat from them. Interview with Gholam-Reza Afkhami, Washington, D.C., March 5, 2004.

29 Interview with Shmuel Bar, Tel Aviv, October 18, 2004.

30 Interview with Yitzak Segev, former Israeli military attaché to Iran, Tel Aviv, October 17, 2004.

31 Israel's de-emphasizing of superpower politics was made evident after the Marxist coup against Haile Selassie in Ethiopia in 1974. As a non-Arab state with a large Jewish minority, Ethiopia played an important role in Israel's doctrine of the periphery. Ethiopia's Cold War orientation was less important to Israel. As a result, Tel Aviv quickly moved to establish ties with the Mengistu government in Addis Ababa after the communist coup to ensure the continuation of its doctrine of the periphery. Iran, on the other hand, viewed the developments in Ethiopia as a successful Soviet bid to gain influence in the Horn of Africa after having been ousted by Sadat from Egypt. Sobhani, *Pragmatic Entente*, 126.

32 Interview with Davoud Hermidas-Bavand, Professor at Shahid Beheshti University and former Iranian diplomat, Tehran, August 8, 2004.

33 Sobhani, *Pragmatic Entente*, 74.

34 Ibid., 71.

35 R. K. Ramazani, "Security in the Persian Gulf," *Foreign Affairs* 4 (1979): 1.

36 Interview with Gholam-Reza Afkhami, an adviser to the Mohammad Reza Shah, Washington, D.C., March 5, 2004.

37 For instance, the same message was delivered to senior American officials in Washington by the Shah in April 1969 immediately after the funeral of President Eisenhower. The Iranian monarch added that an American troop withdrawal from the Persian Gulf following the British departure would be the most logical way of preventing the Soviets from acquiring influence in the region. Since 1949, the U.S. Navy had had a regular but small presence in the Persian Gulf through a base in Bahrain. Alam, *The Shah and I*, 50.

38 Kenneth Pollack, *The Persian Puzzle* (New York: Random House, 2004), 99–100.

39 Walter Isaacson, *Kissinger: A Biography* (New York: Touchstone, 1992), 563.

40 Available at the National Security Archive, http://www.gwu.edu/~nsarchiv/NSAEBB/NSAEBB21/03-01.htm.

41 International Financial Statistics Yearbook, International Monetary Fund, 1991. World Development Report, World Bank, 2003.

CHAPTER 4 Iran's Quest for Supremacy

Epigraph: Interview with a former deputy commander in chief of the Iranian navy, March 16, 2004.

1 R. K. Ramazani, *Revolutionary Iran: Challenge and Response in the Middle East* (Baltimore: Johns Hopkins University Press, 1988), ch. 2.

2 Mohammad Reza Pahlavi, *Answer to History* (New York: Stein and Day, 1980), 142.

3 Interview with former Iranian diplomat under the Shah, Washington, D.C., April 2, 2004.

4 Interview with Gholam-Reza Afkhami, former adviser to Mohammad Reza Shah, Washington, D.C., March 5, 2004. The Shah viewed Iran and Japan as the most advanced nations in Asia; thus he believed Japan should lead in east Asia, while Iran should lead in west Asia. Asadollah Alam, *The Shah and I*, ed. Alinaghi Alikhani (New York: St. Martin's, 1991), 389. Mohammad Reza Pahlavi, *Mission for My Country* (London: Hutchinson of London, 1960), 132.

5 Interview with Charles Naas, Washington, D.C., March 8, 2004.

6 Interview with Afkhami, March 5, 2004.

7 Alam, *The Shah and I*, 185.

8 U.S. Department of State, Bureau of Verification and Compliance.

9 Saudi Arabia's military spending skyrocketed, particularly after 1973, when it grew sevenfold in as many years. The other rising Arab state was Iraq, which, under the leadership of Saddam Hussein, began arming itself to the teeth.

10 Historically, major wars have broken out when the divergence between states' power and their political role becomes intolerable. Disequilibrium is reached in the political order that only war can restore. Simply put, rising states can either be given space by their neighbors or have their power quelled through war. According to Charles Doran, role is the currency of power. It is the state's ability to partake in regional decision-making and advance its interest without resorting to force. Unlike power, however, role is granted to a state by its neighbors by recognizing the legitimacy of the state's interests. As a state's power rises, so does its need to expand its role to partake in decisions that affect its growing sphere of influence. Absent such a role, the state will face great difficulties in sustaining its power. Doran's power cycle theory provides an excellent explanation of the dynamics of role and power. See Charles Doran, *The Politics of Assimilation: Hegemony and Its Aftermath* (Baltimore: Johns Hopkins University Press, 1971).

11 Interview with Afkhami, March 5, 2004.

12 Ibid.

13 Interview with Davoud Hermidas-Bavand, professor at Shahid Beheshti University and former Iranian diplomat, Tehran, August 8, 2004.

14 Interview with former senior Israeli diplomat stationed in Tehran, Tel Aviv, October 31, 2004.

15 Interview with former Iranian diplomat stationed in Israel, Tehran, August 12, 2004. For this very reason, the Shah held the Sultan of Oman in high regard. In June 1976, after a brief visit by the Sultan to Tehran, the Shah told Court Marshall Asadollah Alam that the Arab ruler was "a good sort. He doesn't do a thing without asking our permission." Alam, *The Shah and I*, 495.

16 Kenneth Pollack, *The Persian Puzzle* (New York: Random House, 2004), 104.

17 Hooshang Amirahmadi and Nader Entessar, *Reconstruction and Regional Diplomacy in the Persian Gulf* (London: Routledge, 1992), 230–231.

18 Hooshang Amirahmadi and Nader Entessar, *Iran and the Arab World* (New York: St. Martin's, 1993), 102. Renowned historian Nikki Keddie writes that though Persian-Arab tensions have existed since the Arab conquest of Iran, the paradigm of twentieth-century Persian nationalism incorrectly maintains that enmity between the two peoples is age-old and unchanging. According to Keddie, there is much evidence that premodern Iranians identified more as Shias than Iranians. See Nikki Keddie, *Modern Iran: Roots and Results of Revolution* (New Haven: Yale University Press, 2003).

19 Sohrab Sobhani, *The Pragmatic Entente: Israeli-Iranian Relations, 1948–1988* (New York: Praeger, 1989), 103.

20 Interview with a former deputy commander in chief of the Iranian navy, March 16, 2004.

21 Phone interview with Ambassador Fereydoun Hoveyda, former head of the Permanent Mission of Iran to the UN, Washington, D.C., March 3, 2004.

22 Phone interview with Abbas Maleki, Iranian deputy foreign minister in the early and mid-1990s, Geneva, January 27, 2005.

23 Sobhani, *Pragmatic Entente*, 104.

24 Interview with Hermidas-Bavand, August 8, 2004.

25 Interview with Deputy Minister M. Vakilzadeh, Washington, D.C., February 28, 2004.

26 CIA Intelligence memorandum, "Iran: The Shah's Lending Binge," December 1974. Available at the National Security Archives.

27 Interview with Iran's former Deputy UN Ambassador Mehdi Ehsassi, Tehran, August 3, 2004.

28 Sobhani, *Pragmatic Entente*, 77.

29 Interview with a former deputy commander in chief of the Iranian navy, March 16, 2004.

30 William Quandt, *Peace Process* (Los Angeles: University of California Press, 1993), 148.

31 Sobhani, *Pragmatic Entente*, 96. Phone interview with Soli Shavar, professor at Haifa University, Haifa, October 28, 2004.

32 Israel was a valued strategic asset to Iran in the sense that it "absorbed so much of the Arab energy." Interview with Afkhami, March 5, 2004. Iran knew that "a strong Israel would divert the Arab countries toward looking at [Israel] as a bigger threat than Iran." Interview with a former deputy commander in chief of the Iranian navy, March 16, 2004.

33 Interview with Yitzak Segev, Tel Aviv, October 17, 2004.

34 According to a former Iranian intelligence officer, from Tehran's perspective Egypt went from rival and enemy to ally in less than two years as a result of the rise of Sadat. Interview with former Iranian intelligence officer, Washington, D.C., March 14, 2004.

35 Shahram Chubin and Mohammad Fard-Saidi, "Recent Trends in Middle East Politics and Iran's Foreign Policy Options," *The Institute for International Political and Economic Studies* (August 1975): 79.

36 Having just won suzerainty of the Persian Gulf from the British—a God-sent gift, according to an Iranian diplomat—the Shah was in no mood to hand it over to the Americans or the Soviets. Phone interview with Hoveyda, March 3, 2004.

37 Interview with a former deputy commander in chief of the Iranian navy, March 16, 2004.

38 Iran's role as the guarantor of security in the Gulf necessitated the Soviet Union's exclusion from the region. "We certainly could see the dangers of a Soviet presence in the Persian Gulf; we definitely didn't want that." Interview with former Iranian ambassador to South Africa, New York, February 26, 2004. While Iran could not match Moscow's power, it could prevent the Soviet Union from finding a pretext to enter the warm waters of the Persian Gulf. "The Shah always thought [the reemergence of the great powers in the Gulf] would be very bad for Iran and for the region." Interview with Afkhami, March 5, 2004.

39 *Documents of the United States Embassy in Tehran,* Volume 8, 1979, 65.

40 Interview with Ehsassi, August 3, 2004.

41 Pollack, *Persian Puzzle,* 105.

42 Interview with Afkhami, March 5, 2004.

43 R. K. Ramazani, "Iran and the Arab-Israeli Conflict," *Middle East Journal* 3 (1978): 421.

44 Sobhani, *Pragmatic Entente,* 84.

45 Samuel Segev, *The Iranian Triangle* (New York: Free Press, 1988), 82.

46 Alam, *The Shah and I,* 326.

47 Kayhan, December 1, 1973; cited in Ramazani, "Iran and the Arab-Israeli Conflict," 418–420.

48 Alam, *The Shah and I,* 325–326. Interview with a former deputy commander in chief of the Iranian navy, March 16, 2004.

49 Interview with former Iranian ambassador to South Africa, New York, February 26, 2004.

50 Interview with Alinaghi Alikhani, former minister of finance under the Shah, Washington, D.C., April 7, 2004.

51 Sobhani, *Pragmatic Entente,* 89.

52 Interview with former Iranian ambassador to South Africa, New York, February 26, 2004.

53 Phone interview with Hoveyda, March 3, 2004.

54 Phone interview with Soli Shavar, professor at Haifa University, Haifa, October 28, 2004.

55 Interview with Ehsassi, August 3, 2004.

56 Interview with a former deputy commander in chief of the Iranian navy, March 16, 2004. Interview with former Iranian diplomat stationed in Israel, Tehran, August 12, 2004.

57 Mustafa Alani, "Probable Attitudes of the GCC States Towards the Scenario of a Military Action Against Iran's Nuclear Facilities," Gulf Research Center, 2004, 11.

CHAPTER 5 **Sealing Demise in the Moment of Triumph**

Epigraph: Interview with Yaacov Nimrodi, Savion (Tel Aviv), October 19, 2004.

1 Interview with former senior Israeli diplomat stationed in Tehran, Tel Aviv, October 31, 2004.

2 Secret memorandum from the U.S. embassy in Iran, June 21, 1977. Available at the National Security Archives.

3 Interview with Uri Lubrani, Tel Aviv, October, 2004. Mage publishers recently published an English translation of the *Shahname.*

4 Samuel Segev, *The Iranian Triangle* (New York: Free Press, 1988), 83–84.

5 Phone interview with Soli Shavar, Haifa, October 28, 2004.

6 Segev, *Iranian Triangle,* 87–88.

7 R. K. Ramazani, "Iran and the Arab-Israeli Conflict," *Middle East Journal* 3 (1978): 420–421.

8 Interview with former senior Israeli diplomat stationed in Tehran, Tel Aviv, October 31, 2004.

9 The Kurds are indigenous to a contiguous geocultural region that includes adjacent parts of Iran, Iraq, Syria, and Turkey. Smaller communities can also be found in

Lebanon, Armenia, and Azerbaijan. The ancient Greek historian Xenophon referred to the Kurds in Anabasis as "Kardukhi . . . a fierce and protective mountain-dwelling people" who attacked Greek armies in 400 B.C.

10 Interview with Eliezer Tsafrir, Tel Aviv, October 16, 2004.

11 Interview with Iran's former Deputy UN Ambassador Mehdi Ehsassi, Tehran, August 3, 2004.

12 Interview with Tsafrir, October 16, 2004.

13 David Kimche, *The Last Option* (New York: Maxwell MacMillan International, 1991), 189.

14 Nader Entessar, "Israel and Iran's National Security," *Journal of South Asian and Middle Eastern Studies* 4 (2004): 2–4.

15 The Israeli-Iranian-Kurdish collaboration steadily intensified during the 1960s. In late 1965, Israeli military instructors set up permanent camps in northern Iraq to train the Kurdish guerillas. After the 1967 war, the volume of Israeli arms shipments further increased as Soviet-made arms captured from Egypt and Syria were shipped to Barzani's men, and, in 1969, as a result of increased tensions between Iran and Iraq over the Shatt-el-Arab/Arvand Rud waterway, which separates the two countries north of the Persian Gulf, Tehran sent regular Iranian forces dressed in Kurdish clothing into Iraqi territory to support the Kurds against Iraq. In early 1970, a breakthrough in the negotiations between Baghdad and Mustapha Barzani that would end the Kurdish rebellion in northern Iraq was in the making. This deeply concerned the Shah, who feared that without the Kurdish problem, Iraq would concentrate its forces on the Iranian border. Barzani failed, however, to win a deal with the Iraqi government, and the rebellion continued, as did Israel and Iran's support for it. Sohrab Sobhani, *The Pragmatic Entente: Israeli-Iranian Relations, 1948–1988* (New York: Praeger Publishers, 1989), 46–47. Interview with Alinaghi Alikhani, former minister of finance under the Shah, Washington, D.C., April 7, 2004. Kimche, *Last Option,* 194.

16 Kenneth Pollack, *The Persian Puzzle* (New York: Random House, 2004), 105.

17 Shahram Chubin and Mohammad Fard-Saidi, "Recent Trends in Middle East Politics and Iran's Foreign Policy Options," *The Institute for International Political and Economic Studies* (August 1975): 87.

18 Sobhani, *Pragmatic Entente,* 86.

19 Kimche, *Last Option,* 194.

20 Interview with Yaacov Nimrodi, Savion (Tel Aviv), October 19, 2004.

21 Interview with Tsafrir, October 16, 2004.

22 Asadollah Alam, *The Shah and I,* ed. Alinaghi Alikhani (New York: St. Martin's, 1991), 415–417.

23 Gary Sick, *October Surprise* (New York: Random House, 1991), 61–62. The division of the strategic waterway dated back to the Constantinople Treaty of 1913 between Iran and the Ottoman Empire. Tehran believed that the treaty had given to Iraq excessive privileges over what was supposed to be an international waterway. The Shah had long sought to renegotiate the treaty, and the two countries almost went to war over the issue in 1969.

24 Alam, *The Shah and I,* 417, 409, 418.

25 Interview with Tsafrir, October 16, 2004.

26 Interview with Gary Sick, New York, February 25, 2004.

27 Interview with Charles Naas, Washington, D.C., March 8, 2004.

28 Interview with a former deputy commander in chief of the Iranian navy, March 16, 2004. In fact, the Shah proudly explains in his book *Mission for My Country* that the relations between the United States and Iran are between two equals, a viewpoint that few in Tehran or Washington concurred with. See Mohammad Reza Pahlavi, *Mission for My Country* (London: Hutchinson of London, 1960), 130.

29 Alam, *The Shah and I,* 417. Kimche, *Last Option,* 195. Interview with former Iranian diplomat stationed in Israel, Tehran, August 12, 2004.

30 Interview with former Iranian diplomat under the Shah, Washington D.C., April 2, 2004.

31 Interview with Tsafrir, 2004.

32 Kimche, *The Last Option,* 195.

33 John A. Conway, "The Kurds and Israel," *Newsweek,* April 7, 1975, 17.

34 Interview with Tsafrir, October 16, 2004. The Iranians themselves didn't have much time; approximately one hundred Iranian pieces of field artillery, as well as countless anti-tank and SAM missiles, had to be destroyed because Tehran did not have time to bring them back across the border. Alam, *The Shah and I,* 419. The Barzani clan also fled to Iran and was given refuge in Karaj, outside of Tehran. The Kurds wanted the cooperation with Israel to continue by having the Israeli air force deliver aid by parachute drops, but Israel deemed the operation impossible without access provided by Iran. The Iraqi army took full advantage of the new circumstances and swiftly launched an offensive against the abandoned Kurds, who suffered a devastating defeat. Hundreds were massacred, and many more were forcibly relocated to the south of Iraq as part of Saddam Hussein's effort to ethnically cleanse northern Iraq of its Kurdish population. Kimche, *Last Option,* 195–196.

35 Interview with former Iranian cabinet minister, Potomac, February 2004. The identity of the minister is withheld for his protection.

36 Interview with a former deputy commander in chief of the Iranian navy, March 16, 2004.

37 Interview with former Iranian ambassador to South Africa, New York, February 26, 2004.

38 Interview with Mehdi Ehsassi, August 3, 2004.

39 Alam, *The Shah and I,* 418.

40 Interview with Alikhani, April 7, 2004. Some Iranian officials have also insisted that the United States was supporting the negotiations behind the scenes and was fully aware of the details. (Interview with former Iranian ambassador to Denmark and Greece, Washington, D.C., April 2, 2004.)

41 Alam, *The Shah and I,* 417–419.

42 Interview with Alikhani, April 7, 2004.

43 Interview with Naas, March 8, 2004.

44 Interview with Henry Precht, former Iran desk officer at the U.S. Department of State, Washington, D.C., March 3, 2004. Iranian diplomats, however, have argued that the United States also expressed satisfaction with the accord since it gave Iran, a U.S. ally, the upper hand against the Soviet-backed Iraqi government. (Interview with Ehsassi, August 3, 2004.)

45 Kimche, *Last Option,* 195.

46   Interview with Tsafrir, October 16, 2004.

47   Interview with Yaacov Nimrodi, Savion (Tel Aviv), October 19, 2004.

48   Sobhani, *Pragmatic Entente,* 108.

49   Interview with former Iranian ambassador to South Africa, New York, February 26, 2004.

50   Tehran's military expenditures tripled between 1973 and 1975, going from $6.1 billion to $15.6 billion.

51   Pollack, *Persian Puzzle,* 108.

52   Interview with former Iranian diplomat serving the government of the Shah, Washington, D.C., April 2, 2004.

53   Interview with Alikhani, April 7, 2004. In addition, the Shah was concerned that the United States would sell Israel Pershing missiles capable of carrying nuclear warheads. Classified Department of State telegram, September 1970. Available at the National Security Archives.

54   Joseph Alpher, "Israel and the Iraq-Iran War," in *The Iraq-Iran War: Impact and Implications,* ed. Efraim Karsh (New York: St. Martin's, 1989), 157.

55   Andrew Parasiliti, "Iraq's War Decisions," Ph.D. diss., Johns Hopkins University, 1998, 36, 85–86.

56   Interview with Gholam-Reza Afkhami, former adviser to Mohammad Reza Shah, Washington, D.C., March 5, 2004.

57   Interview with Davoud Hermidas-Bavand, professor at Shahid Beheshti University and former Iranian diplomat, Tehran, August 8, 2004.

58   Parasiliti, "Iraq's War Decisions," 36.

59   Interview with Tsafrir, October 16, 2004.

60   Interview with a former deputy commander in chief of the Iranian navy, March 16, 2004.

CHAPTER 6 **Megalomania**

Epigraph: Asadollah Alam, *The Shah and I,* ed. Alinaghi Alikhani (New York: St Martin's, 1991), 477.

1   Interview with a former deputy commander in chief of the Iranian navy, March 16, 2004. "Iran had ambitions in that area that Israel could not possibly have. That is the ambition of leadership, the ambition of interactivity, and the ambition of even moving beyond [the Persian Gulf]," according to Afkhami. Interview with Gholam-Reza Afkhami, former adviser to Mohammad Reza Shah, Washington, D.C., March 5, 2004.

2   Interview with former Iranian diplomat stationed in Israel, Tehran, August 12, 2004.

3   Samuel Segev, *The Iranian Triangle* (New York: Free Press, 1988), 73.

4   Sohrab Sobhani, *The Pragmatic Entente: Israeli-Iranian Relations, 1948–1988* (New York: Praeger, 1989), 89.

5   In conservative readings of Shi'ism, non-Shias, including Jews, are considered *najes,* unclean. As Segev pointed out, the anti-Semitism Israelis encountered tended to have religious rather than political roots. Interview with Yitzak Segev, former Israeli military attaché to Iran, Tel Aviv, October 17, 2004.

6   Interview with a former deputy commander in chief of the Iranian navy, March 16, 2004.

7   "We in the Ministry of Foreign Affairs were thinking that we shouldn't go along with the Israelis all the way. . . . I personally never tried to give the Israelis the feeling that I am with them 100 percent," explained a former Iranian deputy UN ambassador. Interview with former Iranian deputy UN ambassador Mehdi Ehsassi, Tehran, August 3, 2004. .

8   Interview with former Iranian diplomat under the Shah, Washington, D.C., April 2, 2004.

9   Sobhani, *Pragmatic Entente*, 86–87.

10   Neither the Shah nor his foreign minister, Ardeshir Zahedi, held the Israelis in high regard. Discussions between them in regards to Israel were often disrespectful and derogatory. Interview with former Iranian diplomat stationed in Israel, Tehran, August 12, 2004.

11   Interview with Henry Precht, former Iran desk officer at the U.S. Department of State, Washington, D.C., March 3, 2004.

12   Interview with former senior Israeli diplomat stationed in Tehran, Tel Aviv, October 19, 2004.

13   Phone interview with Ambassador Fereydoun Hoveyda, former head of the Permanent Mission of Iran to the UN, Washington, D.C., March 3, 2004. In January 1976 the Israeli Foreign Ministry connected the Shah with a Jewish American public relations consultant, Daniel Yankelovich. The efforts to improve Iran's image and mold U.S. public opinion in favor of the Shah's rule were to operate under a new body, called The Center for Media Research, to keep the Israeli dimension of the collaboration out of public sight. But the public relations campaign was a fiasco, partly because of excessive Iranian expectations. By the end of 1976 the Shah lost interest in the project, though he remained convinced that the media in America were under the spell of "World Jewry." "He never came out of this conviction," complained Hoveyda. Asadollah Alam, *The Shah and I*, ed. Alinaghi Alikhani (New York: St. Martin's, 1991), 458, 463–464.

14   Alireza Nourizadeh, "Israel and the Jews: Drawing on Ancient Traditions," *(Beirut) Daily Star*, October 26, 2002.

15   Massoume Price, "A Brief History of Iranian Jews," Culture of Iran, http://www.cultureofiran.com/iranian_jews.php.

16   European Jewish agencies encouraged the migration by offering financial incentives for migrating to Israel. Israeli diplomats refrained from getting involved in the emigration of Iranian Jews to Israel and let it be handled by various Zionist committees. Confidential Memorandum of Conversation, U.S. Second Secretary (Greene) and Israeli First Secretary (Tourgeman) in Tehran, December 22, 1965. Available at the National Security Archives. Unlike other Jewish minorities, Iranian Jews were, for the most part, quite foreign to the ideological tenets of Zionism. One respondent in the Tehran University study explained that his Jewish identity, which remained second to his Iranian identity, came into being only after he arrived in Israel. Hormoz Shahdadi, "Immigration of Iranian Jews to Israel: The Effects of National Identity," *Relations Internationales*, Center for International Studies, University of Tehran (1974), 117–136. Indeed, Israeli leaders were very concerned about the strong Iranian identity of Iranian Jews, as well as their lukewarm support for the state of Israel. According to one official of the Jewish Agency, the Iranian Jewish community was in the 1970s "becoming in-

creasingly Persian" and "not as helpful [toward Israel] as would be desired." Confidential correspondence between U.S. embassy in Tel Aviv and U.S. State Department, April 30, 1976. Available at the National Security Archives.

17 Interview with Ehsassi, August 3, 2004.

18 Interview with Ehsassi, August 3, 2004.

19 Interview with Davoud Hermidas-Bavand, professor at Shahid Beheshti University and former Iranian diplomat, Tehran, August 8, 2004.

20 Interview with former Iranian diplomat, Washington, D.C., April 2, 2004.

21 Phone interview with Hoveyda, March 3, 2004.

22 Alam, *The Shah and I*, 451.

23 Interview with former senior Israeli diplomat stationed in Tehran, Tel Aviv, October 19, 2004.

24 Andrew Parasiliti, "Iraq's War Decisions," Ph.D. diss., Johns Hopkins University, 1998, 37.

25 Alam, *The Shah and I*, 477. Interview with Hermidas-Bavand, August 8, 2004.

26 Interview with a former deputy commander in chief of the Iranian navy, March 16, 2004. Already in 1974 the Shah had shown a propensity for overestimating Iran's standing in international affairs. At the presentation of the incoming West German ambassador's credentials on June 9, 1974, the Shah felt insulted by the German's failure to recognize the distinction between Iran of the past and the Iran the Shah had developed. In a rather undiplomatic fashion, the Shah stated that if "Germany wishes to carry on good relations with Iran her best bet would be to learn to keep her place." Alam, *The Shah and I*, 375.

27 Interview with Hermidas-Bavand, August 8, 2004.

28 Interview with Charles Naas, Washington, D.C., March 8, 2004.

29 Interview with Precht, March 3, 2004.

30 Interview with Yitzak Segev, former Israeli military attaché to Iran, Tel Aviv, October 17, 2004.

31 Interview with Alinaghi Alikhani, former minister of finance under the Shah, Washington, D.C., April 7, 2004.

32 Department of State Scope Paper, August 15, 1967. Available at the National Security Archives.

33 Phone interview with Hoveyda, March 3, 2004.

34 Interview with Ehsassi, August 3, 2004.

35 Alam, *The Shah and I*, 176.

36 Abbas Milani, *The Persian Sphinx* (Washington, D.C.: Mage, 2004).

37 Interview with Minister of Agriculture A. A. Ahmadi, Washington, D.C., February 28, 2004.

CHAPTER 7 The Rise of Begin and the Israeli Right

Epigraph: Documents of the United States Embassy in Teheran, Volume 19, 1979, 4. National Security Archives.

1 William Quandt, *Peace Process* (Los Angeles: University of California Press, 1993), 261.

2 Ilan Peleg, *Begin's Foreign Policy 1977–1983: Israel's Move to the Right* (New York: Greenwood, 1987), 18.

3   Peleg, *Begin's Foreign Policy,* 7, 58.
4   Shlomo Avineri, "Ideology and Israeli Foreign Policy," *Jerusalem Quarterly* 37 (Winter 1986): 4–6.
5   Sohrab Sobhani, *The Pragmatic Entente: Israeli-Iranian Relations, 1948–1988* (New York: Praeger, 1989), 98–99.
6   Peleg, *Begin's Foreign Policy,* 52.
7   Dan Fichter, "Extremists and Pragmatists: Israel's Far Right," *Yale Israel Journal* 3 (2004).
8   Peleg, *Begin's Foreign Policy,* 181–182.
9   Interview with former senior Israeli diplomat stationed in Tehran, Tel Aviv, October 19, 2004.
10 Gary Sick, *All Fall Down: America's Tragic Encounter with Iran* (New York: Random House, 1985), 22. Samuel Segev, *The Iranian Triangle* (New York: Free Press, 1988), 60.
11 Sobhani, *Pragmatic Entente,* 99.
12 Interview with Iran's former Deputy UN Ambassador Mehdi Ehsassi, Tehran, August 3, 2004.
13 Interview with former Iranian diplomat stationed in Israel, Tehran, August 12, 2004.
14 R. K. Ramazani, "Iran and the Arab-Israeli Conflict," *Middle East Journal* 3 (1978): 424.
15 Sobhani, *Pragmatic Entente,* 101.
16 *U.S. News & World Report,* March 22, 1976.
17 "Morocco, Iran Issue Joint Communiqué," *Xinhua,* February 3, 1977.
18 "Iran, Egypt Issue Joint Communiqué," *Xinhua,* March 17, 1977.
19 "Kuwaiti Foreign Minister Visits Iran," *Xinhua,* May 3, 1977.
20 Phone interview with Ambassador Fereydoun Hoveyda, former head of the Permanent Mission of Iran to the UN, Washington, D.C., March 3, 2004.
21 Documents of the United States Embassy in Teheran, Volume 19, 1979, 4. Available at the National Security Archives.
22 Interview with Gholam-Reza Afkhami, an adviser to Mohammad Reza Shah, Washington, D.C., March 5, 2004.
23 Interview with former Iranian ambassador to South Africa, New York, February 26, 2004.
24 Phone interview with Hoveyda, March 3, 2004.
25 Documents of the United States Embassy in Teheran, Volume 19, 1979, 1–3. Available at the National Security Archives.
26 Quandt, *Peace Process,* 270.
27 Interview with Afkhami, March 5, 2004.
28 Arnaud de Borchgrave, "The Shah on War and Peace," *Newsweek,* November 14, 1977, 69.
29 Moshe Dayan, *Breakthrough* (New York: Alfred Knopf, 1981), 106–107.
30 Sobhani, *Pragmatic Entente,* 126–128.
31 Ramazani, "Iran and the Arab-Israeli Conflict," 423–424.
32 *Washington Post,* January 10, 1978.
33 Interview with Afkhami, March 5, 2004. Sobhani, *Pragmatic Entente,* 100.
34 Interview with former senior Israeli diplomat stationed in Tehran, Tel Aviv, October 19, 2004.

35 Iraqi Scud missiles became one of Baghdad's most dreaded weapons later in the Iraq-Iran war. Through Iraq's access to missile technology, it could strike against Tehran itself from Iraqi soil.

36 Borchgrave, "The Shah on War and Peace," 70.

37 Sobhani, *Pragmatic Entente*, 129. The Iraq-Iran war later demonstrated that the Scuds were indeed a devastating weapon that Iran lacked deterrence against or protection from.

38 Interview with a former deputy commander in chief of the Iranian navy, March 16, 2004.

39 Documents of the United States Embassy in Teheran, Volume 19, 1979, 4. National Security Archives.

40 Elaine Sciolino, "Documents Detail Israeli Missile Deal with the Shah," *New York Times*, April 1, 1986. Sobhani, *Pragmatic Entente*, 116.

41 Martin Bailey, "The Blooming of Operation Flower," *Observer*, February 2, 1986, 19; Sciolino, "Documents Detail Israeli Missile Deal."

42 Sciolino, "Documents Detail Israeli Missile Deal."

43 Sobhani, *Pragmatic Entente*, 116.

44 Documents of the United States Embassy in Teheran, Volume 19, 1979, 14. Available at the National Security Archives.

45 *Documents of the United States Embassy in Tehran*, 36 (1979), 29. Sobhani, *Pragmatic Entente*, 119.

46 Sciolino, "Documents Detail Israeli Missile Deal."

47 Interview with a former deputy commander in chief of the Iranian navy, March 16, 2004.

48 Sobhani, *Pragmatic Entente*, 115.

49 Documents of the United States Embassy in Teheran, Volume 19, 1979, 4. Available at the National Security Archives.

50 Interview with Yitzak Segev, former Israeli military attaché to Iran, Tel Aviv, October 17, 2004. Discussion with senior Iranian government official, Paris, January 19, 2006.

51 Interview with Eliezer Tsafrir, who served as the head of the Mossad in Iran and Iraq in the 1960s and 1970s, Tel Aviv, October 16, 2004.

52 Behrouz Souresrafil, *Khomeini and Israel* (London: Researchers, 1988), 38.

CHAPTER 8 **Enter the Sign of God**

Epigraph: Interview with Yitzak Segev, former Israeli military attaché to Iran, Tel Aviv, October 17, 2004.

1 William Sullivan, *Mission to Iran* (New York: WW Norton, 1981), 62.

2 Interview with Eliezer Tsafrir, head of the Mossad in Iran, Tel Aviv, October 16, 2004.

3 Interview with Yitzak Segev, former Israeli military attaché to Iran, Tel Aviv, October 17, 2004.

4 Interview with Israeli official, Tel Aviv, October 2004.

5 Interview with former senior Israeli diplomat stationed in Tehran, Tel Aviv, October 19, 2004.

6 Henry Paolucci, *Iran, Israel and the United States* (New York: Griffon House, 1990), 208.

7 Interview with Israeli official, Tel Aviv, October 2004.

8   Interview with Yitzak Segev, former Israeli military attaché to Iran, Tel Aviv, October 17, 2004.

9   Sohrab Sobhani, *The Pragmatic Entente: Israeli-Iranian Relations, 1948–1988* (New York: Praeger, 1989), 135.

10 Interview with Segev, October 17, 2004.

11 Samuel Segev, *The Iranian Triangle* (New York: Free Press, 1988), 114–115.

12 Paolucci, *Iran, Israel and the United States,* 208.

13 Nader Entessar, "Israel and Iran's National Security," *Journal of South Asian and Middle Eastern Studies* 4 (2004): 4.

14 David Menashri, *Post-Revolutionary Politics in Iran* (London: Frank Cass, 2001), 266.

15 Shireen Hunter, *Iran and the World* (Indianapolis: Indiana University Press, 1990), 40–41.

16 The roots of anti-Israeli sentiment in Iran date back to the creation of the Jewish State itself. Ayatollah Mahmood Taleqani, a leading cleric who later became the first leader of the Friday Prayer after the victory of Islamic Revolution, was the first Iranian intellectual to address the topic. In 1955, he visited the Jordanian-controlled part of Jerusalem for a conference on the Israeli-Palestinian conflict. The trip left a mark on the cleric. Shortly after his eye-opening trip, he wrote a book on the plight of the Palestinians that came to color the Iranian public's view of the conflict. Another influential intellectual who helped shape pro-Palestinian sentiment in Iran was Shams Al-e Ahmad. Though he initially was an admirer of the Jewish State, a visit to the country prompted a reversal in his position. Interview with a former Iranian deputy foreign minister with close ties to Ayatollah Taleqani, August 1, 2004, Tehran.

17 Nikki Keddie, *Modern Iran: Roots and Results of Revolution* (New Haven: Yale University Press, 2003), 232.

18 Phone interview with Nader Entessar, January 25, 2005, Washington, D.C.

19 Entessar, "Israel and Iran's National Security," 5. Menashri, *Post-Revolutionary Politics,* 269.

20 R. K. Ramazani, "Ideology and Pragmatism in Iran's Foreign Policy," *Middle East Journal* 4 (2004): 555.

21 Hunter, *Iran and the World,* 36. Interview with Mahmood Sariolghalam, professor at Shahid Beheshti University and adviser to the Iranian National Security Advisor, August 18, 2004, Tehran.

22 Interview with a prominent Iranian reformist strategist, March 2, 2004, Washington, D.C.

23 Entessar, "Israel and Iran's National Security," 5.

24 Interview with a former Iranian deputy foreign minister, August 1, 2004, Tehran.

25 Entessar, "Israel and Iran's National Security," 5.

26 Behrouz Souresrafil, *Khomeini and Israel* (London: Researchers, 1988), 45.

27 Phone interview with Entessar, January 25, 2005.

28 Confidential State Department telegram from the U.S. embassy in Iran, from October 1979, sent by Chargé d'Affaires Bruce Laingen. Available at the National Security Archives.

29 Interview with a former Iranian vice prime minister, August 1, 2004, Tehran. The deputy foreign minister was part of the Iranian delegation greeting Arafat at the Tehran airport.

30 Souresrafil, *Khomeini and Israel*, 46.

31 Secret communiqué from the U.S. embassy in Tehran, late September 1979. Available at the National Security Archives.

32 A few years later, the PLO and Amal would be fighting bloody battles for control of West Beirut. Entessar, "Israel and Iran's National Security," 6.

33 Souresrafil, *Khomeini and Israel*, 48.

34 Entessar, "Israel and Iran's National Security," 6.

35 Confidential State Department memo, September 30, 1979. Available at the National Security Archives.

36 The PLO maintained friendly relations with the Marxist-Islamist Mujahedeen-e Khalq (People's Mujahedeen) and its leader, Massoud Rajavi, one of Khomeini's most potent rivals. The Mujahedeen leader received Arafat during his second trip to Tehran, for the one-year anniversary of the revolution in February 1980, and pledged his support to the Palestinians by giving Arafat a captured Israeli machine gun. "It was the Palestinian revolution that first placed arms in our hands. But our battles with imperialism and Zionism are still going on. Please accept this machine-gun as a pledge of action from the [Mujahedeen] that, by this means, we will meet one day in a free Jerusalem," Rajavi told Arafat. (Today, pro-Israeli lawmakers such as the ranking member of the House Foreign Affairs Committee, Ileana Ros-Lehtinen, support Rajavi and the Mujahedeen as an alternative to the clerical regime in Tehran even though the group is classified by the U.S. State Department as a terrorist organization.) *Mojahed*, Esfand 6, 1358 (February 28, 1980).

37 Anoushiravan Ehteshami, *After Khomeini* (New York: Routledge, 1995), 129. Souresrafil, *Khomeini and Israel*, 50.

CHAPTER 9 Ideological Shifts, Geopolitical Continuities

Epigraph: Interview with Iranian political strategist, March 2004.

1 Declassified CIA Intelligence memorandum, "Iran: Khomeini's Prospects and Views," January 19, 1979. Declassified on January 23, 1986. Available at the National Security Archives.

2 Shireen Hunter, *Iran and the World* (Indianapolis: Indiana University Press, 1990), 42.

3 Interview with Iranian political strategist, March 2004.

4 Interview with Ambassador Javad Zarif, Iran's ambassador to the UN, New York, April 1, 2004.

5 Declassified CIA Intelligence memorandum, "Iran: Khomeini's Prospects and Views."

6 The role of Khomeini in the initial stages of the hostage-taking is disputed. According to Nikki Keddie, "The takeover, like an earlier one, would have been brief had it not got the support of Khomeini, who saw in it a chance to get rid of the liberal government, radicalize the revolution, and increase his power." Nikki Keddie, *Modern Iran: Roots and Results of Revolution* (New Haven: Yale University Press, 2003), 248–249.

7 Hunter, *Iran and the World*, 113.

8 Interview with former Minister of Finance Dan Meridor, Tel Aviv, October 27, 2004.

9 Samuel Segev, *The Iranian Triangle* (New York: Free Press, 1988), 4.

10 Gary Sick, *October Surprise* (New York: Random House, 1991), 61–63.

11 Interview with David Kimche, Tel Aviv, October 22, 2004.

12 Sohrab Sobhani, *The Pragmatic Entente: Israeli-Iranian Relations, 1948–1988* (New York: Praeger, 1989), 145.

13 Interview with Yitzhak Segev, former Israeli military attaché to Iran, Tel Aviv, October 17, 2004.

14 Israel Shahak, "How Israel's Strategy Favors Iraq over Iran," *Middle East International,* March 19, 1993, 19.

15 Interview with Yossi (Joseph) Alpher, former Mossad official and senior adviser to Ehud Barak, Tel Aviv, October 27, 2004.

16 Joseph Alpher, "Israel and the Iraq-Iran War," in *The Iraq-Iran War: Impact and Implications,* ed. Efraim Karsh (New York: St. Martin's, 1989), 157–159.

17 Ilan Peleg, *Begin's Foreign Policy 1977–1983: Israel's Move to the Right* (New York: Greenwood, 1987), 53.

18 Jakob Abadi, *Israel's Leadership: From Utopia to Crisis* (London: Greenwood, 1993), 64, 82, 155. The survival of the periphery doctrine was guaranteed by Israeli decision-makers' central belief in the inability to make peace with the Arabs. Interview with David Menashri, professor at Tel Aviv University, Tel Aviv, October 26, 2004.

19 Alpher, "Israel and the Iraq-Iran War," 158, 155.

20 Interview with Zarif, April 1, 2004.

21 Seyed Assadollah Athari, "Iranian-Egyptian Relations," *Discourse: An Iranian Quarterly* 2 (2001): 53–55. To this day, diplomatic relations between Egypt and Iran have not been restored. The sticking point is that Iran has renamed a street in Tehran after Lt. Col. Khalid al Islambuli, the Egyptian soldier who assassinated Sadat on October 6, 1981.

22 David Menashri, *Post-Revolutionary Politics in Iran* (London: Frank Cass, 2001), 227.

23 A. Ehteshami and R. Hinnebusch, *The Foreign Policies of Middle East States* (London: Lynne Rienner, 2002), 45.

24 Hunter, *Iran and the World,* 110.

25 Secret Department of State memorandum, U.S. embassy in Tehran, October 1979. Available at the National Security Archives.

26 Interview with former Deputy Foreign Minister Mahmoud Vaezi, Tehran, August 16, 2004. Suspiciousness of Israel was further fueled by Savak prisoners' revelation of Israel's role in training Savak agents in torture techniques. Massoumeh Ebtekar, *Take-over in Tehran* (Vancouver: Talonbooks, 2000), 188.

27 Interview with Gary Sick, New York, February 25, 2004.

28 Sick, *October Surprise,* 61–65.

29 Segev, *The Iranian Triangle,* 5. Sick, *October Surprise,* 71. Behrouz Souresrafil, *Khomeini and Israel* (London: Researchers, 1988), 61–62. Later, Carter managed to win a promise from Begin not to sell Iran any spare parts until the hostages were freed. Sick, *October Surprise,* 141.

30 Sobhani, *Pragmatic Entente,* 147.

31 Souresrafil, *Khomeini and Israel,* 62. Not all Iranian Jews fled the country, though. After meeting with leaders of the Jewish community, Khomeini issued a fatwa—a religious edict—decreeing that Jews and other minorities were to be protected.

32 Phone interview with Nader Entessar, January 25, 2005.

33 "Iran Calls for Stopping Oil Supply to Countries Supporting Israel," *Xinhua*, August 15, 1980.

34 Interview with Bijan Khajepour, Washington, D.C., February 17, 2004.

35 Anoushiravan Ehteshami, *After Khomeini* (New York: Routledge, 1995), 131.

36 Interview with Sick, February 25, 2004.

CHAPTER 10 **Saddam Attacks!**

1 Shireen Hunter, *Iran and the World* (Indianapolis Indiana University Press, 1990), 104.

2 Interview with Ali Reza Alavi Tabar, Tehran, August 21, 2004.

3 Seyed Assadollah Athari, "Iranian-Egyptian Relations," *Discourse: An Iranian Quarterly* 2 (2001): 56.

4 Shireen Hunter, *Iran After Khomeini* (New York: Praeger, 1992), 84, 92, 113.

5 Barry Rosen, ed., *Iran Since the Revolution* (New York: Columbia University Press, 1985), 56–59.

6 This was later demonstrated through the raining of Iraqi Scuds on Tel Aviv during the 1991 Persian Gulf War.

7 Samuel Segev, *The Iranian Triangle* (New York: Free Press, 1988), 124.

8 Anoushiravan Ehteshami, *After Khomeini* (New York: Routledge, 1995), 132.

9 Interview with Amir Mohebian, Tehran, August 19, 2004.

10 Interview with A. A. Kazemi, former Iranian diplomat during the early years of the Khomeini regime, Tehran, August 16, 2004.

11 This was reflected, among other things, in Iran's emerging alliance with secular Ba'athist Syria, as well as in its arms trade with Israel. A. Ehteshami and R. Hinnebusch, *The Foreign Policies of Middle East States* (London: Lynne Rienner, 2002), 47.

12 Nader Entessar, "Israel and Iran's National Security," *Journal of South Asian and Middle Eastern Studies* 4 (2004): 7.

13 Interview with Iranian political strategist, March 2004.

14 Even the most hard-line clerics saw "nothing contradictory with acquiring arms from your enemy." Interview with Iranian political strategist, March 2004. For more details on how Shi'ism permits the existence of contradictions, see Rosen, *Iran Since the Revolution*, xii.

15 Interview with Javad Zarif, Iran's ambassador to the UN, New York, April 1, 2004. Interview with Iranian political strategist, March 2004.

16 Interview with former Deputy Foreign Minister Mahmoud Vaezi, Tehran, August 16, 2004. The more ideological elements of the Iranian regime believed that the Ba'ath Party and Iraq were fighting Iran on behalf of Washington and Tel Aviv. Saddam's invasion of Iran was believed to have been encouraged by Washington, and as a result all U.S. allies, including Israel, were viewed with great suspicion. If Saddam had attacked Iran at the behest of Washington and Tel Aviv, how could Iran have common security interests with Israel, these revolutionaries asked themselves. "At that time, we did not see any real difference between what Saddam Hussein was doing [against Iran], and what America and Israel were doing," a senior Iranian diplomat explained to me. "We put them all in the same category." Interview with Tabar, August 21, 2004. Interview with former Deputy Foreign Minister Mahmoud Vaezi, Tehran, August 16, 2004. Interview with Mustafa Zahrani, February 26, 2004. Interview with Iranian political strategist, March 2004.

17 Interview with Zarif, April 1, 2004.

18 Interview with Gary Sick, New York, February 25, 2004.

19 Interview with Amir Mohebian, Tehran, August 19, 2004.

20 Interview with Kazemi, August 16, 2004.

21 "Call for End to Iran's Links with Israel," *BBC*, November 5, 1984. "Iran Runs 'Destroy Israel' Contest for Children," Associated Press, April 25, 1985. "Iran to Send Iraqi POWs to Lebanon to Fight Israel," Associated Press, June 5, 1981. "Iran Proposes Islamic Army to Fight Israel," Associated Press, April 2, 1982.

22 Interview with Mohebian, August 19, 2004.

23 Interview with Abbas Maleki, Tehran, August 1, 2004.

24 Interview with Tabar, August 21, 2004.

25 Interview with former Iranian official, Tehran, August 2004.

26 Houchang Chehabi, *Distant Relations: Iran and Lebanon in the Last 500 Years* (New York: I. B. Tauris, 2006), 211–213.

27 Ibid., 226.

28 Interview with Vaezi, August 16, 2004. According to Alavi Tabar, who belongs to the reformist faction of the Iranian government, this duality still remains a problem for Iranian foreign policy in general. "Our rhetoric is very harsh, but our policies are soft, while America speaks softly but conducts very harsh policies. . . . Though our rhetoric has been radical, in practice, our behavior has not."

29 Interview with Maleki, August 1, 2004.

30 Haleh Vaziri, "Iran's Involvement in Lebanon: Polarization and Radicalization of Militant Islamic Movements," *Journal of South Asian and Middle Eastern Studies* 16:2 (Winter 1992): 4.

31 Entessar, "Israel and Iran's National Security," 7.

32 Iraq was, after all, an Arab country whose aspirations to replace Egypt as the leading pan-Arab state prevented it from taking a soft stance on Israel. "Our tremendous fear was that Iraq would win that war, and we felt that would have been a terrible threat to Israel's security," Kimche said. "So from purely security point of view . . . we felt we had to do everything to prevent Iraq winning that war." Kimche dismissed the possibility that the arms Israel provided Iran could one day be used against Israel itself, and he confirmed the Israeli view at the time that Iran was not a threat. Interview with David Kimche, Tel Aviv, October 22, 2004.

33 Segev, *Iranian Triangle*, 22. Gen. Raphael Eytan, the chief of staff of the Israeli army at the time, explained Iran's inability to pose a threat to Israel: "If Iran decided to invade Israel, first her forces should cross Iraq and then, they should cross Jordan; in order to get to Israel they should destroy these two countries and when they reach Israel, they would realize that we are neither Iraq nor Jordan and to overcome us would not be possible." Behrouz Souresrafil, *Khomeini and Israel* (London: Researchers, 1988), 79.

34 Interview with David Menashri, professor at Tel Aviv University, Tel Aviv, October 26, 2004. According to Yuval Ne'eman, a right-wing Knesset member, though Iran was not a friendly state, "as far as Israel's security is concerned, Iraq is a far greater danger." Ruth Sinai, "Israel Helps Iran for Strategic and Economic Reasons," Associated Press, December 1, 1986.

35 Interview with Itamar Rabinovich, former adviser to Rabin and Israeli ambassador to the United States, Tel Aviv, October 17, 2004.

36 Interview with former National Security Advisor Robert McFarlane, Washington, D.C., October 13, 2004. "In strict geopolitical terms, if you don't consider regimes, our friend should be Iran, and we should never forget that," argued Itamar Rabinovich, Israel's U.S. ambassador 1993–1996 and a close adviser to Rabin. Interview with Rabinovich, October 17, 2004. Interview with Jess Hordes, director of the Anti-Defamation League's Washington office, Washington, D.C., March 24, 2004.

37 Interview with Kimche, October 22, 2004.

38 Malcolm Byrne, *The Chronology* (New York: Warner Books, 1987), 116.

39 Gary Sick, *October Surprise* (New York: Random House, 1991), 114.

40 "Israel Would Aid Iran in Return for Friendship," Associated Press, September 28, 1980.

41 According to French journalist Pierre Pean, some Israeli military advisers even visited the Iranian front line to evaluate firsthand Iran's capabilities and needs. Entessar, "Israel and Iran's National Security," 7.

42 Sick, *October Surprise*, 114, 167–179, 198.

43 Entessar, "Israel and Iran's National Security," 8.

44 Nikki Keddie, *Modern Iran: Roots and Results of Revolution* (New Haven: Yale University Press, 2003), 81.

45 Ariel Sharon, *Warrior* (New York: Simon and Schuster, 1989), 412–413.

46 Entessar, "Israel and Iran's National Security," 7.

47 Segev, *Iranian Triangle*, 7.

48 Interview with Kimche, October 22, 2004.

49 Sohrab Sobhani, *The Pragmatic Entente: Israeli-Iranian Relations, 1948–1988* (New York: Praeger, 1989), 148. Reza Pahlavi, the son of the Mohammad Reza Shah, had approached Defense Minister Sharon through a Saudi billionaire, Adnan Khashoggi, with a request for Israeli assistance in training and arming Iranian soldiers loyal to the Pahlavi monarchy. The young pretender to the Peacock Throne wanted to train the Iranians in Sudan—far enough to be beyond Tehran's reach—using Saudi funds and Israeli equipment in order to stage a counterrevolution in Iran. Pahlavi had on many occasions sought Israel's assistance in toppling the Khomeini government. His outreach to Israelis who had dealt with the Shah's Iran was extensive, so it was no surprise that he called them personally to urge them to speak out in favor of a coup d'état in Iran and congratulating them when they did so. Sharon quickly lost faith in the abilities of the young Pahlavi, however. Sharon, *Warrior*, 416–417. Segev, *Iranian Triangle*, 11, 82, 7.

50 Interview with Yossi (Joseph) Alpher, former Mossad official and senior adviser to Ehud Barak, Tel Aviv, October 27, 2004.

51 *Sunday Telegraph,* June 14, 1981.

52 Sick, *October Surprise*, 207.

53 "BBC Says Israel Resumed Shipping Arms to Iran," Associated Press, February 1, 1982.

54 Entessar, "Israel and Iran's National Security," 9.

55 Sick, *October Surprise*, 200.

56 "Sharon Reveals Arms Supplies to Iran," *BBC*, May 28, 1982.

57 "Israel Sends Military Equipment to Iran," Associated Press, May 28, 1982.

58 Interview with Zarif, April 1, 2004.

59 Interview with Zahrani, February 26, 2004.

60   "Khomeini's Twenty-fourth August Speech: Israel and Iran's Opponents," *BBC*, August 26, 1981.

61   Interview with Shmuel Bar, Tel Aviv, October 18, 2004.

CHAPTER 11 Scandal

Epigraph: Behrouz Souresrafil, *Khomeini and Israel* (England: Researchers, 1988), 115.

1   Charles D. Smith, *Palestine and the Arab-Israeli Conflict* (New York: St. Martin's, 1996), 284.

2   Lara Deeb, "Hizballah: A Primer," *Middle East Report Online*, July 31, 2006.

3   The importance of the 1982 Israeli invasion of Lebanon to the formation of Hezbollah cannot be overestimated. Had it not been for Israel's invasion, Iran would likely have failed in getting a stronghold in Lebanon, just as it had failed in Iraq and Bahrain. Incidentally, Iran's interest in the Lebanese Shia preceded the Iranian revolution. During Israel's 1978 invasion of Lebanon, the Shah privately expressed great concern about Iran's religious kin. To ease the Shah's worries, the Israelis let an Iranian delegation visit Lebanon to confirm that the Shias were not being mistreated. Interview with former senior Israeli diplomat stationed in Tehran, Tel Aviv, October 31, 2004.

4   Efraim Karsh ed., *The Iran-Iraq War: Impact and Implications* (New York: St. Martin's, 1989), 154. A. Ehteshami and R. Hinnebusch, eds., *The Foreign Policies of Middle East States* (London: Lynne Rienner, 2002), 47.

5   Sohrab Sobhani, *The Pragmatic Entente: Israeli-Iranian Relations, 1948–1988* (New York: Praeger, 1989), 150.

6   Interview with David Kimche, Tel Aviv, October 22, 2004.

7   Interview with Shmuel Bar, Tel Aviv, October 18, 2004.

8   Sobhani, *Pragmatic Entente*, 149.

9   David Kimche, *The Last Option* (New York: Maxwell Macmillan International, 1991), 213.

10   Interview with Yaacov Nimrodi, Savion (Tel Aviv), October 19, 2004. Information also taken from draft of Nimrodi's forthcoming English-language book on this subject.

11   Joyce Battle, "Shaking Hands with Saddam Hussein: The U.S. Tilts Toward Iraq, 1980–1984," *National Security Archive Electronic Briefing Book* No. 82, February 25, 2003.

12   Unclassified State Department memo titled "Iraq Use of Chemical Weapons," November 1, 1983. Available at the National Security Archives.

13   Robert Parry, "Missing U.S.-Iraq History," *Consortiumnews.com*, February 27, 2003. Based on testimony of National Security Council staff member Howard Teicher.

14   Rara Avis, "Iran and Israel," *Economist*, September 21, 1985.

15   Samuel Segev, *The Iranian Triangle* (New York: Free Press, 1988), 161.

16   Interview with Kimche, October 22, 2004.

17   Behrouz Souresrafil, *Khomeini and Israel* (London: Researchers Inc., 1988), 115.

18   Ian Black, "Israel's Longstanding Links with Iran," *Manchester Guardian Weekly*, December 7, 1986.

19   Malcolm Byrne, *The Chronology* (New York: Warner Books, 1987), 72. Based on Senate Intelligence Panel's report. Nimrodi denies this claim and argues that he was brought into the affair in February 1985.

20   Robert C. McFarlane, *Special Trust* (New York: Cadell and Davis, 1994), 19.

21   Interview with former National Security Advisor Robert McFarlane, Washington, D.C., October 13, 2004.

22 Byrne, *Chronology,* 117–118.

23 Ibid., 125.

24 Segev, *Iranian Triangle,* 133.

25 Interview with Nimrodi, October 19, 2004. See also Byrne, *Chronology,* 98.

26 Interview with Nimrodi, October 19, 2004.

27 Kimche, *Last Option,* 220.

28 Interview with Gary Sick, New York, February 25, 2004.

29 Interview with Iranian political strategist, March 2004.

30 Interview with Nimrodi, October 19, 2004.

31 Segev, *Iranian Triangle,* 281.

32 Kimche, *Last Option,* 213. Interview with Nimrodi, October 19, 2004.

33 Interview with Nimrodi, October 19, 2004.

34 Interview with McFarlane, October 13, 2004. "However, that theory was created among ourselves and had no foundation in fact of contemporary events or intelligence material," McFarlane concluded in retrospect.

35 Top-secret memorandum to George Schultz and Caspar Weinberger from Robert McFarlane, June 17, 1985. Available at the National Security Archives.

36 Interview with Nimrodi, October 19, 2004.

37 Kimche, *Last Option,* 211. According to McFarlane, Ledeen's visit with Peres was per Ledeen's own initiative; he was not authorized to speak on behalf of the U.S. government. McFarlane, *Special Trust,* 17.

38 McFarlane confirmed in his testimony before the Senate that Peres had brought up the idea of arms sales with Ledeen in May 1985. Sally Mallison and Thomas Mallison, "The Changing U.S. Position on Palestinian Self-Determination and the Impact of the Iran-Contra Scandal," *Journal of Palestine Studies* 3 (Spring 1987): 101–114. Interview with Nimrodi, October 19, 2004.

39 Segev, *Iranian Triangle,* 138.

40 Interview with Kimche, October 22, 2004.

41 Kimche, *Last Option,* 211. According to Kimche, Israel's primary motivation was to help the United States. "We owe the Americans so much that we have to do our utmost to help them; especially as they have come to us to seek our help," Peres reportedly told Kimche.

42 According to McFarlane, the Israeli envoy suggested that the United States and Israel could collaborate to "accelerate perhaps by one means or another" Khomeini's death. But McFarlane refused any suggestion of U.S. involvement in a plot to assassinate the ayatollah in the strongest possible terms. Kimche, however, vehemently denies having ever made such a suggestion, arguing that McFarlane "put that in the book to discredit Israel and save his own skin." McFarlane, *Special Trust,* 21. Interview with Kimche, October 22, 2004.

43 Interview with McFarlane, October 13, 2004.

44 McFarlane, *Special Trust,* 21.

45 Interview with Nimrodi, October 19, 2004.

46 Segev, *Iranian Triangle,* 157.

47 Interview with Nimrodi, October 19, 2004.

48 Ibid.

49 Kimche, *Last Option,* 216.

50 Byrne, *Chronology,* 601. Based on testimony of Robert McFarlane before the Senate. See also McFarlane, *Special Trust,* 31–35.

51 Kimche, *Last Option,* 213.

52 Interview with Nimrodi, October 19, 2004.

53 Segev, *Iranian Triangle,* 183–184.

54 Interview with Nimrodi, October 19, 2004.

55 Segev, *Iranian Triangle,* 183–184.

56 Interview with Nimrodi, October 19, 2004.

57 McFarlane, *Special Trust,* 46–47.

58 Ibid, 49–50, 52.

59 William Quandt, *Peace Process* (Los Angeles: University of California Press, 1993), 357.

60 Kimche, *Last Option,* 217.

61 Top-secret letter from Peres to Reagan, dated February 28, 1986. National Security Archives.

62 Victor Ostrovsky, *By Way of Deception* (New York: 1990), 330. Segev, *Iranian Triangle,* 249.

63 McFarlane, *Special Trust,* 54.

64 Top-secret Chronology of Events, dated November 18, 1986. Available at the National Security Archives.

65 Segev, *Iranian Triangle,* 270.

66 George Cave, "Why Secret 1986 U.S.-Iran 'Arms for Hostages' Negotiations Failed," *Washington Report on Middle East Affairs* (September/October 1994).

67 McFarlane, *Special Trust,* 54–56.

68 Interview with McFarlane, October 13, 2004.

69 McFarlane, *Special Trust,* 59.

70 Interview with McFarlane, October 13, 2004.

71 McFarlane, *Special Trust,* 61, 65.

72 Cave, "Negotiations Failed." McFarlane, *Special Trust,* 61, 65.

73 In one specific case, Nir received a phone call from Iran's Prime Minister Moussavi on July 20, 1986, informing him of Iranian efforts to release an American hostage nicknamed "the priest." Byrne, *Chronology,* 427.

74 Byrne, *Chronology,* 490. Based on Charles Allen's testimony before the Tower Commission.

75 Top-secret memorandum from Oliver North to National Security Advisor John Poindexter, September 15, 1986. Available at the National Security Archives. American proponents of reaching out to Iran argued along the same lines. Charles Allen of the CIA, who was closely involved in the operations, identified the principal motivation behind the Iranian channel to be "to open up a long-term geo-strategic relationship with Iran." Kimche, *Last Option,* 219.

76 Cave, "Negotiations Failed."

77 Mallison and Mallison, "Changing U.S. Position," 109.

78 Cave, "Negotiations Failed."

79 Quandt, *Peace Process,* 357.

80 Byrne, *Chronology,* 555.

81 Segev, *Iranian Triangle,* 313–314.

82 "Israel Doesn't Pledge Halt to Selling Iran Arms," Associated Press, December 8, 1986.

83 Ruth Sinai, "Peres Says U.S. Initiated Iran Deal, Israel Just Went Along," Associated Press, December 10, 1986.

84 Mary Sedor, "Peres: Arms Sales to Iran Less Than $6 Million in 1985," Associated Press, January 20, 1987.

85 "Israel Bears No Guilt in Iran Arms Sale, Eban Says," Associated Press, February 28, 1987.

86 "Shamir Urges U.S. to Pursue Possible Contacts with Iran," *Washington Post,* February 12, 1987.

87 Ostrovsky, *By Way of Deception,* 329.

88 Scheherezade Faramarzi, "Iran Offers Help Freeing Hostages, Denies Israel in Arms Deal," Associated Press, November 28, 1986.

89 R. K. Ramazani, "Ideology and Pragmatism in Iran's Foreign Policy," *Middle East Journal* 4 (2004): 556.

90 Segev, *Iranian Triangle,* 28.

91 John Rice, "Arabs Switch Focus from Israel to Ancient Enemy Iran," Associated Press, November 14, 1987. In late 1989 reports resurfaced of continued Iranian sale of oil to Israel. Iran vehemently denied the charges, but Tehran was nevertheless blasted by the PLO for its alleged ties with Israel. Associated Press, "Iran Denies Oil Sold to Israel," December 20, 1989.

92 L. Carl Brown, *Diplomacy in the Middle East* (New York: I. B. Tauris, 2004), 249.

93 Lee Stokes, "Iran Says Israel Will Only Respond to Force," United Press International, December 16, 1988.

CHAPTER 12 The Dying Gasp of the Periphery Doctrine

Epigraph: Behrouz Souresrafil, *Khomeini and Israel* (England: Researchers, 1988), 114.

1   Joseph Alpher, "Israel and the Iraq-Iran War," in *The Iraq-Iran War: Impact and Implications,* ed. Efraim Karsh (New York: St. Martin's, 1989), 164.

2   Ibid., 161.

3   Malcolm Byrne, *The Chronology* (New York: Warner Books, 1987), 444.

4   Interview with Yitzhak Segev, former Israeli military attaché to Iran, Tel Aviv, October 17, 2004.

5   Samuel Segev, *The Iranian Triangle* (New York: Free Press, 1988), 232.

6   "U.S. Rejects Rabin Suggestion on Better Relations with Iran," Associated Press, October 29, 1987. Alpher, "Israel and the Iraq-Iran War," 162.

7   Behrouz Souresrafil, *Khomeini and Israel* (London: Researchers, 1988), 114.

8   Alpher, "Israel and the Iraq-Iran War," 163.

9   *AIC Insight* 2 (September 2004). Souresrafil, *Khomeini and Israel,* 114.

10 Alpher, "Israel and the Iraq-Iran War," 159–160. Sohrab Sobhani, *The Pragmatic Entente: Israeli-Iranian Relations, 1948–1988* (New York: Praeger, 1989), 157.

11 Interview with Segev, October 17, 2004.

12 Interview with Javad Zarif, Iran's ambassador to the UN, New York, April 1, 2004.

13 Interview with Eliezer Tsafrir, Tel Aviv, October 16, 2004.

14 Farhang Rajaee, *The Iraq-Iran War: The Politics of Aggression* (Gainesville: University Press of Florida, 1993), 1, 206.

15 Moshe Zak, *Maariv,* August 1, 1988. Cited in Alpher, "Israel and the Iraq-Iran War," 165.

16 Efraim Imbar, "Yitzhak Rabin and Israeli National Security," *Security and Policy Studies,* No. 25, Begin-Sadat (BESA) Center for Strategic Studies, http://www.biu.ac.il/Besa/books/25/analysis.html.

17 Nicolas Tatro, "End of Iraq-Iran War Would Be Bad News for Israel," Associated Press, July 20, 1988.

18 Sobhani, *Pragmatic Entente,* 152.

19 Alpher, "Israel and the Iraq-Iran War," 165. Tamir and Saguy were supported by a pro-Iraq lobby in Washington that sought to convince Israeli leaders that Saddam Hussein's rule was beneficial to Israel. Even before the end of the war, an attempt had been made to align Israel with Washington's thaw with Saddam Hussein. The Jewish State "should develop a pro-Iraqi orientation, which may bear political fruit in the long run," a senior Israeli political source told the Israeli daily *Hadashot* in November 1987. "In recent months, senior Iraqi officials have indicated a willingness to examine the possibility of changing the policy towards Israel if the latter supports Iraq in the [Persian] Gulf War." David Kimche, *The Last Option* (New York: Maxwell Macmillan International, 1991), 231. Ilan Kfir, *Hadashot,* November 13, 1987.

20 Nick Luddington, "Iraq, Israel Call for Closer Ties with Iran; U.S. Wants Hostages Freed," Associated Press, June 5, 1989.

21 "Israel Bought Oil from Iran," Associated Press, December 19, 1989.

22 "State Department: Israel Informed U.S. About Resuming Oil Purchases from Iran," *Jerusalem Post,* December 20, 1989.

23 "Israel-Iran Oil-POW Deal Reported," *World News Digest,* December 31, 1989.

24 "Iran Denies Oil Sold to Israel," Associated Press, December 20, 1989.

25 "IDF Radio Says Israel Made 2.5m Dollar Profit in Oil Deal with Iran," *BBC,* February 22, 1990.

26 Interview with Iranian political strategist, March 2004.

27 "The Gulf Challenges of the Future," Emirates' Center for Strategic Studies and Research, 2005, 163–183.

28 Yahya Sadowski, *Scuds or Butter? The Political Economy of Arms Control in the Middle East* (Washington, D.C.: Brookings Institution, 1993), 63. Anoushiravan Ehteshami, *After Khomeini* (London: Routledge, 1995), 140.

29 Interview with Gary Sick, New York, February 25, 2004.

30 Interview with Abbas Maleki, Tehran, August 1, 2004.

31 Ehteshami, *After Khomeini,* 140.

32 Sadowski, *Scuds or Butter?,* 62.

33 Giandomenico Picco, *Man Without a Gun* (New York: Random House, 1999), 110, 113–114.

34 Interview with Mustafa Zahrani of the Iranian Foreign Ministry, New York, February 26, 2004. Anoushiravan Ehteshami and Raymond Hinnebusch, *The Foreign Policies of Middle East States* (London: Lynne Rienner, 2002), 300, 302.

35 Interview with Zarif, April 1, 2004.

36 Ehteshami, *After Khomeini,* 142. Hooshang Amirahmadi, "The Spiraling Gulf Arms Race," *Middle East Insight* 2 (1994): 48.

37 Shireen Hunter, *Iran After Khomeini* (New York: Praeger, 1992), 131.

38 Interview with former National Security Advisor Brent Scowcroft, Washington, D.C., September 27, 2004.

39 Interview with Deputy Foreign Minister Hadi Nejad-Hosseinian, Tehran, August 12, 2004.

40 Interview with Ali Reza Alavi Tabar, Tehran, August 21, 2004. Interview with Gen. Amnon Lipkin-Shahak, Tel Aviv, October 25, 2004.

41 Interview with adviser to the Iranian National Security Advisor, Tehran, August 2004.

42 Interview with former Deputy Foreign Minister Mahmoud Vaezi, Tehran, August 16, 2004. (The Iranian government views its rhetoric simply as an expression of opinion and not necessarily an action plan. This enables Iran to pursue one policy while portraying itself as the champion of a completely different policy.)

43 Interview with former member of Parliament and lead reformist strategist Mohsen Mirdamadi, Tehran, August 22, 2004.

CHAPTER 13 **The New World Order**

Epigraph: Interview with U.S. Ambassador Daniel Kurtzer, Tel Aviv, October 19, 2004.

1 David Kimche, *The Last Option* (New York: Maxwell Macmillan International, 1991), 236.

2 Interview with former National Security Advisor Brent Scowcroft, Washington, D.C., September 27, 2004.

3 Efraim Halevi, *Man in the Shadows* (New York: St. Martin's, 2006), 33–34.

4 Phone interview with Efraim Halevi, former head of the Mossad, June 17, 2006.

5 Kimche, *Last Option,* 236.

6 The Iranian intelligence services even alerted the Kuwaiti government hours before the Iraqis attacked. Ibid., 233.

7 Shireen Hunter, *Iran After Khomeini* (New York: Praeger, 1992), 126.

8 Paul J. White and William S. Logan, *Remaking the Middle East* (New York: Berg, 1997), 201.

9 John Esposito and R. K. Ramazani, *Iran at the Crossroads* (New York: Palgrave, 2001), 220.

10 Interview with former Deputy Foreign Minister Mahmoud Vaezi, Tehran, August 16, 2004.

11 For a discussion on the significance of Secretary Baker's statement, see R. K. Ramazani, "Move Iran Outside the 'Axis,'" *Christian Science Monitor,* August 19, 2002.

12 Anoushiravan Ehteshami, *After Khomeini* (London: Routledge, 1995), 160. Shahram Chubin, "Iran's Security Policy in the Post-Revolutionary Era," *RAND* (2001), 12. Interview with Mustafa Zahrani of the Iranian Foreign Ministry, New York, February 26, 2004.

13 Esposito and Ramazani, *Iran at the Crossroads,* 151. David Menashri, *Post-Revolutionary Politics in Iran* (London: Frank Cass, 2001), 252. White and Logan, *Remaking the Middle East,* 209. This remarkable shift was captured in a statement by Iran's foreign minister, Ali Akbar Velayati, while on a visit to Moscow in March 1996. Iranian-Russian relations, Velayati said, were "at their highest level in contemporary history." *RAND,* March 7, 1996. Esposito and Ramazani, *Iran at the Crossroads,* 7. Rather than exporting its Islamic revo-

lution to the newly freed states of central Asia, Iran pursued a pro–status quo policy based on economic exchange and cultural—rather than religious—affinity.

14 Ahmed Rashid, *Taliban: Militant Islam, Oil, and Fundamentalism in Central Asia* (New Haven: Yale University Press, 2000).

15 Interview with Amir Mohebian, Tehran, August 19, 2004. The statement resembles the title of one of Khairallah Talfah's pan-Arab writings (Talfah was Saddam Hussein's uncle): "Three things God should not have created: Jews, Persians and mosquitoes."

16 Interview with Mohammad Reza Dehshiri, head of Regional Studies Department, School of International Relations, Iranian Foreign Ministry, Tehran, August 24, 2004.

17 Interview with Mohammad Reza Tajik, counselor to President Khatami and director of the Strategic Studies Center of the President's Office, Tehran, August 25, 2004.

18 Anoushiravan Ehteshami and Raymond Hinnebusch, *The Foreign Policies of Middle East States* (London: Lynne Rienner, 2002), 83. Interview with Iranian political strategist, March 2004.

19 Chubin, "Iran's Security Policy." Interview with Nasser Hadian, reformist strategist in Iran, New York, February 26, 2004.

20 Interview with Javad Zarif, Iran's ambassador to the UN, New York, April 1, 2004.

21 Presentation by Shahram Chubin, Woodrow Wilson Center for International Scholars, November 9, 2004.

22 Interview with Vaezi, August 16, 2004.

23 Interview with Shmuel Limone, Ministry of Defense, secretary of Israel's Iran committee, Tel Aviv, October 18, 2004.

24 *Jerusalem Post*, October 1, 1997.

25 Interview with Mahmoud Sariolghalam, professor at Shahid Beheshti University and adviser to the Iranian National Security Advisor, August 18, 2004, Tehran.

26 Kenneth Pollack, *The Persian Puzzle* (New York: Random House, 2004), 259.

27 Dafna Linzer, "Iran Is Judged 10 Years from Nuclear Bomb," *Washington Post*, August 2, 2005.

28 IAEA Resolution GOV/2006/14, February 4, 2006.

29 Menashri, *Post-Revolutionary Politics in Iran*, 297.

30 Interview with Iranian political strategist, February 2004.

31 Interview with Zarif, April 1, 2004.

32 Interview with Vaezi, August 16, 2004.

33 Interview with Ali Reza Alavi Tabar, Tehran, August 21, 2004.

34 Christopher Boucek, "An Impact Greater Than Its Size: Israeli Foreign Policy in Central Asia," master's thesis, 1999, School of Oriental and African Studies, University of London, 9. Interview with Mustafa Zahrani of the Iranian Foreign Ministry, New York, February 26, 2004.

35 Ehteshami, *After Khomeini*, 154.

36 White and Logan, *Remaking the Middle East*, 203. Hunter, *Iran After Khomeini*, 133. Esposito and Ramazani, *Iran at the Crossroads*, 217. Interview with Gary Sick, New York, February 25, 2004.

37 Hunter, *Iran After Khomeini*, 136. Interview with Siamak Namazi, Atieh Bahar Consulting, Tehran, August 2, 2004.

38 Interview with Scowcroft, September 27, 2004. White and Logan, *Remaking the Middle East*, 202.

39 Hooshang Amirahmadi, "The Spiraling Gulf Arms Race," *Middle East Insight* 2 (1994): 48.

40 Interview with Tabar, August 21, 2004.

41 Amirahmadi, "The Spiraling Gulf Arms Race," 49.

42 Interview with Ambassador Nabil Fahmi, Washington, D.C., October 12, 2004.

43 James Baker, *The Politics of Diplomacy* (New York: Putnam, 1995), 412.

44 Amirahmadi, "The Spiraling Gulf Arms Race," 49. White and Logan, *Remaking the Middle East*, 204.

45 Interview with Shlomo Brom, Jaffee Center for Strategic Studies, Tel Aviv, October 26, 2004. "Israel's strategic position was very much improved," said Ephraim Kam of the Jaffee Center for Strategic Studies at Tel Aviv University. "The collapse of the Soviet Union was very important in the end." Interview with Ephraim Kam, Jaffee Center for Strategic Studies, Tel Aviv, October 26, 2004.

46 Interview with Eynat Shlein, Israeli embassy in Washington, June 1, 2004. Interview with Kam, October 26, 2004.

47 Interview with Ehud Yaari, Jerusalem, October 24, 2004.

48 Max Abrahms, "A Window of Opportunity for Israel?" *Middle East Quarterly* (Summer 2003).

49 Phone interview with Halevi, June 17, 2006.

50 Interview with Israel's former Minister of Finance Dan Meridor, Tel Aviv, October 27, 2004.

51 Interview with Keith Weissman of American Israel Public Affairs Committee (AIPAC), Washington, D.C., March 25, 2004. The war showed that "there is no such thing as Arab unity," according to an Israeli diplomat at the Israeli UN Mission who spoke on condition of nonattribution. Interviewed March 31, 2004, New York.

52 Interview with Brom, October 26, 2004.

53 Interview with Ambassador Daniel Kurtzer, Tel Aviv, October 19, 2004.

54 Interview with Yaari, October 24, 2004.

55 Uri Savir, *The Process: 1,100 Days That Changed the Middle East* (New York: Random House, 1998), 27.

56 David W. Lesch, *The Middle East and the United States* (Boulder: Westview, 2003), 278.

57 Interview with Shai Feldman and Shlomo Brom, Jaffee Center for Strategic Studies, Tel Aviv, October 26 and 27, 2004.

58 Baker, *Politics of Diplomacy*, 415, 428.

59 Halevi, *Man in the Shadows*, 33–34.

60 Baker, *Politics of Diplomacy*, 117, 123, 129.

61 Barry Rubin, "The United States and the Middle East, 1992," *Middle East Contemporary Survey* (1992).

62 Baker, *Politics of Diplomacy*, 423, 125, 131.

63 Phone interview with Halevi, June 17, 2006.

64 Interview with Kurtzer, October 19, 2004.

65 Baker, *Politics of Diplomacy*, 444.

66 Interview with Ambassador Dennis Ross, Washington, D.C., May 29, 2004.

67 Interview with Kenneth Pollack, Washington, D.C., November 29, 2004.

68 Interview with Assistant Secretary of State Robert Pelletreau, Washington, D.C., March 1, 2004.

69 Interview with Scowcroft, September 27, 2004.

70 Interview with Pelletreau, March 1, 2004. Interview with Ross, May 29, 2004.

71 Interview with Scowcroft, September 27, 2004.

72 Interview with Israeli diplomat who spoke on condition of nonattribution, New York, March 31, 2004.

73 Interview with Kurtzer, October 19, 2004.

74 Interview with Tabar, August 21, 2004. "We could have played a positive role in the region. We expected much better behavior [from the United States]," Tabar recalled.

75 Ehteshami and Hinnebusch, *Foreign Policies of Middle East States,* 302.

76 Pollack, *Persian Puzzle,* 254.

77 Ehteshami, *After Khomeini,* 157. Interview with Bijan Khajepour, Atieh Bahar Consulting, Washington, D.C., February 17, 2004.

78 Emma Murphy, "The Impact of the Arab-Israeli Peace Process on the International Security and Economic Relations of the Persian Gulf," *The Iranian Journal of International Affairs* 2 (Summer 1996): 441.

79 Interview with Deputy Foreign Minister Hadi Nejad-Hosseinian, Tehran, August 12, 2004.

80 Interviews with Nejad-Hosseinian, August 12, 2004; Tabar, August 21, 2004; Tajik, August 25, 2004; Namazi, August 2, 2004; and Bijan Khajepour, February 17, 2004. Additional officials who spoke on condition of nonattribution confirmed this.

81 Interview with Namazi, August 2, 2004.

82 Interview with Tajik, August 25, 2004.

83 Fearing that Iraq's disintegration would leave Iran completely unchecked, Washington decided to keep Saddam in power in order to balance Iran. Pollack, *The Persian Puzzle,* 247.

84 Interview with Col. Lawrence Wilkerson, former U.S. Secretary of State Colin Powell's chief of staff, Washington, D.C., October 16, 2006.

85 Interview with Namazi, August 2, 2004.

86 Interview with Masoud Eslami of the Iranian Foreign Ministry, Tehran, August 23, 2004.

87 Interview with Tajik, August 25, 2004. Overall, more than a dozen Iranian officials from all political factions confirmed that Iran was willing to participate in the Madrid conference and that its behavior would have been more conciliatory had it been invited to the conference.

88 Interview with Iranian political strategist, August 2004.

89 Interview with Tabar, August 21, 2004. Interview with Mohebian, August 19, 2004.

90 Interview with Tajik, August 25, 2004.

91 Interview with Ross, May 29, 2004.

92 Interview with Mohebian, August 19, 2004.

93 Interview with Tabar, August 21, 2004. Interview with Mohebian, August 19, 2004.

94 R. K. Ramazani, review of Mahmoud Sariolghalam's *The Foreign Policy of the Islamic Republic,* in *Discourse: An Iranian Quarterly* 2 (2001): 216. Interview with Mohebian, August 19, 2004.

95 *Ettela'at,* September 11, 1993.

96 Interview with Israeli diplomat who spoke on condition of nonattribution, New York, March 31, 2004.

CHAPTER 14 **Trading Enemies**

Epigraph: Interview with Efraim Inbar, Begin-Sadat Center, Jerusalem, October 19, 2004.

1 The damage to Palestinian society was far greater, though, with thousands held under harsh conditions in administrative detention. In addition, the occupied territories were suffering a steep economic decline brought about by the conflict and greatly worsened by Israeli closure during the Persian Gulf War, which had a devastating impact on Palestinians, who up to that point had been overwhelmingly dependent on jobs inside Israel.

2 Uri Savir, *The Process: 1,100 Days That Changed the Middle East* (New York: Random House, 1998), 22.

3 David Makovsky, *Making Peace with the PLO* (Boulder: Westview, 1996), 108.

4 Interview with Israel's former Minister of Finance Dan Meridor, Tel Aviv, October 27, 2004.

5 According to Savir, "The occupation had been forced upon Israel in 1967," and Israel needed to break out of Jabotinsky's "Iron-Wall." Savir, *The Process*, 13, 23.

6 Interview with Itamar Rabinovich, former adviser to Rabin and Israeli ambassador to the United States, Tel Aviv, October 17, 2004.

7 Makovsky, *Making Peace with the PLO,* 83.

8 Max Abrahms, "A Window of Opportunity for Israel?," *Middle East Quarterly* (Summer 2003).

9 Shimon Peres, *The New Middle East* (New York: Henry Holt, 1993), 3. Interview with Shai Feldman, Jaffee Center for Strategic Studies, Tel Aviv, October 27, 2004.

10 Interview with Gen. David Ivry, head of Israel's Iran committee, Tel Aviv, October 19, 2004.

11 Interview with former National Security Advisor Brent Scowcroft, Washington, D.C., September 27, 2004. "On the Brink," *Near East Report,* Washington Institute for Near East Affairs, May 12, 1993.

12 Israel Shahak, *Open Secrets—Israeli Nuclear and Foreign Policies* (London: Pluto, 1997), 82–83.

13 Interviews with Eynat Shlein, First Secretary, Embassy of Israel, Washington, D.C., June 1, 2004; Feldman, October 27, 2004; and Michael Eisenstadt, Washington Institute for Near East Policy, Washington, D.C., June 2, 2004.

14 David W. Lesch, *The Middle East and the United States* (Boulder: Westview, 2003), 277. Interview with Ambassador Dennis Ross, Washington, D.C., May 29, 2004.

15 Peres, *New Middle East,* 12.

16 Emma Murphy, "The Impact of the Arab-Israeli Peace Process on the International Security and Economic Relations of the Persian Gulf," *The Iranian Journal of International Affairs* 2 (Summer 1996): 428, 432–433.

17 Adam Garfinkle, *Politics and Security in Modern Israel* (London: M. E. Sharpe, 2000), 271.

18 Peres, *New Middle East,* 146.

19 Anoushiravan Ehteshami and Raymond Hinnebusch, *The Foreign Policies of Middle East States* (London: Lynne Rienner, 2002), 77.

20 Barry Rubin, *From War to Peace in Arab-Israeli Relations 1973–1993* (New York: New

York University Press, 1994), 4. Makovsky, *Making Peace with the PLO,* 11. Interview with Eisenstadt, June 2, 2004.

21 Charles Smith, *Palestine and the Arab-Israeli Conflict* (Boston: Bedford/St. Martin's, 2001), 440. Savir, *The Process,* 5. Makovsky, *Making Peace with the PLO,* 108. David Kimche, *The Last Option* (New York: Maxwell Macmillan International, 1991), 314.

22 Phone interview with Efraim Halevi, former head of Mossad, June 17, 2006.

23 Smith, *Palestine and the Arab-Israeli Conflict,* 441. Peres, *New Middle East,* 19.

24 Interview with Keith Weissman of American Israel Public Affairs Committee (AIPAC), Washington, D.C., March 25, 2004. Shimon Peres, *Battling for Peace* (New York: Random House, 1995), 284. Peres, *New Middle East,* 2–3.

25 Smith, *Palestine and the Arab-Israeli Conflict,* 440.

26 Makovsky, *Making Peace with the PLO,* 113. Hamas's ascendancy had a decisive impact on Rabin's realization that the long-standing Israeli position of not negotiating with the PLO had to be softened. Herbert C. Kelman, "Some Determinants of the Oslo Breakthrough," *International Negotiation* 2 (1997): 188.

27 Peres, *New Middle East,* 19. Barry Rubin, "The United States and the Middle East, 1992," *Middle East Contemporary Survey* 16 (1992). Makovsky, *Making Peace with the PLO,* 83.

28 Kelman, "Some Determinants of the Oslo Breakthrough," 188.

29 Peres, *New Middle East,* 33–34.

30 Interview with David Kimche, Tel Aviv, October 22, 2004.

31 Murphy, "Impact of the Arab-Israeli Peace Process," 437.

32 Makovsky, *Making Peace with the PLO,* 112. Ambassador Dennis Ross explained the Israeli shift as follows: When "there was a different Iran, you tried to create connections with Iran to counteract what were the threats closer to you. Now [Rabin] was trying to build [a] buffer of states between Israel and the potential threat to Israel [from Iran] . . . [because] the new threat came from the periphery." Interview with Ross, May 29, 2004.

33 Joseph Alpher, "Israel and the Iraq-Iran War," in *The Iraq-Iran War: Impact and Implications,* ed. Efraim Karsh (New York: St. Martin's, 1989), 164, 167n14.

34 Interview with former Minister of Defense Moshe Arens, Tel Aviv, October 21, 2004. One of the thirty-nine Iraqi Scuds that Saddam Hussein launched against Israel hit Moshe Arens's house north of Tel Aviv.

35 Interview with David Menashri, professor at Tel Aviv University, Tel Aviv, October 26, 2004. Interview with Yossi (Joseph) Alpher, former Mossad official and senior adviser to Ehud Barak, Tel Aviv, October 27, 2004.

36 Interview with Alpher, October 27, 2004.

37 Shahak, *Open Secrets,* 54.

38 "Iran Looms as a Growing Strategic Threat for Israel," *Jerusalem Post,* November 21, 1991.

39 Interview with Ephraim Sneh, member of Knesset, Tel Aviv, October 31, 2004.

40 Ephraim Sneh, "An Asymmetrical Threat," *Haaretz,* February 7, 2004.

41 Interview with leading Israeli military commentator, who spoke on condition of anonymity, Tel Aviv, October 17, 2004.

42 Peres, *New Middle East,* 43.

43 AFP, February 12, 1993.

44 "Israel Seeking to Convince U.S. That West Is Threatened by Iran," *Washington Post,* March 13, 1993.

45 Interview with Gary Sick, New York, February 25, 2004.

46 "Israel Focuses on the Threat Beyond the Periphery," *New York Times,* November 8, 1992.

47 Interview with Assistant Secretary of State Robert Pelletreau, Washington, D.C., March 1, 2004.

48 Israel Shahak, "How Israel's Strategy Favors Iraq over Iran," *Middle East International,* No. 446, March 19, 1993, 91.

49 Shai Feldman, "Confidence Building and Verification: Prospects in the Middle East," *JCSS Study* 25 (1994): 167. "Iran Is Going Nuclear, Israel Says," Reuters, September 17, 1992.

50 Reuters, October 25, 1992. "Iran Greatest Threat, Will Have Nukes by '99," Associated Press, February 12, 1993. No evidence had been found at the time that Iran was developing nuclear weapons. To this day Iran has not convinced the IAEA that its nuclear program is solely for peaceful purposes, yet the IAEA has not found evidence of a weapons program, either.

51 Peres, *New Middle East,* 41, 42, 63, 81, 82.

52 Interview with Shmuel Limone, Ministry of Defense, secretary of Israel's Iran committee, Tel Aviv, October 18, 2004.

53 Feldman, "Confidence Building and Verification," 25.

54 Peres, *New Middle East,* 19, 41.

55 Interview with Menashri, October 26, 2004. Menashri was also a member of the Israeli committee on Iran.

56 Interview with David Makovsky, Washington Institute for Near East Policy, Washington, D.C., June 3, 2004.

57 Interview with Shmuel Bar, Tel Aviv, October 18, 2004.

58 Interview with Shlein, June 1, 2004.

59 Peres, *New Middle East,* 19. Shahak, *Open Secrets,* 91. Interview with Ivry, October 19, 2004.

60 Peres, *New Middle East,* 83.

61 "Israel Seeking to Convince U.S. That West Is Threatened by Iran," *Washington Post,* March 13, 1993.

62 "Israel Focuses on the Threat Beyond the Periphery," *New York Times,* November 8, 1992.

63 Interview with Sneh, October 31, 2004.

64 Interview with Kenneth Pollack, Washington, D.C., November 29, 2004.

65 Interview with Weissman, March 25, 2004.

66 Interview with Scowcroft, September 27, 2004.

67 Interview with Ambassador Nabil Fahmi, Washington, D.C., October 12, 2004.

68 Interviews with Bader Omar Al-Dafa, Qatar's ambassador to the United States, Washington, D.C., May 26, 2004; and Fahmi, October 12, 2004.

69 Interview with Israeli diplomat who spoke on condition of nonattribution, New York, March 31, 2004.

70 Feldman, "Confidence Building and Verification," 168. Interview with Dore Gold,

Jerusalem, October 28, 2004. Gold argued that though the military edge was necessary for Israel's survival, it was purely a defensive strategy with no hegemonic ambitions in the political or cultural sense.

71 Interview with Shlomo Brom, Jaffee Center for Strategic Studies, Tel Aviv, October 26, 2004.

72 Yahya Sadowski, *Scuds or Butter? The Political Economy of Arms Control in the Middle East* (Washington, D.C.: Brookings Institution, 1993), 64–65.

73 Paul J. White and William S. Logan, *Remaking the Middle East* (New York: Berg, 1997), 208.

74 Ehteshami and Hinnebusch, *Foreign Policies of Middle East States,* 85.

75 World Military Expenditures and Arms Transfers, U.S. Department of State, Bureau of Verification and Compliance.

76 Interview with former Assistant Secretary of State Martin Indyk, Washington, D.C., March 4, 2004.

77 Eric Margolis, "Israel and Iran: The Best of Enemies," *Toronto Sun,* July 5, 1998.

78 Interview with Weissman, March 25, 2004.

79 Interview with Brom, October 26, 2004.

80 Interview with Ranaan Gissin, Jerusalem, October 31, 2004.

81 Interview with Weissman, March 25, 2004.

82 White and Logan, *Remaking the Middle East,* 205–207.

83 Interview with Fahmi, October 12, 2004.

84 Interview with Barry Rubin, Global Research in International Affairs Center, Tel Aviv, October 18, 2004.

85 Phone interview with Halevi, June 17, 2006.

86 Interview with Israeli expert on Iran who spoke on condition of anonymity, Tel Aviv, October 30, 2004.

87 Interview with Brom, October 26, 2004.

88 AFP, April 5, 1993.

89 Interview with Gen. Amnon Lipkin-Shahak, Tel Aviv, October 25, 2004.

90 Shahak, *Open Secrets,* 82–83.

91 Feldman, "Confidence Building and Verification," 167.

92 Ehteshami and Hinnebusch, *Foreign Policies of Middle East States,* 123.

93 Ehud Sprinzak, "Revving Up an Idle Threat," *Haaretz,* September 29, 1998.

94 Ephraim Kam, lecture at Tel Aviv University, February 2004.

95 Interview with Makovsky, June 3, 2004.

96 Makovsky, *Making Peace with the PLO,* 112.

97 Interview with Ehud Yaari, Jerusalem, October 24, 2004. Israel had to agree to "painful concessions" with its immediate neighbors in order to face the "unattractive cocktail presented by Iran, namely fanaticism, deliberate use of international terrorism, and development of WMDs and means of delivery," Rabin's adviser Rabinovich noted. Interview with Rabinovich, October 17, 2004.

98 Interview with Ross, May 29, 2004.

99 Jim Lobe, "'Strategic Consensus' Redux?" *IPS,* October 4, 2006.

100 "Peres Says Iran Greatest Threat to Arabs," Reuters, November 28, 1993.

101 Peres, *New Middle East,* 91, 146.

102 Radio Monte Carlo, May 16, 1996.

103 Interview with Fahmi, October 12, 2004.

104 Interview with Rabinovich, October 17, 2004.

105 Interview with Efraim Inbar, Begin-Sadat Center, Jerusalem, October 19, 2004.

106 Interview with Makovsky, June 3, 2004.

107 Interview with Indyk, March 4, 2004.

108 Interview with Feldman, October 27, 2004.

109 Interview with Yaari, October 24, 2004.

110 "Israel Seeking to Convince U.S. That West Is Threatened by Iran," *Washington Post,* March 13, 1993.

111 Interview with Inbar, October 19, 2004.

112 Murphy, "Impact of the Arab-Israeli Peace Process," 426.

113 Interview with former National Security Advisor Anthony Lake, Washington, D.C., April 5, 2004.

114 Gary Sick, "The Future of U.S.-Iran Relations," *Middle East Economic Survey,* 21 June 1999, D1–D6.

115 F. Gregory Gause III, "The Illogic of Dual Containment," *Foreign Affairs,* March/April 1994.

116 Kenneth Pollack, *The Persian Puzzle* (New York: Random House, 2004), 263.

117 Interview with Pelletreau, March 1, 2004.

118 Interview with Scowcroft, September 27, 2004.

119 Interview with senior State Department official who spoke on condition of nonattribution, October 2004.

CHAPTER 15 **From Cold Peace to Cold War**

Epigraph: *Mideast Mirror,* March 10, 1995.

1 Shahram Chubin, "Iran's Security Policy in the Post-Revolutionary Era," *RAND* (2001), 10. Interview with Ali Reza Alavi Tabar, Tehran, August 21, 2004.

2 Interview with Deputy Foreign Minister Hadi Nejad-Hosseinian, Tehran, August 12, 2004.

3 Interview with Abbas Maleki, Tehran, August 1, 2004.

4 Interview with Mohammad Reza Dehshiri, head of Regional Studies Department, School of International Relations, Iranian Foreign Ministry, Tehran, August 24, 2004. R. K. Ramazani, review of Mahmoud Sariolghalam's *The Foreign Policy of the Islamic Republic,* in *Discourse: An Iranian Quarterly* 2 (2001): 216.

5 Interview with Mahmoud Sariolghalam, professor at Shahid Beheshti University and adviser to the Iranian National Security Advisor, August 18, 2004, Tehran.

6 Ephraim Kam, speech given at Tel Aviv University, February 10, 2004.

7 Interview with Tabar, August 21, 2004.

8 Interview with Amir Mohebian, Tehran, August 19, 2004.

9 Interview with Nejad-Hosseinian, August 12, 2004.

10 Interviews with Mohebian, August 19, 2004; and Sariolghalam, August 18, 2004.

11 Interview with Davoud Hermidas-Bavand, professor at Shahid Beheshti University and former Iranian diplomat, Tehran, August 8, 2004.

12 Interview with Nejad-Hosseinian, August 12, 2004.

13 David Menashri, "Revolution at a Crossroads," Policy Paper 43, Washington Institute

for Near East Policy, 1997, 81. Shaul Bakhash, "Iran: Slouching Towards the 21," in *The Middle East Enters the Twenty-First Century,* ed. Robert O. Freedman (Gainesville: University Press of Florida, 2002), 57–58.

14   Interview with Mohammad Reza Tajik, counselor to President Khatami and director of Strategic Studies Center of the President's Office, Tehran, August 25, 2004.

15   Clark Staten, "Israeli-PLO Peace Agreement—Cause of Further Terrorism?," *Emergency-Net NEWS,* October 12, 1993.

16   Interview with Masoud Eslami of the Iranian Foreign Ministry, Tehran, August 23, 2004.

17   Reuters, March 5, 1994.

18   Interview with Hermidas-Bavand, August 8, 2004.

19   Interviews with Tajik, August 25, 2004; and A. A. Kazemi, former Iranian diplomat during the early years of the Khomeini regime, Tehran, August 16, 2004.

20   Interview with Mustafa Zahrani of the Iranian Foreign Ministry, New York, February 26, 2004.

21   Interview with Hermidas-Bavand, August 8, 2004.

22   Interview with Tabar, August 21, 2004.

23   Interview with Eslami, August 23, 2004.

24   Interview with Tabar, August 21, 2004.

25   Houchang Chehabi, *Distant Relations: Iran and Lebanon in the Last 500 Years* (New York: I. B. Tauris, 2006), 230.

26   Robert O. Freedman, *The Middle East Enters the Twenty-First Century* (Gainesville: University Press of Florida, 2002), 58. Interview with Shlomo Brom, Jaffee Center for Strategic Studies, Tel Aviv, October 26, 2004.

27   Interview with Iranian political strategist, March 2004.

28   Interview with Brom, October 26, 2004. "Only much later they started to have [*sic*] some kind of relationship with Hamas, although until now I think their relationship with Hamas is much weaker than with the other Islamic groups. . . . But in 1991 it was mainly the Hezbollah."

29   Interview with Ambassador Nabil Fahmi, Washington, D.C., October 12, 2004.

30   "Iran Blasts the PLO," *Washington Post,* April 30, 1994.

31   Marc Perelman, "Israeli Report Calls Argentina Bombing Payback for '92 Raid," *Forward,* July 22, 2005.

32   Interview with Itamar Rabinovich, former adviser to Rabin and Israeli ambassador to the United States, Tel Aviv, October 17, 2004.

33   Interview with Gen. Amnon Lipkin-Shahak, Tel Aviv, October 25, 2004. "Iran began to engage in anti-Israeli global terrorism with the destruction in Argentina, in 1994," Rabinovich recalled. "Terrorism as a global issue became a big issue from our point of view with Iran since 1994." Interview with Rabinovich, October 17, 2004.

34   Interview with Yossi (Joseph) Alpher, former Mossad official and senior adviser to Ehud Barak, Tel Aviv, October 27, 2004.

35   Phone interview with Efraim Halevi, former head of Mossad, June 17, 2006.

36   Interview with Brom, October 26, 2004. "In the suicide bombing that started in 1994–1995, Iran was quite active in pushing the Islamic Jihad to initiate many of these kinds of actions," Brom said.

37 Interview with Rabinovich, October 17, 2004.

38 The State Department provides details regarding the MKO's terrorist activities on its Web site, http://www.state.gov/s/ct/rls/fs/2001/6531.htm.

39 "Iranian Opposition Approaches Israel," *Voice of Israel,* May 1, 1995. "While Israel did not identify itself with the opponents of the Tehran regime," said Nisim Zvili, the Labor Party secretary-general, "it supported the political campaign to halt any assistance to the incumbent Iranian government."

40 Interview with David Menashri, professor at Tel Aviv University, Tel Aviv, October 26, 2004.

41 Interview with leading Israeli military commentator who spoke on condition of anonymity, Tel Aviv, October 17, 2004.

42 Iran-Interlink, http://www.iran-interlink.org/files/News3/May05/interlink040505.htm. The Israeli companies were Intergama Investment group and Kardan Group, using the REEM Teleport and Tel-Aviv Teleport satellites.

43 Anoushiravan Ehteshami and Raymond Hinnebusch, *The Foreign Policies of Middle East States* (London: Lynne Rienner, 2002), 82. Interview with Ephraim Sneh, member of Knesset, Tel Aviv, October 31, 2004. Interview with former Minister of Defense Moshe Arens, Tel Aviv, October 21, 2004.

44 David Makovsky, *Making Peace with the PLO* (Boulder: Westview, 1996), 112.

45 Interview with Menashri, October 26, 2004.

46 Interview with Rabinovich, October 17, 2004.

47 Interview with Israeli diplomat who spoke on condition of nonattribution, Tel Aviv, October 18, 2004.

48 Interview with Ephraim Kam, Jaffee Center for Strategic Studies, Tel Aviv, October 26, 2004.

49 Interview with Efraim Inbar, Begin-Sadat Center, Jerusalem, October 19, 2004.

50 Shai Feldman, *Confidence Building and Verification: Prospects in the Middle East,* JCSS Study No. 25 (Tel Aviv: Jaffee Center for Strategic Studies, 1994), 199.

51 Israel Shahak, *Open Secrets—Israeli Nuclear and Foreign Policies* (London: Pluto, 1997), 64.

52 Eric Margolis, "Israel and Iran: The Best of Enemies," *Toronto Sun,* July 5, 1998.

53 Mahmoud Sariolghalam, "Iranian Perceptions and Responses," *Journal of Political and Military Sociology* 29 (2001): 297.

54 Phone interview with Soli Shavar, Haifa, October 28, 2004.

55 Interview with Gen. David Ivry, head of Israel's Iran committee, Tel Aviv, October 19, 2004.

56 Interview with Gen. Amos Gilad, Tel Aviv, October 31, 2004.

57 Giandomenico Picco, *Man Without a Gun* (New York: Random House, 1999), 232.

58 Interview with Yitzak Segev, former Israeli military attaché to Iran, Tel Aviv, October 17, 2004.

59 Interview with Ehud Yaari, Jerusalem, October 24, 2004.

60 Interview with former Israeli Minister of Finance Dan Meridor, Tel Aviv, October 27, 2004.

61 Interview with Shai Feldman, Jaffee Center for Strategic Studies, Tel Aviv, October 27, 2004.

62 Interview with Gilad, October 31, 2004.

63 Interview with Rabinovich, October 17, 2004.

64 Interview with Alpher, October 27, 2004. "There was a fear that if America talks to Iran, Israel will be left out in the cold," explained Gerald Steinberg, professor at Bar Ilan University in Israel. "The Great Satan will make up with Iran and forget about Israel." Interview with Gerald Steinberg, Jerusalem, October 28, 2004.

65 Interview with Israeli diplomat who spoke on condition of nonattribution, Tel Aviv, October 18, 2004.

66 In 1998 and 1999, for example, Fortune named American Israel Public Affairs Committee (AIPAC) the second most powerful lobby in Washington after AARP (American Association for Retired Persons). On July 6, 1987, the *New York Times* described AIPAC as "a major force in shaping United States policy in the Middle East." The article also stated that "the organization has gained power to influence a presidential candidate's choice of staff, to block practically any arms sale to an Arab country, and to serve as a catalyst for intimate military relations between The Pentagon and the Israeli army. Its leading officials are consulted by State Department and White House policy makers, by senators and generals." David K. Shipler, "On Middle East Policy, a Major Influence," *New York Times,* July 6, 1987.

67 Interview with Alpher, October 27, 2004.

68 Samuel Segev, *Crossing the Jordan* (New York: St. Martin's, 1998), ch. 1.

69 Interview with Jess Hordes, director of the Anti-Defamation League's Washington office, Washington, D.C., March 24, 2004.

70 Interview with Alpher, October 27, 2004.

71 Segev, *Crossing the Jordan,* ch. 1.

72 Interview with Hordes, March 24, 2004.

73 Farideh Farhi, "Economic Statecraft or Interest Group Politics: Understanding U.S. Sanctions on Iran," *The Iranian Journal of International Affairs* 1 (Spring 1997): 67.

74 Interview with Feldman, October 27, 2004.

75 Shahak, *Open Secrets,* 84.

76 Efraim Karsh, "Israel's Imperative," *Washington Quarterly* 3 (2000): 155.

77 Reuters, September 12, 1994.

78 Interview with Kenneth Pollack, Washington, D.C., November 29, 2004. Kenneth Pollack, *The Persian Puzzle* (New York: Random House, 2004), 260.

79 Emma Murphy, "The Impact of the Arab-Israeli Peace Process on the International Security and Economic Relations of the Persian Gulf," *The Iranian Journal of International Affairs* 2 (Summer 1996): 426. Interview with Keith Weissman of American Israel Public Affairs Committee (AIPAC), Washington, D.C., March 25, 2004.

80 Interview with former National Security Advisor Brent Scowcroft, Washington, D.C., September 27, 2004.

81 Reuters, December 15, 1994.

82 Reuters, January 6, 1995.

83 UPI, January 1, 1995.

84 Interview with Pollack, November 29, 2004.

85 John Esposito and R. K. Ramazani, *Iran at the Crossroads* (New York: Palgrave, 2001), 203.

86 Text of Warren Christopher speech, "Maintaining the Momentum for Peace in the Middle East," Georgetown University, October 25, 1994.

87 *Mideast Mirror,* March 10, 1995.

88 Paul J. White and William S. Logan, *Remaking the Middle East* (New York: Berg, 1997), 199.

89 Interview with Ambassador Daniel Kurtzer, Tel Aviv, October 19, 2004.

90 Pollack, *Persian Puzzle,* 260.

91 Ibid., 268–270.

92 Ami Ayalon, *Middle East Contemporary Survey* (1994).

93 Interview with Weissman, March 25, 2004.

94 Interview with Rabinovich, October 17, 2004.

95 Interview with Pollack, November 29, 2004.

96 Interview with Bijan Khajepour, Washington, D.C., February 17, 2004.

97 Lamis Andoni, "When Iran Hedges Closer, U.S. Pushes Away," *Christian Science Monitor,* April 7, 1995.

98 Colin Barraclough, "Iran Seeks Oil Partners, U.S. Firms Can't Join the Dance," *Christian Science Monitor,* December 12, 1995.

99 Pollack, *Persian Puzzle,* 271.

100 Interview with Weissman, March 25, 2004.

101 "Comprehensive U.S. Sanctions Against Iran: A Plan for Action," *AIPAC Report,* April 2, 1995.

102 John Greenwald, "Down Goes the Deal," *Time,* March 27, 1995.

103 "Clinton's Anti-Iran Move," *Christian Science Monitor,* May 2, 1995.

104 Statement by Secretary of State Christopher at the White House, May 1, 1995.

105 Pollack, *Persian Puzzle,* 273.

106 "Clinton's Anti-Iran Move," *Christian Science Monitor,* May 2, 1995.

107 Pollack, *Persian Puzzle,* 259–260.

108 Interview with Ambassador Dennis Ross, Washington, D.C., May 29, 2004.

109 Associated Press, May 9, 1995.

110 "Greatest Threat from Iran Says Peres," *Jerusalem Post,* May 10, 1995.

111 Interview with Ross, May 29, 2004.

112 Interview with Weissman, March 25, 2004. G. Moffett, "Push to Widen Libya Sanctions Riles U.S. Allies," *Christian Science Monitor,* January 24, 1996. Pollack, *Persian Puzzle,* 270.

113 Intimately involved in every step of the deliberations on the bill, which became known as ILSA (the Iran Libya Sanctions Act), American Israel Public Affairs Committee (AIPAC) was the only lobby group at the table when the Ways and Means Committee in the House discussed the bill. Farhi, "Economic Statecraft," 66.

114 White House Fact Sheet, August 6, 1996.

115 Testimony by Assistant Secretary of State Pelletreau before the House International Relations Committee, May 2, 1995.

116 Gary Sick, "The Future of U.S.-Iran Relations," *Middle East Economic Survey,* June 21, 1999.

117 Interview with Weissman, March 25, 2004.

118 Comments by Martin Indyk at a public debate at Cooper Union, New York City, September 28, 2006.

119 Interview with Sneh, October 31, 2004.

CHAPTER 16 **With Likud, the Periphery Doctrine Returns**

Epigraph: Interview with Dore Gold, Jerusalem, October 28, 2004.

1 Kenneth Pollack, *The Persian Puzzle* (New York: Random House, 2004), 245.
2 Emma Murphy, "The Impact of the Arab-Israeli Peace Process on the International Security and Economic Relations of the Persian Gulf," *The Iranian Journal of International Affairs* 2 (Summer 1996): 435.
3 Interview with Ephraim Kam, Jaffee Center for Strategic Studies, Tel Aviv, October 26, 2004. Interview with Efraim Inbar, Begin-Sadat Center, Jerusalem, October 19, 2004. "Iran Rallies Against Peace," *Near East Report WINEP,* January 24, 2000.
4 Interview with Itamar Rabinovich, former adviser to Rabin and Israeli ambassador to the United States, Tel Aviv, October 17, 2004.
5 "Iran Rallies Against Peace," *Near East Report WINEP,* January 24, 2000.
6 Interview with Keith Weissman of American Israel Public Affairs Committee (AIPAC), Washington, D.C., March 25, 2004.
7 Interview with former Assistant Secretary of State Martin Indyk, Washington, D.C., March 4, 2004.
8 Ibid. Other American officials were less impressed with Iran's cunning and more critical of Washington's own conduct. According to one senior official who preferred to remain unnamed: "I think it is a serious misreading of what happened to say that Iran outsmarted us. If we were in a moment of serious dominance on November 1, 1991 [the day after the Madrid conference], why didn't we exploit it better? Why didn't we fix the Arab-Israeli crisis? Why didn't we succeed if everything was going our way? Six months later Shamir was out of office, so we didn't have that excuse. We had marginalized Arafat. So he wasn't a factor. How is that Iran's doing? I would be more self-critical in my analysis. I think it is really wrong and self-exculpatory to say that Iran outsmarted us by choosing terror. Of course they would choose terror, that's all they had left. Of course they would go for the bomb, and go to exactly where they have to go for the expertise to do it, Pakistan and North Korea. I hope our Iran experts would know that. I don't think we're so stupid not to know."
9 Interview with Ambassador Daniel Kurtzer, Tel Aviv, October 19, 2004.
10 Reuters, November 7, 1995.
11 Reuters, November 5, 1995.
12 Reuters, February 8, 1996.
13 *Israel Line,* February 15, 1996.
14 Reuters, March 7, 1996.
15 Reuters, April 8, 1996. Binyamin Netanyahu, Peres's rival in the elections, did not want the public to conclude that terror attacks in Israel would help him win the elections and reacted by seeking American and German support to send a strong message to Iran and Syria. AFP, April 8, 1996.
16 Interview with Weissman, March 25, 2004.
17 Interview with Shlomo Brom, Jaffee Center for Strategic Studies, Tel Aviv, October 26, 2004.
18 Interview with an Israeli military officer who participated in the Iran Committee meetings. He spoke on condition of nonattribution. Tel Aviv, October, 2004.
19 "Israeli Election Draws Mixed Reactions," CNN, May 30, 1996.
20 Interview with Ehud Yaari, Jerusalem, October 24, 2004.

21 Interview with Yossi (Joseph) Alpher, former Mossad official and senior adviser to Ehud Barak, Tel Aviv, October 27, 2004.

22 Interview with Dore Gold, Jerusalem, October 28, 2004.

23 Interview with Weissman, March 25, 2004.

24 Interview with Shmuel Limone, Ministry of Defense, secretary of Israel's Iran committee, Tel Aviv, October 18, 2004.

25 Interview with Alpher, October 27, 2004.

26 Interview with Gen. David Ivry, head of Israel's Iran committee, Tel Aviv, October 19, 2004.

27 Interview with Limone, October 18, 2004.

28 Interview with Marshal Breger, professor at Catholic University, Washington, D.C., October 11, 2004.

29 Interview with Limone, October 18, 2004.

30 Interview with Gen. Amos Gilad, Tel Aviv, October 31, 2004.

31 Interview with Shmuel Bar, Tel Aviv, October 18, 2004.

32 Interview with Inbar, October 19, 2004.

33 Uzi Arad, "Russia and Iran's Nuclear Program," *Jerusalem Issue Brief,* April 28, 2003.

34 Interview with Brom, October 26, 2004.

35 Interview with leading Israeli military commentator who spoke on condition of anonymity, Tel Aviv, October 17, 2004.

36 Interview with Gilad, October 31, 2004.

37 Interview with Yaari, October 24, 2004.

38 Interview with Gold, October 28, 2004.

39 Aluf Ben, "A Change in Israeli-Iranian Relations," *Haaretz,* November 10, 1996. David Menashri, *Post-Revolutionary Politics in Iran* (London: Frank Cass, 2001), 296.

40 "Israel Looks Again at Iran Relations," Channel 2, November 22, 1996. Lubrani's efforts resulted in the CIA being allocated $18 million to destabilize the Iranian government. Pollack, *Persian Puzzle,* 273.

41 Interview with Gold, October 28, 2004.

42 "Likud said to seek understanding with Iran," *RAND,* July 24, 1996. IDF Radio, November 10, 1996. *Xinhua,* September 13, 1996. *Xinhua,* September 28, 1996.

43 *Jerusalem Post,* September 9, 1997.

44 Speech by Prime Minister Benjamin Netanyahu to a Joint Session of the United States Congress, Washington, D.C., July 10, 1996.

45 Interview with Gold, October 28, 2004.

46 Interview with Indyk, March 4, 2004.

47 Reuters, August 28, 1997.

48 Interview with Barry Rubin, Global Research in International Affairs Center, Tel Aviv, October 18, 2004.

49 Interview with Gold, October 28, 2004.

50 Ibid.

51 Interview with Weissman, March 25, 2004.

52 Interview with Bar, October 18, 2004.

53 Interview with Weissman, March 25, 2004.

54 Interview with Gold, October 28, 2004.

55 Ibid. According to Gold, 50–70 percent of Hamas funding came from Saudi Arabia.

56 IDF Radio, November 10, 1996.

57 Interview with Gilad, October 31, 2004.

58 IDF Radio, November 10, 1996.

59 Interview with Israel's former Minister of Finance Dan Meridor, Tel Aviv, October 27, 2004.

60 Interview with Amir Mohebian, August 19, 2004. Interview with former Deputy Foreign Minister Mahmoud Vaezi, Tehran, August 16, 2004.

61 Reuters, June 25, 1996.

62 Interview with former member of Parliament and lead reformist strategist, Mohsen Mirdamadi, Tehran, August 22, 2004.

63 "Iran Helps Free Hostages," AFP, April 29, 1996.

64 Interview with leading Israeli military commentator who spoke on condition of anonymity, Tel Aviv, October 17, 2004.

65 IDF Radio, November 10, 1996.

66 Reuters, July 22, 1996.

67 Interview with Iranian political strategist, New York, February 26, 2004.

CHAPTER 17 **Khatami's Détente**

Epigraph: President Mohammad Khatami, interviewed on CNN, January 7, 1998.

1 Anoushiravan Ehteshami and Raymond Hinnebusch, *The Foreign Policies of Middle East States* (London: Lynne Rienner, 2002), 302.

2 Kayhan Barzegar, "Détente in Khatami's Foreign Policy and Its Impact on Improvement of Iran-Saudi Relations," *Discourse: An Iranian Quarterly* 2 (2002): 160–167.

3 Saudi Crown Prince Abdullah's speech at eleventh OIC Summit, Tehran, December 10, 1997.

4 Reuters, March 25, 1997.

5 Interview with Ambassador Nabil Fahmi, Washington, D.C., October 12, 2004.

6 *Xinhua,* June 24, 1997. Reuters, April 2, 1997.

7 David Menashri, *Post-Revolutionary Politics in Iran* (London: Frank Cass, 2001), 243.

8 *Xinhua,* November 1, 1997.

9 Reuters, November 11, 1997.

10 R. K. Ramazani, "Ideology and Pragmatism in Iran's Foreign Policy," *Middle East Journal* 4 (2004): 558.

11 "Transcript of Interview with Iranian president Mohammad Khatami," CNN, January 7, 1998.

12 Ali Ansari, *Confronting Iran* (New York: Basic Books, 2006), 155–156.

13 *Dow Jones,* May 27, 1997.

14 Interview with David Makovsky, Washington Institute for Near East Policy, Washington, D.C., June 3, 2004.

15 The White House, Office of the Press Secretary, "Remarks at the Millennium Evening: The Perils of Indifference: Lessons Learned from a Violent Century," released April 12, 1999.

16 Bulent Aras, "Turkish-Israeli-Iranian Relations in the Nineties: Impact on the Middle East," *Middle East Policy* 3 (2000): 156. For instance, the Anti-Defamation League and the Conference of Presidents of Major American Jewish Organizations opposed the Clinton administration's decision to lift the ban on imports of caviar, Persian rugs, and

pistachios from Iran. "Israel, U.S. Jewish Lobby Disagree on Iran Sanctions," UPI, September 22, 2000.

17 "U.S. Move to Engage Iran Worries Supporters of Israel," JTA, June 22, 1998. Ansari, *Confronting Iran,* 142–143.

18 "Washington Event Boycott Said Censure of U.S.-Iran Moves," Israeli TV, June 18, 1998.

19 Interview with Dore Gold, Jerusalem, October 28, 2004. Interview with Yossi (Joseph) Alpher, former Mossad official and senior adviser to Ehud Barak, Tel Aviv, October 27, 2004.

20 Federal News Service, February 28, 1997.

21 Reuters, March 4, 1997.

22 Reuters, March 26, 1997.

23 Dore Gold, "Middle East Missile Proliferation, Israeli Missile Defense, and the ABM Treaty Debate," *Jerusalem Letter-Jerusalem Center for Public Affairs,* May 15, 2000.

24 Reuters, May 28, 1997.

25 Interview with Makovsky, June 3, 2004.

26 Phone interview with Foreign Minister Shlomo Ben-Ami, May 21, 2006.

27 *Israel Line,* August 26, 1997.

28 Reuters, November 16, 1997. Efraim Karsh, "Israel's Imperative," *Washington Quarterly* 3 (2000): 160. At the same time, Israel purchased American F-15i's, a fighter-bomber capable of reaching Iran. *Dow Jones,* September 17, 1997.

29 Interview with Ranaan Gissin, Jerusalem, October 31, 2004.

30 Interview with Alpher, October 27, 2004. Interview with David Menashri, professor at Tel Aviv University, Tel Aviv, October 26, 2004. At this stage, adherence to the periphery doctrine was stronger within the Likud.

31 Interview with Ephraim Sneh, member of Knesset, Tel Aviv, October 31, 2004.

32 "Israel Finds New Ally to Stop Iranian Nuclear Bomb," *Independent,* December 29, 1995.

33 Ilan Berman, "Israel, India, and Turkey: Triple Entente?" *Middle East Quarterly* 4 (2002).

34 Interview with Alpher, October 27, 2004.

35 Interview with Gissin, October 31, 2004.

36 Erich Marquardt, "U.S. Seeks to Ostracize Iran," *Asia Times,* September 30, 2004.

37 Interview with Gissin, October 31, 2004.

38 Interview with Gen. Amos Gilad, Tel Aviv, October 31, 2004.

39 Interview with Gold, October 28, 2004.

40 Interview with Gilad, October 31, 2004.

41 Interview with Sneh, October 31, 2004.

42 *Jerusalem Post,* September 9, 1997.

43 "Splits in Israel over Iran," *Yediot Aharonot,* December 15, 1997.

44 John Esposito and R. K. Ramazani, *Iran at the Crossroads* (New York: Palgrave, 2001), 206. "Netanyahu Working to Prevent U.S. Policy Shift on Iran," *Haaretz,* December 15, 1997.

45 Reuters, June 10, 1997.

46 "Israeli-Iranian Trade Ties Reportedly 'Extensive,'" *Yediot Aharonot,* January 15, 1999.

47 *Voice of Israel,* May 28, 1997. *Dow Jones,* August 22, 1997.

48 Interview with Deputy Foreign Minister Hadi Nejad-Hosseinian, Tehran, August 12, 2004.

49 "Netanyahu Rejects Sharon Initiative to Discuss Debt to Iran," *Tel Aviv Globes,* February 1, 1998.

50 Ramazani, "Ideology and Pragmatism," 557.

51 Menashri, *Post-Revolutionary Politics in Iran,* 288.

52 Interview with Bijan Khajepour, Washington, D.C., February 17, 2004.

53 Interview with Iranian political strategist, March 2004.

54 Interview with Ali Reza Alavi Tabar, Tehran, August 21, 2004. Prominent reformists, including President Khatami's brother, Mohammad Reza Khatami, are often more anti-Israeli than the conservatives. Also, Mohtashamipour, the founder of Hezbollah, belongs to the Reformist camp.

55 Menashri, *Post-Revolutionary Politics in Iran,* 294. "A bowl warmer than the soup" is an Iranian expression equivalent to the English saying, "Being more Catholic than the pope."

56 Khatami's election was decisive for Iran's change of attitude toward terror as a political tool. Gary Sick, "Iran: Confronting Terrorism," *Washington Quarterly* 4 (2003): 93.

57 Transcripts of Track-II meetings held in northern Europe. Author attended one of the meetings in August 2003 as an observer.

58 "Transcript of Interview with Iranian President Mohammad Khatami," CNN, January 7, 1998.

59 Kenneth Pollack, *The Persian Puzzle* (New York: Random House, 2004), 315.

60 Interview with Khajepour, February 17, 2004.

61 Interview with Iranian political strategist, March 2004.

62 Transcripts of Track-II meetings held in northern Europe.

63 Interview with Davoud Hermidas-Bavand, professor at Shahid Beheshti University and former Iranian diplomat, Tehran, August 8, 2004.

64 Interview with Abbas Maleki, Tehran, August 1, 2004.

65 Nejad-Hosseinian, who held a cabinet position in the Rafsanjani government, pointed out that Rafsanjani followed the same policy. "Our position is that we have our views of Israel, but that we will not impose those views on the Palestinians. We will respect their decision, but we may not support it. It's been there throughout the 1990s. Both Khatami and Rafsanjani had it." Interview with Nejad-Hosseinian, August 12, 2004.

66 Interview with Mohammad Reza Dehshiri, head of Regional Studies Department, School of International Relations, Iranian Foreign Ministry, Tehran, August 24, 2004. According to Nejad-Hosseinian, Iran would "have no moral position to object" to an agreement accepted by the Palestinians and would as a result "have no choice but to accept it." Interview with Nejad-Hosseinian, August 12, 2004.

67 AFP, February 26, 1998. Reuters, May 2, 1998.

68 Transcripts of Track-II meetings held in northern Europe.

69 AFP, February 17, 1998. Jalali later denied that the meeting had taken place. AFP, February 18, 1998.

70 Reuters, February 1, 1998.

71 *Xinhua,* February 1, 1998.

72 *Haaretz,* June 20, 1999. Former Foreign Minister Shlomo Ben-Ami does not recall having received such an offer from the Iranians. Phone interview, May 21, 2006.

73 *AIC Insight* 2 (2004).

74 Mark Katz, "Iran and America: Is Rapprochement Finally Possible?," *Middle East Policy* 4 (2005): 61.

75 Interview with Gerald Steinberg, professor at Bar Ilan University in Israel, Jerusalem, October 28, 2004.

76 AFP, April 5, 1993.

77 Phone interview with Ben-Ami, May 21, 2006.

78 H. E. Chehabi, ed., *Distant Relations: Iran and Lebanon in the Last 500 Years* (London: I. B. Tauris, 2006), 230.

79 Interview with Gen. Amnon Lipkin-Shahak, Tel Aviv, October 25, 2004.

80 "Iran Told Hezbollah to Act Inside Israel," *Haaretz,* March 29, 2000.

81 Phone interview with Ben-Ami, May 21, 2006.

82 Ibid.

83 Interview with Gold, October 28, 2004. Tel Aviv feared that Washington, motivated by lucrative business opportunities in Iran, would overlook Israeli concerns and end its policy of isolating Iran.

84 Phone interview with former head of Mossad, Efraim Halevi, June 17, 2006. "There is always a degree of apprehension, of concern that there might be an American concession of sorts which otherwise would not have been contemplated."

85 Phone interview with Ben-Ami, May 21, 2006.

86 Interview with Israel's former Minister of Finance Dan Meridor, Tel Aviv, October 27, 2004.

87 "U.S. Move to Engage Iran Worries Supporters of Israel," JTA, June 22, 1998.

88 Israel was careful not to come across as too dismissive of the reformist winds in Iran and expressed cautious optimism regarding the elections. "Israel Cautiously Welcomes Election Results in Iran," *Xinhua,* February 20, 2000.

89 "Beilin: Time to 'Reassess' Iran Relations," *Haaretz,* April 5, 2000.

90 Interview with Makovsky, June 3, 2004.

91 "Softer Israeli Policy Sees Iran as 'Threat, Not Enemy,'" *Haaretz,* July 8, 1999.

92 David Makovsky, *Making Peace with the PLO* (Boulder: Westview, 1996), 112.

93 "Israel Condemns Recent 'Terrorist' Attacks in Iran," *Yediot Aharonot,* March 17, 2000.

94 "Israel Says Iran Missile Test Reflects Nuclear Ambitions," UPI, July 15, 2000.

95 "Israel Rejects Talks with Iran: Former FM," *Xinhua,* September 26, 2000.

96 Interview with Iranian reformist strategist, February 2004.

97 Phone interview with Ben-Ami, May 21, 2006.

98 Bill Samii, "Iran Welcomes Israeli Withdrawal," *RFE/RL Iran Report,* May 29, 2000.

99 Bill Samii, "Israeli Withdrawal Leaves Questions Unanswered," *RFE/RL Iran Report,* June 5, 2000.

100 Safa Haeri, "Iran Tells a Bewildered Syria Hezbollah Must Play It Cool," Iran Press Service, May 29, 2000.

101 "Israel: Source Says Iran Inciting 'Terrorist Acts' to Spoil Political Process," *Voice of Israel,* July 23, 2000.

102 Phone interview with Halevi, June 17, 2006.

103 Phone interview with Ben-Ami, May 21, 2006.

104 See Clayton Swisher, *The Truth About Camp David: The Untold Story About the Collapse of the Middle East Peace Process* (New York: Nation Books, 2004), and Hussein Agha and Robert Malley, "Camp David: The Tragedy of Errors," *New York Review of Books,* August 9, 2001.

105 Interview with Robert Malley, Washington, D.C., April 22, 2004.

106 Remarks by Yoram Schweitzer, delivered at the Iranian Challenge Seminar, the Jaffee Center for Strategic Studies, Tel Aviv University, February 19, 2004.

107 "Iran: Official Welcomes Egypt's, Jordan's Decisions on Ties with Israel," *RAND,* November 22, 2000.

108 "Khamenei Calls for Muslim Unity Against Israel," *Voice of the Islamic Republic of Iran,* December 27, 2000.

109 "Intifada Helps Iran Warm Ties with Arab World," Reuters, March 6, 2001.

110 "Israel: Security Sources Say Iran Funding Some of Fatah's Activists," *Voice of Israel,* July 11, 2001.

111 "Iran Wants War-Crimes Court to Try Israel," AFP, November 19, 2000.

112 *Israel Line,* February 4, 1999.

113 AFP, May 2, 1998, April 10, 1999.

114 E-mail interview with former European ambassador to Iran, who spoke on condition of nonattribution, January 2005.

CHAPTER 18 **Betrayal in Afghanistan**

1 Interview with Deputy Foreign Minister Hadi Nejad-Hosseinian, Tehran, Aug 12, 2004. "It's illogical to tie the solution of a small problem to solving a much bigger problem!" he told me in his Tehran office.

2 "Israel to Face Iran Alone When U.S. Lifts Sanctions," *Haaretz,* February 19, 2001.

3 Confirmation hearing of Gen. Colin Powell as secretary of state, January 17, 2001.

4 Interview with Ambassador James Dobbins, Washington, D.C., October 24, 2006.

5 Interview with Col. Lawrence Wilkerson, Secretary of State Colin Powell's chief of staff, Washington, D.C., October 16, 2006.

6 "Israel to Face Iran Alone When U.S. Lifts Sanctions," *Haaretz,* February 19, 2001.

7 Testimony of Howard Kohr to the House International Relations Committee, May 9, 2001.

8 "Renew ILSA: Let the Real Moderates Win in Iran," *WINEP,* June 14, 2001.

9 Iran and Israel continued to exchange accusations, but Tehran had toned down its poisonous rhetoric and focused more on isolating Israel internationally by, for instance, urging Muslim states to help push for an international ban on arms sales to Israel. "Iran: Foreign Minister Calls for Weapons Sanction against Israel," *RAND,* August 20, 2001.

10 Flynt Leverett, "Illusion and Reality," *American Prospect,* September 12, 2006.

11 Gareth Porter, "How Neocons Sabotaged Iran's Help on al-Qaeda," *IPS,* February 23, 2006.

12 Leverett, "Illusion and Reality."

13 Interview with Yossi (Joseph) Alpher, former Mossad official and senior adviser to Ehud Barak, Tel Aviv, October 27, 2004.

14 Patrick Bishop, "Worried Israel Feels Spurned as the West Courts Iran," *Daily Telegraph,* September 26, 2001.

15 Letter by the Project for the New America Century to President George Bush, September 20, 2001. Other prominent neoconservatives who courted the Bush administration with the idea of invading Iraq include Bernard Lewis and Fouad Ajami.

16 Porter, "How Neocons Sabotaged Iran's Help on al-Qaeda."

17 Ibid.

18 Kenneth Pollack, *The Persian Puzzle* (New York: Random House, 2004), 346–347.

19 Interview with Wilkerson, October 16, 2006. Interview with Dobbins, October 24, 2006.

20 Speech by Ambassador James Dobbins to the New America Foundation, Washington, D.C., August 24, 2006. Interview with Javad Zarif, Iran's ambassador to the UN, New York, October 12, 2006. Pollack, *Persian Puzzle,* 347. Michael Hirsh and Maziar Bahari, "Blowup? America's Hidden War with Iran," *Newsweek,* February 19, 2007. The interim constitution put Hamid Karzai in power in Afghanistan. This was not an uncontroversial decision. Several Afghani warlords refused to recognize his authority. One such warlord was Ismail Khan, whose close ties to Iran were well known. To remove any doubt of Tehran's wishes, Iran's foreign minister attended Karzai's inauguration and brought Ismail Khan with him just to make sure no one doubted that he was going to support Karzai.

21 "Iranian diplomats who dealt with U.S. counterparts during this period indicated that there was interest in Tehran in using this cooperation to effect a broader opening to the United States." Leverett, "Illusion and Reality."

22 Interview with Dobbins, October 24, 2006.

23 Interview with Zarif, October 12, 2006.

24 Interview with Wilkerson, October 16, 2006.

25 Speech by Dobbins to the New America Foundation, August 24, 2006.

26 Interview with Dobbins, October 24, 2006. Gareth Porter, "How Neocons Sabotaged Iran's Help on al-Qaeda," *IPS,* February 23, 2006.

27 James Bennet, "Sharon Invokes Munich in Warning U.S. on 'Appeasement,'" *New York Times,* October 5, 2001.

28 Jack Donnelly, "Nation Set to Push Sharon on Agreement," *Boston Globe,* October 10, 2001.

29 "Majlis Deputy Says Israel Angered by Iran's Current Foreign Policy Posture," *Aftab-e Yazd,* September 29, 2001. Another lawmaker, Mohsen Armin, echoed the same views in an interview with *Norooz.* "Reformist Official Comments on National Security, Ties with USA, Israel," *Norooz,* November 17, 2001.

30 Christopher Hitchens, "Minority Report," *Nation,* November 14, 1988, 482.

31 Jim Lobe, "Ledeen's Way," *IPS,* July 3, 2003.

32 Michael Ledeen courted the pro-monarchist Iranian opposition in the United States and appeared regularly on the exiled satellite TV stations operating out of Los Angeles. Though only two decades earlier he had been intimately involved in facilitating arms sales to the clerical regime in Tehran, he now portrayed himself as a champion of the Iranian student movement.

33 Edward Herman and Gerry O'Sullivan, *The "Terrorism" Industry* (New York: Pantheon, 1989), 161.

34 Joshua Micah Marshall, Laura Rozen, and Paul Glastris, "Iran-Contra II?," *The Washington Monthly,* September 2004.

35 Laura Rozen, "Three Days in Rome," *Mother Jones,* July/August, 2006. Seymour M. Hersh, "Moving Targets," *New Yorker,* December 15, 2003.

36 Marshall, Rozen, and Glastris, "Iran-Contra II?"

37 Pollack, *The Persian Puzzle,* 350–351.

38 Ali Ansari, *Confronting Iran* (New York: Basic Books, 2006), 186. Pollack, *Persian Puzzle,* 351.

39 Interview with Dobbins, October 24, 2006. Interview with Zarif, October 12, 2006. Interview with Wilkerson, October 16, 2006.

40 *AIC Insight* 2 (2004).

41 Interview with Wilkerson, October 16, 2006.

42 Porter, "How Neocons Sabotaged Iran's Help on al-Qaeda."

43 Gary Sick, "Iran: Confronting Terrorism," *Washington Quarterly* 4 (2003): 90. Wilkerson argued that Iran's inclusion was motivated more by the need of a third country for rhetorical purposes than an actual belief that the regime in Iran belonged to the same category as those in Iraq and North Korea. Interview with Wilkerson, October 16, 2006.

44 Ansari, *Confronting Iran,* 186–187.

45 Scott Peterson, "Pragmatism May Trump Zeal as Iran's Power Grows," *Christian Science Monitor,* July 6, 2006.

46 Pollack, *The Persian Puzzle,* 353.

47 Interview with Dobbins, October 24, 2006.

48 Ansari, *Confronting Iran,* 186.

49 Speech by Dobbins to the New America Foundation, August 24, 2006.

50 Interview with Dobbins, October 24, 2006.

51 Interview with Wilkerson, October 16, 2006.

52 "Israel to Ask World to Declare Iran Terror-Supporting State," *Voice of Israel,* January 4, 2002.

53 "Israel Compiles 'Black Book' on Iran, Says Peres," AFP, January 26, 2002.

54 "Khatami Urges World to Boycott Israel," *RAND,* January 29, 2002.

55 "Iran to Revenge with Missiles If Israel Bombs Nuclear Plant," Tass, February 7, 2002.

56 "Washington Wants Israel to 'Cool It' over Iran: Report," AFP, February 6, 2006.

57 "Iran Not an Enemy for Israel, Says National Security Chief," AFP, February 18, 2006.

CHAPTER 19 **Snatching Defeat from the Jaws of Victory**

Epigraph: Interview with leading Israeli military commentator, who spoke on condition of anonymity, Tel Aviv, October 17, 2004.

1 Neil Mackay, "Bush Planned Iraq 'Regime Change' Before Becoming President," *Sunday Herald,* September 15, 2002.

2 "Rebuilding America's Defenses: Strategy, Forces and Resources for a New Century," *Project for the New American Century,* September 2000. See http://www.newamerican century.org/RebuildingAmericasDefenses.pdf.

3 After the war, many Israelis have concluded that the invasion of Iraq worked to Israel's detriment. Yuval Diskin, the chief of the Israeli internal security service, the Shin Bet, told a crowd of Israeli settlers in February 2006 that a strong dictatorship in Iraq would be preferable to the present chaos there. "I'm not sure we won't miss Saddam," he said. "Israel 'May Rue Saddam Overthrow,'" *BBC,* February 9, 2006.

4   Magdi Abdelhadi, "Israel 'Trains Iraqi Kurd Forces,'" *BBC,* September 20, 2006. "Israelis Training Kurds in Northern Iraq—Report," Reuters, December 1, 2005.

5   "Israel Sets Up Iran as Next Target for the U.S.," *Manchester Guardian Weekly,* February 13, 2002.

6   Eric Margolis, "After Iraq, Bush Will Attack His Real Target," *Toronto Sun,* November 10, 2002.

7   *Newsweek,* August 19, 2002.

8   Interview with Javad Zarif, Iran's ambassador to the UN, New York, October 12, 2006.

9   Kenneth Pollack, *The Persian Puzzle* (New York: Random House: 2004), 353.

10 Interview with a senior Iranian politician who spoke on condition of nonattribution, Tehran, August 2004.

11 Michael Ledeen, "Let's Talk with Iran Now," *New York Times,* July 19, 1988.

12 See Laura Rozen's blog, http://www.warandpiece.com/blogdirs/001070.html.

13 Pollack, *The Persian Puzzle,* 354–355.

14 Gregory Beals, "A Missed Opportunity with Iran," *Newsday,* February 19, 2006.

15 Bernard Gwertzman, "Leverett: Bush Administration 'Not Serious' About Dealing with Iran," *Council on Foreign Relations,* March 31, 2006.

16 Gordon Corera, "Iran's Gulf of Misunderstanding with U.S.," *BBC,* September 25, 2006.

17 "Iran: Hardline Daily Dismisses Saudi Plan for Recognizing Israel," *Resalat,* February 26, 2002.

18 The reference to the Mujahedin is clarified on the White House Web site, which states that "Iraq shelters terrorist groups including the Mujahedin-e-Khalq Organization (MKO), which has used terrorist violence against Iran and in the 1970s was responsible for killing several U.S. military personnel and U.S. civilians." See http://www.whitehouse.gov/infocus/iraq/decade/sect5.html.

19 Connie Bruck, "Exiles: How Iran's Expatriates Are Gaming the Nuclear Threat," *New Yorker,* March 6, 2006, 56. Andrew Higgins and Jay Solomon, "Iranian Imbroglio Gives New Boost to Odd Exile Group," *Wall Street Journal,* November 29, 2006.

20 Gareth Porter, "Cheney-Led 'Cabal' Blocked 2003 Nuclear Talks with Iran," *IPS,* May 28, 2006.

21 Interview with Col. Lawrence Wilkerson, Secretary of State Colin Powell's chief of staff, Washington, D.C., October 16, 2006.

22 Porter, "Cheney-Led 'Cabal.'"

23 According to the Iranian version of the story, Iran did not make the proposal; rather, it responded to an American proposal (see Appendix B). The Iranians say that on April 27, 2003, Ambassador Kharrazi received an American proposal that spelled out the contours of a grand bargain. The exact source of the proposal is unknown, but they say it was a high-level State Department official, most likely Undersecretary of State Richard Armitage or Assistant Secretary of State William Burns. Kharrazi notified the supreme leader, Ayatollah Khamenei, who asked Ambassador Zarif to make amendments to the proposal and return it. No U.S. official has confirmed this version of the story, though some have said it is not entirely unlikely. It is conceivable that some senior State Department officials feared that the ease with which Iraq had been defeated would prompt Washington hawks to push for a swift expansion of the war into Iran. By initiating negotiations with the Iranians, these war plans would be derailed. Alterna-

tively the Iranians, through interaction with U.S. diplomats, may have learned of the draft U.S.-Iran peace plan drafted by the State Department at the request of Colin Powell immediately after September 11. The Iranians may have been unaware that the plan never received Bush's approval and as a result may have perceived it as an official U.S. proposal.

24 Gwertzman, "Leverett: Bush Administration 'Not Serious.'" It was via the Swiss that Iran in early 2002 had sent a memo to Washington insisting on its innocence in the *Karine A* affair.

25 The author advised Congressman Bob Ney on foreign policy matters at the time.

26 Guy Dinmore, "Washington Hardliners Wary of Engaging with Iran," *Financial Times*, March 16, 2004.

27 Corera, "Iran's Gulf of Misunderstanding with U.S." Interview with Wilkerson, October 16, 2006.

28 Gareth Porter, "Burnt Offering," *American Prospect*, June 6, 2006.

29 Interview with Wilkerson, October 16, 2006. Porter, "Cheney-Led 'Cabal.'"

30 Porter, "Burnt Offering."

31 Interview with Wilkerson, October 16, 2006.

32 Dinmore, "Washington Hardliners." Interview with Wilkerson, October 16, 2006.

33 Kessler, "In 2003, U.S. Spurned Iran's Offer of Dialogue." Gwertzman, "Leverett: Bush Administration 'Not Serious.'"

34 Corera, "Iran's Gulf of Misunderstanding with U.S."

35 Glenn Kessler, "Rice Denies Seeing Iranian Proposal in '03," *Washington Post*, February 8, 2007.

36 Beals, "A Missed Opportunity with Iran."

37 Porter, "Cheney-Led 'Cabal.'"

38 Interview with Bijan Khajepour, Washington, D.C., February 17, 2004.

39 Guy Dinmore, "U.S. Rejects Iran's Offer for Talks on Nuclear Programme," *Financial Times,* June 15, 2003.

40 Interview with Masoud Eslami of the Iranian Foreign Ministry, Tehran, August 23, 2004.

41 Interview with adviser to the Iranian National Security Advisor, August 2004, Tehran.

42 Interview with Iranian Foreign Ministry official, Tehran, August 2004.

43 Interview with Mohammad Reza Tajik, counselor to President Khatami and director, Strategic Studies Center of the President's Office, Tehran, August 25, 2004. Interview with adviser to the Iranian National Security Adviser, August 2004, Tehran.

44 At the dinner, Ambassador Zarif qualified the Iranian request for "U.S.-Iran relations based on mutual respect" to mean Iran's inclusion in regional decision-making, particularly a Persian Gulf security arrangement. Author attended the dinner as an observer invited by one of the congressmen.

45 Michael Ryan Kraig, "Realistic Solutions for Resolving the Iranian Nuclear Crisis," *The Stanley Foundation Policy Analysis Brief,* January 2005.

46 Interview with leading Israeli military commentator who spoke on condition of anonymity, Tel Aviv, October 17, 2004.

47 William Kristol, "The End of the Beginning" *Weekly Standard* 8:34 (May 12, 2003).

48 Reuel Marc Gerecht, "Regime Change in Iran?" *Weekly Standard*, August 5, 2002.

49 Jim Lobe, "Neo-cons Move Quickly on Iran," *IPS*, May 26, 2003.

50 Porter, "Burnt Offering." Flynt Leverett also questioned the validity of the intelligence claiming an Iranian role in Saudi bombings during a panel discussion at the Center for American Progress, December 15, 2006.

51 Interview with Zarif, October 12, 2006.

52 The Iranian Jewish Public Affairs Committee is a small organization headquartered in Los Angeles. Its policy positions tend to be close to those of American Israel Public Affairs Committee (AIPAC).

53 Mark Benjamin and Eli Lake, "Senator Asks $50M to Aid Iran Dissidents," UPI, April 8, 2003.

54 Marc Perelman, "New Front Sets Sights on Toppling Iran Regime," *Forward,* May 16, 2003.

55 Interview with Keith Weissman of American Israel Public Affairs Committee (AIPAC), Washington, D.C., March 25, 2004.

56 "Brownback Presses French Not to Turn Over Iranian Opposition Figures," Brownback press release, June 20, 2003.

57 Interview with senior Iranian official who spoke on the condition of nonattribution, Tehran, August 2004.

58 Corera, "Iran's Gulf of Misunderstanding with U.S."

59 Interview with Menashe Amir, head of the Israeli Radio's Persian Service, Jerusalem, October 24, 2004.

60 Interview with Ephraim Sneh, Tel Aviv, October 31, 2004.

61 Interview with leading Israeli military commentator who spoke on condition of anonymity, Tel Aviv, October 17, 2004.

62 Interview with Hadi Nejad-Hosseinian, Tehran, August 12, 2004.

CHAPTER 20 Facing the Future, Facing Reality

Epigraph: Joschka Fischer, "The Case for Bargaining with Iran," *Washington Post,* May 29, 2006.

1 The United States has with much success maintained strategic relations with states it opposes ideologically. A case in point is Saudi Arabia, with which the United States has maintained a very close and strategic relationship for many decades even though the Saudi Kingdom has been ruled for this entire period by the most austere and repressive Wahhabi sect of Sunni Islam.

2 Interview with Joseph Alpher, Tel Aviv, October 27, 2004. Many Iranians recognized Israel's fear of improved U.S.-Iran relations. "The more the U.S. saw Iran and Iraq as threats, the greater Israel's strategic security became," argued Masoud Eslami. Interview with Masoud Eslami of the Iranian Foreign Ministry, Tehran, August 23, 2004.

3 Interview with Shlomo Brom, Jaffee Center for Strategic Studies, Tel Aviv, October 26, 2004.

4 In his "Ideology and Pragmatism in Iran's Foreign Policy," R. K. Ramazani argues that, historically, pragmatism has triumphed over ideology in Iranian foreign policy. See *Middle East Journal* 4 (2004): 549–559.

5 Interview with Mohsen Mirdamadi, former member of Parliament and lead Reformist strategist, Tehran, August 22, 2004.

6 Ray Takeyh, "Iranian Options: Pragmatic Mullahs and America's Interests," *National Interest* 73 (2003): 51.

7 *RAND,* April 12, 2003. It is noticeable, however, that Rafsanjani sought to present his argument as an ideologically based criticism against the emphasis on *vazifeh.*

8 Phone interview with Abbas Maleki, Iranian deputy foreign minister in the early and mid-1990s, Geneva, January 27, 2005.

9 Mahmoud Sariolghalam, "Justice for All," *Washington Quarterly* 3 (2001): 115. "No leadership, however strong, can act against [Iran's] geopolitical rationale," Sariolghalam wrote.

10 Barry Rubin, "Iran: The Rise of a Regional Power," *The Middle East Review of International Affairs* 10, no. 3 (September 2006).

11 Phone interview with Ben-Ami, May 21, 2006.

12 Mohammad Quchani, "The Jewish Issue Is Not Our Issue," *Sharq,* March 1, 2006.

13 Anderson Cooper, CNN, September 21, 2006.

14 Interview with Keith Weissman of American Israel Public Affairs Committee (AIPAC), Washington, D.C., March 25, 2004.

15 Dafna Linzer, "Iran Is Judged 10 Years from Nuclear Bomb," *Washington Post,* August 2, 2005.

16 Interview with Itamar Rabinovich, former adviser to Rabin and Israeli ambassador to the United States, Tel Aviv, October 17, 2004.

17 Dafna Linzer, "Past Arguments Don't Square with Current Iran Policy," *Washington Post,* March 27, 2005.

18 On May 30, 2006, the 144 countries in the Non-Aligned Movement issued a statement upholding Iran's right to uranium enrichment. Mark Heinrich, "Iran: No Global Consensus Against It Despite Pressure," Reuters, June 14, 2006.

19 Marc Perelman, "U.S. Pursues Diplomacy on Iran Nukes," *Forward,* January 27, 2006.

20 Herb Keinon, "Israel 'May Go It Alone' Against Iran," *Jerusalem Post,* August 24, 2006.

21 Eric Fingerhut and Debra Rubin, "Iran, Hamas Dominate AIPAC," *Washington Jewish Week,* March 9, 2006.

22 Ron Kampeas, "With Time Short on Iran Nukes, AIPAC Criticizes Bush Approach," JTA, December 4, 2005.

23 Transcript of Online *Newshour,* March 18, 2004, http://www.pbs.org/newshour/bb/international/jan-june04/elbaradei_3-18.html.

24 Interview with Shmuel Limone, Ministry of Defense, secretary of Israel's Iran committee, Tel Aviv, October 18, 2004.

25 Interview with Javad Zarif, Iran's ambassador to the UN, New York, April 1, 2004.

26 "I don't believe that they are doing it [pursuing the nuclear option] to nuke Israel," Ben-Ami told me. "I have been saying that in Israel for quite some time, and it has never been very popular. Let us put it this way: Of course Israel should not be interested in Iran having a nuclear bomb. But then, having said that, one should try to see what is really behind the march to a nuclear capacity." Phone interview with Ben-Ami, May 21, 2006.

27 Interview with Shai Feldman, Tel Aviv, October 27, 2004.

28 Interview with Ehud Yaari, Jerusalem, October 24, 2004.

29 Phone interview with Halevi, June 17, 2006. "The Iranians are not irrational. They hold extreme views, but they are not irrational," Brom added. Interview with Brom, October 26, 2004.

30 Phone interview with Reuven Pedatzur, director of the Galili Center for Strategy and National Security, Tel Aviv, November 24, 2005.

31 Interview with Gerald Steinberg, professor at Bar Ilan University in Israel, Jerusalem, October 28, 2004. See also Project Daniel, a 2003 survey commissioned to assess the threat to Israel from other states in the Middle East. It was prepared by a high-powered team of Israeli foreign policy and military experts. The report was submitted to Prime Minister Ariel Sharon and was discussed among Israel, the United States, and NATO.

32 "Iran: Expediency Council Office Says Israel Distorted Its Chairman's Remarks," *RAND*, January 2, 2002.

33 Students of American history will note an eerie similarity with what Richard Nixon called his "madman theory." In search of a way to end the Vietnam War on terms favorable to the United States, Nixon told his advisers that it would be useful to let word slip out, as a bluff, that Nixon was so obsessed with the Communists that he'd do anything to win the war, including the use of nuclear weapons against Hanoi. See Seymour Hersh, *The Price of Power* (New York: Summit Books, 1983), 52–53.

34 *International Crisis Group Report,* November 24, 2004.

35 Interview with adviser to the Iranian National Security Advisor, August 2004, Tehran.

36 Israel similarly believed that India, mindful of its conflict with Muslim Pakistan, was fighting the laws of geopolitics by refusing to recognize Israel and establish security ties with it.

37 Interview with Ephraim Sneh, member of Knesset, Tel Aviv, October 31, 2004.

38 Interview with Menashe Amir, head of the Israeli Radio's Persian Service, Jerusalem, October 24, 2004.

39 Interview with Ranaan Gissin, Jerusalem, October 31, 2004. Former Defense Minister Moshe Arens agreed and argued that every regime in Iran will pursue the nuclear option, and thus that there is very little the outside world can do to stop Tehran. Interview with former Minister of Defense Moshe Arens, Tel Aviv, October 21, 2004.

40 Uzi Arad, "Russia and Iran's Nuclear Program," *Jerusalem Issue Brief,* April 28, 2003.

41 Interview with Gen. Amnon Lipkin-Shahak, Tel Aviv, October 25, 2004.

42 Interview with Gen. Amos Gilad, Tel Aviv, October 31, 2004.

43 Matthew Kalman, "Israel Set War Plan More Than a Year Ago," *San Francisco Chronicle,* July 21, 2006.

44 Max Blumenthal, "Birth Pangs of a New Christian Zionism," *Nation,* August 8, 2006. Uzi Mahnaimi, "Humbling of the Supertroops Shatters Israeli Army Morale," *Sunday Times,* August 27, 2006.

45 Roee Nahmias, "Hizbullah: We Were Surprised by Israel's Response to Kidnapping," *YNews,* August 26, 2006.

46 Interview with Javad Zarif, Iran's ambassador to the UN, New York, October 12, 2006.

47 Michael Slackman, "Iran Hangs in Suspense as the Conflict Plays Out," *New York Times,* July 29, 2006.

48 Guy Dinmore, "Experts Challenge White House Line on Iran's Influence," *Financial Times,* July 18 2006.

49 Slackman, "Iran Hangs in Suspense."

50 Interview with Gerald M. Steinberg, *Council on Foreign Relations,* August 1, 2006. See http://www.cfr.org/publication/11215/.

51 Ze'ev Schiff, "Tehran's Role Is Extensive," *Haaretz,* July 16, 2006.

52 Mahnaimi, "Humbling of the Supertroops."

53 Interview with Zarif, October 12, 2006.

54 Hassan M. Fattah, "Fearful of Iran, Arab Leaders Criticize Militants," *New York Times,* July 17, 2006.

55 "Dampened Trust? A Conversation with Nawaf Obaid," *SUSRIS,* August 22, 2006.

56 James D. Besser and Larry Cohler-Esses, "Iran-Israel Linkage by Bush Seen as a Threat," *The Jewish Week,* April 21, 2006.

57 Interview with Zarif, April 1, 2004.

58 Anne Barnard, "Iranians Debate Parameters for a Global Role," *Boston Globe,* September 5, 2006.

59 Joschka Fischer, "The Case for Bargaining with Iran," *Washington Post,* May 29, 2006.

60 Shlomo Ben-Ami, "The Basis for Iran's Belligerence," *Haaretz,* September 7, 2006.

61 Interview with Brom, October 26, 2004.

62 Interview with Shmuel Limone, Ministry of Defense, secretary of Israel's Iran committee, Tel Aviv, October 18, 2004.

63 Interview with Shmuel Bar, Tel Aviv, October 18, 2004.

64 Interview with Gilad, October 31, 2004.

65 Interview with Sneh, October 31, 2004. "We have no choice but to be superior to our immediate environment, because if we don't, we will be crushed. They will not wait a day," Yaari argued. Interview with Yaari, October 24, 2004. "There is a sense in Israel that it is much better to be alarmist, to be untrusting. Because anytime you stick your neck out or at all take a step forward, it is so easy to be proven wrong. And when you are proven wrong, you jeopardize the safety of the nation," Pollack noted. Interview with Kenneth Pollack, Washington, D.C., November 29, 2004.

66 Interview with Limone, October 18, 2004.

67 Interview with Feldman, October 27, 2004.

68 Interview with Limone, October 18, 2004.

69 David Ivry, "War Against Terror, Dilemmas of Values and Legality," *The Fisher Institute for Air and Space Strategic Studies,* April 2004, 2.

70 "Israel's Strategic Future—The Final Report of Project Daniel," *A Journal of Politics and the Arts* 3 (2004).

71 Interview with Bar, October 18, 2004.

APPENDIX A: IRAN'S MAY 2003 NEGOTIATION PROPOSAL TO THE UNITED STATES

The Iranian authorities sent the following negotiation proposal to the United States via the Swiss in May 2003.

Iranian aims:
(The US accepts a dialogue **"in mutual respect"** and agrees that Iran puts the following aims on the agenda)
- **Halt in US hostile behavior and rectification of status of Iran in the US:** (interference in internal or external relations, "axis of evil", terrorism list.)
- **Abolishment of all sanctions:** commercial sanctions, frozen assets, judgments (FSIA), impediments in international trade and financial institutions.
- **Iraq:** democratic and fully representative government in Iraq, support of Iranian claims for Iraqi reparations, respect for Iranian national interests in Iraq and religious links to Najaf/Karbal.
- **Full access to peaceful nuclear technology, biotechnology and chemical technology.**
- Recognition of **Iran's legitimate security interests** in the region with according defense capacity.
- **Terrorism:** pursuit of anti-Iranian terrorists, above all MKO and support for repatriation of their members in Iraq, decisive action against anti-Iranian terrorists, above all MKO and affiliated organizations in the US.

US aims: (Iran accepts a dialogue **"in mutual respect"** and agrees that the US puts the following aims on the agenda)
- **WMD:** full transparency for security that there are no Iranian endeavors to develop or possess WMD, full cooperation with IAEA based on Iranian adoption of all relevant instruments (93+2 and all further IAEA protocols)
- **Terrorism:** decisive action against any terrorists (above all Al Qaida) on Iranian territory, full cooperation and exchange of all relevant information.
- **Iraq:** coordination of Iranian influence for activity supporting political stabilization and the establishment of democratic institutions and a non-religious government.
- **Middle East:**
  1) stop of any material support to Palestinian opposition groups (Hamas, Jihad etc.) from Iranian territory, pressure on these organizations to stop violent action against civilians within borders of 1967.

2) action on Hizbollah to become a mere political organization within Lebanon

3) acceptance of the Arab League Beirut declaration (Saudi initiative, two-states-approach)

Steps:

I.   communication of **mutual agreement on the following procedure**

II. **mutual simultaneous statements** "We have always been ready for direct and authoritative talks with the US/with Iran in good faith and with the aim of discussing—in mutual respect—our common interests and our mutual concerns based on merits and objective realities, but we have always made it clear that, such talks can only be held, if genuine progress for a solution of our own concerns can be achieved."

III. **a first direct meeting** on the appropriate level (for instance in Paris) will be held **with the previously agreed aims**

    a. of a **decision on the first mutual steps**

- **Iraq:** establishment of a common group, active Iranian support for Iraqi stabilization, US-commitment to actively support Iranian reparation claims within the discussions on Iraq foreign debts.
- **Terrorism:** US-commitment to disarm and remove MKO from Iraq and take action in accordance with SCR1373 against its leadership, Iranian commitment for enhanced action against Al Qaida members in Iran, agreement on cooperation and information exchange
- Iranian general statement "to support a peaceful solution in the **Middle East** involving the parties concerned"
- US general statement that "Iran did not belong to 'the axis of evil'"
- US-acceptance to halt its impediments against Iran in international financial and trade institutions

    b. **of the establishment of three parallel working groups** on disarmament, regional security and economic cooperation. Their **aim is an agreement on three parallel road maps,** for the discussions of these working groups, each side accepts that the other side's aims (see above) are put on the agenda:

        1) **Disarmament:** road map, which combines the mutual aims of, on the one side, full transparency by international commitments and guarantees to abstain from WMD with, on the other side, full access to western technology (in the three areas)

        2) **Terrorism and regional security:** road map for above mentioned aims on the Middle East and terrorism

        3) **Economic cooperation:** road map for the abolishment of the sanctions, rescinding of judgments, and un-freezing of assets

    c. of agreement on a time-table for implementation

    d. and **of a public statement after this first meeting on the achieved agreements**

APPENDIX B: ORIGINAL U.S. DRAFT NEGOTIATION PROPOSAL

According to the Iranian version, Tehran did not initiate the proposal but rather responded to an American proposal. In the Iranian response, changes were made only to the section describing the Iranian aims with the negotiation, while the U.S. aims were left untouched. The original U.S. draft follows.

<u>Iranian aims:</u>
(The US accepts a dialogue **"in mutual respect"** and agrees that Iran puts the following aims on the agenda)
- **US refrains from supporting change of the political system by direct interference from outside**
- **Abolishment of all sanctions:** commercial sanctions, frozen assets, refusal of access to WTO
- **Iraq:** pursuit of MKO, support of repatriation of MKO-members, support of Iranian claims for Iraqi reparations, no Turkish invasion in North Iraq, respect for Iranian national interests in Iraq and religious links to Najaf/Karbal.
- **Access to peaceful nuclear technology, biotechnology and chemical technology**
- Recognition of **Iran's legitimate security interests** in the region with according defense capacity.
- **Terrorism:** action against MKO and affiliated organizations in the US

<u>US aims:</u> (Iran agrees that the US puts the following aims on the agenda)
- **WMD:** full transparency for security that there are no Iranian endeavors to develop or possess WMD, full cooperation with IAEA based on Iranian adoption of all relevant instruments (93+2 and all further IAEA protocols)
- **Terrorism:** decisive action against any terrorists (above all Al Qaida) on Iranian territory, full cooperation and exchange of all relevant information.
- **Iraq:** coordination of Iranian influence for activity supporting political stabilization and the establishment of democratic institutions and a non-religious government.
- **Middle East:**
  1) stop of any material support to Palestinian opposition groups (Hamas, Jihad etc.) from Iranian territory, pressure on these organizations to stop violent action against civilians within borders of 1967.
  2) action on Hizbollah to become a mere political organization within Lebanon

3) acceptance of the Arab League Beirut declaration (Saudi initiative, two-states-approach)

Steps:

I. communication of **mutual agreement on the following procedure**

II. **mutual simultaneous statements** "We have always been ready for direct and authoritative talks with the US/with Iran with the aim of discussing—in mutual respect—our common interests and our mutual concerns, but we have always made it clear that, such talks can only be held, if genuine progress for a solution of our own concerns can be achieved."

III. **a first direct meeting** on the appropriate level (for instance in Paris) will be held **with the previously agreed aims**

    a. of a **decision on the first mutual steps**

- **Iraq:** establishment of a common group, active Iranian support for Iraqi stabilization, US-commitment to resolve MKO problem in Iraq, US-commitment to take Iranian reparation claims into the discussions on Iraq foreign debts.
- **Terrorism:** Iranian commitment for enhanced action against Al Qaida members in Iran, agreement on cooperation and information exchange
- Iranian general statement "to support a peaceful solution in the **Middle East** involving the parties concerned"
- US-acceptance of Iranian access to WTO-membership negotiations

    b. **of the establishment of three parallel working groups** on disarmament, regional security and economic cooperation. Their **aim is an agreement on three parallel road maps,** for the discussions of these working groups, each side accepts that the other side's aims (see above) are put on the agenda:

        1) **Disarmament:** road map, which combines the mutal aims of, on the one side, full transparency by international commitments and guarantees to abstain from WMD with, on the other side, access to western technology (in the three areas)

        2) **Terrorism and regional security:** road map for above mentioned aims on the Middle East and terrorism

        3) **Economic cooperation:** road map for the abolishment of the sanctions and solution of frozen assets

    c. and **of a public statement after this first meeting on the achieved agreements**

APPENDIX C: LETTER FROM AMBASSADOR GULDIMANN TO THE U.S. STATE DEPARTMENT

The following is the letter from Tim Guldimann, the Swiss ambassador to Iran, to the U.S. State Department, dated May 4, 2003, explaining the background and authenticity of the Iranian grand bargain proposal.

1. On **April 21, I had a longer discussion with Sadeq Kharrazi** who came to see me (S.Kh. is the Iranian Ambassador in Paris, former Deputy FM and nephew of the Foreign Minister, his sister is married to the son of the Religious Leader Khamenei). **During this discussion a first draft of the enclosed Roadmap was developed.** He said that he would discuss this with the Leader and the Foreign Minister.

2. On **May 2, I met him again for three hours. He told me that he had two long discussions with the Leader on the Roadmap.** In these meetings, which both lasted almost two hours, only President Khatami and FM Kharrazi were present; "we went through every word of the this [*sic*] paper". (He additionally had a series of separate meetings with both).—The question is dealt with in high secrecy, therefore no one else has been informed, (S.Kh. himself has become also very discreet in our last contacts).—S.Kh. presented the paper to the Leader as a proposal, **which he had discussed with a friend in Europe who has close contacts with higher echelons in the DoS.** The Leader explicitly has asked him whether this is a US-proposal and S.Kh. denied this, saying that, if it is accepted, this friend could convey it to Washington as the basis for opening the bilateral discussion.

3. Then S.Kh. told me that the Leader uttered some **reservations** as for some points; the President and the Foreign Minister were very positive, there was no problem from their side. Then he said "They (meaning above all the Leader) agree with 85%–90% of the paper. But everything can be negotiated." (By 'agree' he meant to agree with the points themselves referred to as 'US aims' in the Roadmap, and not only to agree that the US puts these points on the agenda)—"There is a clear interest to tackle the problem of our relations with the US. I told them, this is a golden opportunity, one day we must find a solution".—Then S.Kh. asked me whether I could present the enclosed Roadmap very confidentially to someone very high in the DoS in order to get to know the US-reaction on it.—He asked me to make some minor changes in the Roadmap draft of our previous meeting, we re-wrote for instance the Iranian

statement on the Middle-East, and he said that he thinks, that this statement would be acceptable—"the peace process is a reality".

4. Then he said: "If the Americans agree to have a **discreet bilateral meeting on the basis of this Roadmap, then this meeting could be arranged very soon. In this meeting our remaining reservations could be discussed as well as the US would bring in their reservations on this paper.** I am sure that these differences can be eliminated. If we can agree on a Roadmap to clarify the procedure, as a next step it could already be decided in this first meeting that the two Foreign Ministers could meet for starting the process" along the lines of the Roadmap "to decide on how to proceed to resolve everything from A till Z". — Asked whether the meeting between the two foreign ministers has been agreed by the Leader, he said "Look, if we can agree on the procedure, I believe honestly that it is O.K. for the meeting of the foreign ministers in Paris or Geneva, there is soon an occasion."—Asked whom he thinks would participate in the first discreet meeting, he mentioned Armitage, referring to the positive positions of the latter on Iranian democracy.—I told him that I think that this is impossible, but then he mentioned a meeting these days between Khalilzad and Zarif (Ambassador to the UN) in Geneva on terrorism and said it could be a similar level from the DoS and on their side maybe him or Zarif or both.

5. When I tried to obtain from him a precise answer on what exactly the Leader explicitly has agreed, **he said that the lack of trust in the US imposes them to proceed very carefully and very confidentially.** After discussing this problem with him I understood that they want to be sure that if this initiative failed, and if anything about the new Iranian flexibility outlined in it became known, they would—also for internal reasons—not be bound to it.—However, I got the **clear impression that there is a strong will of the regime to tackle the problem with the US now and to try it with this initiative.**

INDEX